ESSENTIALS OF ALTERNATIVE DISPUTE RESOLUTION

Susan R. Patterson, Esq.
D. Grant Seabolt, Jr., Esq.

Second Edition

Copyright © 2001
All rights reserved.
Pearson Publications Company
Dallas, Texas

Website: Pearsonpub-legal.com

ISBN 0-929563-63-8

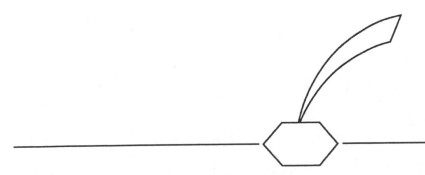

Essentials of Alternative Dispute Resolution is designed as a textbook for classroom use. The information contained herein is intended only for education and informational purposes.

Table of Contents

Chapter One

Introduction to Alternative Dispute Resolution

Introduction

Alternative Dispute Resolution (ADR) means the use of various processes and techniques to settle a dispute without court adjudication – in other words, without appealing to a judge or jury to decide the outcome. ADR can be an alternative to trial and, in some cases, to litigation. In the case of labor disputes, it may be an alternative to a strike. If the parties resolve their differences before a lawsuit is filed, or a strike is called, further conflict is avoided. In other situations, filing suit or calling a strike serves as a means of bringing the parties (back) to the bargaining table, as well as structuring the negotiations that follow. Even when trial is inevitable, ADR can be used to eliminate ancillary issues, resolve matters of evidence and procedure, and generally reduce the tension between the parties.

Historical Perspective

The founders of the United States were deeply concerned that citizens have the power and the means to redress their grievances with one another and with the government in an acceptable and orderly manner. Consequently, they provided for the establishment of courts and the appointment of judges, and gave everyone the right to trial by jury. They also devised a legal system that was "adversarial" in nature. That system assumes that if each party is required to argue the superiority of his or her claims over the claims of the other party before a neutral tribunal that decides the outcome, the parties to a lawsuit are more likely to achieve a just and fair outcome. Consequently, the parties must marshal evidence and prepare their arguments, often at considerable expense, in order to persuade a judge or jury that they should prevail. The outcome is usually a "winner-take-all" judgment, amounting to an award of a sum of money or the right to have whatever is in dispute (e.g., patent right, performance of a contract). Nevertheless, the system leaves the parties free to settle their dispute outside of the courtroom at any point short of a court-rendered decision. If the parties settle and move for a dismissal of their suit, in most cases the court loses all jurisdiction over the matter.

Given the obvious time and expense associated with litigation and the explosive growth and expansion of the American population in the 18th and 19th centuries, it is not surprising that our system of adversarial justice soon had its detractors.

For example, as early as 1776, the president of the graduating class at Yale College (later renamed Yale University) cautioned his fellow graduates about the pitfalls of "going to law."[1]

Abraham Lincoln, himself a gifted trial lawyer, lectured law students: "Discourage litigation. Persuade your neighbors to compromise whenever you can. Point out to them how the nominal winner is often the real loser."[2]

Early in the 20th century, Roscoe Pound, an influential legal scholar and law professor, warned that the "uncertainty, delay and expense, and above all, the injustice of deciding cases upon points of practice...have created a deep-seated desire to keep out of court."[3]

Despite growing concern about the effectiveness of the American system of justice, alternative methods for resolving disputes had only limited use – confined primarily to unionized labor disputes – until the 1960s when ADR began to make tremendous gains in popularity within the American legal community and the public. The modern ADR movement can trace its conceptual beginnings to the Pound Conference convened in 1976 by the American Bar Association. At the conference, a Harvard law professor, Frank E.A. Sanders, proposed a dispute resolution system that encompassed a variety of processes that would utilize the method most appropriate to each dispute. Although Professor Sanders' views ran counter to the training of most lawyers that a public court is the inevitable forum for resolving disputes, his ideas and leadership helped launch the contemporary ADR movement.

Many reasons have been offered to explain why those concerned with justice were open to the possibility and promise of ADR. Most observers agree, however, that the increasing cost and incidence of lawsuits have fueled the search for alternatives to litigation. Several factors explain these increases:

1. The inflation of the 1970s and 1980s had a corresponding effect on legal fees and expenses.

2. The maturing of the baby boom generation born after World War II dramatically increased the number of potential litigants.

    ♦ In the commercial sector, growing economic competition caused many businesses to resort to the courts in order to control and even punish their competitors.

    ♦ In the legislative arena, laws passed during the 1970s, 1980s and 1990s increased individual rights and with them the types of actions that aggrieved parties could bring. For example, the Americans With Disabilities Act (ADA) created new rights for disabled persons and new requirements for those who deal with the disabled, especially employers and public accommodations. New consumer legislation also made it easier for parties to prove in court that they had been wronged. "Lemon laws," provided consumers with the means to prove that a car dealer had committed fraud by selling a defective automobile.

In response to the growing number of lawsuits, public courts were added at federal, state and local levels, but never enough to keep up with ever-increasing demand. Therefore, the interest in and development of alternatives continued.

Exercises

1.   What is your attitude about the American system of civil justice? Do you think it works well? Why or why not? What has influenced your opinions?

2.   Have you or anyone close to you ever been involved in a lawsuit, including a divorce or child custody/support matter? What was the controversy and what was the result? Do you think the result was fair? Where did the process work well? Work poorly? How? Could ADR have improved the experience, and how? Explain your response.

3.   Before starting this course, what did you know about ADR? How would you describe your attitude toward ADR right now (e.g., enthusiastic, neutral, unimpressed, skeptical, etc.)? What has influenced your attitude?

Four Themes of the ADR Movement

Scholars who study ADR have identified four general themes within the ADR movement that help explain its recent development, popularity and direction:

♦   First, people involved in disputes at all levels of society are looking for quick, simple, confidential, and inexpensive methods to resolve their differences.

♦   Second, the legal community made up of attorneys, judges, law scholars and lawmakers, has become increasingly concerned about the need to conserve scarce court services for the resolution of complex business and commercial disputes, and to find more appropriate forums for resolving less complex matters such as consumer complaints and some family issues.

♦   Third, those concerned with social and civil rights desire to make justice more accessible to disadvantaged members of society who cannot afford the costs and delays of traditional litigation.

♦   Fourth, there is the widespread desire to develop higher-quality techniques for resolving disputes that will focus on the underlying needs of the disputing parties, empower them to mutually resolve their differences, and result in more satisfactory outcomes.[4]

Common to all four themes in the ADR movement is the belief that traditional litigation, while critical to the American system of justice, is appropriate for resolving some disputes and inappropriate for others. Understanding the various methods of dispute resolution and knowing which method(s) to use in a given case are important skills for lawyers, paralegals and other dispute counselors to learn.

Furthermore, ADR offers paralegals the opportunity to become more actively involved in dispute resolution, as compared with litigation, because in many cases ADR does not constitute "the practice of law." More and more paralegals are becoming arbitrators and mediators, or they accompany clients to administrative hearings, ADR proceedings, and other nonjudicial forums that permit the use of nonattorney advocates. (See Chapter Eight for a fuller discussion of paralegal opportunities in ADR.)

In order to understand ADR and its importance in today's legal environment, let's look briefly at the nature of disputes, the use of litigation to resolve disputes, and the various types of ADR that will be explored in more detail in this book.

The Meaning of "Dispute"

Analysts who study conflict describe a dispute as a claim that party A has against party B that is rejected either completely or partially by party B.[5] At the heart of the claim is a grievance that A has against B. The grievance is rooted in A's belief that B has denied to A something to which A is entitled.[6]

For example, suppose Tim, a computer analyst at a local company, discovers that his salary is lower than those of other analysts at the company. Naturally, he becomes concerned. He notes that his skills, education, length of employment and productivity equal or exceed those of his peers. Consequently, he concludes that he is being treated unfairly and deserves a higher salary.

In short, what started for Tim as an uneasy feeling that he was being mistreated has developed into a grievance against the employer that is supported by information Tim has accumulated. Tim can choose to ignore his grievance or he can communicate it to his employer. People often decide not to pursue their grievances, which is probably the most frequently used form of "dispute resolution." In Tim's case, if he wants to proceed, he must translate his grievance into a claim that he has a right to compensation commensurate with his peers. If Tim's employer accepts his claim and raises his salary, the matter is settled. But if Tim gets nothing, or less than he asked for, he and his employer have a dispute.

Disputes between people are a normal part of human interaction. Wherever people gather together, whether in families, clubs, teams, religious organizations, businesses, jobs, towns, political parties, nations, or international coalitions, disagreements will emerge, and some will evolve into full-blown fights. Disputes are an expression of our differences and, by airing them, we have the opportunity to better understand one another and to resolve those differences in ways that

♦ restore the peace

♦ clarify relationships

♦ engender skills and rules for dealing with one another in the future and

♦ ultimately reinforce our community and its values.

Conversely, if we squander the opportunity, disputes will likely escalate, destroying relationships and possibly even life and property. This missed opportunity, in turn, will isolate the combatants in their entrenched positions and fracture the community even more.

Exercise

Do you agree that airing disputes provides a way for people to better understand one another? Think of a situation in your own life when this has happened. How was the matter resolved? Did any neutral third party assist in the resolution of the dispute? Did you learn dispute resolution skills from the experience and, if so, what skills did you learn? How have you applied those skills to other situations?

Litigation and Trial as a Means of Dispute Resolution

Because disputing can be so costly, human beings have devised many systems and tools for resolving conflicts. Filing a lawsuit is probably the most complex, formal, and costly approach.

Let's return for a moment to Tim, our aggrieved employee. To settle his dispute with his employer, Tim may try to negotiate with his employer or use internal grievance procedures in the company to pursue his claim. If he is unsuccessful and asks a court of law to vindicate him, the case becomes a civil legal dispute.

Tim, as the plaintiff, will file a formal complaint with the court stating his right to fair treatment, that his employer has treated him unfairly and violated his rights, and that he is entitled to compensation. Tim's employer, who is the defendant, will file an answer, explaining why Tim's claim is without merit and further stating any defenses that he has to support his position. The parties will then gather evidence and prepare their respective sides of the case for presentation at trial. Filing suit, preparing for and participating in trial, and collecting or paying any judgments awarded by the judge or jury is called litigation.

The civil law process of filing a lawsuit, described above, is one response by society to conflict among its members. It is a publicly supported process of dispute resolution designed to redress the claims of private parties and provide remedies. One party to a dispute states his or her grievance in terms of a right to which he or she is entitled (e.g., the right to comparable pay for comparable skills and work, as in the example above), and uses the power of the state to force the other party to either defend against the claim or concede the fight. Disputing parties become adversaries in a process that is designed to determine clear winners and losers. Litigation has been likened to a ritualized game played according to formal rules, called civil procedure (or criminal procedure in the case of a criminal matter). These rules are imposed impartially on all "players" regardless of their religion, race, net worth, or any other characteristic, and are supposed to equalize the parties before the court, no matter how unequal they may be in power and wealth outside of the courtroom.

All litigation does not end in a decision at trial. In fact, the number of lawsuits filed that are resolved by a judge or jury verdict is 10% or less depending on jurisdiction.* The remainder are settled at some point short of a trial verdict.

For each suit that goes the distance, however, the court relies on how similar cases have been decided in the past to determine an appropriate outcome for the current dispute. Reliance on precedent ensures a certain predictability of result for litigants and potential litigants. When a dispute arises, if precedent is on your side, you may be more willing to bring (or remain in) a lawsuit because you know that you are likely to win at trial.

---

* Information is based on a review of literature about alternative dispute resolution in which the authors cite statistics from various jurisdictions from 1985 through 1994. The lowest number quoted was 2% and included both civil and criminal matters, while the highest number quoted was 10% for civil lawsuits only.

Conversely, if you are sued and determine that precedent is against you, the most prudent course of action may be to settle early to avoid the cost of litigation and a judgment at trial that may exceed the amount you can settle for now. Similarly, if you have a grievance but determine that precedent is on the other side, you may either forgo your dispute entirely or seek some other means to get what you want from the other party.

At least in theory, the courts of the United States and the various states are available to everyone equally. In fact, public justice is often too costly and takes too long for the average disputant. It is not uncommon, for example, to wait two years or longer from the point a suit is filed until trial. Add to that the period of time from when the dispute first arose until suit was filed, and the total can easily exceed three years. For most parties, who want to get on with their lives, this is too long to live in a state of unresolved conflict. In addition, the only remedy that most courts can provide a person is to award a one-time amount of money, which may not be the most appropriate solution. In the example above, what Tim wanted was a fair salary in the future. However, a court can only award him past damages. Furthermore, Tim wanted to keep his job and to continue to enjoy an amicable relationship with his employer. Unfortunately, none of these alternatives can be guaranteed by a court, and they may not be possible after the acrimony of a lawsuit. Consequently, Tim may want to consider alternatives to litigation to air his grievance and persuade his employer to see things his way.

Alternatives to Trial and Litigation

Just as all litigation does not end in trial, so also every dispute does not end in litigation. There are many ways to resolve disagreements, some of which are discussed below.

Ignoring the Problem

Some people choose to disregard their disagreements as the quickest and cheapest solution to their problem. In fact, this approach is probably the most frequently used method of dealing with disputes. The disputant may have asked an attorney to evaluate the problem, only to learn that there is no law that can be invoked that will translate the dispute into a lawsuit. In many other cases, disputants won't even bother to consult with an attorney. Either way, they simply decide to disregard the problem.

In the early 1990s, the American Bar Association (ABA) conducted a Comprehensive Legal Needs Survey among 3000-plus moderate and lower-income American households regarding their perceived legal needs.[7]

Approximately half of all respondents reported a legal problem ranging from consumer, housing and domestic issues to problems dealing with immigration, veteran's benefits and small business matters. Of this group, 38 percent of lower income, and 26 percent of moderate income households took no action of any sort. Of these, one-third believed that seeking legal assistance would not help, or would cost too much. Nearly 20 percent minimized their problem in some manner, or claimed that they did not want to make trouble.

As the ABA study showed, most of us simply choose to live with our problems unresolved. Sometimes, we are able to remove ourselves from the scene of conflict. Employees who are being discriminated against or sexually harassed get new jobs, Patients who have been misdiagnosed to their detriment go to another doctor. Retailers stuck with shoddy merchandise buy their inventory elsewhere.

Generally, however, we choose to live in the midst of the conflict because we perceive that the cost of solving the problem is greater than the cost of leaving it unresolved. In the hubbub of our busy and complicated lives, we learn to "pick our fights." Unfortunately, conflict that is avoided or ignored is not without costs, which at the moment may not be apparent. The stress of unresolved conflict takes a toll on our future physical and psychological health. Furthermore, conflicts often escalate, and tomorrow or next year the situation is worse. In short, leaving disputes unresolved may not be so cheap after all.

Self-Help

Self-help is another way in which people frequently deal with disputes. Self-help employs some approach outside the normal channels of dispute resolution, and usually involves unilateral action. For example, a landlord may decide to remove a delinquent tenant's possessions and change the locks rather than pursue an eviction action in court. However, such a self-help measure may be illegal. If local law requires an eviction action before forcibly entering and removing a tenant's personal property, the landlord's self-help remedy may be efficient but it is clearly illegal. When self-help takes the form of violence, it is almost always illegal. Killing an estranged spouse is a violent, illegal alternative to divorce.

Informal Methods of Dispute Resolution

Between the extremes of a trial verdict and ignoring the problem, society has developed many informal methods of settling disagreements. For example, in the Sunni Muslim villages of Lebanon where a strong bond exists between all members of the community, disputes are aired in the street, and neighbors shout arguments and ideas from their doorways and rooftops. As one commentator put it, "arriving at settlement is not only high drama, but it is also public entertainment."[8]

For millennia, disputants have sought out wise and revered persons to settle their differences, whether a family matriarch or patriarch, a village elder, a priest or the local landholder. Today, similar authority is vested in professionals such as ministers, priests, teachers, school principals, counselors, physicians, social workers and others.

While these professionals may be able to assist in the resolution of family conflicts and other personal matters, they are ill-equipped to deal with disputes arising out of complex economic and business relationships or matters involving technical or scientific evidence. In short, they are unable to provide the structure to air complex disputes, and often lack sufficient experience in the subject matter to help disputing parties define and resolve the issues.

Internal and Administrative Means of Dispute Resolution

Groups of specially selected persons also provide dispute resolution services. Internal grievance committees are often formed within companies, unions, political units and other organizations to hear and resolve disputes and prescribe appropriate remedies.

For example, most colleges and universities have an academic appeals committee to which students who face expulsion due to poor grades may appeal their cases. Large corporations will appoint neutral ombudsmen to hear and resolve employee or customer complaints before they turn into lawsuits against the company. Likewise, governmental agencies that provide benefits to citizens have instituted procedures to hear cases brought by recipients whose benefits have been reduced or denied.

In many situations, a court will not hear a suit brought by a party who has not first exhausted his or her internal or administrative remedies. The advantages of internal remedies are many. In addition to being quicker and much less costly than litigation, disputes are usually heard by people who are experienced and trained in the subject matter of the dispute and who understand the context in which the dispute arose. The techniques used by these internal and administrative groups often resemble those employed by ADR or are creative adaptations tailored to the situation. Nevertheless, these forums often lack the neutrality of ADR, because the person or panel hearing the dispute is employed or appointed by the company or the agency involved.

Exercises

> 1. Identify situations from your own life or the life of someone you know where a dispute has been resolved through:
>   ✓ ignoring the problem
>   ✓ self-help
>   ✓ informal methods
>   ✓ internal administrative mechanisms
>
> 2. Given each particular situation in No. 1, above, why was the particular dispute resolution method chosen? What was the resolution in each situation and how satisfactory was it? Would some other method have achieved a better result and, if so, why?

ADR

Disputes that cannot be ignored, or resolved through internal or administrative processes, must be resolved through other methods of resolution.

ADR as a Legal Phenomenon

More and more people are turning to ADR as their first choice, with litigation and other legal remedies viewed as a last resort. They are often encouraged by people within the ADR movement who are "anti-legal," in that they view the American legal system as incapable of delivering justice. Nevertheless, it is important to note that today, most ADR occurs in the context of a lawsuit, or at least "within the shadow of the law. There are several reasons for this:

a. First of all, one of the parties may have already instituted legal action or is threatening to do so. "Legal action" includes filing a lawsuit or resorting to some other remedy sanctioned by law, such as a labor strike. It also includes proceedings instituted by government agencies to enforce rules and regulations.

b. Second, if a lawsuit or some other action has been instituted, the court or administrative agency involved may require that the matter be referred to ADR.

c. Third, even disputes brought voluntarily to a nonlegal ADR provider have legal underpinnings. For example, a local mechanic summoned to mediation by an angry customer for installing used, rather than new, auto parts is likely to decline to participate if the statute of limitation on the customer's claim expired three months ago. Furthermore, agreements reached through the use of informal, nonlegal dispute resolution are enforceable as contracts in a court of law.

d. Finally, ADR has, and continues to be, the topic of a great deal of legislation. The federal government, all of the states and most of the U.S. territories have passed laws requiring or encouraging the use of ADR in the resolution of a wide variety of disputes. Many other countries and international tribunals have promulgated similar laws and resolutions. Other statutes establish, and in some cases fund, ADR agencies at both the federal and state level. In addition, laws have been enacted to regulate ADR, including setting standards of performance, qualification and training for the people who provide ADR, requiring confidentiality of ADR proceedings, providing for the enforcement of ADR-negotiated agreements, and much more.

There is a nonlegal strain in the ADR movement that recognizes that unresolved conflict of any sort is not good for the earth or the people who inhabit it. ADR techniques are being advanced in a variety of areas to solve problems that do not involve legal claims. Therapists teach negotiation to married couples and employ mediation to resolve family disputes. Corporations and other large organizations use ADR techniques to promote teamwork and improve performance. School-age children are taught how to mediate playground fights.

Nevertheless, ADR remains primarily a phenomenon of legal mechanisms and thinking, as well as an alternative to them. For these reasons, the discussion in this text will approach ADR accordingly. Furthermore, most paralegals will encounter ADR within the employ of a legal entity, be it a law firm, corporate legal department, government agency or court. If the paralegal is an ADR professional, or works for one, much of the business will come from the legal sector.

Forms of ADR   ADR is not one single form or process of dispute resolution, but rather a concept that embraces and offers a variety of methods from which disputing parties may choose. Every year the list of methods grows longer as more and more variations are devised to fit the circumstances of a particular dispute or type of dispute, as well as to mitigate the weaknesses of more traditional forms of ADR. Some forms of ADR are nonadjudicatory, leaving it to the parties or their attorneys to decide the best resolution to their problems. Negotiation, the most commonly used form of ADR, involves no third-party intervention at all.

While not a complete list, the six primary types of ADR presently in use in the United States, as well as many other countries, are:

♦   negotiation

♦   mediation

♦   arbitration

♦ minitrial

♦ summary jury trial (SJT), and

♦ moderated settlement conference (MSC).

Other forms of ADR that occur less frequently include:

♦ private judging, sometimes called "rent-a-judge," an alternative that is gaining in popularity

♦ "early neutral evaluation" (ENE), a process created by legislation to explore settlement as early as possible in the life of a lawsuit

♦ "multi-door courthouse," a court-administered program that encompasses a variety of processes and utilizes the method most appropriate to each dispute

♦ med-arb, a combination of methods that begins with mediation and resorts to binding arbitration only if mediation is unsuccessful

♦ arb-med, a combination of both methods that begins with arbitration. An award is formulated, but not issued until a follow-up mediation has failed to achieve a settlement

♦ "baseball arbitration," a form of "high-low" arbitration where each party submits an offer and the arbitrator simply selects one of them as the more appropriate. Thus, parties have an incentive to submit proposals that are reasonable for fear the arbitrator will choose the other party's offer.

♦ "conciliation," a term that is used extensively in older statutes and regulation, and which is often used interchangeably with "mediation." Generally, conciliation does not involve expanded meetings between the parties and the neutral.

One of the ways to understand and characterize ADR methods is to arrange them on a horizontal line from left to right, based on how much control the parties to a dispute have over the ultimate decision or solution. The following chart places the various methods of dispute resolution discussed in this chapter on such a continuum, from ignoring the problem on the left, to judicial and legislative decision making on the right. The chart categorizes the methods based on whether they are private or public solutions.

CONTINUUM OF CONFLICT MANAGEMENT AND RESOLUTION APPROACHES

Ignoring the Problem	Non-violent or Violent Direct Action	Informal Discussion & Problem Solving	Negotia-tion Mini-Trial ENE	Concili-a-tion Media-tion	SJT MSC ENE Non-Binding Arbitra-tion	Adminis-trative Hearing/ Decision	Binding Arbi-tration Private Judging	Judicial Decision	Legislative Decision
Private Decision Made by the Parties					Advisory Decision	Private 3rd Party Decision		Legal/Public 3rd Party Decision	

Negotiation   Negotiation is an informal process where two or more parties, or their agents, attempt to resolve a dispute through discussion and bargaining. No outside, neutral third party is involved, and the parties control the outcome. There are no rules, no required procedures or methods, and no one can compel another to participate. Furthermore, if negotiations break down, the parties can always try again tomorrow, or suspend negotiations and resort to some other, more stringent form of dispute resolution such as arbitration or litigation. Negotiation takes place in private, and any offers made during negotiation are inadmissible in court to prove liability or the amount of damages.

Mediation   Mediation is a form of negotiation that is assisted by an impartial third party called a mediator. The mediator, who has no authority to resolve the dispute, helps the parties to communicate and to work out a solution to their problem. The mediation process provides a means for disputants to candidly express their concerns and positions to the mediator in confidence. Knowing how both sides view the dispute, the mediator can then suggest options that the parties may not have considered. In some cases, the mediator may propose a settlement design to the parties.

Arbitration   Arbitration is a forum where the parties present their case to an impartial arbitrator or panel of arbitrators who renders a specific award. Arbitration is similar to litigation, but somewhat less formal. The discovery process is abbreviated, often at the discretion of the arbitrator. Rules of procedure are usually agreed upon by the parties. In arbitration, the ruling of the arbitrator can be binding or nonbinding, depending upon the desire of the parties. If the parties choose or the court orders binding arbitration, the parties may be able to appeal the decision of the arbitrator to a court of law. Generally, however, there must have been a serious error or other strict grounds for appeal.

Due to the influence of the American Arbitration Association and other similar organizations, more and more contracts contain mandatory dispute resolution clauses that require the parties to settle any disputes arising under the contract through binding arbitration. Arbitration is the most popular forum for the resolution of commercial disputes. Despite its popularity, arbitration is often criticized for "splitting the baby" rather than seeking more creative solutions. The results of arbitration may be private or public, depending upon the case.

Minitrial   Minitrial is a technique to facilitate negotiated settlements. It is especially well-suited to cases involving highly complex, technical issues where trained experts are in the best position to find a resolution.[9] The minitrial, which uses trial-like procedures, is usually presided over by a moderator who has been hired by the parties, and who is generally an expert in the subject matter of the dispute. The proceedings are attended by executives from each side to the dispute who have the authority to settle the matter. The lawyers present their clients' cases in summary form, then depart, leaving the executives to discuss whether a negotiated settlement is possible. The moderator may act as a mediator, and may issue an advisory opinion if both sides and the moderator agree that such an opinion would be helpful. The responsibility for resolution of the dispute rests with the parties, however. Minitrial proceedings are confidential, and no transcripts are made, nor are records kept.

Summary Jury Trial

The summary jury trial (SJT) is a forum for evaluating a case and developing realistic settlement options. It is most effective when used early in the life of a dispute or lawsuit. SJT uses a mock jury that issues a nonbinding, advisory "verdict," allowing the parties to see how a real jury might respond to their case. The advisory verdict is used as a basis for settlement negotiations. Judges sometimes order the parties to use SJT as a final attempt to encourage settlement before a full-blown trial. An SJT is confidential and private.

Moderated Settlement Conference

Moderated Settlement Conference (MSC) proceedings are similar to mini-trials, except that an MSC uses a panel of advisors, usually attorneys, who issue an advisory opinion at the end of the summary presentation. This opinion, which presents a legal analysis of the case, is then used as a guide for further settlement discussions. After the attorneys have presented the factual and legal arguments of their clients' cases, the panel questions them and their clients, then deliberates and renders an evaluation of the strengths and weaknesses of each case. They may also provide a dollar or percentage range for settlement.[10]

Private Judging

Parties who prefer the structure and adversarial nature of litigation, but who want to speed up the process and also control who hears the case, might choose private adjudication, an ADR method that most closely resembles trial. Called "rent-a-judge" in many jurisdictions, the proceeding is a full-blown trial that is presided over by a judge, often retired from the bench, whom both sides have selected and whose fee for service is shared equally by the parties. The trial is held at a private location, out of the public view.

Conciliation

Although not discussed in this book, "conciliation" generally means a highly informal method of dispute resolution where the parties meet with a neutral third party to discuss how the dispute might be settled. It can also be used as a synonym for ADR. The term, "conciliation," is more likely to occur in articles, texts, and statutes that predate the modern ADR movement.

The following chart compares court adjudication to the various methods of ADR discussed above.

COMPARISON OF ADR TO COURT ADJUDICATION				
	ADJUDICATION	**NEGOTIATION**	**MEDIATION**	**ARBITRATION**
DESCRIPTION	Judge or jury decides which side will prevail after hearing factual proofs and arguments; decision is binding subject to appeal; proceeding and results are public	Direct communications among parties to arrive at some settlement of a matter; if agreement is reached, it is enforceable as a contract; proceeding and results are private	Mediator(s) assists the disputing parties in negotiating a settlement; if agreement is reached, it is enforceable as a contract; proceeding and results are private	Arbitrator or panel of arbitrators listens to all sides to a dispute and renders a decision and award based on the facts of the case and the law; decision may be nonbinding but is usually binding, subject to appeal to a court of law; may be public or private
	MINITRIAL	**SUMMARY JURY TRIAL**	**MODERATED SETTLEMENT CONFERENCE**	**PRIVATE JUDGING**
	Trial-type event; attorneys for parties present their cases in summary form; presided over by neutral who is an expert in subject matter of dispute. After presentation of cases, parties with authority to settle meet to negotiate agreement; enforceable as a contract; proceedings are private; results are private and non-binding	Summary of proofs and arguments is presented to a jury panel by each side in the dispute. Panel listens and renders advisory, nonbinding verdict in order to assist parties to reach a settlement; can be private or public	Abbreviated trial where attorneys for parties present their cases in summary form; presided over by a panel of three lawyers who give an advisory opinion. After presentation of the case, parties meet to negotiate an agreement; enforceable as a contract; proceedings are private; results are private and nonbinding	Private judge conducts a trial and decides all or part of the case; decision is sometimes supported by findings of fact and conclusions of law; proceedings are private; results are private and nonbinding unless judicial enforcement is sought
	ADJUDICATION	**NEGOTIATION**	**MEDIATION**	**ARBITRATION**
THIRD-PARTY NEUTRAL	Impartial judge and jury acting under authority of the government; parties, through their attorneys, have limited power to select jury and little control over which judge will hear case; usually has no expertise in subject matter of the dispute	No third-party facilitator	Impartial third-party facilitator who is selected by the court, a neutral agency or the parties; may be layperson, paralegal, lawyer or former judge; often specializes in subject matter of dispute	Neutral individual or panel either imposed by court or selected by a neutral agency or the parties; generally has no special expertise in subject matter with key exceptions, such as labor arbiter
	MINITRIAL	**SUMMARY JURY TRIAL**	**MODERATED SETTLEMENT CONFERENCE**	**PRIVATE JUDGING**
	Moderator selected by parties; often has specialized expertise in subject matter of dispute	A mock jury panel (generally six persons) chosen from same group from which public courts choose their jurors	Three-member panel; often lawyers selected by court or by a neutral agency; parties have unlimited number of strikes until they achieve a satisfactory panel	Former or retired judge, often with experience in specialized area applicable to subject matter of the case

COMPARISON OF ADR TO COURT ADJUDICATION				
	ADJUDICATION	**NEGOTIATION**	**MEDIATION**	**ARBITRATION**
ROLE OF THIRD-PARTY NEUTRAL	Judge decides issues of procedure (e.g., admissibility of evidence); judge or jury renders a verdict favorable to only one side	None	Helps parties to identify and clarify issues, identify settlement options and negotiate a settlement; may draft the final agreement	Render a decision and an award based on principle and supported by a reasoned opinion
	MINITRIAL	**SUMMARY JURY TRIAL**	**MODERATED SETTLEMENT CONFERENCE**	**PRIVATE JUDGING**
	Hears presentation and upon request by parties, provides expert evaluation of case to the parties to be used to negotiate and reach settlement; may also mediate negotiations	Jury panel listens and renders a verdict. May not be told that their verdict is merely advisory	Hear presentation and evaluate strengths and weaknesses of case; issue an advisory opinion to parties; may also assist in negotiations	Conduct a bench trial and render a verdict
	ADJUDICATION	**NEGOTIATION**	**MEDIATION**	**ARBITRATION**
ROLE OF LAWYERS	Formulate case strategy and remedies; aggressively present client's case to the judge and jury	Attorneys for parties negotiate on behalf of their client; draft final agreement	May present case summary at opening session; may draft or review the final agreement; prepare client for mediation and support client during session	May present case and cross-examine opposing witnesses
	MINITRIAL	**SUMMARY JURY TRIAL**	**MODERATED SETTLEMENT CONFERENCE**	**PRIVATE JUDGING**
	Formulate case strategy and make abbreviated presentation of client's best case; prepare and assist client with negotiation; draft final agreement	Present summary of their client's case in same manner as would be presented in court. Advise clients regarding negotiation	Formulate case strategy and make abbreviated presentation of client's best case; prepare and assist client with negotiation; draft final agreement	Present case in same manner as in a court trial

COMPARISON OF ADR TO COURT ADJUDICATION				
	ADJUDICATION	**NEGOTIATION**	**MEDIATION**	**ARBITRATION**
ROLE OF PARTIES	May testify; otherwise listen to case presentation but may not interject into court proceeding	Parties may negotiate directly with one another or participate with their attorneys in negotiation sessions; approve decision or ratify attorney decision	Present their case, vent feelings, tell story and may negotiate directly with other party; identify settlement options; approve mutually agreeable settlement	May present case and testify; if decision is nonbinding, can continue negotiation after rendition of a decision
	MINITRIAL	**SUMMARY JURY TRIAL**	**MODERATED SETTLEMENT CONFERENCE**	**PRIVATE JUDGING**
	Listen to case presentation; negotiate directly or with their attorneys; party representatives should be individuals who have authority to settle the case	Parties may testify; otherwise, role is similar to role at trial - listen and give feedback and approve next steps such as to negotiate or proceed to public trial	Listen to case presentation; negotiate directly or with their attorneys	May testify
	ADJUDICATION	**NEGOTIATION**	**MEDIATION**	**ARBITRATION**
PRIMARY USE	All types of disputes	All types of disputes	Where parties want personal/professional relationship to continue; multiparty litigation; where legal remedies are limited	Where a decision is needed and parties prefer that it be made by a third party
	MINITRIAL	**SUMMARY JURY TRIAL**	**MODERATED SETTLEMENT CONFERENCE**	**PRIVATE JUDGING**
	Complex commercial disputes where expert neutral is a plus and where parties are likely to maintain business relationship into the future	Useful to understand how a jury might react, e.g., dramatic client or case, no settled law. Also useful to distill lengthy presentation to most effective points	Where a neutral, professional legal advisory opinion is needed, often because negotiations are at an impasse	Where parties want a trial but also want faster results, more control over selecting the judge and avoid publicity; often used to try selected issues that comprise part of the dispute

COMPARISON OF ADR TO COURT ADJUDICATION				
	ADJUDICATION	**NEGOTIATION**	**MEDIATION**	**ARBITRATION**
NATURE AND SCOPE OF PROCEEDING	Uses formalized and highly structured rules; restricted presentation of evidence; use of witnesses; for defendant proceeding is involuntary	Usually informal and unstructured; unbounded presenting of evidence; no use of witnesses; participation is voluntary; outcome is private; can resolve entire matter or portion thereof	Usually informal and unstructured; unbounded presenting of evidence; no use of witnesses; participation is voluntary unless ordered by court; outcome is private; can resolve entire matter or portion thereof	Formalized, structured and adversarial proceeding; voluntary, contractual or court-ordered participation
	MINITRIAL	**SUMMARY JURY TRIAL**	**MODERATED SETTLEMENT CONFERENCE**	**PRIVATE JUDGING**
	Informal and loosely structured with procedural rules set by the parties; participation is voluntary	Less structured than adjudication and with limited evidence and witnesses; may be voluntary or court-ordered	Usually informal and loosely structured; participation is voluntary or by court order	Use rules of procedure and evidence with some flexibility if the parties agree; participation is voluntary

Newer Forms of ADR

Because it is so flexible, ADR is forever inventing itself into new methods and procedures. Recent variations include:

Med-Arb

Often two or more types of ADR are combined to form a hybrid. One example is known as med-arb, which combines mediation and arbitration. In med-arb, the parties begin with mediation and agree that if mediation is unsuccessful, either the mediator will make the decision that resolves the dispute, or the parties will proceed to arbitration using a different third person as arbitrator. In the latter case, the process is usually called med-then-arb. In both cases, the decision of the mediator or arbitrator is usually binding on the parties.

Mediation Against the Box

Another form of ADR that combines mediation and arbitration is called "mediation against the box." The parties begin by arbitrating the dispute. The arbitrator makes a decision but seals the award in an envelope. The parties then proceed to mediation, fully informed of the strengths and weaknesses of their own, and the other side's case. Only if the parties fail to resolve their dispute through mediation is the envelope opened and the arbitrator's award made binding.

Early Neutral Evaluation

Early neutral evaluation (ENE) is the name of a program being used in various federal district courts to help facilitate settlement. ENE sessions are non-binding evaluation conferences attended by the parties, their attorneys and a neutral member of the bar who has extensive litigation experience and is likely to be an expert in the subject matter of the lawsuit. The session occurs early in the pretrial period of the lawsuit so that the parties can use what they learn during the session to expedite discovery and other pretrial activity. Designed to save time and money associated with litigation, the session also serves as a way to get the parties talking together in the presence of a neutral third person early in the process.

Neutral Factfinder Parties involved in highly technical disputes are turning more and more to neutral factfinders to resolve key factual issues on which the dispute hinges. The factfinder is almost always an expert in his or her technical field rather than a legal expert. Furthermore, the factfinder is agreed to and employed by all parties to the dispute, who also decide whether the expert's findings will be binding or nonbinding. Examples include an appraiser employed to determine the value of a business, a structural engineer employed to determine factors contributing to a building collapse, or an accountant employed to trace a complex commercial transaction. The factfinder's determinations can motivate the parties to settle. Even if litigation ensues, using an expert factfinder can ultimately save on litigation costs because the parties can stipulate to key facts rather than spend time and money educating a judge or jury unfamiliar with the technical area involved.

Advisory Opinion In cases that turn more on how the law will be interpreted and applied to the facts, parties will often use a panel of neutral legal experts familiar with the area of law involved. The attorneys for the parties will present their cases to the panel who will evaluate what they heard, make their report, and then attempt to facilitate negotiations based on their evaluation.

High-Low Summary Jury Trial This is a binding form of summary jury trial where the parties establish a high and low range for the award. After hearing the case, the jury makes a binding award within the range established earlier by the parties. This method encourages plaintiffs to compromise at the upper end of the range and the defendants to compromise at the lower end.

Ombuds Programs Although ombuds programs are not new they are cropping up more and more. These programs utilize neutral ombuds who investigate grievances and report both their findings and recommendations to the decision making person or group who hired them. These programs differ from other ADR forms in that the neutral is also the investigator. Ombuds programs are often used by large corporations and other large institutions to investigate employee grievances. Cities will sometimes provide ombuds services to area employers.

ADR Architect ADR architects are experts in ADR who are employed by the parties to a dispute to design an ADR process tailor-made to the parties and the issues involved.

The Benefits of ADR

Over the past 20 years, the extensive use of a wide variety of ADR methods has clearly demonstrated that private processes are effective in achieving fair and just resolutions to conflict. Apart from the advantages of efficiency, speed and reduced costs, ADR has also demonstrated that it is capable of achieving results that meet the needs of all the parties involved, at least in some measure.

At the beginning of this chapter, we identified four goals that have motivated the development of ADR. In recent years, each of those goals has been met to some degree.

1. ADR has clearly provided people with quick, simple, confidential, and inexpensive methods to resolve their differences. This is especially so for individuals at middle and lower income brackets who can least afford litigation.

2. ADR has freed up court resources by diverting many simpler and more commonplace disputes to alternative methods, leaving the courts to handle the more complex cases, or those requiring a precedential result. Nevertheless, ADR has matured to the point that it is making inroads even into complex matters and those involving great public policy issues.

3. ADR has proved highly amenable to defending the rights of disadvantaged members of society. By focusing the parties on mutual interests and settlement, ADR is not only resolving the immediate dispute, it is also instilling in people the confidence that future conflict can be managed.

4. Finally, ADR is empowering people to mutually resolve their differences and to be willing to consider settlement options that allow everyone to achieve at least some of their goals.

The Drawbacks to ADR

ADR, which is essentially a form of private justice, is not a substitute for the public system of law in the United States. That system, backed by the authority of the government, provides the standard of justice and fair play that ADR must live up to. It also provides guidance in settling current disputes by providing legal precedent. Judges can look to how courts have decided similar disputes in the past to determine what would be an appropriate outcome in a current matter. Thus, reliance on precedent helps to insure that disputes of a particular type will be dealt with in a similar manner from court to court, county to county, and state to state. Furthermore, legal precedent provides parties with a basis for determining their chances at trial and whether it would be better to settle now. A settlement agreement is to an important extent a prediction of what a judge or jury would decide.

Some critics of ADR warn that the growing use of private justice will thwart the development of legal precedent and thus undermine the power of the courts to bring about positive social change. For example, the 1954 Supreme Court case of *Brown v. Topeka Board of Education*[11] allowed black children to attend school with white children and prohibited segregation in public schools throughout the United States. The shock wave of that decision was a powerful stimulus to the civil rights movement that followed. Furthermore, it raised questions about the constitutionality of all other laws that permitted racial segregation in public-supported institutions and facilities. If *Brown* had been settled privately through ADR, the case would never have reached the Supreme Court, and the legal and social revolution that followed might never have happened.

A third problem involves the remedies available through ADR. In many cases, ADR can fashion remedies that are tailor-made to the situation and which a court would be unlikely to award. In other situations, however, damages that are severe enough to deter dangerous behavior in the future may not be available through ADR, and can only be awarded by a court of law.[*] Therefore, ADR may not be appropriate for particularly egregious cases of fraud, intentional torts, or violent criminal activity.

---

[*] Arbitrators in New York, Indiana, Colorado, and Arkansas may not award punitive damages in cases that do not involve interstate commerce, and other states have not decided the issue. Furthermore, the parties may have expressly provided in their agreement to arbitrate that the arbitrator is not permitted to assess punitive damages.

Proponents of ADR often point to its success rate at achieving outcomes that are more likely to satisfy the parties involved, as compared with adjudication. Nevertheless, studies show that ADR works best when the parties are truly motivated to resolve the dispute themselves. In other words, parties predisposed to settle turn to ADR, while the more contentious proceed to the courthouse. This is not an inappropriate outcome, but should be taken into account when comparing the advantages and disadvantages of public versus private justice.

So far, the public is largely unaware of the availability of ADR to resolve conflict. Most citizens are not involved in lawsuits or do not encounter problems significant enough to invoke the arbitration provision in the contracts that they may have signed. In the ABA study of the legal needs of moderate and lower income Americans, mentioned above, only 20 percent of all households were aware of the availability of mediation services to resolve common disputes.[12] Thus, one additional drawback to ADR may be its relative obscurity.

Conclusion

As ADR continues to evolve, more and more people will use it to resolve a broader and broader range of disputes. Law schools routinely offer ADR training and in some schools such training is mandatory. Today, few attorneys would dismiss the merits of ADR, and in some jurisdictions, the duty to inform clients of ADR is written into codes of professional responsibility that govern the conduct of lawyers. As the following chapters will show, ADR offers alternatives, choices, and empowerment to those involved in disputes that take less time, cost less money, and may produce a more satisfactory outcome than other, more traditional and formal approaches to dispute resolution.

Nevertheless, in order for ADR to accomplish good results, parties and their advisors need to understand which techniques are most compatible with their needs and how to use them. ADR offers to parties a way to examine their disagreements, understand how they arose, and work together to settle their differences amicably.

Overview of Future Chapters

This text is structured so that the student can gain an understanding of each ADR method, how it works, when and where it can be used, and the advantages and disadvantages of each approach. The text also discusses the relationship of each method to litigation.

♦ Chapter Two examines how parties can use negotiation to settle their dispute rather than resort to a decision by a judge or jury.

♦ Chapters Three and Four examine mediation, which is negotiation assisted by a neutral third party.

♦ Chapter Five explores arbitration, which is similar to litigation and yet very different, in that the parties retain control over many important aspects of the proceedings.

♦ Chapter Six examines various methods of ADR used by parties to test settlement strategies so that they can better determine whether or not to proceed to trial.

♦ Chapter Seven shows how ADR is applied to specific types of disputes.

♦   Chapter Eight explores in more detail the role of the paralegal in ADR
    within the context of each ADR method, and will discuss career possibilities
    available in ADR. The chapter will also explore the future of ADR.

♦   Finally, the Appendices provide various reference materials that should
    prove helpful not only in a course on ADR but in practice as well.

Exercises

> 1. Do you think that attorneys should have a duty to inform clients of ADR?
>   Why or why not?
>
> 2. Many less populated and rural countries throughout the United States
>   have few if any ADR resources available. In what ways might this fact
>   affect the quality of justice available to litigants? Do you think that state
>   legislatures, state bar associations, the AAA, and others have a duty to
>   provide cost effective ADR resources to outlying counties? Why or why
>   not? How?

Sources

[1] Timothy Dwight (1776), *in* M. Bloomfield, American Lawyers in a Changing Society 1776-1876, at 39 (1976).

[2] A. Lincoln's Notes for a Law Lecture (July 1, 1850), *in* C. Cooper and B. Meyerson, A Drafter's Guide to Alternative Dispute Resolution (1991).

[3] R. Pound, The Causes of Popular Dissatisfaction with the Administration of Justice, 29 A.B.A. Rep. 395 (1906), *reprinted in* 70 F.R.D. 79 (1976)

[4] J. Murray, A. Rau and E. Sherman, *Processes of Dispute Resolution - The Role of the Lawyers, Notes for Teachers*, I-13 (1990).

[5] Miller and Sarat, *Grievances, Claims, and Disputes: Assessing the Adversary Culture*, 15 Law & Soc'y Rev. 525, 526 (1980-81).

[6] *Id.*

[7] American Bar Association, Legal Needs and Civil Justice, A Survey of Americans, Major Findings of the Comprehensive Legal Needs Study (1994).

[8] R. King's View From the Bench: ADR and Justice in the 1990s, Dispute Resolution and Democracy in the 1990s: Shaping the Agenda, Proceedings (October 19-22, 1989) *in* Soc'y of Prof. in Disp. Resol. (1989).

[9] S. Leeson and B. Johnston, *Ending It: Dispute Resolution in America*, 114 (1988).

[10] A. Greenspan, *Handbook of Alternative Dispute Resolution*, 11 (1990).

[11] *Brown vs. Board of Education of Topeka, Shawnee County, Kan.*, 347 U.S. 483, 74 S.Ct. 686, 98 L.Ed. 873 (1954).

[12] American Bar Association, Legal Needs and Civil Justice, A Survey of Americans, Major Findings of the Comprehensive Legal Needs Study (1994).

Chapter Two

Negotiation

Introduction

Negotiation is the "process of submission and consideration of offers until [an] acceptable offer is made and accepted."[1] Negotiation has also been defined as "communication for the purpose of persuasion."[2] Negotiation, which is the most fundamental form of dispute resolution used in our legal system today, occurs when two or more people, or their representatives, bargain together without the intervention of any neutral third party.

People negotiate all the time. From two people deciding what movie to see, to the representatives of labor and management bargaining over a labor contract, people everywhere attempt to reach agreement in order to manage the matters of daily life and commerce. Negotiating is a way people avoid conflict, or a way we resolve conflict that has already occurred.

In legal situations, negotiation occurs either between the parties to a dispute, or through their representatives. As long as the parties themselves do the negotiating, they directly determine the outcome. If their representatives negotiate for them, the representatives will influence and shape the results. Nevertheless, the parties usually must ratify the accord that their representatives reach in order for the agreement to have legal and lasting effect.

Negotiation is both a distinct method of dispute resolution and a technique that is employed in almost every other form of ADR that will be considered in this book. Summary jury trials, mini-trials and moderated settlement conferences could each be characterized as the prelude to negotiating. Mediation is negotiation assisted by a neutral third party. Because negotiation is central to ADR, the ideas discussed in this chapter will assist the reader in better understanding and differentiating the various ADR methods covered in this text.

Legal Negotiating

This chapter is about negotiation to settle legal disputes. It assumes that the parties to a dispute have been unsuccessful at negotiating on their own and have turned to professional advocates to champion their respective causes and to represent them in future bargaining. Legal negotiating differs from other forms and uses of negotiation in several ways:

1. With legal negotiating, the law provides a blueprint for building a settlement. The negotiator researches the law that pertains to a dispute in order to ascertain the relative rights, duties, claims, defenses and damages available to the parties. He or she then works with the client and the other side to devise a settlement based largely on that research. Bargaining is highly influenced by the outcome that the parties believe they would likely achieve if they went to trial.

2. Legal negotiations tend to be rich in information, because the negotiators have access to the facts and data they need to either prosecute or settle their dispute. Generally speaking, people settle when they have enough information to make an informed decision about their chances. The law, and specifically the rules of civil procedure, provide the authority to "discover" information possessed by the other side that will enable each party to better assess its own case, and devise a negotiation strategy.

3. Legal bargaining is conducted by lawyers who are experienced negotiators. Negotiation is part and parcel of a lawyer's trade and, in fact, most lawyers are constantly engaged in negotiation. Relationships with clients are shaped by negotiation over matters such as fees and the scope of representation. Lawyers bargain with their associates and support staff in order to get their work done. Attorneys who write contracts use negotiation to hammer out the terms of agreement. Administrative lawyers bargain with government regulators on behalf of their clients. Criminal attorneys bargain with prosecutors about crimes to be charged and punishments to be accepted. Civil trial lawyers negotiate with judges and with opposing counsel over issues of procedure and evidence. And, of course, litigation lawyers use negotiation ultimately to settle the vast majority of disputes that they are hired to handle, often on the eve of trial or even after trial has begun. Furthermore, lawyers study about negotiation and frequently take classes to improve their bargaining skills.

Negotiation Law and Policy

Although the American system of justice, both civil and criminal, provides for adjudication and trial by jury, public policy favors the voluntary settlement of disputes. At no time did the founders expect that all disputes would end up in court. Furthermore, philosophical values inherent in democracy uphold the notion that people can decide what is best for themselves and their associates.

Settlement negotiations are promoted by the justice system in primarily three ways:

1. First, the Federal Rules of Civil Procedure (FRCP) encourage and permit federal courts to order the parties to a lawsuit to participate in court-sponsored, pretrial conferences for a variety of purposes including "facilitating the settlement of the case."[3] FRCP Rule 16 further provides that the participants at a pretrial conference may consider and take action with respect to "the possibility of settlement or the use of extrajudicial procedures to resolve the dispute."[4]

   The annotations to Rule 16 note that it has become commonplace to discuss settlement at pretrial conferences in order to ease crowded court dockets and save money for both the litigants and the courts. The annotations explain that "[a]lthough it is not the purpose of [FRCP] Rule 16(c)(7) to impose settlement negotiations on unwilling litigants, it is believed that providing a neutral forum for discussing the subject might foster it."[5]

   FRCP Rule 16 also provides that the parties at a pretrial conference may consider "the advisability of referring matters to a magistrate or master."[6]

   Magistrates and masters are empowered to rule on matters of evidence and, therefore, can greatly influence the course of negotiations by deciding what evidence will and will not be allowed at trial. Parties with the weaker evidence are inclined to favor negotiations rather than trial.

Masters and magistrates can also serve as neutral third parties at settlement negotiations. According to annotations to the Rule, "a judge ... may arrange, on his own motion or at a party's request, to have settlement conferences handled by ... a magistrate." Furthermore, "[r]equests for a conference from a party indicating a willingness to talk settlement normally should be honored, unless thought to be frivolous or dilatory."[7] Nevertheless, the annotations recognize that a settlement conference may not always be compatible with a discussion of other pretrial matters and, therefore, "a separate settlement conference may be desirable."[8] Most of the 50 states and the U.S. Territories include provisions similar to FRCP Rule 16 in their rules of civil procedure.

2. Second, the Federal Rules of Civil Procedure also provide that the failure to accept a reasonable offer of settlement may result in the rejecting party's having to pay the costs associated with trial.[9] Rule 68 declares that at any time more than 10 days before the trial begins, the defendant may serve upon the plaintiff an offer, which includes payment of plaintiff's costs up to that point and which, if accepted, becomes the judgment of the court. However, if plaintiff rejects the offer and later is awarded less at trial, plaintiff must pay defendant's costs from the time the offer was made.[10] Thus, the rule supports the making and accepting of realistic offers of settlement and imposes sanctions for failure to take such offers seriously. Two-thirds of the states and the District of Columbia have rules that are similar to FRCP Rule 68.

3. Another manner in which the law promotes settlement is to disallow into evidence any offers to settle a case, including the fact that an offer was made, the nature or amount of the offer, to whom the offer was extended, any statements or behavior surrounding the offer, or any other information about it.[11] The concern of the drafters of the Federal Rules of Evidence (FRE) was that such offers would be used to prove that the offering party was admitting liability, as well as the amount of that liability.[12] The Advisory Committee on the Rules noted that Rule 408 was intended to promote compromise and settlement of disputes.[13] Furthermore, they considered that offers of settlement were likely to be motivated by a desire for peace and closure and, therefore, were irrelevant as concessions of weakness of position.[14] All other U.S. jurisdictions have similar rules.

4. A fourth way that law and policy support negotiated settlements is to permit judges and juries to award prejudgment interest for certain damages such as lost wages and medical expenses.[15] Rather than allow the defendant to have, in effect, the use of plaintiff's money during the time a case is pending, the defendant is required to pay not only the damages but interest thereon from the date of loss.[16] The risk of incurring substantial interest charges is designed to encourage the defendant to make an early and reasonable offer in settlement of the case.[17]

5. Finally, the law promotes negotiation by requiring in some cases that the parties bargain in "good faith." This is especially true in labor law dealing with the negotiations between unions and management.* For a fuller discussion of mandatory participation in settlement negotiations and good faith bargaining, see Chapter Four, *Mandatory Participation in Mediation*.

The Negotiation Climate

While the law provides a structure within which to build a negotiated settlement, much of the process of negotiation is shaped by cultural and psychological principles that influence how people interact with one another. Attorneys often assume that they will be successful at negotiation. After all, attorneys, like people everywhere, have been relating to their fellow human beings for all their lives. "How hard can it be?" most lawyers ask.

In fact, successful bargaining takes patience, training, and practice. Negotiation is a process comprising various and distinct phases that a good negotiator will recognize, understand and orchestrate. Negotiation involves a certain amount of ritual, and the stages of negotiation must evolve naturally. A common mistake in negotiating is trying to cut the process short before the parties have reached the point, intellectually and emotionally, where they are ready to settle. A patient bargainer who permits the process to unfold is more likely to obtain expeditious settlement agreements than the impatient negotiator who tries to needlessly accelerate the process.[18]

Experts who study and teach negotiating have made the following observations about the climate in which negotiation usually takes place.

1. First, the atmosphere in which negotiation of disputes occurs is usually full of tension. Even under the best of circumstances, it is an uncomfortable process for most Americans, primarily because we place such a high value on being forthright about our opinions and feelings. Consequently, most people do not like to bargain. They prefer instead to know up front the terms involved in a transaction or relationship, which they are then free to accept or reject. Any American who has ever bought a car or traveled to parts of the world where haggling over the price of merchandise is acceptable learns very quickly just how easily we acquiesce to the demands of the other party. Because of our aversion to bargaining, we are poor negotiators. Furthermore, we know it, and we expect our opponents to take advantage of us because of it.

2. Second, the parties involved in negotiating frequently place very different values on the dispute. Furthermore, they will measure value in many different ways, including the amount of money at stake, the concessions they may demand or be required to make, whether or not the outcome will enhance or detract from their ego, how much emotional energy they will have expended to reach a settlement, etc.

---

* The National Labor Relations Act, for example, requires that the parties meet at reasonable times and confer in good faith with respect to wages, hours, and other terms and conditions of employment. 29 U.S.C. §158(a)(5), (b)(3)

Remember Tim, the computer analyst from Chapter One who believed that he was being treated unfairly by his employer? In negotiating his claim with the boss, Tim will place more than a raise in salary on the line. Even if he achieves his short-term objective, he may still eventually lose his job and with it his financial security. He risks being branded as a troublemaker, which could stymie his career. If he gets less than what he wants, he will lose face with his associates and possibly even with his family and friends. If Tim's dispute turns into a lawsuit, he must hire a lawyer with no guarantee that any settlement he may be awarded will cover his costs.

Compare Tim's situation to that of his employer. If the company is large and profitable, the possibility of a lawsuit will be a minor annoyance with very little at risk. Conversely, if the company is small and privately owned, the threat of costly litigation must be weighed against the risk of acquiescing to demands that could set a precedent for other employees to emulate. Ultimately, the company may be forced out of business by employee demands and lawsuits it cannot afford.

3. Parties to a dispute are likely to misunderstand what is important to their opponents – in other words, what the other side really wants. Most disputants assume that the other side is looking only for the highest (or lowest) possible monetary settlement. Consequently, they will fail to see, for example, that their opponent wants an apology or recognition for a past achievement, desires that the relationship between them will survive the dispute, is weary and wants to settle, or some other less tangible but nevertheless valuable result. In their pursuit for the highest (or lowest) possible monetary settlement, disputants are likely also to overlook their own, intangible, but equally important needs.

4. Another phenomenon that contributes to the negotiation climate is the expectation that very little will be accomplished from negotiating and that the best that can be hoped for is to arrive at some "split the baby" compromise that satisfies no one. Furthermore, in almost every negotiation, one of the parties will feel a greater need to settle, because the negotiation process makes them more uncomfortable or because they feel a greater need to avoid the risk of not settling. People involved in conflict are more likely to focus on what they have to lose rather than on what they have to gain. Yet studies show that participants who approach negotiation with confidence in the process and high expectations of what can be achieved usually get better and more satisfying results.

5. Finally, the differences in the experience, values and expectations of the attorneys on the one hand and their clients on the other contribute significantly to the negotiation climate. An attorney is more likely to be experienced at negotiation and therefore will feel more in control, less anxious, better able to read the signals and know from previous cases when and how the current case will settle.

Ego involvement is also likely to vary. The attorney may view negotiation in a businesslike manner, while the client may be angry and looking for vindication or revenge. Or the attorney may relish the opportunity to verbally annihilate an opponent, while the client just wants a fair and expeditious settlement. A competent attorney-negotiator will ascertain these differences, help the client understand the process and put the client's needs first.

Exercises

1. Do you consider yourself a good negotiator? If so, what is it about your personality or behavior that makes you effective? If not, what makes you ineffective?

2. How does knowledge about the subject matter of the negotiation improve your ability to negotiate?

3. People often approach negotiating with a sense of fear or apprehension. What do you think they are afraid of?

4. Having a vested interest in the outcome of a negotiation can affect how we approach the process. Discuss the negotiation atmosphere in the following circumstances from the standpoint of each of the parties:
    - ✓   college roommates choosing three toppings to order on a pizza
    - ✓   a married couple deciding where to go to dinner
    - ✓   a young college graduate, recently employed in his or her first job, negotiating the price of a new car
    - ✓   a commercial cleaning company responding to the demands of its largest customer to reclean two entire floors of an office tower after the new tenants complained
    - ✓   a Fortune 500 company who is a defendant in a toxic tort class action suit considering a settlement offer from the plaintiffs
    - ✓   a diplomat negotiating the release of hostages held by a terrorist group that is withholding food from its prisoners
    - ✓   a felon facing a possible federal sentence of life without parole negotiating the terms of a plea bargain with a shorter sentence.

Approaches to Negotiating

Negotiations vary not only in the values, expectations and attitudes that the players bring to the table, but in the overall approach to the task of negotiating. Generally speaking, there are two ways to view a negotiation, *distributive* and *interest-based*.

Distributive Negotiation

Distributive negotiation assumes that the parties to a dispute have a fixed amount of resources that they must divide between them. Therefore, the more one side gets, the less will be left for the other. Many lawsuits involve a sum of money that the parties must divide. In some situations, the maximum amount available is predetermined by insurance caps and similar mechanisms. In others, the ceiling figure is limited only by the resources of the defendant.

In either situation, however, the plaintiff knows the minimum she will accept while the defendant knows the maximum that he will pay. This approach to negotiating has also been called "positional" negotiating[19] because each party comes to the table with a predetermined position or result in mind. Thus, the scope of the dispute and the possible outcomes are limited to the positions that each party initiates. Distributive/positional negotiating focuses on what each party is willing to give or take in order to settle. The goal is to gain the most concessions from the other party.

Interest-Based Negotiating

Interest-based negotiating, on the other hand, is collaborative. It assumes that underneath the issues on the table are other interests that need to be identified and satisfied. It also assumes that the parties may have some interests in common that they can solve together. For this reason, it is also called "integrative negotiating." In a patent infringement suit, for example, the plaintiff, a small and underfunded manufacturer, seeks to establish his patent rights and also obtain a sum of money to compensate him for lost sales due to the defendant's knockoff product. The defendant, on the other hand, who is well funded and has access to a lucrative new market, is less concerned about paying damages and more concerned about retaining the right to continue selling his product. By employing collaborative, integrative negotiating, the parties should be able to uncover each other's underlying interests. The manufacturer may be able to negotiate the sale of his patent for a top price. Or the parties may discover that by joining forces in business, they can achieve more together than on their own.

The Camp David Accord signed by Israel and Egypt in 1979 offers a well-known example of integrative, interest-based negotiating. During the 1967 Six-Day War, Israel gained control of the Sinai Peninsula, a large desert area separating the two countries. Over the years, Israel and Egypt attempted unsuccessfully to negotiate the return of the land to Egypt, primarily by drawing conflicting boundary lines on maps and trying to bully one another into conceding. In 1979, then-United States President Jimmy Carter proposed a peace conference between Israel and Egypt designed to enable the two sides to redefine their positions based on what they valued the most. For Israel, this meant restoring and preserving the security of its pre-1967 southern border. For Egypt, on the other hand, which felt emasculated by the loss of its land, it meant regaining its sense of sovereignty. To meet the interests of both parties, Israel and Egypt creating a demilitarized Sinai under Egyptian civilian control. Israel could again feel secure without a military presence abutting her southern border, and Egypt could again feel whole.

It is important to note that a distributive approach to negotiating is not wrong, nor is an interest-based approach applicable to all disputes. As indicated above, many disputes are only about money. That's all the defendant has to offer and that's all the plaintiff wants. There is no ongoing relationship or other factors present that would cause the parties to have common interests or mutually compatible needs. In these situations, a distributive approach is highly appropriate.

Styles of Negotiating

Just as there are two approaches or ways of viewing a negotiation, there are also two primary styles of negotiating, *competitive* and *cooperative*.

Competitive Negotiation

A competitive negotiator views negotiation as a battle to be won. The goal is to make the greatest possible gains for his or her side, to the detriment of the other. A competitive negotiator views the interests of the parties as antagonistic and does not consider that they may have interests in common. The competitive negotiator uses intimidation to raise the level of tension in order to gain concessions. Yet, at the same time he or she concedes little. The competitive negotiator tends to see all disputes as distributive in nature, and is often able to win large monetary settlements for clients.

Cooperative Negotiation

In contrast, the cooperative negotiator attempts to identify and create several alternative solutions to a dispute that will leave all the parties at least somewhat satisfied. While the cooperative negotiator hopes to gain most of what is important to his or her client, the negotiator realizes that he or she must help the other side to achieve at least some of its objectives. A humiliated opponent is beneficial to no one. In contrast to the competitive negotiator, the cooperative bargainer makes reasonable demands and responds positively to well-reasoned arguments from the other side. Not surprisingly, the cooperative negotiator is most effective and most comfortable with interest-based bargaining.

The following chart compares competitive and cooperative negotiating.[20]

COMPETITIVE NEGOTIATING	COOPERATIVE NEGOTIATING
Tries to maximize tangible gains for one side to the detriment of the other	Tries to maximize what each side attains, both tangible and intangible
Believes that the interests of the parties are antagonistic	Believes that the parties share common values that need to be discovered and emphasized
Takes an adversarial approach	Takes a problem-solving approach
Relies on adversarial tactics	Relies on thorough knowledge of the facts of the case
Attempts to isolate the opposition	Draws opponents together as joint problem solvers
Goal is to win as much as possible	Goal is a mutually agreeable solution that is fair to all parties
Makes high opening demands and sticks with them	Seeks reasonable results based on the common interests of the parties
Demands concessions as a condition to continue, but seldom concedes	Makes realistic demands and yields to reasonable arguments
Invests ego in positions taken during negotiation which must be defended at all cost	Separates ego from positions taken during negotiation
Defines the problem as being the other party's actions and attitudes	Separates the people from the problem
Manipulates and intimidates opponent with threats, confrontation, argument, and abrasive communication style	Reasons with opponent; uses non-confrontational debating techniques and a firm but pleasant communication style

Exercises

1. In each of the scenarios in the exercises on page 26, question 4, which style of negotiating, competitive or cooperative, is likely to be employed by each of the parties involved? Why?

2. In each of the scenarios in the exercises on page 26, question 4, what competing interests are the parties likely to have. What common interests are the parties likely to have that, if maximized, could improve the outcome?

Negotiation Styles

Each style of negotiation involves certain advantages, but also risks.

Competitive Negotiation Benefits and Drawbacks

In disputes where the issues are clear-cut, the stakes are well-defined, one party is significantly more powerful than the other, and/or the parties have no ongoing relationship, a competitive approach to negotiating can quickly bring a dispute to its inevitable conclusion. Also, a competitive negotiator may be better prepared to deal with competitive tactics used by the other side and, therefore, is less likely to be rattled or misled by such tactics.

On the other hand, the competitive negotiator relies on tension, fear, threat and manipulation, which are powerful yet largely uncontrollable factors. Reliance on competitive tactics tends to minimize the value of thoroughly analyzing the merits of the dispute and identifying all possible solutions. Also, the anger and fear engendered by competitive negotiating impedes the flow of information between the parties.

Thus, the competitive negotiator risks being unprepared and unable to exchange information that could help his or her client. The competitive negotiator also risks being unable or unwilling to recognize solutions that emerge during negotiation that could be beneficial to both parties. Competitive negotiation tends to be hard on relationships and may result in either no settlement or settlements that are dissatisfying to the parties and, therefore, difficult to enforce. It can also be distasteful enough to dissuade the parties from seeking early settlement in future disputes, preferring instead the relative orderliness of a civil trial rather than the hand-to-hand combat of competitive negotiations.

Cooperative Negotiation Benefits and Drawbacks

Cooperative negotiating holds the promise of achieving settlements that are satisfactory to all the parties and not just to one side. In disputes that involve several issues and a variety of possible outcomes, cooperative negotiators are more likely to identify and seek trade-offs that will leave each side feeling satisfied. For example, an insurance company may be more willing to agree to a higher settlement if the payout is over many years rather than in one lump sum. A noncustodial parent may agree to fewer weekend visits that disrupt everyone's schedules, if he or she can have the children at Christmas and all summer. Cooperative negotiating is also more likely to promote positive relations between the parties in the future.

Nevertheless, the cooperative negotiator also faces risk. He or she may be perceived as weak by the other negotiator, who responds by escalating the competition. A cooperative negotiator who is relying on the good will of all the parties may be unable to recognize manipulation, and to defend against competitive tactics. The cooperative negotiator also risks giving away too much information that will damage the client's position and foreclose possible solutions. Consequently, the cooperative negotiator may inadvertently escalate the competition, weaken the client's position and sabotage the process.

Also, because cooperative negotiating relies on thorough research and analysis of a dispute, this approach to negotiation can take more time and cost the client more money. Furthermore, cooperative negotiation requires substantial skill and knowledge of the process, which many clients cannot afford and many negotiators do not possess.

Studies show that only one-fourth of all attorneys consistently use a competitive approach to negotiating.[21] Furthermore, cooperative negotiators are more capable than their counterparts at employing competitive tactics when necessary. In theory, competitive negotiators will use whatever style(s) will enable them to "win"; in fact, they tend to use competitive tactics exclusively. Even though competitive negotiators often produce larger settlements for their clients, cooperative negotiators are viewed as more effective by other lawyers, perhaps because their negotiations are less likely to break down and end in nonsettlement or subsequent actions to collect a judgment. Nevertheless, negotiators who successfully combine the strengths of both approaches are most likely to achieve both a high rate of settlement and maximum results.

Combining Styles of Negotiating

Frequently, a negotiation will begin cooperatively, during which time the parties each gain important concessions that are not costly to the other side. Eventually, however, the parties reach the more distributive issues in their dispute, where concessions become significantly more costly. This is the point where agreement must be reached, for example, on which heir will get the farm, which parent will be awarded custody of a child, or how much money an injured party will receive. As a result, the parties are likely to switch to a more competitive style of bargaining in an attempt to get what they want.

Take the case of a building contractor facing significant, unanticipated cost overruns on construction of an elementary school. The school district sues him for failure to complete construction. During negotiation, the contractor recommends that he be permitted to substitute less expensive materials that are of comparable quality. As each type of material is discussed, the contractor and school district either grant or deny the other's request, or identify alternatives that are satisfactory to both. The result of this process is a modified building plan that generally satisfies the client and provides the contractor with a modest profit.

The school district now demands that construction be completed by the beginning of the next school year. The contractor, knowing that he will sustain a loss if he is forced to complete the building within that time period, asks for an extension and is refused. Both sides switch to a more competitive style of negotiating and begin to bargain hard for their respective positions.

At risk is the accord that they have reached regarding the modified building plan, and the possibility of more costs and delays if negotiations break down and the case proceeds through the courts. Neither side can afford an impasse; conversely, both sides believe that they have conceded enough. The challenge is to be both firm and also open to alternatives in the spirit of cooperation that characterized the earlier phase of negotiation.

Exercise

> In each of the scenarios in the exercises on page 26, question 4, what are the benefits and drawbacks of both competitive and cooperative negotiating under the circumstances? How could a negotiator combine the two styles to achieve a good result for all the parties? How would you negotiate each situation?

Phases of Negotiations

Earlier in this chapter, negotiation was described as a process comprising various and distinct phases. There are essentially six phases in a typical negotiation.[22]

I.   Preparation Phase
II. Preliminary Phase
III. Information Phase
IV. Competitive/Distributive Phase
V. Closing Phase
VI. Cooperative/Integrative Phase

The discussion that follows implies that negotiation takes place in one formal session. Keep in mind, however, that negotiation usually involves several sessions, some of which are in person and others over the telephone and by fax and e-mail. Furthermore, negotiations may break off at any point in the process. Nevertheless, consecutive sessions tend to build on one another and eventually should reach the closing and integrative phases with a minimum of backtracking.

I. Preparation Phase

Success in any enterprise depends on solid preparation. For the negotiator this means:

♦ researching the facts of the case and the applicable law

♦ understanding the position(s) of the client in the dispute

♦ identifying and thinking through all possible arguments that support the client's position

♦ thoroughly probing what the client wants to achieve in the case and prioritizing those goals as essential, important, or merely desirable

♦ determining the probable outcome of the case if a negotiated settlement is not achieved

♦ developing a strategy and plan for negotiations

♦ reviewing the plan with the client and obtaining all necessary approval or authority from the client to negotiate according to the plan.

First of all, it is critical that an advocate have a thorough enough understanding of a case to know what the client wants, and to assess what he or she can reasonably expect, given the strengths and weaknesses of the claims being made. At the beginning of a case, most clients fully expect that a jury will side with them. Furthermore, clients generally couch their goals in terms of what a jury can award – usually a sum of money.

An effective advocate will provide a client with a realistic assessment of both the strengths and weaknesses of the case. The advocate will also probe for additional interests, besides just money damages, that if met will help compensate the client. Some of those interests might include[23]

♦ being listened to and understood

♦ receiving an apology or an expression of sympathy

♦ maintaining an ongoing relationship with the other party after the dispute is resolved

♦ preserving or reestablishing the client's position, role or reputation

♦ keeping the dispute and its outcome confidential

♦   shaming the other party publicly

♦   proving once and for all that the client is right.

Paralegals who conduct intake interviews or who have ongoing contact with clients can provide valuable assistance to attorneys in gathering objective and subjective information about the case, and in providing feedback about the client's needs and desires.

Once an advocate has a thorough understanding of the client's case, he or she will turn to the opponent's. An effective negotiator will attempt to understand the opponent's position, both legally and personally, and will think through how to respond to every anticipated argument. Good negotiators will neither underestimate the opponent's weaknesses nor overestimate their own strengths. The curse in any dispute is to assume that you have the upper hand.

Next, a conscientious negotiator will carefully plan strategy and tactics from opening offer to final agreement. This includes establishing an "aspiration level," which is a measurement of the best possible results that the negotiator believes can be attained. An effective aspiration level is high but reasonable, and one which the negotiator can defend objectively and with confidence. In addition, the negotiator will also identify the lowest level of results that will be acceptable. The distance between the aspiration level and the minimum acceptable level is called the "settlement range." The goal in negotiation is to settle as close to the aspiration level as possible. Naturally, it is important that the negotiator also estimate the settlement range of the other side.[*]

If the case is particularly complex, from both a legal and factual standpoint, a negotiator may have difficulty formulating a realistic settlement range until at least some discussion and negotiation has occurred. The more talking that takes place between the negotiators, the better educated each will be about the case and the other side, and therefore, the better able they will be to develop a realistic settlement range, as well as evaluate their opponent's range of expectations. Sometimes, negotiators will develop a written statement of their aspiration level for presentation to the other side. Called a settlement brochure, it will often include pictures and other graphics designed to legitimize and reinforce the client's opening position. A well-drafted settlement brochure, which is often prepared, in part, by the paralegal assigned to the case, can go a long way in convincing the opponent that the client's expectations are realistic and supportable.

Finally, in order to understand the consequences of nonsettlement, the negotiator must determine the best and worst alternatives to a negotiated agreement. If the case goes to trial, a jury may award more than the client's aspiration level. Yet, continuing the litigation could consume much of the award. Conversely, the jury may award nothing, or less than the opponent's last offer. Furthermore, waiting for a trial and jury verdict could take many more months or even years.

---

[*]   In a typical example, a plaintiff may hope for $100,000 but will settle for as little as $50,000. Conversely, the defendant may hope to settle for as little as $25,000 but will pay $75,000. Consequently, if settlement occurs it will happen when the parties agree on some figure between $50,000 and $75,000. Much of what occurs in negotiation is designed to discover the other party's settlement range and to determine if they will, in fact, go higher (or lower) than their original positions.

The negotiator will also need to estimate the BATNA and WATNA of the other side.[*] Paralegals can provide valuable assistance in assessing alternatives to negotiation by conducting research into local jury awards and other matters that will help the negotiator estimate possible results at trial.

Tips from the Experts

♦ Know what the client wants and why.

♦ Estimate what the opponent wants and why.

♦ Of all the arguments that can be made, decide which ones will be the most effective

♦ Develop a concession pattern; either a series of small concessions or a few major position changes

♦ Determine if the opening position is high enough; higher expectations usually achieve better results.

♦ Role-play the negotiations.

♦ Check out your opponent's reputation as a negotiator.

II. Preliminary Phase

The preliminary phase is the opening of the negotiation session when the parties will introduce themselves and exchange professional and personal information. It is also the first opportunity to establish the tone of the negotiation as competitive or cooperative, unfriendly or congenial. During this phase, the attorneys will develop a better understanding of who they are up against, including how knowledgeable the other side is about the essential facts of the case and the substantive law that governs the dispute. Ideally, the attorneys will have established a cordial working relationship before any formal session, however.

Some instructors of negotiating caution students that the preliminary phase actually begins when the attorneys first contact one another about the case. Every communication from that point forward provides an opportunity to set the tone of future negotiating, to learn important information about the other side, and to begin to extract concessions from them. These concessions include, for example, stipulation of facts, hearing schedules, and the times and locations for formal negotiation sessions. While they may seem innocent at the time, nevertheless, these early concessions establish a pattern of giving in that an effective negotiator will attempt to continue when negotiations turn to more substantive issues.

Early communications can also inadvertently give away valuable information to the opponent. Consequently, all members of the client's legal team should be instructed regarding their roles in gathering information and influencing the negotiating climate.

---

[*] Authors will often refer to the "best alternative to a negotiated agreement" as the BATNA, and the "worst alternative to a negotiated agreement" as the WATNA.

Because paralegals will often communicate with their counterparts to convey messages and deal with administrative matters related to discovery, hearings and negotiation sessions, they need to be especially sensitive to how they can influence negotiating. Paralegals should be cordial and yet cautious about what they say. At the same time, they should listen carefully and learn as much as possible about how the other side is thinking and feeling about the matter.

The clients may or may not be present during formal negotiations. Their presence is one of the strategic decisions that the attorneys and their clients must make. In determining whether or not to involve the client, a negotiator must consider many factors, including not only what the client may say but what sorts of nonverbal clues he or she is apt to give and how this might influence the negotiation either positively or negatively. Some clients may be so emotionally involved in the dispute that their presence is likely to be disruptive and their behavior difficult to control. In other cases, a client may be unable to attend or be too weak to endure a long and rigorous negotiation. Conversely, a client may be able to provide important factual information during the course of negotiating and, therefore, his or her presence is essential. One side may choose to send only their attorney(s), leaving the other to decide whether their client should or should not be included. When clients are present at negotiation sessions, it is critical that they be well-prepared ahead of time as to what their role(s) will be, what to expect from the other side, and how to comport themselves.

Tips from the Experts

♦ Maintain control of the logistics such as where and when negotiations will take place, when the next telephone conversation will take place, etc. Remember the "home court advantage."

♦ Orchestrate all communications with the other side. It's all part of the negotiations.

♦ Consider using a team approach – two negotiators or a paralegal to assist. It adds strength in numbers, another voice, and another set of eyes and ears.

♦ Showcase a sympathetic client. Take him or her along to a negotiation session to humanize the dispute.

III. Information Phase

During the information phase the emphasis should be on understanding the opponent's position and their underlying needs and desires. Generally, the parties attempt to gain as much information as possible about each other while revealing as little as possible about themselves. Successful negotiators will control this process, giving out just enough information to keep the negotiations moving forward, while avoiding revelations that will damage their position. Too much information too soon may cause the process to get ahead of the players and result in nonsettlement. For example, if the negotiator quickly and easily reveals the client's settlement range, the other side is unlikely to take it seriously and will assume that the true range is much different. It is also important to anticipate what questions the other side will ask and how best to respond.

Effective negotiators will ask open-ended questions that seek to learn the what, when, why and how of the case, rather than ask questions that can be answered with "yes" or "no." The goal is to induce the other side to keep talking and reveal as much information as possible. A good negotiator will listen intently and also pay careful attention not only to what is being said but to the wealth of verbal and nonverbal communication that is going on at the same time. For example:[24]

- Frequent clearing of the throat usually means the speaker is about to make a false statement.

- Highly deliberate words enunciated slowly and carefully often mean the speaker is intentionally misrepresenting the truth.

- A high-pitched voice conveys anxiety.

- Rubbing the eyes is often a signal that the person is having difficulty accepting what is being said or offered.

- Crossed arms and legs suggest that the person is feeling defensive.

- Drumming the fingers on a table usually signals impatience.

- Placing the hand over the heart is a way for a speaker to appear credible, while open and uplifted hands convey sincerity.

- Hand wringing, sweating, and frequent blinking usually mean the person is feeling extreme tension.

- Taut lips signal the party is feeling anxious and frustrated.

- Leaning back and assuming a relaxed posture says the person is feeling confident.

- Affirmative head nodding can mean agreement, or it can mean, "Let's move on."

- Shaking one's head from side to side can mean disagreement with what is being said, or it may mean that one is lying.

- Use of words such as "to be truthful" and "candidly" usually means the person is being neither.

Negotiation training will almost always include extensive instruction in how to read, and also send, nonverbal communication to advantage. Paralegals who attend negotiations should be trained in these matters in order to provide skilled listening and observation assistance to the attorneys involved.

During the information phase, the parties usually will reveal their initial offers. This occurs even when the negotiators are trying to employ an integrative, nondistributional approach to negotiating. The difference is that in integrative negotiating, opening positions are viewed as amendable because the parties are open to reasonable arguments from the other side. Nevertheless, beginning positions are almost always higher than the clients' aspiration levels.

Tips from the Experts

- Keep the other side talking.

- Determine what information will be kept absolutely confidential – no exceptions. All else is revealable at the appropriate time.

♦ Block inquiries into sensitive areas, e.g., give general answers to specific questions and vice versa; answer a question with a question.

♦ Communicate the client's less significant and controversial demands first. This helps to build cooperation and a pattern of compromise.

♦ Reveal the client's demands slowly – even reluctantly. They will be more believable.

♦ Question the other side's demands. Ask why each demand is important.

IV. Competitive/ Distributive Phase

Fortified with information about the opponent, this is the point when each side attempts to gain as many concessions as possible from the other. Concessions tend to be made in response to a party's evaluation of his or her own situation, as well as an evaluation of the position, options and capabilities of the other side. Consequently, the negotiators will attempt to influence these perceptions. As the reader might have guessed, this is the phase when negotiators are most likely to use competitive tactics such as argument, warnings, threats, challenges, manipulation, silence and other similar tactics. At the same time, successful negotiators will try to appear even-handed, objective, and back up their demands with logical-sounding arguments.

During the distributive phase, the negotiators will take turns making offers and justifying why each offer is reasonable. If the other side buys the argument, they will concede ground and come up (or down) on their offer. Unless one of the parties has an especially strong case or forces the other side to make major concessions through the use of competitive tactics, early negotiations are likely to be characterized by small concessions and little movement toward compromise.

Therefore, for the negotiations to be successful, one of the parties must make an offer closer to his or her settlement range. For example, in the footnote example above on page 32, if plaintiff opened at $150,000 and defendant countered with $10,000, and after several offers and counter offers the parties have progressed to only $125,000 and $18,000, respectively, plaintiff may want to reduce her demand to $95,000 in order to induce defendant to make a similar concession and raise his offer to $25,000. Thus, the negotiations will, in effect, begin again with both of the parties within their settlement ranges, and only $70,000 rather than $140,000 apart.

Tips from the Experts

♦ Stick to your concession strategy. Don't be tricked into making major position changes you did not plan.

♦ Have a good argument for every demand, and a good argument for every concession.

♦ Explain your arguments. Don't just state them conclusively.

♦ After each major concession, check your position with your BATNA. Do the same for major concessions by your opponent.

♦ Don't threaten the opponent, but do point out the natural consequences if they stubbornly stick to their demands.

- Don't fall for the "dire predictions" ploy; e.g., "We'll have to take at least fifteen depositions and demand ten years' worth of records if we are forced to go to trial." Ask yourself how likely the opposing client will be to pay for all that discovery.

- Use promises rather than threats – "I'll come down if you'll come up."

- Keep the opponent talking; then listen, watch and keep still.

- Communicate succinctly. Don't ramble.

- Don't reveal if you have final authority to settle. Always claim you must check with the client first. This way you can come back and ask for more.

- Beware of negotiators who put themselves at your mercy, hoping that you will soften your demands. Stay tough.

- Take breaks to restore your composure and sense of perspective.

V. Closing Phase

When the parties realize that an agreement within their respective settlement ranges is likely, they enter the closing phase and become committed to settling. The initial temptation is to rush ahead and concede too much too soon. The second reaction is to become fearful about the possibility of conceding too much. Good negotiators will carefully pace this phase of the process, and through the use of conciliatory tactics, encourage the opponent to close the gap that remains.

Tips from the Experts

- Be patient. Don't move too quickly to closure.

- Stay calm. Don't employ any disruptive tactics at this point.

- Make sure you have attained all possible benefits for your client. Don't leave anything on the table.

- Don't make any unreciprocated final concessions. Close the gap together.

- Help your opponent close the gap by suggesting an "out," e.g., "I know you're concerned what your client will think. But I'm sure that we can both explain to our clients the benefits of our agreement."

VI. Cooperative/ Integrative Phase

At this point everyone is likely to be exhausted. Nevertheless, there may remain some alternative tradeoffs that should be explored. For example, an insurance company may agree to pay a larger settlement if it can pay the award in installment payments rather than a lump sum. A contractor might offer to complete a stalled construction job in exchange for a lower monetary settlement. Likewise, a noncustodial parent may offer substantially higher child support payments in exchange for a smaller lump sum divorce payout. When all possible agreement has been reached, the accord should be written down and executed by the parties.

Tips from the Experts

- Suggest to the opponent that both sides first initial the agreement reached and then discuss ways to improve the deal.

- Be prepared with some possible trade-offs and present them to the other negotiator.

Negotiation Case Study

The following negotiation case study involves a contract dispute "with a twist." As with most contract matters, money is a major issue. Consequently, parties and negotiators must be prepared to do the mathematics necessary to evaluate their own alternative positions as well as those of the other side. Contract matters often involve other issues besides money, however, as you will see. Exercises have been inserted within the case to help you analyze and understand the issues involved as the story unfolds.

Phelps Energy desired to drill several wells on land that it had leased from a rancher. Phelps had six months remaining on its lease with the landowner to complete the wells or lose the lease for which it had paid over $1,500,000. After studying geological surveys of the lease, Phelps decided to drill six wells on the property. The project was supported by a group of physician/investors who had limited experience in oil and gas investments and were more than a little nervous about the speculative nature of petroleum exploration ventures.

Because Phelps had drilled many times before in the general area where its lease was located, it dispensed with the step of obtaining bids from drillers and instead, sought out Aztec Exploration to drill the wells. Aztec was a small, three-year-old oil and gas exploration firm with a reputation for hard work, honest dealing and high-tech equipment. Although Phelps had never dealt with Aztec before, and typically did not deal with drillers in business for less than five years, the energy company decided to gamble on Aztec because of its solid reputation. Naturally, Aztec was excited about the nod from Phelps, which was bigger than any company they had serviced so far. Aztec knew that if it did a good job, Phelps would use them in the future.

Phelps drew up a standard industry contract for Aztec's services. The contract stated the price to be paid to Aztec by Phelps, inclusive of Aztec's profit. Phelps based the price on standard industry norms and on its experience drilling in the area. The contract included no additional language about if and how the price could or would be modified. The contract also contained an integration clause asserting that the written document encompassed the entire agreement between the parties.

Under the terms of the contract, Phelps provided Aztec with geological studies indicating the nature of the layers of earth through which Aztec had to drill, along with the projected locations of the oil reservoirs below the surface. Using the geological studies and oil industry norms, Phelps estimated the cost of drilling each well at $100,000, which included $50,000 for supplies and labor, and a projected profit for Aztec of approximately $50,000 per well. This brought the total projected drilling cost to $600,000. Under the terms of the contract, Phelps paid Aztec one-half of this amount ($300,000) at the start of the project so that Aztec would have sufficient funds to pay subcontractors and suppliers. Phelps agreed to pay Aztec the remaining $300,000 at the rate of $50,000 per well as each well was completed. Nevertheless, due to the state-of-the-art equipment used by Aztec, the actual drilling costs projected by Aztec were $40,000 per well, which increased Aztec's projected profit to $60,000 per well.

Exercise

> Based on what you know so far, make a list of Phelps' likely objectives and concerns about the project. Make a list of Aztec's likely objectives and concerns.

During initial drilling of the first well, Aztec determined that the geological study provided by Phelps was inaccurate and that the reservoirs were at least 2,000 feet deeper than originally estimated. In addition, they discovered that the layers of earth below the surface had denser rock than indicated. As a result, Aztec estimated that it would expend $25,000 more per well, which increased its projected costs per well to $65,000 ($40,000 + $25,000).

Faced with unanticipated costs of $150,000 ($25,000 per well X 6 wells) that Aztec blamed on Phelps, the driller directed the company's attorney to draft a letter to Phelps outlining Aztec's request for an additional $150,000. The detailed letter provided Phelps with a thoughtful description of Aztec's analysis and findings concerning the geological nature of the field and compared those findings to the erroneous survey provided by Phelps. Despite the reasonableness of Aztec's letter, the Phelps attorney responded a few days later refusing Aztec's request and reasserting the terms of the contract whereby Aztec had agreed to drill six wells at $100,000 per well.

Exercises

1. a. Prepare a chart, outlining the numbers discussed above, that compares the various assumptions of each of the parties and each of the scenarios we know about so far. How many columns will you need? Consider the following 12 scenarios:

   1-2   original assumptions used by Phelps

   3-6   revised assumptions of Phelps in light of the new geological information:
   - ✓   if Phelps absorbs the additional costs, or
   - ✓   if Aztec absorbs the additional costs

   7-8   original assumptions used by Aztec in light of its state-of-the-art technology

   9-12   revised assumptions of Aztec in light of the new geological information:
   - ✓   if Phelps absorbs the additional costs, or
   - ✓   if Aztec absorbs the additional costs.

Tip #1: Prepare two columns for each scenario, the first showing assumptions per well and the second showing totals for the entire project.
Tip #2: Number your columns consecutively from left to right. This makes it easier to compare columns that are not next to one another.
Tip #3: Drop the last three zeros from your figures when preparing your chart, and don't use decimal points.

   b. How many rows will your chart have? (Hint: at least 3, if you include one each for Aztec's costs, Aztec's profits, and Phelps' total outlay.)

2. Analyze your chart. From Phelps' standpoint, how much less is Aztec's profit per well if Aztec absorbs the additional costs? (Subtract column 5 from column 3) What is the answer from Aztec's point of view using its original state-of-the-art assumptions? (Subtract column 11 from column 9) What is the spread of profit for Aztec, per well and overall? What is the spread of outlay for Phelps, per well and overall? Whose spread is wider from a percentage standpoint?

3. Compare Phelps' advance of $300,000 to Aztec's projected costs. Assuming that Phelps believes Aztec's revised cost projections of $25,000 per well, what is the total shortfall based on Phelps' cost estimate of $50,000 per well? What is the shortfall based on Aztec's estimate of $40,000 per well?

4. Based on Phelps' reply to Aztec's demand for more money, what should Aztec do? Should they suspend drilling? File a lawsuit? Call Phelps and ask for a meeting? Discuss the pros and cons of each of these alternatives and others you may identify. What is the likely outcome of each of these courses of action?

5. Under the circumstances, do you think that Phelps is being unfair? How would a judge or jury likely react to any claims by Aztec that Phelps was being unfair?

At the time Aztec signed the Phelps contract, Aztec was experiencing serious cash flow problems, its bank line of credit had been frozen, and no additional sources of capital appeared to be available to the fledgling company. Unknown to Phelps, Aztec deposited the original $300,000 advanced by Phelps into its general operating account, from which it paid expenses and bills on other projects. In addition, an IRS lien was attached to Aztec's bank account. After the lien was satisfied, only $100,000 remained in the Aztec account.

When Phelps refused to advance Aztec an additional $150,000, the driller realized that it had enough money to barely complete four wells, even with the $50,000 well completion payments from Phelps. In order to finish the job, Aztec estimated that it needed an additional $140,000. Naturally, it loathed the thought of absorbing the higher drilling costs, due to Phelps' inaccurate geological data. However, it feared even more the possibility of being sued by Phelps if the energy company learned of Aztec's misuse of its funds, which seemed inevitable under the current circumstances. If Phelps sued, it would likely file claims for breach of contract, as well as fraud and conversion. At stake were consequential damages of several million dollars if Phelps asked for the return of its $300,000 advance, the loss of $1,500,000 for the oil and gas lease, and lost profits from wells that were never drilled. In addition, Aztec faced punitive damages that could equal or exceed three times the amount of consequential damages.

Exercises

1. Based on the information revealed about Aztec's misuse of Phelps' funds, what additional objectives and concerns does the driller have? Add them to the list you started in the first exercise, above. If Phelps learns of Aztec's actions, what additional concerns and objectives would the energy company likely have?

2. How and under what circumstances is Phelps most likely to learn of Aztec's misuse of funds? How can Aztec keep its action a secret? Will they be successful?

3. What bargaining chips has Aztec lost due to its misuse of funds? How would a judge or jury react now to any claims by Aztec that Phelps was being unfair?

Upon receipt of Phelps' letter of refusal, Aztec's management met with the company attorney to plan strategy. The first order of business was to run the numbers and project their cash flow problems if Phelps continued to refuse to advance any more funds. The following chart was prepared for review.

Chart No. 1	Beginning Balance	(Less) Drilling Costs	Before Completion Payment	Plus Completion Payment	Ending Balance
Well # 1	$100,000	($65,000)	$35,000	$50,000	$85,000
Well # 2	$85,000	($65,000)	$20,000	$50,000	$70,000
Well # 3	$70,000	($65,000)	$5,000	$50,000	$55,000
Well # 4	$55,000	($65,000)	($10,000)	$50,000	$40,000
Well # 5	$40,000	($65,000)	($25,000)	$50,000	$25,000
Well # 6	$25,000	($65,000)	($40,000)	$50,000	$10,000

Exercises

1. Based on the chart, do you agree with Aztec's earlier assessment of its shortfall at $140,000? What alternative conclusions are suggested by the numbers?

2. Assuming that Aztec tries to negotiate with Phelps, what would you recommend as its
    - ✓ aspiration level?
    - ✓ minimum acceptable result?
    - ✓ settlement range?

3. What is Aztec's best alternative to a negotiated settlement (BATNA)? In other words, what is the standard against which any offers from Phelps should be measured? For example, can Aztec
    a. walk away from the contract and refund the advance?
    b. subcontract to another driller with more cash?
    c. find another source of capital?
    d. call Phelps' bluff and sue?
    e. some combination of a-d?
    f. come clean, expecting that Phelps will fork over the extra money rather than lose its $1.5 million lease?
    g. declare bankruptcy and seek protection from the court?
    h. skip the country?
    i. other alternatives?

4. What is Aztec's worst alternative to a negotiated settlement (WATNA)? In other words, if Aztec can't negotiate a settlement, what is the worst that will happen? (Remember, Phelps does not yet know about Aztec's misapplication of funds.) For example, what if
    a. Aztec lost the contract and had to refund the advance?
    b. Aztec sued Phelps for breach of contract and lost?
    c. Aztec was sued by Phelps on contract claims only and Aztec lost?
    d. Phelps learned of Aztec's misapplication of funds and sued the driller for $20 million in compensatory damages, plus punitive damages?
    e. other consequences?

5. Based on what you know about Phelps, what is its aspiration level, minimum acceptable result, and settlement range? What is its BATNA and WATNA?

Given the chart above, Aztec realized that it needed only an additional $45,000 to complete all six wells. Consequently, the company defined its minimum acceptable result, aspiration level and settlement range as follows:

♦ minimum acceptable result: $45,000 additional advance from Phelps

♦ aspiration level: $150,000 additional advance from Phelps

♦ settlement range: $45,000 - $150,000

Aztec's management also discussed alternatives to a negotiated settlement, and concluded that it had a fair chance of raising additional capital from one or more private investors who would be unlikely to scrutinize Aztec's records and discover its handling of Phelps' advance. The cost of private money would be substantial, however, and could take too much time to raise. In Aztec's opinion, its worst alternative was for Phelps to file suit and, through discovery, learn of Aztec's mishandling of funds.

Aztec's attorney was directed to call Phelps and propose a meeting between the principals of the two companies and their attorneys. Phelps agreed to the meeting, which was scheduled in just three days. The attorney for Aztec felt that the driller needed to convince Phelps that its request for additional money was reasonable. Therefore, the legal staff quickly assembled documentary evidence supporting Aztec's conclusions regarding the geological formations through which it must drill. The evidence included the report of an expert witness called in to review Phelps' material as well as Aztec's findings. The attorney also felt that Aztec should stress the argument that the Phelps/Aztec contract viewed Phelps' completion payments of $50,000 per well as a release of profit to Aztec rather than as financing for work in progress. Consequently, Aztec prepared the following chart for presentation to Phelps in order to bolster its argument.

Chart No. 2	Beginning Balance	*(Less)* Drilling Costs	Ending Balance
Well # 1	$300,000	($75,000)	$225,000
Well # 2	$225,000	($75,000)	$150,000
Well # 3	$150,000	($75,000)	$75,000
Well # 4	$75,000	($75,000)	$0
Well # 5	$0	($75,000)	($75,000)
Well # 6	($75,000)	($75,000)	($150,000)

Exercises

1. Based on the chart, above, what amount of money would you ask from Phelps as a reasonable and fair additional advance?

2. Do you feel that Aztec is being dishonest to base its cost projections on Phelps' estimates of $50,000 per well rather than Aztec's projections of $40,000 per well?

At the negotiation session, senior management from both companies and their attorneys were present. The meeting took place at the offices of Phelps, primarily because Aztec had no conference room large enough to accommodate all of the participants. Nevertheless, Aztec opened the talks by stating that Phelps had provided inaccurate geological data. It then presented its geological information in considerable detail along with the chart, above. Aztec concluded its presentation by refusing to continue work on the Phelps' wells unless more money was immediately forthcoming from Phelps. In response, Phelps asked Aztec to complete the drilling of at least three wells, and upon completion, Phelps would consider paying some undisclosed amount of additional monies. After a fair amount of discussion and finger pointing in which Phelps inquired on more than one occasion about Aztec's cash position, the meeting adjourned without agreement.

Over the next 24 hours the two sides met separately to reassess their positions. In the Phelps meeting, concern was expressed that their investors were looking for a return on their investment, and that failure to get at least some of the wells into production might cause the group to turn against them. Because drilling had commenced, the lease was automatically extended for another year. Nevertheless, the investors were getting nervous.

In the Aztec meeting, relief was expressed that Phelps had not learned about Aztec's mishandling of funds. Furthermore, they were encouraged by Phelps' indications that it might be willing to advance more monies. Feeling off the hook in terms of their WATNA, the possibility of having to "eat" some of the additional costs no longer seemed so unpalatable, provided Aztec could get enough funds to complete the project. Therefore, Aztec's president called Phelps and offered to continue talking.

The same group met the following day. Aztec again opened the meeting, this time by offering to complete at least three wells without an additional advance. However, the driller declined to do any more work unless more money was forthcoming from Phelps. In response, Phelps offered to release the first $50,000 completion payment now if Aztec would finish the first three wells in one month. A considerable amount of discussion ensued about the feasibility of drilling three wells in such a short time frame, with Aztec stressing the difficult geology and Phelps playing it down. The group adjourned for lunch.

Over barbecue, the Aztec team felt exhilarated that Phelps had tipped its hand regarding the fact that time was just as important to them as money. They also agreed that drilling three wells in one month was "no problem." Down the street, the Phelps group expressed amazement about Aztec's sudden willingness to drill three wells without any assurance of more money, and wondered if some of its initial $300,000 advance might have found its way into other projects. Somebody mentioned the possibility of suing Aztec if that was the case. However, the idea was dismissed because Aztec didn't have a "deep pocket," and furthermore Phelps needed to get several wells into production as soon as possible.

When the negotiation reconvened, Aztec accepted Phelps' offer of $50,000 immediately in completion payments in exchange for drilling three wells in one month, provided Phelps would also assume 50% of the additional costs of production, payable now. Phelps countered with an offer to assume 50% of all substantiated costs above $50,000 per well, payable at the end of the total project. Aztec expressed mock gratitude for Phelps' willingness to assume some of the costs associated with its own inaccurate geological data. Aztec then noted that Phelps was again asking the driller to assume the higher costs it would incur due to an accelerated drilling schedule. Seeing Aztec's point, and also sensing the possibility of saving money in the long run, Phelps revised its counter offer by agreeing to make an immediate one-time payment of $45,000 toward added costs on top of the $50,000 advance completion payment.

Realizing that it had exacted $95,000 out of Phelps, which was more than enough to complete all six wells, without relinquishing completion payments, Aztec's attorney offered to draft a memorandum of intent on the spot to be initialed by the parties, and to follow up with a typed agreement for signing by the CEO of each company. As the attorney pulled out a legal pad, Phelps' president decided to try one more gambit. Would Aztec agree to complete all six wells in three months rather than six if Phelps immediately released the remaining $250,000 in completion payments into an escrow account, from which Aztec could draw with approval from Phelps? Aztec's president nodded vigorously in agreement.

Exercises

1. As a result of the negotiation, what did each side accomplish? How close did each side get to its aspiration level?

2. What alternatives emerged during the negotiation that were not anticipated during the preparation phase?

3. At what point in the negotiation did the preliminary phase begin? The information phase? The competitive/distributive phase? The closing phase? The cooperative/integrative phase?

4. Identify the tactics in the negotiation that you would consider to be characteristic of distributive/positional bargaining? Characteristic of integrative/collaborative bargaining?

5. What is the likely result of this negotiation in terms of the future? Will Aztec and Phelps do more business together? How are they apt to treat one another and what policies and procedures will be instituted to avoid more problems?

Matching Negotiation Tactics to the Dispute

In choosing the best negotiation tactics for each phase of bargaining, negotiators must consider both the nature of the dispute and the participants involved. Disputes, and parties, tend to fall into certain broad classifications that influence the choice of negotiation strategies that will work best. Below are described several different ways to classify both disputes and parties. The discussion is not exhaustive, but it should alert the reader to some of the more important factors that influence choice of negotiation strategies. As you consider each one, think about which negotiating tactics would be most appropriate to achieve settlement under the circumstances, and why.

1. *Disputes based on highly conflicting interpretations of the facts.*

Many disputes are based on different versions of the same story. In a dispute over a will, for example, the adult children of the defendant claim that their brother unduly influenced the parent to execute a will in his favor by visiting her frequently, helping her with financial matters, providing transportation and, ultimately, compelling her to leave everything to him. The brother, on the other hand, claims that he was fulfilling his duty to a parent who was ignored and forgotten by her other children. Think about how family dynamics have and will continue to influence this dispute? What is at stake besides money and property? Remembering that a judge or jury may be asked to determine whether the decedent was unduly influenced, is it possible or even necessary for the parties to agree on the facts? How will the size of the estate influence the attitude and behavior of the parties or their attorneys at a negotiation session to resolve the dispute?

2. *Disputes where the success or failure to reach agreement affects whether or not the parties will deal with each other in the future.*

Many business disputes involve parties who rely on one another for their success. For example, in a contract dispute between a manufacturer and a parts supplier, the manufacturer knows that if she is unable to settle, she can always purchase comparable parts at similar prices in the future from other sources. How will this fact influence her attitude toward her opponent during the negotiation and willingness to make concessions? But what if the manufacturer knows that her adversary is the only producer of the part, or that other producers charge significantly higher prices and that failure to settle will adversely impact her company in the future? What impact is this limitation likely to have on the attitudes of the parties? What if the manufacturer is a major customer of the supplier or, conversely, the supplier cannot meet the high demand for his product?

3. *Disputes where future dealings between the parties are highly likely, whatever the outcome of the current disagreement.*

Typical examples include disputes between divorcing parents of minor children, union leaders and management, or business partners who hope to continue to do business together in the future. Emotions often run high in disputes involving parties who have had intense and long-term relationships prior to the dispute. Feeling wounded and caught up in the past, they will often declare at the outset of negotiation that their position is non-negotiable.

What negotiation style and tactics are likely to break down entrenched positions? What roles should the parties play in the negotiation, or should their respective attorneys or spokespersons do the negotiating? Disputes such as these are most likely to be resolved if negotiations proceed deliberately and patiently. But can the parties afford to be patient when they know that small children, unemployed workers or business customers are being adversely affected by their stalemate?

4. *Disputes between large institutions and individuals.*

The story in Chapter One concerning Tim, the disgruntled and underpaid systems analyst, characterizes the disparity of bargaining power that often exists between employers and employees when disputes arise. Personal injury suits brought by individuals against major corporations are another example of unequal bargaining power that influences negotiation strategy. Juries, composed of ordinary citizens, are frequently sympathetic to the individual plaintiff, provided he or she can afford to go to court against the seemingly unlimited resources of the corporate opponent.

Large institutions often have no incentive to settle because they can afford a trial. Plaintiffs know this and are hesitant to file a lawsuit unless they have an especially strong case. If they do file they are likely to find that negotiations are not taken seriously by their opponent, who can wait them out and wear them down.

In some cases, a group of plaintiffs injured in similar ways by the same company will bring a class action. Asbestos and breast implant litigation of the 1990s are examples of class action litigation. In what ways would a class action, or the threat of a class action, influence negotiation between a large corporation and a group of aggrieved individuals by changing the balance of power between the parties?

Disputes with large corporations often involve critical public policy issues such as discrimination or worker safety that can also attract the close attention of the media. Should worker/plaintiffs negotiate a private, confidential settlement when so much is at stake, or should they take their case to trial? What is the likely impact of media attention on negotiations?

5. *Disputes where the parties involved in negotiation may or may not have the authority to settle.*

Parties who are individuals or representatives of smaller companies are more likely to have the power to settle a matter during negotiation. Conversely, larger companies may send middle managers who must report to their superiors, or senior managers who must gain the approval of the board of directors for any negotiated agreement. Where government is a party, the representative may be required to submit the settlement to an elected counsel or committee before the matter is finalized. How forthcoming, creative and flexible is one party likely to be knowing that the other side can or cannot make the final decision? What if neither side can make the final decision?

6. *Disputes where the judge to whom a case is assigned, or the jurisdiction and venue, are significant factors in the possible outcome of a suit at trial.*

Negotiated settlements are often a prediction of how a judge or jury will decide a case. The quality of judging varies from highly competent to incompetent. Furthermore, judges are susceptible to prejudice despite their oath of impartiality. Sometimes a judge will dislike one of the lawyers involved in a case due to past dealings. Even when a jury will make the ultimate decision, a judge has significant influence on how smoothly a case will proceed and on critical matters such as choice of law, timing and evidence. Juries also vary.

From jurisdiction to jurisdiction, the size of personal injury awards tends to vary depending upon the sympathies of the citizens who typically make up the jury pool. In commercial cases, some jurisdictions are notoriously pro-business while others have the reputation for being pro-consumer. The race, wealth and gender of the parties may be important factors that will influence both the attitude of the court and the verdict typically reached by jury. Federal versus state jurisdiction may also be an issue, and the chances of commencing or continuing suit in one or the other can significantly influence how a case might be settled. Most of these factors are beyond the control of the parties and their attorneys. How is possible jury hostility or an ignorant or prejudiced judge likely to influence the course of a negotiation? How can a party mitigate circumstances such as these that are beyond his or her control and still achieve a fair settlement through negotiation?

7. *Disputes characterized by how attorneys will be paid for their services.*

Attorneys get paid in many different ways for providing representation and, unfortunately, method of payment can influence how an attorney proceeds with a negotiation. For example, some attorneys receive a percentage of any monetary settlement, while others work for a fixed fee. Many are paid by the hour, whatever the outcome. *Pro bono* attorneys work for nothing.

The Ethics of Negotiating

Negotiating presents many interesting and perplexing ethical questions. The discussion that follows attempts to raise several of the more important ethical questions and is not intended to be conclusive. Ethics will be explored throughout this book in relationship to each of the methods of ADR.

The Model Rules of Professional Conduct that govern attorney behavior, and the behavior of paralegals who work for attorneys, require that "a lawyer shall not knowingly make a false statement of material fact or law to a third person."[25] The Model Code of Professional Responsibility requires that "a lawyer shall not engage in conduct involving dishonesty, fraud, deceit, or misrepresentation."[26] Yet, the essence of effective negotiating is the ability to mislead and, at the same time, not be misled.

Good negotiators are masters at misleading their opponents about their true positions, especially concerning their settling range. Negotiators will insist that the offer on the table is the last one or that their client has authorized them to go no higher (or lower). Negotiators will often overstate their client's case, such as the amount of pain and suffering the client has endured, or the value of the client's property. False flattery to gain concessions or feigned anger to generate guilt are typical negotiator tactics. Negotiators even engage in behavior designed to intimidate or harass the opponent, despite a prohibition in the Model Rules against the use of tactics that "have no substantial purpose other than to embarrass, delay, or burden a third person…"

A certain amount of "puffing" is expected in negotiations. Furthermore, nearly every negotiator will occasionally use competitive tactics to make gains for the client. However, advocates who are consistently histrionic, and who use harsh and abrasive tactics most of the time, may achieve high settlements for their clients but they do so at the risk of their professional relationships. Attorneys are likely to avoid negotiations in future case with "junkyard dog" lawyers, preferring to go to trial rather than face the discomfort and humiliation of face-to-face confrontation.

Eventually, the abrasive negotiator may be trapped into litigating nearly every case simply because settlement negotiations have been foreclosed by his or her rude and offensive behavior. Also, he or she is unlikely to obtain referrals from other lawyers who don't want to expose their colleagues to such negative tactics.

Negotiators also engage actively in withholding facts and information from their opponent. Standard ploys include changing the subject when asked a direct question, or providing answers that don't really address the question. Attorney-negotiators who discover that their opponent is ignorant about the law that governs the dispute may feel no duty to offer enlightenment.

In litigation, an attorney who does not inform the judge about the applicable law, however favorable or unfavorable it might be to the client, is subject to sanctions. Yet the same standard does not apply in negotiating, even when the opponent's ignorance of the law might result in their settling for much less than a court of law would almost certainly award.

Unfortunately, very little guidance is provided in the law or the various codes of professional behavior to unravel the ethical dilemmas presented by negotiating. Commentary on the Model Rules of Professional Conduct declares that:

> Whether a particular statement should be regarded as one of fact can depend on the circumstances. Under generally accepted conventions in negotiation, certain types of statements ordinarily are not taken as statements of material fact. Estimates of price or value placed on the subject of a transaction and a party's intentions as to an acceptable settlement of a claim are in this category.[27]

Apparently, there are levels of truth and different types of facts. Is the commentator also suggesting that negotiators can get away with telling less than the truth because we all know they don't mean it? What about those who support an "end-justifies-the-means" argument? One writer on the topic has suggested that truth should be a function of "the consequences, and the skill and expectations of the opponent."[28] Because negotiating is more art than science, and because the mix of players, legal issues, expectations and other factors is often dissimilar to any other negotiation, bargaining ethically often means discovering and testing new rules as one goes along. As readers learn about other forms of ADR, they are encouraged to think about the norms of human behavior that apply and whether it is possible to reach settlement without sacrificing important ethical values.

Exercises

<blockquote>

1. How do you feel about negotiators using each of the tactics described above to achieve the upper hand for themselves or their clients, and why? What about:
   - ✓ claiming (falsely) that the offer on the table is the last one?
   - ✓ claiming that your client has aches and pains that, in fact, he or she does not have?
   - ✓ flattering the opponent by asserting that you know him or her to have a reputation as a fair and reasonable person?
   - ✓ feigning anger and stomping out of the negotiation when it reaches an impasse?
   - ✓ berating and belittling your opponent?

2. When, if ever, would each of the tactics described in No. 1, above, be appropriate, and why?

3. If you were a negotiator facing each of the tactics described in No. 1, above, how would you respond?

</blockquote>

When to Initiate Negotiations

Knowing when to initiate negotiations with the other side in a dispute is an important skill for lawyers. Sense of timing is critical in orchestrating the ultimate settlement of any disagreement. Generally, an attorney gets involved in a dispute after the problem has emerged and developed, sides have formed, and at least to some extent, the positions of the parties have become set. It is also highly likely that the two sides have stopped talking to one another.

The act of hiring an attorney or enlisting the aid of a third-party advocate means that the parties believe they can no longer handle the problem on their own. By this time, unfortunately, simple solutions that might have solved the problem initially are no longer possible. More complex solutions are needed, and they are likely to be costly in terms of money, time and emotional energy. The challenge for the third-party advocate is to move as quickly and expeditiously as possible before the range of possible solutions narrows even further and costs escalate.

After the attorney or advocate has developed a basic understanding of the dispute and what the client wants, he or she will often call the other party or his or her attorney to get a feeling for their side of the story and to see if any basis for an immediate settlement exists. If this proves fruitful, phone calls, fax messages and other informal communications will continue until a settlement is worked out or an impasse is reached. Many consumer disputes are settled in this manner.

The next step, at least in certain disputes, is to send a demand letter, wherein one party notifies the other of their legal claim, and outlines what it will take to satisfy the claim. The purpose of the letter is to put the other party on notice that if some settlement is not reached currently, the aggrieved party intends to file a lawsuit. The demand letter presents the parties and their attorneys with another opportunity to explore settlement. The tone of the letter should be designed to motivate the other party to consider settlement before costs and risk escalate further, and to leave the door open for more conversation. If a positive response is received to this communication, the parties, through their attorneys, will continue settlement negotiations. If not, or if there is an impasse, the aggrieved party will generally file a lawsuit.

A lawsuit provides each side with the opportunity and means to obtain information from the other party that was unavailable during the earlier stages. Called discovery, it involves gathering facts and evidence so that the parties can more fully understand the dispute and build a case. Discovery and other pretrial activities provide valuable opportunities for the attorneys to confer and to initiate negotiations at appropriate points. Generally speaking, negotiation should be initiated when either party believes that he or she possesses enough information to make an informed decision about how the case should be settled. Thus, if discovery turns up strong evidence for one side, the other side should probably seek to negotiate a settlement rather than lose more ground and risk, and spend more money on litigation.

Ideally, the parties will have reached settlement well before a suit comes up for trial. Unfortunately, it is not uncommon for attorneys' fees and costs to equal or significantly exceed the value of the claim by the time trial is imminent. In a recent case, for example, a homeowner with a claim against her insurance company for $6,500 spent $6,000 before she ever got to trial. She had earlier rejected a settlement offer of $2,500, despite her attorney's pleas to accept. Proving her point eventually cost her nearly $10,000.

In another matter, one company sued another for business interference, and their combined expenses at the time of trial exceeded $1.1 million for a claim that totaled $1.5 million. It is often the cost of discovery and building a case that forces many parties to settle before trial. Another motivator is the growing uncertainty that most parties experience as their opponent learns more and more about them. Settlement becomes a way to mitigate the risk of losing later at trial when someone else (judge or jury) will make the decision.

The Difficulty of Early Settlement

Despite growing concern about the escalation of lawsuits and the adversarial nature of litigation, early settlement is often very difficult to achieve. There are many reasons why this is the case:

1. As discussed above, by the time attorneys get involved, the parties have generally done a fair job of escalating their dispute to a crisis point.

2. In order to "legalize" the matter, the lawyers repackage the dispute in categorical terms based on rights, duties and damages. The parties get labeled as thief, defaulter, bankrupt, deadbeat, malingerer, tortfeasor, etc. Legalizing and labeling legitimize the dispute and tend to exacerbate the bad feelings between the parties.

3. Each side usually will deluge the other with mountains of discovery requests, hoping to intimidate their opponent into settling. This and other similar tactics create resentment because of the time and costs involved in answering questions and producing documents.

4. It is difficult for counsel, in the midst of litigation, to change gears and dispassionately negotiate a mutually beneficial outcome to the dispute. Furthermore, communications and correspondence between the lawyers, which are often threatening and caustic, can actually poison the relationship between them and prevent the cooperation required to achieve a negotiated settlement.

5. Litigators often approach early settlement sessions with little or no planning or preparation of the case or of their client, and with an expectation of failure.

6. Clients are more likely to encourage a continuation of the lawsuit early in the process. Only later, after great expense or the emergence of new distractions will they become amenable to settlement. Unfortunately, they may still be inclined to gamble on trial rather than settlement as the only way to obtain reimbursement for at least some of their costs. Attorneys with unpaid invoices to the client, likewise, may encourage trial for the same reason.

7. Finally, the attorneys might want to keep the lawsuit going in order to collect more fees, even though such a rationale is unethical.

As one writer put it, "Often, considering settlement involves a pill of such bitterness that no one will dare to broach the subject of swallowing it."[29] Clearly, the challenge ahead for ADR, in general, and negotiation proponents in particular, is to continue to train attorneys and other advocates in effective negotiating, to encourage the use of negotiation as early as possible and to develop and disseminate workable strategies for managing conflict better.

The next two chapters deal with mediation, which is negotiation assisted by an impartial third party. Mediation embodies the principles of cooperative, integrative negotiating, and can often overcome the obstacles that prevent successful negotiations early in a lawsuit.

Sources

[1] *Gainey v. Brotherhood of Railway. and S.S. Clerks, Freight Handlers, Exp. & Station Employees*, 275 F.Supp. 292, 300 (E.D. Pa. 1967).

[2] S. Goldberg, F. Sander and N. Roberts, *Dispute Resolution, Negotiation, Mediation, and Other Processes*, 17 (1992).

[3] Fed. R. Civ. P. 169(a)(5).

[4] Fed. R. Civ. P. 16(c)(7).

[5] Fed. R. Civ. P. 16(c)(7), advisory committee's note.

[6] Fed. R. Civ. P. 16(c)(6).

[7] Fed. R. Civ. P. 16(c)(7), advisory committee's note.

[8] *Id.*

[9] Fed. R. Civ. P. 68.

[10] *Id.*

[11] Fed. R. Evid. 408.

[12] *Id.*

[13] Fed. R. Evid. 408, advisory committee's note.

[14] *Id.*

[15] J. Murray, A. Rau, and E. Sherman, *Processes of Dispute Resolution*, 161-162 (1988).

[16] *Id.*

[17] *Id.*

[18] C. Craver, *Effective Legal Negotiation and Settlement*, 1 (1994).

[19] R. Fisher, W. Ury and B. Patton, *Getting to Yes,* 4-5 (2d ed. 1991).

[20] Adapted from charts comparing negotiating styles *in* C. Craver, *Effective Legal Negotiation and Settlement* (1994), R. Fisher, W. Ury, and B. Patton, *Getting to Yes*, 9-13 (2d ed. 1991), and J. Murray, A. Rau, and E. Sherman, *Processes of Dispute Resolution II-3 -II-6* (*Notes for Teachers*, Supplement 1990).

[21] G. Williams' quote, Legal Negotiation and Settlement, 51 (1983) *reprinted in* J. Murray, A. Rau and E. Sherman, *Processes of Dispute Resolution 80* (*Notes to Teachers*, Supplement 1990).

[22] C. Craver, *Effective Legal Negotiation and Settlement*, 47ff (1994).

[23] *Id.*

[24] *Id.*, at 29ff.

[25] Model Rules of Professional Conduct Rule 4.1(a) (1983).

[26] Model Code of Professional Responsibility 1-102(A)(4)(1980).

[27] *Id.*, at 7-101(A)(1); *see also id.*, at 7-102(A)(1).

[28] Murray, Rau, and Sherman, *supra*, at 200.

[29] *Alternative Dispute Resolution Techniques*, § 3.067 (W. Hancock ed. 1996).

Chapter Three

Mediation

Introduction

Mediation has been described as assisted or facilitated negotiation.[1] During a mediation session, the parties to a dispute attempt to negotiate a settlement with the assistance of a third party called a mediator, who is neutral toward the parties and the outcome of the dispute. The mediator listens to the parties, empathizes with them, encourages them to vent their feelings when appropriate, presses the parties to face facts, urges them to listen and commends them when they try to accommodate the other party.[2] The mediator helps the disputants to define the problem and identify possible solutions. However, the mediator has no power to impose a decision on the parties.

With the exception of negotiation, mediation differs from all other forms of ADR that will be considered in this text in one critical way. Mediation is a process specifically designed to achieve settlement during the proceedings. In contrast, arbitration, mini-trial, summary jury trial, and private judging are trial-like hearings designed to induce settlement after the proceeding has concluded. Disputants are motivated to settle because the hearing has provided them with a better assessment of what the outcome of their case might be if it were tried in a court. Thus, the possible legal outcome is the standard against which all other outcomes are measured.

Mediation, on the other hand, relies on cooperative negotiating to identify and promote solutions jointly devised by the parties, and which an arbitrator or court may be unlikely to award or impose. While the possible outcomes at trial may influence a mediated settlement design, especially if a lawsuit has been filed or is anticipated, other standards may be even more influential.

Mediation and Negotiation Compared

Negotiation and mediation share a commitment to the notion that disputing parties can bargain together to resolve their differences. Nevertheless, mediation differs from negotiation in several critical ways:

1. First, the actual parties to a legal dispute almost always participate actively in the mediation session(s). The purpose of mediation is to provide a forum in which the parties can devise solutions to their problems. Therefore, their presence is critical to the process. By comparison, negotiation usually takes place among the representatives* of the parties, who inform their clients of the results of the latest round, and consult with them regarding the next steps to be taken.

---

* Because mediation is a nonlegal process, it is frequently employed in situations where a lawsuit is not anticipated. Likewise, many mediation professionals have no legal training. In addition, many of the parties who resort to mediation come on their own, unaccompanied by a representative. In Chapters Three and Four, both of which deal with mediation, the individuals who are disputing will be called "disputants," or "parties," interchangeably. However, if the text assumes that the parties are represented by others, they may also be called "clients." The persons who represent them will be referred to as "representatives," or "advocates," interchangeably. However, if the context assumes that a lawsuit has been filed or is anticipated, the term "attorney" may also be used.

2. Second, mediation is presided over by a person who is neutral, has no prior involvement in the dispute, and who generally has no authority to decide the case. Negotiation, on the other hand, almost always involves only the parties and/or their advocates. No impartial person is involved. Furthermore, the advocates are likely to have been involved with the parties in the past and will continue their involvement into the future.

3. Third, in the context of litigation, mediation is generally an extra procedure that is inserted into the process in an attempt to achieve a better and/or earlier resolution. Even when mediation is ordered by a court, cooperation in the process is voluntary, and an uncooperative party will usually not be sanctioned for failing to participate in a meaningful manner. By comparison, negotiation is an integral part of litigation along with pleadings, discovery and other procedural aspects of litigation. And even though participation in negotiation is "voluntary," in some situations a party can be sanctioned by a court for failing to negotiate in good faith.

4. Fourth, mediation is usually a structured, in-person, self-contained event that lasts several consecutive hours or days and may involve other persons such as expert witnesses. Consequently, mediation must be planned, scheduled, executed and paid for, and for these reasons, usually occurs only once and occasionally twice during a dispute. Also, mediation generally occurs well before trial. Conversely, negotiation is informal, usually involves only the parties or their representatives, can occur via mail, telephone, fax and e-mail, as well as face-to-face, and frequently involves many episodes over several days, weeks, months and even years. In the context of a lawsuit, negotiations can be concurrent with trial and can continue right up to the point that the jury returns with a verdict.

5. Finally, mediation embodies the values and employs the techniques of cooperative negotiation. The entire process is designed to neutralize both the impulse to bargain competitively and the effects of prior competitive negotiations between the parties. Thus, mediation limits the range of bargaining techniques available to disputants and their attorneys. Pure negotiation, on the other hand, provides a wider array of models and techniques for bargaining, and in this respect, may have broader application to a larger variety of disputes and parties.

When compared to mediation, negotiation is often inefficient, slow to unfold, and therefore unsuccessful at achieving a settlement that is satisfactory to all the parties. One text on the topic made the following criticism of negotiation:[3]

♦   Negotiation usually occurs without any deadlines or a sense of urgency.

♦   Negotiation involves interrupted and easily distorted communication from advocate to client to advocate and back again.

♦   Negotiation does not give the opposing side the opportunity to meet and hear the other party until a deposition is taken.

♦   Negotiation cannot mitigate personality conflicts between the advocates and, in fact, tends to exacerbate them.

♦   Negotiation is easily influenced by fee arrangements and other self-interests of the advocates.

♦ Negotiation may prevent the parties from taking their offers to one another seriously because of suspicion of any proposal by a self-interested opponent.

♦ Negotiation can occur between the advocates with little or no input from the clients, thus raising the issue of whether the clients have been adequately represented.

♦ Negotiation tends to make clients anxious as they face the inevitable delays, lack of information, and lack of sustained attention to their case that busy advocates are unable to provide.

The Origins of Mediation

The use of mediation to settle disputes is as old as organized human society and as new as the modern mediation movement. It most likely began when a friend or family member first intervened in a controversy in order to keep the peace. The intervenor sought to use his or her influence to adjust or neutralize the differences between the disputing parties. Legal historians speculate that mediation preceded any formal system of justice and most likely provided the model for the development of courts of law. In some societies, litigation in the courts was viewed as a less desirable alternative to a mediated settlement. In China, during the Confucian era, using an intermediary was considered the socially proper way to settle disputes.[4] The intermediary would shuttle back and forth between the disputants conveying the respective claims of the parties until the parties achieved a solution.[5]

In Anglo-Saxon England, before the Norman Conquest in 1066 A.D., disputing parties could mediate their differences even after a court had rendered a judgment in the matter, provided they did so before the judgment was finalized.[6] Faced with full knowledge of the court's conclusion as to who would win and who would lose, the parties would weigh the likely consequences, and if they preferred a different outcome, they would negotiate or mediate a settlement of their own. In one dispute, for example, where a landowner won the right at trial to evict a trespasser who sought to collect on an old debt owed by the landowner, the parties, nevertheless, chose to mediate their differences. As a result, the trespasser agreed to leave peacefully and the landowner agreed to pay the debt. Even though the landowner had "won" at trial, she knew that the trespasser would continue to make trouble if he was not appeased. Therefore, she chose to mediate the dispute rather than accept the court's judgment.[7] The modern technique of arb-med is similar to this ancient practice (see page 10).

The Modern Mediation Movement

The modern mediation movement has generated much renewed interest in mediation as a "consensual alternative to legal remedies."[8] It is predicated on the notion that agreements voluntarily arrived at will be more satisfying to the parties and more likely to be followed.[9] Furthermore, modern mediation permits the parties to fashion their own solutions rather than be bound by legal solutions that are often inflexible,[10] and almost always one-sided in the sense that the winner takes all. Modern mediation focuses as much on the process as it does on the ultimate decision reached by the parties. By permitting people to resolve their disputes without recourse to judges, juries and other mechanisms of state power, the parties feel empowered as citizens, and learn how to build relationships based on respect, trust and understanding rather than on laws and rules set down by others.[11]

Critics of the mediation movement express concern, however, that mediation may not be appropriate for all disputes. For example, in disputes involving parties with unequal bargaining power, such as a large corporation versus an hourly employee, or a nursing home versus an elderly patient, the less powerful party may need the protection that a court of law can provide. If the weaker party opts instead for mediation, he or she may be intimidated by the stronger opponent and settle for substantially less than a court-rendered judgment would have provided or permitted.

Like all movements and trends, mediation is not monolithic. Even among its proponents there is considerable disagreement about where and when mediation should be used, whether mediation should be supervised by the courts, whether it should be mandatory or purely voluntary, what style of mediation is most effective, whether mediators should be passive or aggressive participants in the process, if mediators should conform to certain training standards or be certified, and so forth.

Furthermore, alternative dispute resolution in general, and mediation in particular, is becoming more and more the subject of legislation at both the federal and state levels, which contributes to its complexity. Lawmakers are actively attempting to regulate how ADR is practiced in order to ensure just and fair outcomes. More important, they are enacting statutes that require disputing parties to attempt to resolve their problems through the use of a variety of ADR techniques before they ask a court to settle the dispute for them.

More and more courts are referring lawsuits to mediation. One of the purposes of doing so is to save court costs associated with discovery. Even though most cases settle before trial, negotiations usually occur very late in the life of a lawsuit, often "on the courthouse steps." By then, the courts and the clients have incurred much of the costs associated with setting the ground rules for discovery and actually gathering the evidence. In fact, some experts estimate that between 80% and 90% of litigation costs go for discovery. Thus, any method that would achieve earlier settlement would save clients money and help to conserve precious judicial resources.

Dallas County, Texas, provides an excellent example of how court-ordered ADR can save resources. In 1987, the Texas legislature passed a statute providing for ADR for cases filed in Texas state courts, either on the court's own motion or the motion of the parties. The 13 district courts of Dallas County embraced the statute and over the next several years developed an active ADR referral program. In 1992, for example, over 6,000 cases in the civil district courts of Dallas county were referred to mediation and, of these, 4,800 settled.

Noting that most of these settlements occurred much earlier in the lawsuits than normally would have occurred via traditional negotiation, one prominent area mediator estimated that these mediated settlements saved clients as much as $96 million, based on an average savings of $20,000 in discovery costs per case. The corresponding savings to the court has not been estimated, but the amount would be substantial.

Exercises

1. Find out whether or not any courts in your county have a process and program for referring civil lawsuits to mediation. If not, has the idea ever been considered and, if so, why was it rejected? If one or more courts does refer cases to mediation, how many cases were referred to mediation in the past twelve months and what was the settlement rate?

2. What is the general opinion among the legal community in your area concerning the use of mediation to resolve disputes? Is mediation approved for certain types of disputes (e.g., family law matters) but not for others? What reasons are given for these opinions? Distinguish, if possible, between those who view mediation favorably and those who are less favorable, in terms of age, gender, profession, type of law practiced, etc.

A Typical Mediation Session

Let's take a look at a typical mediation session involving parties to a lawsuit.

1. Initiating Mediation

Like most forms of ADR, mediation occurs for one of three reasons:

(1) the parties agree to mediate at the time the dispute arises,

(2) the parties have agreed in writing to mediate any disputes that may arise between them in the future, generally concerning a contract between them, or

(3) a court orders the parties to mediate.

In the first two cases, the parties will usually select a mediator at the time a dispute arises, often at the suggestion of one of the parties. In the case of a previously executed written agreement to mediate, the contract may name a mediator or mediation service that the parties agree to use. In the case of court-mandated mediation, referred to as "court-annexed" mediation, the court will appoint a mediator.

Nevertheless, the parties can usually reject at least one court-appointed mediator without cause, and they may be able to reject others, provided they have sufficient grounds for their request, such as conflict of interest. Parties can sometimes also request the appointment of a particular mediator or mediation service, provided all the parties agree. Mediators may or may not be attorneys, and in some court-annexed programs, lawyers are excluded from the ranks of available mediators.[12]

Once a mediator is selected, the mediation session will be scheduled, and the parties will be notified to attend.

2. Costs and Timing

The cost of a mediator's services varies widely. A fee of $700 per party, per day of mediation, plus a nominal administrative fee is not uncommon. Other mediators charge an hourly rate or a flat fee based on the number of participants. It is estimated that between 80% and 90% of mediations settle in one day or less; therefore, the cost of mediation for each party is generally less than $1,000, and usually lower. Community-based, not-for-profit mediation services, which often use voluntary mediators, may be free of charge, or cost as little as $25 per party, regardless of ability to pay.

The attorneys for the parties and the mediator will estimate how long they expect the mediation to last and will schedule their time accordingly. Mediators assigned to small claims court may mediate dozens of disputes in a single day, whereas complex matters, such as environmental suits may take many sessions over several months. When mediation is ordered by the court, the order will also specify a time frame during which the mediation session should occur, usually based on when the next pretrial court appearance is scheduled.* If the parties settle, the appearance is canceled and everyone, including the court, saves time and money.

3. Briefing the Mediator

At an appropriate point before the mediation session, the mediator will submit to the parties a request for information about the case. Some mediators prefer to know very little about the dispute and the parties before the mediation session, believing that too much information will cause them to lose their objectivity and to take sides.[13] Other mediators desire to see copies of the pleadings, critical documentary evidence such as applicable contracts and depositions, a summary of the testimony of any witnesses who may attend the mediation, a history of the negotiations to date, and so forth. They may also request a brief statement from each party of their assessment of the issues involved and the strengths and weaknesses of their case, and perhaps a copy of any pertinent case opinions that are on point.[14]

In cases that are relatively straightforward, sufficient information can usually be exchanged during the mediation session to successfully conduct the mediation. Limited premediation discovery may be necessary on specific issues so that a party can formulate a settlement position. In complex cases and in those involving many parties, however, more information is likely to be sought in advance of mediation and therefore, premediation discovery may be extensive. Mediators who require significant presession information do so for several important reasons.

a. First, they want to be educated about the dispute to save time at the session.

b. Second, in the case of highly complex matters, premediation preparation may be the only way for the mediator to master the issues well enough to be effective at mediating the dispute.

c. Third, mediators want the parties, and especially their advocates, to objectively evaluate the case before the mediation session is held. Thus, everyone will be better prepared to mediate in a realistic and efficient manner.

---

* See Appendix 5 for an example of a court mediation order.

4. Accommodations

The mediator generally has the responsibility of providing, or arranging for the mediation facilities, preferably in a neutral location. Facilities will usually consist of a larger general conference room and two or more smaller "caucus" rooms. Mediators who devote most or all of their time to mediation will frequently provide facilities specially designed to accommodate the needs of mediation, including food service areas, offices where participants may make phone calls and conduct other business during the often long hours of mediation, and other specialized accommodations. Some may even provide completely separate waiting rooms and suites when it is essential that the parties not encounter one another except in joint sessions.

Opening Session

A mediation session almost always commences with a joint session involving the parties, their representatives, and the mediator, who moderates the session. No court stenographers are present, and the session is conducted without the use of formal rules of evidence or procedure.

Introduction of Participants and Process

Typically, the representatives at a mediation will have experienced mediation before, perhaps even with this mediator. However, the experience is likely to be new to the parties. In the ideal situation, the parties will have been briefed ahead of time by their representatives on what to expect and how to conduct themselves during mediation.

The opening session has several purposes, including to

- introduce the participants
- review the process
- establish the rules to be followed
- permit the parties to tell their version of the dispute
- exchange information
- allow the parties to express how they feel
- quickly identify areas of agreement and disagreement.[15]

The mediator usually begins by welcoming the parties, making introductions and providing some background information in order to establish rapport with the participants. Next, the mediator will explain the process of mediation and outline what the parties can expect from the session. The mediator will also describe his or her role in the mediation, and the role of each of the other participants. Participants will be assured that everyone will stay until an agreement is reached, written down and signed, or until the mediator declares either a deadlock or the need to continue another day.

During the opening session, the mediator will cover the ground rules for mediation, including the need to allow the other party to finishing speaking, the need to remain seated during joint sessions, and housekeeping matters such as bathroom and smoking breaks, refreshments, lunch, etc.

These rules, including the use of joint sessions, private caucuses, and other procedural matters, are often negotiated ahead of time by the parties or their representatives. In other cases, the parties will use rules promulgated by a court or an outside ADR agency.[*]

A mediator will usually stress three critical matters during opening remarks:

1. *No Imposed Agreement*

It is essential that the parties understand that the mediator will not impose an agreement on them or make up their minds for them. The mediator will emphasize that it is his or her job to assist the parties to come to an agreement on their own by helping them negotiate with one another. Often, this point is difficult to get across. For one, disputants see the mediator as an authority figure and someone with special knowledge and skills. Therefore, it is not uncommon for them to seek the mediator's approval of their ideas and decisions as the mediation proceeds. Two, if the parties have turned their dispute over to their attorneys and the courts, they may have difficulty taking back control. Some may not want it back, while others may be afraid that they will make a bad decision or be coerced into conceding.

2. *Confidentiality*

The second matter that a mediator will stress concerns confidentiality. The parties are assured that anything that is said or revealed during the mediation, including any information provided to the mediator prior to mediation, will be confidential and will not be used against them at trial if they are unable to settle their dispute. Furthermore, the mediator cannot be called by any of the parties to testify about the matter. The outcome of the mediation will also be confidential, whether or not an agreement is reached.

If the mediation is by court order, in most jurisdictions the only information that a mediator can reveal to the court is whether or not the matter settled. The mediator is required to keep confidential the terms of any agreement. Conversely, a mediator generally cannot reveal to a judge why a case did not settle or any other information about the case or the parties that the mediator learned as a result of the mediation. Finally, the parties are assured that anything they say to the mediator in private will not be revealed to the other side without their express permission to do so.

3. *Decision Makers Must Attend*

The third critical matter that a mediator will stress is the need to have decision makers present at the mediation. A mediator will generally seek assurances both before mediation and during the opening session that the attendees have the authority to settle the dispute. Naturally, if the named plaintiff and defendant in a lawsuit are present, this should pose no problem. However, if one or more of the named parties is a corporation or other entity, the mediator will need to confirm that the party representing the entity at the mediation has full authority to settle the matter without first seeking the ratification of parties who are not present.

---

[*] See Appendix 8, which sets forth the Commercial Mediation Rules of the American Arbitration Association.

Opening Statements by the Parties

Once the mediator has concluded the opening remarks and instructions and answered any questions, the participants, beginning with the complaining party, are invited to make a statement describing how they see the dispute and the basis for their point of view. These opening statements give all the other participants the chance to hear each party's version of the facts and a firsthand account of the strengths of each party's position. Generally speaking, the parties should not state their demands at this point. However, the opening statement does provide an opportunity for the parties to describe their underlying interests. For example, an injured employee may express her desire to fully recover and return to work, or for her employer to find ways to avoid similar on-the-job accidents in the future. A divorcing parent may express concern that custody and visitation arrangements will minimize any disruption for the children.

Although the parties are encouraged to take part in opening statements, it is not uncommon for the advocates present to speak for their clients during the joint meeting, with the clients adding additional information, if necessary. At this early stage, clients are still feeling emotionally caught up in the conflict and are distrustful of one another and of the process. They may be reluctant, therefore, to speak to the entire group. One approach used by some advocates to draw out the client is to pose questions to him or her about the dispute, which the client answers in his or her own words.

Opening statements are most effective if they are well-organized, expressed confidently, addressed to the other party (not to the advocates or to the mediator), and are nonaccusatory. Participants are encouraged not only to share information and express opinions during opening remarks, but in some cases to also "vent" their emotions. For many people locked in a dispute, just being able to tell their opponent how angry or hurt they are is part of the solution.

After a participant has had a chance to speak, the mediator will ask questions and will often restate the key points made by each party. When both sides have had a turn at presenting their case, and the mediator has gained an adequate grasp of the facts and the issues involved, the mediator will then guide the parties in exploring alternatives for settlement and in assessing those alternatives. With the help of the advocates, the mediator will also assist the parties to assess the likely results if no mediated agreement is reached and the case proceeds to trial or some other forum for resolving disputes, such as binding arbitration. Once again, the mediator will stress the value of the settlement being controlled by the parties rather than outsiders to the dispute.

The goal of the mediator, in addition to achieving a settlement, is to aid the disputants to sharpen the issues, establish priorities, find points of agreement and reduce their antagonism so that they are better able to seriously consider alternative solutions to their dispute. In this respect, the mediator employs a cooperative rather than a competitive style of negotiation. This style attempts to take the focus off the people and their demands and to refocus on the problem and on the underlying interests of the parties.

Private Caucus   In some cases, the parties will adjourn to separate, private caucuses after the joint session. The mediator will meet with each side, shuttling back and forth between the caucuses, conveying information and messages from one side to the other until a settlement is reached or an impasse declared. It is not uncommon for a mediator to meet five to ten times with each side, depending upon the complexity of the dispute.

Private caucuses provide opportunities for the parties to share sensitive information with the mediator. For example, they may reveal hidden interests that they want kept confidential, vent feelings they would not have expressed in joint sessions, or discuss options they might not have taken seriously in the presence of the other parties. The private caucus relieves the parties of the need to posture and to trade offers back and forth that characterize face-to-face negotiating. As a result, they may discover that they are much closer to the other side than originally thought.[16]

The private caucus enables the mediator to gain the trust and confidence of the participants. As compared with joint sessions, private caucuses also enable the mediator to more aggressively challenge the parties regarding their positions, and to persuade them to hear what the other side is saying. Mediators who employ a more "activist" style will often push participants to settle, or may even promote a particular position (e.g., advocate joint custody of children over sole custody), while other mediators will remain completely neutral throughout. If the parties are especially hostile toward one another, or if one of the parties is seriously intimidated by the other, the private caucus may be the only way for the mediation to proceed.[17]

Private caucuses are not always necessary to achieve settlement through mediation. Sometimes the participants will remain in joint session, adjourning only once or twice to meet privately with the mediator to discuss matters in confidence or to explore why the process has reached an impasse. Nevertheless, private caucuses are especially helpful when there are several parties to a dispute, where the matter is highly complex and involves many issues, where there is significant disparity in power among the parties (e.g. large corporation vs. an employee or individual consumer), or when the parties are being abusive and threatening toward one another (e.g., divorce disputes). In addition, because the advocates for the parties tend to do the talking in joint sessions, private caucusing is one way to get the parties actively involved in the process.

Closure   During the later stages of mediation, the mediator usually calls for a renewed analysis of the issues and interests of the parties in order to determine if the proposed settlement truly satisfies them.[18] Closure may take place in private caucus, or the mediator may call the parties together for a final session. There are three possible outcomes:

1. a negotiated settlement

2. impasse or

3. an agreement to continue the mediation at a later time.

If a negotiated settlement is reached, many mediators will insist that the agreement be committed to writing and signed before the participants are allowed to leave. The written agreement constitutes a contract and later, if one of the parties fails to perform, the other can bring an action for breach of contract, or seek other available legal remedies. Except for settlements regarding divorce, child custody and certain other matters, the agreement is usually not entered by the court as a judgment.

Generally, the attorneys rather than the mediator will (should) draft the agreement. A mediator, especially if he or she is an attorney, has an inherent conflict of interest in drafting agreements between opposing parties. Furthermore, attorney mediators risk compromising their neutrality if they draft the agreement. In some jurisdictions, nonattorney mediators who draft settlement agreements for disputes where a lawsuit is involved are engaging in the unauthorized practice of law.

Mediation Case Study

Following is a practical case study that illustrates how two companies can resolve their disputes through mediation.

Tri-State Paving Contractors obtained a substantial contract to pave the entire parking lot of a large office complex, which was managed by Universal Management Company. The total contract price exceeded $400,000. Work commenced and was approximately 95% completed, when a meeting was held between Universal and Tri-State to discuss the final items to be finished in order to release the final payment. These "punch list" items were discussed with a representative from Universal, along with Universal's project supervisor, Jane Dunn. Dunn and Tri-State's president, Steve Phillips, walked the entire project together and discussed a verbal "punch list." They then proceeded to Universal's offices and met with Herb Simmons, the manager for the property.

Phillips left the meeting with the understanding that the only items to be completed to authorize the final progress payment of $50,000 and release of the 10% holdback of $40,000 were the items that were verbally discussed during the inspection tour with Dunn. Simmons and Dunn left the meeting with the understanding that the inspection visit and the verbal punch list was a preliminary punch list and that they would prepare a final one to be distributed later.

A week or so passed and the anticipated progress payment of $50,000 was not made. Accordingly, Phillips called Dunn demanding the payment. In response, Dunn sent a punch list of approximately 120 items, as opposed to the 18 discussed during the inspection tour. Phillips felt that he had been "had" and refused to do any of the punch list items until the progress payment was made. He did offer to wait on the holdback money until the originally discussed 18 items were completed.

Before any more discussions could be held, Simmons authorized a suit to be filed against Tri-State. In that suit, Universal contended that the work, overall, was not of the grade and quality that was expected for a high-class office complex, and that to repair and replace defective work done and to complete work not completed would cost approximately $120,000, for which a claim was made against Tri-State. Tri-State counterclaimed for its $50,000 progress payment and $40,000 holdback. Of course, both sides claimed attorney's fees.

The parties exchanged interrogatories and requests for production. Prior to beginning depositions, however, they determined that it might be a good idea to try mediation to see if the case could be resolved. The parties agreed on the mediator and appeared in the mediator's offices. At the beginning of the mediation, the mediator made opening remarks citing mediator's neutrality and that the mediator took no position as to the merits of the parties respective claims. The mediator emphasized the confidential aspects of the mediation and that nothing that the parties said in the mediation could be used in any further discovery proceeding or at trial.

The mediator also told the parties that they needed to be prepared to discuss settlement. In that regard, the parties should have available representatives who could enter into binding settlement proposals, and who would have the authority and discretion to agree to or reject what the other side wanted, or anything in between. Both sides assured the mediator that they had such authority, and their respective counsel, who were also present, concurred. The mediator also emphasized to the parties that it would take time to conduct the mediation and that the mediator would not waste their time; however, the mediator asserted the right to be the "eternal optimist." Therefore, the mediator also asked and received permission to be the one to declare an impasse, rather than the parties. The mediator then asked each side to make opening remarks and emphasized that these were not jury arguments but were to be statements of fact or opinion or collateral circumstances that impacted the settlement value of the case. The mediator also indicated to the parties that there would be caucuses in which the mediator would meet with each side outside the presence of the other to discuss matters in private and to convey and discuss settlement proposals in a protected atmosphere.

The parties made brief opening statements, emphasizing their various claims and their respective concerns as to why the other side could not recognize the legitimacy of their claims. During the initial caucus with Universal, the mediator determined that Universal's version of events was much different than that of Tri-State's, and that Universal considered their building to be a first-class building that had received a third-class paving job. The mediator noted that work had been going on for approximately six months and apparently no written complaints had been received from Universal about the work. Without admitting such, Simmons indicated that Tri-State could tell on their own that the work was not up to par and that he anticipated that when the defects were pointed out, Tri-State would do the remedial work necessary to bring it up to the expected quality level. He also indicated that the bids for $120,000 to complete the work were based upon written specifications and photographs, and that no bidder had actually walked the project.

The mediator then caucused with Tri-State and determined that Tri-State acknowledged that some problems were apparent, but it was their opinion that the problems were within the acceptable standards of work in the industry and that Universal was simply being "too picky." They also cited a long history of doing business with Dunn on other projects in which they'd had no problems, and speculated that Dunn was simply being controlled by Simmons. They also were adamant that they needed to be paid their money.

After completing the initial caucuses, the mediator determined that the parties were so polarized that it would not be productive to have them make initial offers and publish them to each other. Accordingly, the mediator suggested a two-step process. The first step involved meeting together in the general session room and going over the 120 deficiencies alleged by Universal. Secondly, the mediator would solicit simultaneous offers from each side but would keep the offers to himself until such time, in the mediator's judgment, that the offers would not be "insulting" to the parties. At the general session, the 120-item punch list was reviewed in detail. Approximately 35 items were eliminated as being acceptable. The vast majority of the remaining items involved the method of surfacing the parking lot, which involved a difference between a highly smooth surface and one that was somewhat granular.

The mediator recaucused with Universal and pointed out that none of the specifications that Universal had given to Tri-State made any reference to "visual specifications," other than citing a neat, uniform appearance. Simmons again said that it was obvious to him what "neat" and "uniform" meant even though his definitions differed from what Phillips thought they meant. Universal also indicated that they did not desire to have Tri-State come back on the property and complete the work and, therefore, they would be willing to compromise their claims by a deep discount, especially since they had $90,000 of monies otherwise due to Tri-State under the contract.

The mediator then went back and discussed matters with Tri-State. Tri-State understood that prospective jurors could look at the pictures and determine in their own mind that the work was not acceptable, even though it may meet industry standards. Tri-State was also concerned that they had a continuing warranty liability to Universal for another year, even if they were to resolve the issue over the current work done. Therefore, a judgment that awarded them a sum of money for the work done would still not prevent another dispute over a warranty claim in the future.

Accordingly, there was some value to having the warranty obligations eliminated. Both sides acknowledged that the attorneys' fees, costs and expenses (including expert witness fees), could approach or exceed $20,000 per party if the case went to trial.

In a normal mediation, a mediator would have solicited offers from each side and have conveyed them back and forth until such time as the parties reached an agreement. In this particularly unique circumstance, the mediator made a judgment call. The mediator floated an initial "mediator's proposal" to the parties. This was done by way of a written ballot on which the parties could mark either "yes" or "no," or offer an alternative proposal.

If both sides marked "yes," the matter was concluded and a settlement agreement would be drafted. If both sides marked "no," then discussions would also continue, but the side refusing the offer would not be told that the other side accepted it. If one side offered an alternative proposal, then the mediator was authorized to convey that proposal to the other side.

The mediator suggested on the ballot that each side "walk away" from their claims – that is, take nothing on claims, counter claims and attorneys' fees. In addition, Tri-State would have no continuing obligation under contract for warranty work. In response to the mediator's proposal, Universal agreed to the walk-away, but Tri-State countered with a request for $45,000, which was communicated to Universal. Since Tri-State was not allowed to know that Universal had initially agreed to the walk-away, Universal decided to make a demand for $60,000 from Tri-State, which was conveyed to Tri-State.

A series of offers and counteroffers ensued until the parties were approximately $28,000 apart, with Tri-State demanding $13,000 and Universal asking $15,000. At that time, the mediator once again proposed a walk-away from both sides. Again, Universal agreed; however, Tri-State insisted on the $8,000, which was the amount owed to a subcontractor. The mediator met with Universal and determined that they would not agree to paying Tri-State any more money and, therefore, they authorized the mediator to communicate to Tri-State that they agreed to the walk-away. The mediator then communicated to Tri-State this information along with Universal's announced intentions to negotiate no further beyond the walk-away. After some consultation among client and counsel, Tri-State also agreed to the walk-away.

The parties then met and outlined their agreements. Tri-State requested that there be a confidentiality agreement and that they have copies of all the photographs from the walk-through inspection to discuss with their subcontractors, which Universal agreed to. Universal was relieved by the settlement because it had held back a sufficient amount of money to complete the project to a level that was acceptable. Likewise, Tri-State could live with the settlement in that they had finality to the matter, they avoided a huge counter claim, and they were relieved of any further obligation to do any warranty work on the property, which they assumed would be substantial.

Exercise

> Now that you have seen how mediation works, and reviewed a typical case study, how would you compare mediation to adjudication in a court of law? In developing a comparison, consider the following factors:
> - ✓ level of compromise
> - ✓ source of the rules
> - ✓ flexibility of the process
> - ✓ relevance of the parties' interests, values, goals and aspirations
> - ✓ relevance of the law
> - ✓ relevance of the facts
> - ✓ focus – on the past or toward the future
> - ✓ effect on relationship of the parties
> - ✓ role of the advocates representing the parties
> - ✓ role of the neutral third party.

The Role of the Mediator

The above description and case study of a typical mediation set forth in general terms the role of the mediator during the various stages of a mediation. We have seen how the mediator acts as a rule maker for the mediation, establishing procedures that are firm and yet flexible. The mediator seeks to understand the strengths and weaknesses of each side's case so as to play devil's advocate. The mediator also acts as a consultant to the parties, encouraging them to develop a wide variety of settlement options and then helping them select the options that will motivate the other side to settle. Finally, the mediator acts as messenger, bearing offers and information back and forth between the parties.

In addition to these general roles, all successful mediators have several attributes in common. While the following discussion is not exhaustive, it focuses on those elements that are critical to achieving good outcomes through mediation.

The successful mediator is neutral.

Throughout our discussion of mediation, we have emphasized that a mediator is a neutral third party. It is critical that a mediator continually demonstrate neutrality through words and behavior. Before the mediation begins, a conscientious mediator will avoid being seen alone with one party or the other. A mediator who knows one of the advocates, but not the others, will approach them all in the same professional manner. During joint sessions, the mediator will give each of the parties equal time and will not sit too closely to one side or the other, or listen more intently to what one party has to say. The mediator will summarize fairly and accurately what a party has said without adding words of judgment. During private caucuses the mediator will scrupulously maintain the confidentiality of each of the parties by communicating to the other side only what the parties desire to communicate. While the mediator may urge a party to face facts or to take seriously what the other side is saying, he or she will never belittle a party or in any way appear to approve more of one more than the other.

The successful mediator is an advocate for the process.

Rather than being an advocate for any of the parties involved in a dispute, the mediator is an advocate for the process of mediation. As the embodiment of that process, the mediator must remain positive and energetic, and through words and actions instill in the parties the belief that their dispute can be resolved in a way that is fair to all. The mediator will patiently explain the process to the parties, answer their questions and seek to allay their fears. He or she will establish fair ground rules for the mediation and consistently enforce them. The mediator will fully explore the facts of the case and the viewpoints of the parties in order to be better equipped to help the parties fashion a good settlement.

During private caucuses the mediator will pay attention to the signals from the parties and their attorneys concerning their underlying interests. If the mediator believes that a party or an advocate is not acting in that party's best interest, the mediator will communicate those concerns and, if necessary, suspend the session. Finally, the mediator will not declare a deadlock until every reasonable effort has been made to identify and break the impasse.

The successful mediator is empathic.

One of the critical differences between mediation and trial is the ability of the fact finder to demonstrate empathy toward the parties. Typically, a judge or jury remains silent during a trial and can neither ask questions nor express concern. Furthermore, fact finding at trial will focus only on that information deemed to be relevant in determining which party should prevail. In contrast, as the mediator gathers facts and elicits information from each party concerning the dispute, he or she will listen intently, encourage elaboration, and express concern. A successful mediator will allow the parties to tell their stories in their own way and in their own words. The mediator will also be open to digressions even when they do not appear to be relevant to the matter at hand. The speaker probably has some need to express these ideas, and furthermore, they may also contain clues about the party's underlying needs and interests that can be factored into the settlement.

The successful mediator is persuasive.

Mediators achieve settlement through persuasion rather than by imposing a settlement on the parties, as in arbitration or at trial. Furthermore, the persuasion employed is usually a process rather than a series of impassioned speeches at the end of mediation designed to compel the parties to settle. The successful mediator will almost always begin early in the mediation to seek concessions from the parties. These early concessions usually involve "low-cost" matters that are relatively easy for the parties to grant. For example, a divorcing parent may agree to give up Christmas with the kids in exchange for Thanksgiving and Easter. Nevertheless, these early concessions establish momentum that the mediator will attempt to escalate, progressing from the less costly matters to the more critical. The parties are not unaware of what is happening and will probably follow the mediator's lead as they gain confidence in the process to bring the dispute to a head and achieve either resolution or deadlock.

The successful mediator keeps the negotiations on track.

A good mediator will keep the process of negotiation moving forward. He or she will be sensitive to the feelings of the participants and will often act as a balm when someone is upset. Conversely, a good mediator will be the agent of reality and stress the importance of being realistic about the alternatives to agreement. In transmitting messages back and forth between the parties, an effective mediator will be adept at communicating negative messages in positive terms. He or she will also control the tension created by mediations. Mediation is usually an intense experience for the parties, in part because they feel the pressure to settle, and because they control the terms of settlement. Consequently, all successful mediators employ various techniques to break the tension and keep the atmosphere positive. These include the use of humor and time out, for example. Also, by controlling the pace of the mediation, the mediator can lower or raise the level of tension and thus keep the process moving forward.

The successful mediator varies the approach.

An effective mediator will also vary the approach he or she uses to fit the dispute and the parties involved. For example, in a personal injury matter the mediator will most likely focus on the settlement amount and payout, whereas in a dispute over child custody and support, the mediator will pay equal attention to fostering a positive, long-term relationship between the parents.

Some disputes may require a significant amount of pre-mediation preparation on the part of the mediator, especially if the dispute involves highly technical matters or if there is no clear pattern within the jurisdiction of jury awards involving similar facts and circumstances. Conversely, other disputes are simpler or more commonplace, the possible outcome at trial is more predictable, or the mediator has extensive experience in handling similar matters. In these situations, exhaustive preparation by the mediator will be unnecessary.

If a controversy involves a party who has been seriously injured or feels highly victimized, the mediator may need to provide that party with the opportunity to express hurt and anger. Likewise, the mediator may stress settlement options that include intangible "payments" such as an apology or expression of sympathy by the other party. By comparison, in a dispute between two seasoned business owners, it is unlikely that hurt feelings and residual emotions will even be an issue.

The successful mediator searches for the parties' agreement.

Although a mediator must vary his or her approach, which includes the occasional need to recommend options and push the parties toward agreement, a successful mediator will not make the decision for the parties. Doing so would undermine the whole notion of mediation as a party-oriented process in which the disputants solve their problem together. In fact, a mediator may not be able to make a good decision for the parties, even if asked to. According to Tom Arnold, a Houston-area mediator, arbitrator and professor of ADR, during the process of mediation, the mediator

> . . . "normally receives much unreliable partisan hearsay testimony and rank speculation, receives no legal briefs, cross-examines no witnesses, often is not a lawyer but a person from the subject industry, sometimes is a lawyer not informed of the subject industry's customs or recent case law etc., so his or her judgment is in grave risk of error . . ."[19]

The successful mediator will, if necessary, abort the mediation.

If the parties become deadlocked during mediation, an effective mediator will determine, first, if the deadlock can be surmounted and, if not, call off the mediation when it is clear that further deliberations will not break the impasse. He or she will end the mediation also if one of the parties is being harmed by the process. A mediated agreement that is based on distorted evidence, that disregards the law, and that is clearly unfair will not be permitted by an effective mediator.

According to William Simkin, a mediator of labor disputes, an effective mediator will have

- the patience of Job
- the sincerity and bulldog characteristics of the English
- the wit of the Irish
- the physical endurance of a marathon runner
- the broken-field dodging abilities of a halfback
- the guile of Machiavelli
- the personality-probing skills of a good psychiatrist
- the confidence-retaining characteristics of a mute
- the hide of a rhinoceros, and
- the wisdom of Solomon.[20]

Exercises

1. If, during a mediation, a mediator comes to believe that one party in a lawsuit is much more at fault than the other, has the mediator ceased to be neutral? If yes, why? If not, why not? How can a mediator avoid taking sides and favoring the less blameworthy party?

2. Parties frequently fear that mediation will force them to accept a resolution that is unfair. How can a mediator allay these fears, both at the outset of the mediation session and as the session progresses?

3. Do you think that it is appropriate for a mediator to develop a solution and present it to the parties? If not, why not? If yes, what are the risks in doing so, and how can a mediator avoid them?

4. When a party is angry and in need of venting his or her feelings, how and when can a mediator facilitate this without causing the mediation to break down?

5. Based on William Simkin's list, what type of training and experience would enable a mediator to cultivate these characteristics?

The Role of the Attorney/ Advocate in Mediation

If the parties involved in a dispute have retained attorneys or another type of advocate, mediation has the effect of giving the dispute back to the parties, at least temporarily, in order to provide them the opportunity to resolve the matter themselves. On the surface it may appear, therefore, that advocates are extraneous to the process. In fact, mediation provides advocates and the staff who support them with a unique opportunity to zealously represent their clients. Advocates who understand mediation and how to support clients involved will provide those clients with a competitive edge over opponents who are advised by advocates who know only how to litigate. Likewise, paralegals who also understand mediation and the role played by the advocate will be in a better position to lend effective support to the client and the process.

Unfortunately, many advocates come to mediation unprepared.[21] They have no game plan, no careful study of the alternative settlement options of either their client or the opponent, no preparation of the client for mediation, and little or no understanding of how mediation works.[22] What follows is a discussion of the type of actions that a competent advocate will take in order to effectively represent his or her client during mediation.

Presuit Analysis and Counseling

When an advocate is hired to represent a party involved in a dispute, the advocate must first gather facts about the case from the client in order to counsel him or her on the best alternatives available to resolve the problem. As will be discussed in the next chapter, the client's problem may be addressed by legislation or regulation that encourages or mandates that a claimant try mediation or some other form of ADR first. The legislation may even provide the services of a particular mediation service at little or no cost to the parties. Advocates should always check local laws and rules to see if they impact the client's case in any way.

In addition to legislation and regulation, many states and state bar associations have adopted resolutions and promulgated rules that require attorneys to inform their clients of the availability of alternative dispute resolution procedures.* Attorneys can even be held liable in malpractice for failing to inform clients of ADR, if the court finds that the jury award in the matter exceeded the likely outcome of a mediated settlement.[23] Clients anticipating litigation should also be counseled that all forms of dispute resolution involve risk, especially if the resulting decision is final. Even a mediated agreement, once signed, is an enforceable contract by either party. However, if a procedure such as mediation is attempted and no resolution is reached, the parties are free to pursue other means including litigation. Of course, the longer the dispute continues, the greater the cost to the client in time, money and emotions.

Presuit Intervention

When evaluating a new case, an advocate should determine whether early intervention will resolve the matter. Mediation is one form of intervention that can be used effectively even before a lawsuit has been filed. In some cases, if the dispute involves a written contract or agreement between the parties, the contract may contain a provision requiring any dispute arising under the contract to first be mediated. These provisions are usually independent of the rest of the contract. Therefore, if one of the parties repudiates the contract, the ADR provision is still enforceable.

Even where early mediation is not required by contract, research shows that presuit mediation is on the rise, because the parties have not yet fully abdicated the dispute to their attorneys. They still feel in control and thus capable of forging their own settlement using the structure that mediation can provide. Also, presuit mediation can save discovery time and money, because the mediator acts as fact finder and therefore may be able to get enough of the story out on the table for the parties to reach an agreement.

---

* The Texas Lawyer's Creed, adopted by the Texas Supreme Court in 1989, recites in Section II, "I will advise my client regarding the availability of mediation, arbitration and other alternative methods of resolving and settling disputes." See also the Rules of Professional Conduct, Rule 2.1, adopted by the Colorado Supreme Court in 1993.

For these reasons, the advocate for a party should consider contacting counsel for the other and proposing that they and their clients consider negotiating a resolution through the use of mediation.

Early Intervention After Filing Suit

If a suit is filed, the advocate team should plan ahead regarding when would be a judicious time to propose mediation and what basic discovery would be needed in order to adequately assess the case and decide if and how to settle the matter. In this way the advocate can save discovery costs while at the same time facilitating mediation. As before, the attorney should contact the other lawyer to either propose mediation, or if court-mandated, to select a mediator and discuss ground rules.

Selecting a Competent Mediator

One of the most important ways in which an advocate can zealously represent clients is to select competent mediators who consistently facilitate fair and just settlements. An advocate should be thoroughly familiar with available mediators in the area, their specialties, fees, styles and approaches to mediation. Paralegals and other support staff are in an excellent position to gather this information from among their peers, as well as firsthand by volunteering at community mediation centers where professional mediators may also volunteer, supervise or serve on committees and boards. In some cases, it may be helpful to hire a mediator with specialized knowledge in the subject matter of the dispute, especially if it involves technological, scientific, or other esoteric matters such as intellectual property or international law.

Providing the Mediator with Information

Once a mediator has been selected, the legal team will need to provide any information requested by the mediator. In some cases, this may be a complete file on the matter including pleadings, pertinent discovery, case law and other documents. In other situations, the mediator may ask only for a position paper from the advocate evaluating the strengths and weaknesses of the case, from his or her perspective. Typically, a legal team will not develop a thorough perspective on a case until most discovery is completed. Therefore, the team needs to anticipate the mediator's request and be prepared.

Paralegals who have been interacting with the client or gathering and analyzing discovery will be invaluable in helping the advocate to evaluate the case and develop a realistic position paper. Position papers are usually kept confidential by the mediator; however, some advocates will also exchange with their opponents settlement briefs that present the strengths of their case, including facts and legal authority supporting their conclusions. Position papers and settlement briefs also can provide the basis for presenting a client's case during the opening joint session.

Preparing the Client for Mediation

It is critical that a client be well prepared for mediation. The advocate team should meet ahead of time with the client, brief him or her on what to expect, and fully explain the process of mediation. The client needs to understand that the mediation could be the last day of the lawsuit, so he or she must be willing to seriously consider settlement. The advocate should share his or her assessment of the case with the client, review the client's demands and underlying interests and identify settlement options, including the client's "bottom line." The advocate and client also need to discuss what could happen if the mediation fails, including both the best and the worst scenario. For example, is it likely that the client could get more in court? Conversely, what are the chances of a take-nothing judgment?

The advocate and client need to decide who will make the opening statement and what will be emphasized. If the client expects to respond to questions from the advocate, the questions and answers should be reviewed. The client should also be advised on not making an offer too soon. In some cases, the advocate may want to "showcase" the client. For example, in a case involving a consumer who had been defrauded in the purchase of an automobile, the fact that the consumer/client was not fluent in English needs to be demonstrated to the participants during the opening joint session.

In private caucus, the client should be prepared to listen, reevaluate his or her case with an open mind, answer the mediator's questions,[*] explain feelings, attitudes, motivations and goals, and try to be sympathetic toward the other side. The client also needs to understand that if the mediation does not go well, the suit will proceed and nothing will have been lost.

Finally, clients who are represented by an attorney should be counseled concerning how that attorney will behave during mediation. Clients expect attorneys they hire to champion their cause and to behave in an adversarial manner toward the other side. Consequently, a client can be confused or even alarmed when the attorney behaves in a conciliatory manner during joint sessions, or appears to take the opponent's side during private caucus discussions. Clients should understand that such behavior by counsel is appropriate during mediation. Because mediation strives to satisfy the essential needs of all the parties, and not just one of them, it is critical that the parties understand their opponent's point of view. By playing "devil's advocate" or pointing out the strengths of the other side's case, the advocate can assist the client to see the dispute through the eyes of their opponent. Nevertheless, the client should be assured that if the case does not settle through mediation, the attorney will resume a more adversarial posture during further litigation and trial.

---

[*] The following mediator questions are adapted from *Advocacy in Mediation*, by Tom Arnold, in the October 1994 proceedings of the Society of Professionals in Dispute Resolution, at 19:

1. ◆ How do you feel about the dispute and about the other parties?
2. ◆ What do you really want from the resolution of this dispute? Put your wants and desires in priority.
3. ◆ What do you feel are your rights?
4. ◆ After hours of mediating what will the other side likely offer?
5. ◆ What fact or law in your case would you like to change?
6. ◆ What are the risks in your case? What scares you the most?
7. ◆ What does the other side think of their case? Of yours?
8. ◆ What does it feel like to be in their shoes? In yours?
9. ◆ What is limiting your freedom to settle this case?
10. ◆ How important is a future relationship with your opponent?
11. ◆ What do you think of your chances at trial? Their chances?

Preparing the Opening Statement   The advocate should prepare the opening statement or assist the client to do so, making sure that it is a strong and positive presentation of the client's case. The opening statement should strike a balance between an interest in settlement and a willingness to litigate,[24] but without threatening the other side. Likewise, the party or advocate presenting the statement should avoid using pejorative terms, ridiculing their opponent, or making accusations. Such tactics will only "poison the well" from which the client hopes to later obtain a favorable settlement. A typical statement will take five to fifteen minutes and should be addressed to the other party, not the mediator or the other party's attorney. At the courthouse, attorneys try to persuade judges and juries, whereas in mediation, the party being persuaded is the opponent. This is a much tougher job and requires all of the advocate's powers of persuasion.

Counseling the Client in Private Caucus   Those periods of time during private caucuses when the mediator is conferring with the other side can provide the advocate with an excellent opportunity to analyze how the mediation is going, learn more about the client's interests and priorities, and counsel the client accordingly. Together, the advocate and client should analyze the information that the mediator has communicated so far, looking for clues about what the other side is thinking and what sort of settlement they might find acceptable. They should also attempt to anticipate what they will hear next from the mediator and how they should react. The advocate should continue to probe the client to uncover any new interests and changes in the client's priorities.

Meeting Privately with the Mediator   Sometimes it is helpful for an advocate to meet alone with the mediator. Either the advocate or the mediator can initiate a private session. For example, an advocate may sense that the client has unrealistic expectations about what he or she will settle for. By meeting privately, the advocate and mediator can devise a strategy to help the client assess the strengths and weaknesses of the case more objectively. Conversely, a mediator may sense that the advocate has unrealistic expectations regarding the outcome of the case, or the advocate is placing his or her interests ahead of the client (e.g., discouraging settlement in order to continue the litigation and collect more fees).

By meeting privately with the advocate, the mediator can discuss these concerns without embarrassing or humiliating the advocate in the client's presence. A good mediator will always be respectful of the advocate-client relationship. Sometimes, all the advocates involved will meet with the mediator in joint session to clarify issues and to work through an impasse.

Settling   At the end of the mediation, the parties are generally presented with the choice of accepting an agreement that meets some, or even most, of their interests or continuing the dispute. The advocates should be prepared to give an opinion regarding the proposed settlement based on whether or not it meets the essential needs identified during mediation and, if so, whether their client can reasonably expect to improve the outcome by continuing the dispute. If not, then the advocates should attempt to persuade their clients to settle.

Preparing the Settlement Agreement

If a settlement is reached, the advocates should anticipate assisting in drafting the agreement, even if the hour is late. Although many mediators permit agreements to be drafted and signed days and even weeks later, the advocates should make sure their clients initial a tentative agreement before "buyer's remorse" sets in. Conversely, if an advocate feels that the settlement is imprudent, he or she may want to delay drafting any agreement until the client has either committed to the settlement or rejects the offer.

Exercises

After reviewing the mediation case study that begins on page 63 of this chapter, answer the following questions and complete the following tasks. If necessary, supply facts and circumstances that will enable you to answer the questions posed.

1. What steps could the parties and their attorneys have taken to avoid having to file and defend a lawsuit? What about when the parties first became involved with one another; during the time when the work was progressing; when the management company first concluded that the work was unsatisfactory?

2. Assume you are the attorney for the management company. Assume also that the management company has complained directly to Tri-State about the alleged poor quality of its work, that you have sent a letter of complaint to Tri-State's attorney threatening a lawsuit, and that Tri-State's attorney has responded in writing disavowing the allegations and demanding final payment. Prepare what you would say to Tri-State's attorney if you called to propose that the parties mediate the dispute now rather than waiting until after suit has been filed. If you were Tri-State's attorney how would you respond to the proposal, and why?

3. Assume suit has been filed. From the standpoint of each of the parties, when would be the best time to propose mediation and why? What discovery would you recommend that each party complete before proceeding to mediation, and why?

4. From the standpoint of each of the parties, what type of mediator would you select, and why? What qualifications and experience should the mediator possess?

5. Outline a position paper for each of the parties that will be presented to the mediator.

6. Outline a settlement brochure for each of the parties that will be given to the opposing attorney.

7. Assume that you are the attorney for the management company. What would you say to your clients to prepare them for mediation? What would you say if you were counsel to Tri-State?

8. Assume you are the mediator. Prepare an opening statement.

9. Prepare the opening remarks that counsel for each of the parties will make at the initial joint session. If you were counsel for each of the parties, would you want the client to also make some opening statements? If not, why not? If so, why, and what would you expect them to say?

10. Assume that you are Tri-State and that the mediator has asked you in private caucus each of the questions in the footnote on page 73. How would you respond? If you were the management company, how would you respond? *exercises cont'd*

Ethical Issues and Standards of Conduct in Mediation

The practice of mediation raises many ethical issues about the conduct of mediators that are of critical importance to the parties who use mediation, to the courts and to the public. Mediators are potentially powerful people to whom much is entrusted. Like all professionals in similar positions, including physicians, lawyers, counselors, teachers, ministers and others, mediators can accomplish great good or great harm, depending upon how they conduct themselves and perform their duties.

As we have seen in the preceding chapter, standards of practice for mediators are of concern to legislators. Most states have passed laws requiring that mediators be neutral, maintain confidentiality and permit the parties to make their own decisions.[25]* Some states have also passed laws regarding minimum training requirements. However, these laws cannot and do not reach many of the deeper ethical issues that confront mediators. While statutes and regulations can define legal expectations for a mediator, they do not necessarily define ethical behavior.

The promulgation of ethical standards of conduct is usually the job of professional groups and organizations that are concerned about promoting public confidence in their particular profession and providing practitioners with general guidelines for their conduct. The American Bar Association (ABA) was one of the first groups to adopt standards of practice for mediation. Aimed primarily at lawyers involved in family mediation, the ABA Standards of Practice for Lawyer Mediators in Family Disputes set out six duties of a mediator, including the duty to:

1. define and describe the process of mediation and its costs before the parties reach an agreement to mediate;

2. maintain confidentiality of information obtained through mediation unless the parties consent to disclosure;

3. remain impartial at all times including to disclose any conflicts of interest;

4. ensure that the participants make decisions based upon sufficient information and knowledge;

5. suspend or terminate mediation whenever continuation of the process would harm one or more of the participants; and

6. advise each of the participants to obtain legal review prior to reaching any agreement.

---

* "[A mediator] may not compel or coerce the parties to enter into a settlement agreement." "[T]he impartial third party may not disclose to either party information given in confidence by the other and shall at all times maintain confidentiality with respect to communications relating to the subject matter of the dispute." "Unless the parties agree otherwise, all matters, including the conduct and demeanor of the parties and their counsel during the settlement process, are confidential and may never be disclosed to anyone, including the appointing court" (Texas Civil Practice and Remedies Code Annotated § 154.053).

This early ABA code was concerned that parties fully understand the process of mediation including any tradeoffs with other approaches to dispute resolution. It also envisioned the mediator as an aggressive participant who could make settlement suggestions and draft proposals for the parties to consider. The mediator was charged with the responsibility to make sure that the participants understood the law as it pertained to their case. To that end, the mediator could define the legal issues and apply the law to the facts of the dispute, provided he or she did not direct or dictate the decision of the parties. The mediator could also draft the settlement agreement for review by counsel to the parties. One of the important contributions of this early code was that it recognized that lawyers could act as mediators.

Another early code was promulgated by the Society of Professionals in Dispute Resolution (SPIDR), a not-for-profit organization for third-party neutrals and others interested in ADR. Their Ethical Standards of Professional Responsibility, adopted in 1986, focused especially on the process of mediation. The mediator was charged with the responsibility of expediting the process, avoiding anything that would impugn the integrity of the process, anticipating the possibility of using more than one method of ADR to resolve a dispute, and advising the parties accordingly.

Reflecting the increasing maturity of ADR, SPIDR's Standards recognized the possibility that parties and others interested in the outcome of the dispute may not be represented at the mediation, and it was the responsibility of the mediator to inform the principal parties of the problem. Recognizing the growing independence of ADR from the legal profession, the Standards also included statements regarding the need of neutrals to support the ADR profession, to help educate new practitioners and the public, and to provide pro bono services. The Standards also included a section on advertising and solicitation of mediation appointments.

Since these early efforts, additional codes have been promulgated by various professional ADR organizations. Several state courts and bar associations have published ethical codes for mediators. Unfortunately, they often leave important questions unanswered, such as fees, advertising and other issues of concern to those engaged in a profession that is independent of the law. They also are not enforceable against third-party neutrals engaged in private, non-court-referred ADR.

In 1992, the American Arbitration Association and SPIDR teamed up with the litigation and ADR sections of the American Bar Association to develop the Model Standards of Conduct for Mediators, which are reprinted in their entirety in Appendix 11. This new code, which was first published in 1995, draws on many past codes, and also takes into account issues and problems that have surfaced in mediation over the years. The Model Standards are composed of nine canons, as follows:

*Model
Standards of
Conduct for
Mediators*

I.   SELF-DETERMINATION: A MEDIATOR SHALL RECOGNIZE
     THAT MEDIATION IS BASED ON THE PRINCIPLE OF SELF-
     DETERMINATION BY THE PARTIES.

Canon I does not preclude a mediator from providing information to
participants about the process of mediation, raising issues related to the dispute
and helping the parties explore options. Also, a mediator is not required to
personally ensure that each party makes a fully informed choice with regard to
any settlement agreement. Nevertheless, a mediator should counsel participants
about the importance of consulting other professionals before making a final
decision.

II. IMPARTIALITY: A MEDIATOR SHALL CONDUCT THE
     MEDIATION IN AN IMPARTIAL MANNER.

Canon II recognizes that mediation is enhanced when the parties have
confidence in the impartiality of the mediator. Therefore, a mediator must
decline to serve, or withdraw, if he or she is unable at any time to mediate
impartially.

III. CONFLICTS OF INTEREST: A MEDIATOR SHALL DISCLOSE
     ALL ACTUAL AND POTENTIAL CONFLICTS OF INTEREST
     REASONABLY KNOWN TO THE MEDIATOR. AFTER
     DISCLOSURE, THE MEDIATOR SHALL DECLINE TO
     MEDIATE UNLESS ALL PARTIES CHOOSE TO RETAIN THE
     MEDIATOR. THE NEED TO PROTECT AGAINST CONFLICTS
     OF INTEREST ALSO GOVERNS CONDUCT THAT OCCURS
     DURING AND AFTER MEDIATION.

Canon III defines a conflict of interest as a dealing or relationship that might
create an impression of possible bias. The standard for disclosure is any actual
or potential conflict that is reasonably known to the mediator, or *reasonably
could be seen* as raising a question about impartiality.

IV. COMPETENCE: A MEDIATOR SHALL MEDIATE ONLY WHEN
     THE MEDIATOR HAS THE NECESSARY QUALIFICATIONS
     TO SATISFY THE REASONABLE EXPECTATIONS OF THE
     PARTIES.

Canon IV deals with the difficult issue of training and competence. It cautions
mediators that they should hold themselves out as mediators only if they have
the competency to mediate effectively, which includes the "requisite training
and experience." A mediator has an affirmative duty to make information
available to parties regarding their experience and training. Mediator sources
that distribute lists also have a duty to inform the public and parties about the
requirements that a mediator must meet to appear on a list. Finally, a court or
agency that appoints mediators has a duty to ensure that each mediator is
qualified for the particular mediation.

V. CONFIDENTIALITY: A MEDIATOR SHALL MAINTAIN THE REASONABLE EXPECTATIONS OF THE PARTIES WITH REGARD TO CONFIDENTIALITY.

Canon V places confidentiality within the control of the parties by requiring that a mediator keep silent about any matter that a party expects to be confidential. Thus, the parties can make their own rules. For this reason, it is important that the mediator discuss confidentiality with the participants. Nevertheless, Canon V provides that a mediator is to keep settlement offers and agreements, party behavior, and other such matters confidential.

VI. QUALITY OF THE PROCESS: A MEDIATOR SHALL CONDUCT THE MEDIATION FAIRLY, DILIGENTLY, AND IN A MANNER CONSISTENT WITH THE PRINCIPLE OF SELF-DETERMINATION BY THE PARTIES.

Canon VI charges the mediator with the responsibility to ensure a quality process, which includes diligence and procedural fairness. A mediator should accept an assignment only if he or she has the time to commit. In order to maintain neutrality and not confuse the parties regarding the role of the mediator, he or she should not give professional advice. A mediator is required to withdraw to avoid furthering illegal activity, and withdraw or postpone a session if a participant cannot fully participate.

VII. ADVERTISING AND SOLICITATION: A MEDIATOR SHALL BE TRUTHFUL IN ADVERTISING AND SOLICITATION FOR MEDIATION.

Mediator advertising should be truthful and should avoid making promises and guarantees. A mediator may not claim the endorsement of an organization unless that organization has a procedure for qualifying mediators and the mediator has been duly granted status under them.

VIII. FEES: A MEDIATOR SHALL FULLY DISCLOSE AND EXPLAIN THE BASIS OF COMPENSATION, FEES, AND CHARGES TO THE PARTIES.

Fees are to be disclosed before mediation begins, and should be reasonable, based on the mediation service to be provided. Factors include type and complexity of the matter, expertise of the mediator, time required, customary rates in the community and so forth. Fees should not be contingent upon the results, and referral fees are forbidden. Canon VIII encourages the use of written fee agreements, and provides that unearned fees should be returned.

IX. OBLIGATIONS TO THE MEDIATION PROCESS: MEDIATORS HAVE A DUTY TO IMPROVE THE PRACTICE OF MEDIATION.

Canon IX declares that mediators have an obligation to use their knowledge of their craft to help educate the public about mediation, to make it accessible, to correct abuses, and to improve their own skills.

Exercise | The following chart sets out some of the ethical questions and dilemmas that a mediator faces, and attempts to answer according to these Model Standards.[26] Cover the answers in the right-hand column and answer each of the questions posed in the left-hand column using the Model Standards reprinted in Appendix 11. Then compare your answers to those supplied by the authors. Do you agree with the answers provided? Are there other responses that the mediator could have ethically made?

	QUESTION/DILEMMA	ETHICAL RESPONSE
1	At a social function a guest tells you of a lawsuit her attorney just filed on her behalf, which he hopes to take into mediation.	Although you can advertise your services as a mediator, you may not solicit a specific case or matter.
2	You get a court referral involving a judge who doesn't really believe in mediation and is openly skeptical of agreements reached using ADR.	Consider withdrawing. To be successful, mediation requires the confidence of those who will rely on the outcome, including a judge who may be asked to enter judgment based on the agreement.
3	The court appoints you because it believes that you can come up with a good settlement solution and convince the parties of your point of view.	Withdraw if the judge cannot be convinced that the parties must make their own decisions.
4	A close relative of yours is likely to be named as an expert witness in the case you have been asked to mediate.	Consider withdrawing, or at least require the relative to decline to provide expert advice. It is your duty to avoid conflicts of interest.
5	It will be difficult to fit the mediation into your schedule.	Withdraw if you cannot give the mediation sufficient time. The interests of the parties come first.
6	The parties are unwilling to pay the amount of the fee that you charge.	Reduce your fee to a level acceptable to the parties, provided that doing so does not prejudice you against the parties. Alternatively, withdraw if the fee question may sour the process.
7	One of the attorneys offers you a portion of any settlement reached.	You may not charge or accept a fee based on the outcome.
8	One of the parties objects to the fact that you participated in the reelection campaign of the judge assigned to the case.	Withdraw. A mediator must avoid even the appearance of partiality. Furthermore, you may not serve if a party feels that a conflict exists.
9	The attorney for one of the parties questions your qualifications to mediate this particular dispute.	You should withdraw if there are any serious questions about your qualifications, or if you feel unqualified.
10	One of the attorneys suggests that you skip much of the opening session in the interest of saving time.	Decline the suggestion. The mediator must protect the integrity of the process. The parties need to understand the process and agree to the rules. Furthermore, the opening session is a critical part of the process of building rapport and trust, and exchanging information.
11	You learn that one of the parties present does not have the authority to settle the case.	Do not convene the session unless the appropriate parties are present.
12	One of the parties insists that the mediation be completed by noon.	Do not convene the mediation. Adequate time must be reserved for the process to work.
13	One of the participants privately informs you of his bottom-line demand and then tells you he has nothing more to say.	Do not convene the mediation, or terminate it if already under way. All parties must be able to participate meaningfully.

	QUESTION/DILEMMA	ETHICAL RESPONSE
14	In private caucus, counsel for one of the parties insists that the client let him do all the talking.	Do not convene the mediation, or terminate it if already under way. All parties must be able to participate meaningfully.
15	One of the parties is emotionally overwrought and cannot be consoled.	Do not convene the mediation, or terminate it if already under way. All parties must be able to participate meaningfully.
16	One of the parties, a large corporation, sends a representative with authority to settle but with no knowledge of the case.	Do not convene the mediation, or terminate it if already under way. All parties must be able to participate meaningfully.
17	One of the attorneys brings a court reporter to record the proceedings.	Send the court reporter away. A mediator should not permit the recording of mediation proceedings.
18	When you call the judge to report that the case didn't settle, the judge presses you for details.	Decline to give details, unless all of the parties have agreed to the disclosure. Everything about the proceedings is confidential including what was said and how people behaved. You are required only to report if the case settled or reached impasse.
19	Your secretary inserts your notes from the mediation into a file clearly marked with the name of the case and places it in an unlocked filing cabinet.	Render all identifying information anonymous before filing the notes and maintain confidentiality in the storage and disposal of records.
20	During mediation you accidentally tell one side something that was said by the other that you did not have express permission to share.	Immediately inform the parties of what happened. If you or one of the parties believe that the mediation has been irretrievably compromised, terminate the mediation.
21	In a divorce and child custody mediation, one of the parties informs you that his wife has physically abused their daughter.	If state law requires, you must disclose that information to the proper authorities. You should inform the parties of your intent to disclose the information. It is likely that the mediation will have been compromised and, if so, you should terminate the proceedings.
22	You take a serious dislike to one of the parties and have a hard time keeping your patience with him.	Consider terminating the mediation if you cannot fairly commit to and aid all the parties in reaching a settlement.
23	Well into a mediation you discover that, unknown to you, your former law partner represented one of the parties during the period of the partnership.	Reveal the conflict of interest immediately to all of the parties, and obtain their consent to continue; otherwise, terminate the mediation.
24	One of the parties is representing herself, while the other side is represented by three able attorneys. During private caucus the *pro se* party asks you for your legal opinion about the case.	Before convening the mediation you should ascertain the preparedness of the pro se party to mediate and advise that party about the risks of proceeding without independent counsel. Nevertheless, you should decline to give legal advice. Rather, refer the party to an attorney or some independent source of legal information and advice (e.g., an attorney-prepared brochure that outlines the applicable state law).
25	One of the parties asks for your best guess regarding what the other side will settle for.	Decline to state your opinion. At an appropriate time in the proceedings you may express your sense about the other side's readiness to settle, but not how much, unless you have been authorized to make an offer.
26	One of the parties is holding onto important information requested in discovery that the party believes is privileged (but you don't).	Encourage disclosure of the information, and proceed with the mediation.

	QUESTION/DILEMMA	ETHICAL RESPONSE
27	You learn that one of the attorneys has lied about the availability of critical documents properly requested by the other side.	Terminate the mediation without revealing to the other party why you have done so. If rules governing attorney conduct so provide, you should report the lawyer's unethical behavior to the appropriate professional disciplinary authority in your state.
28	The case does not settle and is tried in a court of law. One of the parties subpoenas you to testify about what you learned during the mediation.	Upon receiving the subpoena, you should inform counsel for both parties that, due to the confidentiality afforded mediation and mediators in your state, you cannot be required to testify. You may have to file a motion for a protective order if the party persists.
29	The parties are unable to reach settlement through mediation and they ask you to arbitrate the matter (recommend a settlement).	A mediator may later arbitrate a dispute if the parties agree and the mediator believes that he or she can do so without bias toward either party.
30	The parties reach an impasse.	Postpone, recess or terminate the mediation.
31	The parties reach an agreement but one of them wants to leave before the agreement has been written down and initialed.	Encourage the party to remain while the agreement is prepared.
32	Six weeks after a mediation involving a dispute over the construction of an office building, you are solicited by the developer to invest in the next project.	Decline to invest. You must maintain even the appearance of a conflict of interest regarding the concluded mediation.

Qualification Standards for Mediators

In addition to ethical standards, another means of regulating a profession is by requiring that practitioners either comply with various requirements of training and experience, and/or obtain a license to practice ADR. A major concern underlying the interest in training and performance criteria for mediators is the need to provide the public with a high level of professionalism in the practice of mediation, as well as a means of enabling the public to determine which mediators meet professional standards.

Fueling the interest in qualification standards are the dozens of membership-based organizations for mediators who are concerned not only about the profession but who also want to promote their organization by offering credentials to members who meet their standards. A third influence is the fact that ADR is closely related to the legal profession, where attorneys not only must comply with standards of ethical conduct and responsibility, they must also obtain a law degree from an accredited law school and pass a stringent examination in order to be admitted to the practice of law. (Alabama and perhaps one or two other states permit graduates of nonaccredited law schools to take the bar exam and be admitted to the practice of law.)

Opponents of qualification standards and credentials for ADR professionals argue that our society is in need of more and more mediators, and qualification requirements create barriers of entry for people who want to offer their services, especially on a voluntary basis. They also argue that a good mediator is effective largely due to natural attributes that cannot be taught. Proponents, on the other hand, point out that the influx of untrained and unmonitored people into the profession will confuse the public and downgrade the public trust in mediation and, therefore, standards and enforcement mechanisms are needed.

Training and Experience Standards

The most aggressive activity in the development of training and experience-based standards for mediators can be found in those states where the civil courts promote ADR and aggressively use it to control court dockets. Courts will often require mediators to meet certain requirements in order to receive court referrals. Family mediators are often expected to have additional training in psychology or family counseling. In Florida, mediators of insurance claims must possess a graduate degree in psychology, counseling, business or economics, be a lawyer admitted to the Florida bar, and have been actively engaged in mediation for four years, plus take 40 hours of additional training and pass an exam.

Texas is proposing to go one step farther and offer a special designation to mediators who meet certain training and performance standards. Under the leadership of the ADR section of the State Bar of Texas, which comprises one of the largest groups of mediators in the country, a proposal has been advanced to offer credentials to Texas mediators who meet certain requirements. Those requirements will include:

a. completion of a minimum of 40 hours of mediation training,

b. education about the ADR section's ethical guidelines for mediators via a three-hour course on the topic, and agreement to adhere to those guidelines,

c. completion of at least 20 mediations after completing mediation training,

d. commitment to complete 10 hours annually of continuing education relating to mediation and mediation ethics,

e. agreement to be governed by and to participate in a feedback and grievance procedure established by the ADR section of the bar, and

f. agreement to engage in self-study on mediation and ethical issues, and self-evaluation on mediation techniques.

The requirements are designed to enable the public to identify well-trained mediators who are aware of their ethical obligations, and who will be governed by a grievance procedure to handle complaints. The proponents of the Texas proposal envision a voluntary program that does not require credentials to practice mediation in the state. Furthermore, applicants need not be attorneys or members of the state bar. The program will be administered by a committee that will include representatives of the mediation community and of consumers of mediation, and application fees will be kept low.

It remains to be seen whether states and organizations with proposals for training and experience standards will be successful at implementing effective guidelines that the public comes to rely on. The debate will center to a large extent on the issue of training and advanced degrees versus performance criteria (e.g., number of mediations; types of mediations). Commentators argue that 40 hours of training is much too little. Furthermore, studies show that advanced education does not seem to affect settlement rates or satisfaction with the outcome.

On the other hand, performance criteria based on the number of mediations conducted are misleading because they do not specify the difficulty of the mediations. For example, a person who has mediated five complex disputes each involving millions of dollars in damages is likely to be more qualified to mediate business disputes than a small claims mediator who handles dozens of cases each day involving no more than $2,000 each.

Exercises

1. What do you think of the Texas criteria? Are they too strict or too easy? What criteria would you recommend and why?

2. What do you think of the idea of a mediator complaint process? What would constitute mediator malpractice? What penalties should be given and how can they be enforced?

3. Do you agree with the opponents of qualification standards that they only impede the entry of people into the profession? If not, why not? If so, why do you say that?

License to Practice ADR

So far, no U.S. jurisdiction either requires or offers a license to practice ADR as a third-party neutral, whether as a mediator, arbitrator, private judge, neutral advisor, etc. Discussions regarding licensure are motivated primarily by the perceived need to enforce ethical standards in much the same way that state bar associations regulate, enforce and sanction attorneys licensed to practice law. Proposed license requirements tend to be much more stringent and restrictive than those required for certification only.

It remains to be seen whether any jurisdiction will legislate an ADR license requirement in the future. Nevertheless, in 1995, the Commission on Qualifications for the Society of Professionals in Dispute Resolution recommended against the licensing of mediators for five reasons:

1. The state of knowledge is nascent concerning what qualifications practitioners require to provide effective dispute resolution services.

2. Government licensure risks establishing arbitrary standards that could unnecessarily limit party choice of practitioners and limit access to the field by competent individuals.

3. Licensure could work toward domination of the field by an exclusive group.

4. Licensure could inappropriately "freeze" the standards in a fluid field.

5. The field of dispute resolution practice is as varied and broad as the range of human relationships. Competence in one field (i.e., family disputes) does not assure competence in an unrelated field (i.e., labor disputes).[27]

Exercises

1. Do you think that ADR professionals should be licensed? Why or why not?

2. How could licensure lead to domination of the field by an exclusive group, as the SPIDR report claims?

3. Based on the development of standards of practice in ADR so far, do you think we know enough right now to set licensing standards? Explain your answer. If you had to write a bill proposing licensing standards for mediators, what would the bill require?

4. Right now, lawyers, physicians, dentists, and other licensed professional groups all must satisfy basic requirements regardless of the specialties they later pursue. Are there standards and requirements that apply to all ADR practitioners regardless of specialization? What are those? Can ADR professional standards be measured. If so, how?

Measuring Success in Mediation

Since the beginning of the modern ADR movement, mediation has become the most popular alternative dispute resolution technique currently in use. Nevertheless, it is still unclear why some mediated disputes settle and others don't. Another issue involves the definition of "success." Is a mediation successful merely because it achieves settlement, or should success also include the satisfaction of the parties, the fairness of the outcome, or some other measure? There are nearly as many opinions on these issues as there are mediators.

Most social scientific research into the factors that strongly influence success or failure in mediation have focused on rate of settlement, simply because it is the easiest to measure. Yet, even this research has been inconclusive. Recently, however, researchers have began to isolate some of the variables that most dramatically affect the outcome of mediation. In one study reported in the *Ohio State Journal on Dispute Resolution*, the researcher studied more than 500 mediations in the construction industry, both public and private, legal and nonlegal.[28] The research measured the following factors that contribute to settlement:

A. Situational Factors

♦ type of dispute

♦ issues involved (e.g., contract changes, delays, poor workmanship, nonpayment)

♦ amount in controversy

♦ intensity of the dispute

♦ length and complexity of the dispute including the number of separate issues involved

♦ number of parties involved in the dispute

♦ characteristics of the parties, including motivation to settle, expectations and ability to pay

B. Mediator Characteristics

♦ personal characteristics (e.g., age, gender, personality, training, professional status)

♦ number of mediators involved (some mediations use more than one)

♦ quality and skill of the mediator(s)

♦ amount of premediation fact finding by mediator

♦ number and type of intervention techniques employed (e.g., private caucus, pressuring to settle)

C. Procedural Features

♦ timing (when mediation occurs in the life of a dispute)

♦ whether or not a lawsuit or demand for arbitration has been filed

♦ duration of the mediation (e.g., hours, one day, several days)

♦ source of the request for mediation (e.g., court, one of the parties, mandated by contract)

♦ source of the rules applied (e.g., American Arbitration Association rules, court-defined rules, parties develop their own rules)

♦ amount of discovery that has occurred

The results of this study reached the following conclusions:

1. The most influential factor was the source of the mediation rules used. Mediations conducted using rules developed by the parties themselves, rather than imposed or adopted from the outside, were significantly more likely to settle.

2. The longer the mediation lasted, the more likely that the parties would settle, and in full. In other words, successful mediations take time.

3. The larger the amount in controversy, the less likely the dispute was resolved. Nevertheless, this was the only factor equated with the complexity of the dispute that seemed to matter. For example, mediations that dealt with many issues or highly technical matters were just as likely to settle as simple, single-issue disputes.

4. High-quality mediators who used a variety of strategies and creative techniques to move the process along and keep the parties talking were more likely to achieve success.

The researcher concluded that the relevance of the mediation procedure cannot be underestimated. If the parties perceive the mediation process as fair, they are more likely to settle. Furthermore, by negotiating their own rules they are learning to trust one another, which pays off when negotiation over the substantive issues begins. In addition, if they keep at it and if the mediator is sufficiently creative in designing and directing the process, the outcome is highly likely to be positive.

The next chapter will continue the discussion of mediation with a review of mediation legislation.

Sources

[1] S. Leeson and B. Johnson, *Ending It: Dispute Resolution in America*, 133 (1988).

[2] N. Rogers and C. McEwen, *Mediation: Law, Policy, Practice*, 1-1 (1994).

[3] *Id.*, at 4-10, 11.

[4] Northrop, *The Mediational Approval Theory of Law in America Legal Realism*, 44 Va. L.Rev. 347 (1958).

[5] *Id.*, at 349.

[6] V. Sanchez, *Towards a History of ADR: The Dispute Processing Continuum in Anglo-Saxon England and Today*, 11 Ohio St. J. on Disp. Resol. 1 (1996).

[7] *Id.*, at 27.

[8] J. Murray, A. Rau and E. Sherman, *Processes of Dispute Resolution*, 248 (1989).

[9] *Id.*

[10] *Id.*

[11] Fuller, *Mediation – Its Forms and Functions*, 44 S.Cal.L. Rev., 305, 308, 325-26 (1971).

[12] Cal. Civ. Proc. Code § 4607(d) (West Supp. 1994); Kan. Stat. Ann. § 23-603 (1996).

[13] E. Odum, The Mediation Hearing: A Primer, *reprinted in* Palenski and Launer, *Mediation: Contexts and Challenges* (1986).

[14] E. Galton, *Mediation: A Texas Practice Guide*, 55 (1993) by American Lawyer Media LP, 1-800-456-5484, ext. 157.

[15] L. Singer, *Settling Disputes*, 23 (1994).

[16] B. Roth, R. Wulff, and C. Cooper, *The Alternative Dispute Resolution Practice Guide*, § 23:6 (1993).

[17] L. Singer, *supra*, at 23.

[18] B. Roth, R. Wulff and C. Cooper, *supra*, at § 23:18.

[19] T. Arnold, Mediation Outline: A Practical How-To Guide for Mediators and Attorneys, *reprinted in* Alternative Dispute Resolution Techniques 4.020 (W. Hancock ed. 1996).

[20] W. Simkin, *Mediation and the Dynamics of Collective Bargaining* (1971).

[21] T. Arnold, *Advocacy in Mediation*, Soc'y Disp. Resol., Oct. 1994, at 5.

[22] *Id.*

[23] *Garris v. Severson, Merson, Berke & Melchior*, 205 Cal App 3d 301, 252 Cal Rptr 204 (2d Dist. Ct. 1988), (*op withdrawn*, 1989 Cal LEXIS 529).

[24] M. Lewis, *Advocacy in Mediation: One Mediator's View*, Disp. Resol. Mag., at 7 (Fall 1985).

[25] *Id.*, at 11-2.

[26] B. Sparks and H. Simpson, Sex, Lies, Videotape, and Advocacy: Common Ethics Problems in Mediation (Feb. 1996) (unpublished presentation to the Dallas Bar Association ADR section).

[27] Society of Professionals in Dispute Resolution Commission on Qualifications, Report No. 2: Ensuring Competence and Quality in Dispute Resolution Practice, 9-10 (1995).

[28] D. Henderson, *Mediation Success: An Empirical Analysis*, 11 Ohio St. J. on Disp. Resol. 105 (1996).

Chapter Four

Mediation Law and Policy

Introduction

The preceding chapter introduced mediation to the student, described a typical session, reviewed a typical case study and discussed the critical roles played by the mediator and the attorney/advocate in the mediation process. This chapter will review ADR legislation at the federal and state level in order to provide an understanding of how laws and regulations have profoundly influenced the way mediation is used to resolve disputes and to promote government social policy.

Caveats

1. The following discussion focuses on law and regulation dealing with mediation. Nevertheless, because many of the same statutes and rules cover arbitration, conciliation, and other forms of ADR as well, it is difficult to isolate mediation from the mix, nor is it necessary. While mediation is unique, it is part of the larger ADR scene, which legislators seek to promote and regulate.

2. Terms such as "mediation," "conciliation," and "arbitration" as they occur in federal and state statutes, often have different meanings from jurisdiction to jurisdiction.* Furthermore, some statutes describe a process that looks like arbitration or some other form of third-party decision making, but which is labeled as mediation and conciliation. Likewise, people with arbitrator-like powers are sometimes labeled "mediators." When reviewing ADR laws and regulations, the reader should pay careful attention not only to the terms used but also to the descriptions of the processes and powers to be employed.

3. The term "conciliation" as it is used in statutes and regulations, is used

   (a) to mean a highly informal method of dispute resolution involving a discussion between the parties in the presence of a neutral third party, or

   (b) as a synonym for "alternative dispute resolution" encompassing many techniques designed to reach a decision or agreed settlement.

   Conciliation has also been called "mediation without caucusing."

Mediation and the Law

Legislation is one of the important ways that society responds to movements and trends that influence the lives of its citizens. When a movement begins to grow, legislation will be passed to establish and fund programs aimed at promoting it. Likewise, legislation will seek to regulate the movement in order to maximize its positive potential and to minimize any harm it might cause. Court cases will also influence and shape a movement by testing the legitimacy and sufficiency of the legislation, and in some situations, will make new law.

---

* For example, Michigan has court-directed "mediation," which is more akin to arbitration. If the plaintiff rejects the "mediator's" findings and, at trial, is awarded no more than 110% of the mediator's recommended award, the plaintiff must pay the other side's attorney fees and costs.

The legislative response to ADR generally, and mediation in particular, follows this pattern. Since the late 19th century, federal, state, and local lawmakers have enacted statutes and drafted regulations creating and funding mediation programs, both inside and outside government agencies. They have passed resolutions encouraging the use of mediation and, in some cases, even mandated its use. In addition, efforts have been made to regulate mediation in the following ways:

♦ by establishing standards of professionalism and training for mediators,

♦ by defining the scope of confidentiality in mediation,

♦ by providing for the enforcement of mediated agreements, and

♦ by addressing other issues concerning the quality and accessibility of mediation.

Finally, many of the statutes that lawmakers have passed have been influenced and tested by judicial decisions. The volume of law dealing with mediation is already substantial and continues to increase at a rapid rate. Legal professionals and mediators need to be well-versed in mediation law in order to adequately represent and serve clients, as well as to satisfy what the law requires.

Early Developments in Mediation Legislation

Early legislation aimed at fostering the use of mediation and regulating its practice tended, like all legislation dealing with any issue or problem, to promote specific social policies that legislators found to be desirable. Mediation as a way to resolve disputes first caught the public's attention near the beginning of the 20th century when conflicts developed between corporate management and labor that threatened to seriously disrupt the American economy. The government stepped in, and through legislation sought to create a framework in which the various factions within industry could engage in dialogue and settle their arguments.[1]

Binding arbitration was, and still is the principal means provided by this and later legislation dealing with organized labor disputes. However, as early as 1898, Congressional action authorized the use of mediation and conciliation for resolving union and management disputes. In 1913, the federal government established the Board of Mediation and Conciliation for railroad labor matters, later renamed the National Mediation Board in 1934.[2] In that same year, the Newland Act[3] encouraged the use of mediation for collective bargaining. This and other legislation reflected the belief that voluntary settlement, which is the essence of mediation, aided society because it had the power to do more than just end strikes. Rather, it also helped to prevent strikes by instructing the parties in how to negotiate effectively.[4]

Some of the earliest court-sponsored ADR programs were based on the belief that ADR could produce more cost-effective settlements, as well as greater satisfaction among the disputing parties with the settlement achieved.[5] Family-related lawsuits were often the target of these early court-promoted efforts. For example, in the 1940s and 1950s various states passed statutes establishing programs to foster the reconciliation of couples who had filed for divorce. Although most of these programs were unsuccessful, they provided the structure for family law mediation that developed a decade later.[6]

Legislation was also passed that provided ADR at the community level where many felt it could do the most good. Community-based mediation services began primarily in the 1960s, often with grants from "War on Poverty" programs of the federal government. Sponsors of these local mediation services, both then and now, included churches, charities, schools, local government, police, youth clubs, civil rights organizations, and other similar groups. Citizens involved in disputes were encouraged to seek the aid of these sources to settle their disagreements before they hired a lawyer, initiated a lawsuit, or took the law into their own hands. The services that developed during this era tended to be motivated by various social and political ideals which were often identified in the legislation that created them, including:

♦ the desirability of having people resolve their own disputes;

♦ a distrust of government that was seen as tending to impose unworkable solutions on the community;

♦ a conviction that courts were not responsive to poor and minority citizens and communities;

♦ a belief that relationships within a community were more important than the relationship of the community with the outside system; and

♦ a belief that lawyers were often elitist, expensive, and a part of the system.[7]

In 1972, Congress established through the Department of Justice the Community Relations Service, which was aimed at mediating civil rights disputes in prisons, schools, and other community arenas. The program sought to harness the power of mediation for a noble purpose – to reduce racial discrimination and promote racial harmony.

Modern Trends in Mediation Law

Today, mediation continues to be the topic of considerable legislation at both the federal and state levels. Most statutes and regulations can be categorized in one or more of the following ways:

♦ prescribe the use of ADR by government agencies to make and enforce rules;

♦ encourage or mandate referral of lawsuits to ADR by the courts;

♦ establish programs or agencies that provide ADR services;

♦ provide for the use of ADR in certain types of common, recurring disputes (e.g., labor, small claims, divorce);

♦ clarify the legal status of some aspects of ADR, such as confidentiality of proceedings, enforcement of agreements, etc.

As with earlier laws dealing with ADR, most recent legislation also attempts to promote specific social policies, which are often set forth in the text of the legislation. The peculiar nature of mediation, including its voluntariness, creativity, and flexibility, is evident in the text of many mediation statutes. Drafters appear to have carefully crafted these laws to permit parties to choose or reject mediation without penalty. They also tried hard not to overprescribe how the process should work.

In many cases, legislation permits the use of other forms of ADR besides mediation. Arbitration and conciliation are the most frequently included alternative methods. Nevertheless, the malleable nature of mediation appears to have been the predominant consideration in shaping much of this legislation. Arbitration, which is the focus of a considerable amount of legislation on its own, will be discussed in Chapter Five.

Federal Mediation Law

What follows is a discussion of some of the more important federal legislation concerning mediation and mediation-type mechanisms. In the past two decades, the federal government has wholeheartedly embraced ADR and has provided an important model for the states to emulate. Furthermore, it has provided funding and guidance to the states for the development of local ADR services. The administrative agencies of the federal government, especially, have turned to ADR to supplement more formal, costly and time-consuming procedures for hearing complaints or dealing with people and companies that are not complying with regulatory requirements. In order to facilitate the use of ADR, each government agency is required to develop a policy with regard to the representation of parties by persons who are not attorneys. Consequently, it is not uncommon for paralegals to be advocates in ADR proceedings before federal agencies.[8]

Negotiated Rulemaking

The focus of most federal legislation and regulatory activity dealing with mediation is within agencies of the federal government. One of the important uses of mediation at the federal level is "negotiated rulemaking." When Congress passes a law and the president signs it, the law is referred to an agency of the executive branch for implementation and enforcement. The agency drafts rules and regulations that set out the procedures and other mechanisms to implement the law. For example, Congress may enact a law and provide funding for immunization of school-age children. However, it is Health and Human Services (HHS) that will develop the programs and procedures to inoculate children, allocate funds, monitor activity and report on results. HHS will also draft additional rules as needed after the programs are implemented. Both during and after the development of these rules and regulations, questions and conflicts will inevitably arise. Likewise, many people will have a direct interest in, and be affected by the outcome of these conflicts, including governors and others within state government, school boards, school superintendents and principals, local healthcare providers, parents and school-age children.

Under Title 5 of the United States Code, mediation can be used at two levels in the rulemaking process. First, when a rule is proposed and the head of the agency determines that the use of negotiated rulemaking will "enhance the rulemaking process," he or she will establish a committee to negotiate and develop the rule.[9] By law, the committee is to be made up of people who are significantly affected by the rule, or their representatives.[10] Therefore, the agency will publish its intention to set up a committee in order to attract interested parties who must apply for membership on the committee.[11] Once the committee is established, a facilitator will be selected who will impartially assist the members in conducting discussions and negotiations.[12] The purpose is to draft a rule that is both effective and has the widest possible base of support.

ADR also plays a role after rules and regulations are drafted and in place. If a dispute arises over rights, privileges and obligations of individuals under a rule, the law provides that alternative means of dispute resolution, including mediation, may be used to resolve the matter.[13] Several states have adopted negotiated rulemaking modeled after the federal statute. For example, see Montana Negotiated Rulemaking Act § 2-5-101.

Administrative Dispute Resolution Act

Notwithstanding the above, all agencies of the federal government that directly serve the public have developed administrative procedures, including hearings, to resolve disputes between the agencies and private parties. The procedures are designed to ensure citizens due process of law as guaranteed by the Fifth Amendment to the Constitution of the United States. For example, the Social Security Administration provides procedures for individuals to follow who believe that they have been wrongfully denied benefits. Unfortunately, administrative proceedings, which are intended to resolve disputes informally and inexpensively, have become increasingly formal, costly, and lengthy. In addition, the federal government was overwhelmed by lawsuits filed each year in which it was named a party. Consequently, Congress enacted the Administrative Dispute Resolution Act (Public Law No. 101-552) in 1990, which was designed to promote decisions that are "faster, less expensive, and less contentious" and which can lead to "more creative, efficient, and sensible outcomes."[14] [See Appendix Two for the text of relevant portions of the Act.]

Believing that "an increased understanding of the most effective use of [alternative dispute resolution procedures] will enhance the operation of the Government and better serve the public,"[15] Congress provided that each agency "shall adopt a policy that addresses the use of alternative means of dispute resolution and case management"[16] in connection with adjudication, rulemaking, enforcement actions, issuing and revoking licenses or permits, contract administration, and litigation.[17]

Executive Order on Civil Justice Reform

Effective in January 1992, Executive Order No. 12778 directed government litigators to make greater efforts to seek settlements before filing lawsuits against violators of federal law and regulations. The Order encouraged litigators to obtain ADR training and to use ADR techniques to obtain compliance and thus forego litigation. In response, litigators at such agencies as the Environmental Protection Agency, Federal Communication Commission, Internal Revenue Service, Interstate Commerce Commission, Department of Labor, Health and Human Services, Equal Employment Opportunity Commission and the Department of Justice instituted programs to implement the Order.

Federal Mediation and Conciliation Service

In 1947 Congress created the Federal Mediation and Conciliation Service (FMCS) under the Department of Labor.[18] The purpose of the FMCS was to "assist parties to labor disputes in industries affecting commerce to settle such disputes through conciliation and mediation."[19] The FMCS was seen as an enhancement to the obligation of labor and management to bargain collectively over issues of unfair labor practices.[20]

Over the years the FMCS developed considerable skill, resources and successes with mediating difficult and complex matters. As a result, Congress amended the Labor Management Relations Act to make the FMCS available to all federal agencies in the resolution of disputes.[21] Procedures under negotiated rulemaking and the Administrative Dispute Resolution Act, discussed above, encourage federal agencies to use the FMCS for a variety of matters including evaluating how ADR might best be used, establishing procedures for ADR, and identifying third-party neutrals.

District Court Expense and Delay Reduction Plans

Court-sponsored ADR, which is usually referred to as "court-annexed" ADR, has always been seen as a way to reduce the cost of resolving disputes and therefore, to make justice accessible to people who could not afford traditional litigation. Lately, however, legislation has been equally concerned with conserving court time and costs. The Civil Justice Reform Act (CJRA),[22] passed by Congress in 1990, requires every federal district court to devise a plan to curtail the costs and shorten the time involved in most litigation. In response to the CJRA, every federal court provides for some form of alternative dispute resolution. For example:

♦ Under the Local Court Rules of the United States District Court for the Eastern District of Texas, a management conference will be held within 120 days after the defendant has filed an answer in the case. The management conference will be presided over by a "judicial official" who shall "determine the efficacy of referring the case to alternative dispute resolution." If the official determines "that the case probably will benefit from alternative dispute resolution," he or she has the discretion to refer the case to mediation, voluntary mini-trial, summary jury trial before a judicial officer, or any other ADR program designated for use in the district.

♦ In contrast, the Local Court Rules for the United States District Court for the Western District of Texas require the parties to submit a report "evaluating whether alternative dispute resolution is appropriate in the case." Counsel must certify that their clients have been informed of available ADR procedures. Even if the parties do not agree voluntarily to attempt mediation, the court can order the parties to participate.

In addition to providing for referral to mediation, each District Court Expense and Delay Reduction Plan is to provide a neutral evaluation program for the presentation of the legal and factual basis of a case to a neutral court representative at a nonbinding conference conducted early in the litigation. The neutral will be selected by the court, and the conference must be attended by parties or party representatives with authority to make binding decisions.

Alternative Dispute Resolution Act of 1998

In 1998, the President signed into law the Alternative Dispute Resolution Act of 1998. The Act requires each federal district court to create an ADR program. The Act replaces an earlier pilot program that permitted federal district courts to establish ADR programs but did not make it mandatory. According to the House Report concerning the Act, its purpose is to "provide the federal courts with the tools necessary to present quality alternatives to expensive federal litigation." In support of the Act, Congress found that if properly supported, ADR produces greater satisfaction, innovation and efficiency in achieving settlements and reduces court caseloads.

The Act not only requires that each federal district court create an ADR program, it must also provide litigants with at least one court-annexed ADR program. The list of programs in the Act include mediation, arbitration, mini-trial and early neutral evaluation; however, other methods appear to be permitted. A court *may* order ADR, except that it *may not* order arbitration or mini-trial without the consent of all of the parties and their attorneys. A court *may* exempt certain cases after consulting with members of the bar or the U.S. District Attorney. A court *may* also *require all litigants* to participate, but this is restricted to mediation, early neutral evaluation, and voluntary arbitration. Regarding arbitration, it *may not* refer cases alleging a violation of the U.S. Constitution, cases based on U.S.C. Section 1343 (civil rights or elective franchise), or where relief sought exceeds $150,000. Finally, all courts are required to adopt rules protecting the confidentially of ADR proceedings, communications, and results.

The full text of the Act and the Congressional reports pertaining to it can be found at http://thomas.loc.gov.

Community Relations Service

Several federal laws provide for the use of ADR in resolving civil rights disputes. Under Title 42 of the United States Code, Congress established the Community Relations Service "to provide assistance to communities and persons therein in resolving disputes, disagreements, or difficulties relating to discriminatory practices."[23] Specifically, the Community Relations Service is to provide "conciliation assistance" in confidence and without publicity.[24] Mediation, conciliation, and other forms of ADR are also available to people who have been discriminated against in housing,[25] in employment,[26] due to age,[27] due to disability,[28] and in other ways.

Dispute Resolution Act

As the costs and delays associated with traditional litigation increased during the 1980s and 1990s, Congress became concerned about Americans involved in minor disputes for whom the mechanisms of dispute resolution were "largely unavailable, inaccessible, ineffective, expensive, or unfair." Congress passed the Dispute Resolution Act to help the states provide community-based dispute resolution mechanisms to promote the expeditious settlement of minor disputes.[29] As Congress noted, while each individual dispute may be relatively small, "taken collectively such disputes are of enormous social and economic consequences."[30]

The Act provides that times and locations are to be convenient,[31] that provision should be made for people with language barriers and disabilities,[32] that the procedures be readily understandable,[33] and that the availability of community-based ADR be well publicized.[34] These programs often provide the training ground for new mediators. Most mediators in these programs are volunteers, and many are paralegals and other nonattorney professionals.

International Mediation

The federal government not only promotes the use of ADR domestically, it also endorses it internationally. Any casual follower of the national news will observe United States officials shuttling back and forth between Washington and the capitals of countries that threaten us or our allies, attempting to broker deals and keep the peace. All of this activity carries out the "policy of the United States to adjust and settle its international disputes through mediation or arbitration, to the end that war may be honorably avoided."[35]

Mediation Law at the State Level

Based on a review of state laws, it is fair to say that ADR, including mediation, has definitely caught the attention of state legislatures. Every state plus Puerto Rico and the District of Columbia has enacted legislation providing for ADR, including mediation. By 1995, the number of individual state laws dealing with ADR exceeded 300, and that number continues to increase rapidly.

Court-Annexed ADR

Much of the interest and focus on mediation legislation at the state level is on the courts rather than on administrative rulemaking and enforcement. More and more state and local courts are providing for the use of ADR. A survey in 1990 by the National Center for State Courts found that over 1,200 state courts had ADR programs.[36] By the mid-1990s, over twenty states had enacted comprehensive legislation requiring courts to promote ADR in one way or another. Some states, including Florida and Indiana, mandate that almost every civil case filed in a state court be referred to mediation or nonbinding arbitration. Most of the others stop short of requiring courts to refer. Like federal legislation, state statutes promoting court-annexed ADR seek to reduce the cost of resolving disputes and to make justice more accessible.

Texas provides a typical example of state legislation establishing court-annexed ADR. Chapter 154 of the Texas Civil Practice and Remedies Code declares that it "is the policy of this state to encourage the peaceable resolution of disputes. . . . and early settlement of pending litigation through voluntary settlement procedures."[37] The statute then provides that "it is the responsibility of all trial and appellate courts and their court administrators to carry out the policy. . . ."[38]

In order to fulfill this responsibility, Texas courts may refer pending disputes to ADR on their own motions as well as on the motions of a party.[39] ADR includes mini-trial, moderated settlement conferences, summary jury trials, and arbitration, as well as mediation.[40] The Texas statute includes provisions for the appointment, qualifications, standards, duties and compensation of "impartial third parties."[41] It also deals with confidentiality, the enforceability of written settlement agreements, and the gathering of statistical information on referred disputes.[42]

In response to the Texas statute, courts around the state drafted local rules in much the same way that federal courts responded to the CJRA, discussed above. Local rules tend to concentrate on issues concerning referral of cases to ADR, including factors that a court must consider in determining if a case is suitable for ADR.[*]

---

[*] For example, the Local Rules of the Travis County [Texas] District Court provide that cases considered appropriate for referral to ADR include all cases in which notice of dismissal for want of prosecution has been given. Factors for the court to consider with regard to all active cases include the subject matter of the case, the amount in controversy, the complexity of the case, the number of parties, their interest in pursuing settlement through ADR, the availability of ADR procedures and the likelihood of settlement through ADR. See also, *Downey v. Gregory*, 757 S.W.2d 524, 525 (Tex. App.-Houston [1st Dist.] 1988, no writ), for a list of factors to be considered by a court when referring a matter to ADR.

Exercises

> 1. Review the laws of your state to determine if the civil courts have annexed ADR. If so, what amount of power does the law give to judges to refer matters to ADR? What types of ADR are available under the statute? What sorts of disputes are the focus of the statute?
>
> 2. Call the district clerk or ADR coordinator for the civil courts in your county. Ask how many cases are referred annually to ADR. What is the result in terms of earlier settlements? To what extent do attorneys in your area support ADR and cooperate fully?
>
> 3. According to local court rules, how are mediators and arbitrators chosen? What qualifications and requirements must they fulfill?

Community-Based ADR Programs

In addition to court-annexed mediation programs, state legislators have continued to establish new community-based mediation programs aimed at promoting peace and preserving community values. These programs seek to provide a means for families, relatives, neighbors, friends and local businesses to resolve their disagreements with one another without recourse to the legal system where disputes are costly to litigate and likely to escalate. Many of these programs are funded, in part, by the federal government. For example:

♦ Florida law provides for the establishment of Citizen Dispute Settlement Centers designed to provide "an informal forum for the mediation and settlement of disputes." The statute provides that the Centers will be established upon the recommendation of the chief judge of the local judicial circuit in consultation with county commissioners. The Centers mediate disputes brought to them by the parties and also referred to them by law enforcement agencies, the courts, the state attorney and other agencies.[43]

♦ The California Business and Professional Code § 465 declares that "community dispute resolution programs and increased use of other alternatives to the formal judicial system may offer less threatening and more flexible forums for persons of all ethnic, racial, and socioeconomic backgrounds. These alternatives, among other things, can assist in the resolution of disputes between neighbors, some domestic disputes, consumer-merchant disputes, and other kinds of disputes in which the parties have continuing relationships." The statute provides for the development of community programs, their development, funding, evaluation.[44]

♦ The Illinois General Assembly found that "unresolved disputes which individually may be of small social or economic magnitude are collectively of enormous social and economic consequence; and that seemingly minor conflicts between individuals may escalate into major social problems unless resolved early in an atmosphere in which the disputants can discuss their differences through an informal yet structured process; and that there is a compelling need in a complex society for dispute resolution centers in which people can participate in creating lasting resolutions to ongoing conflicts. . . ."[45] The Act provides for grants of up to $200,000 per center per year, sets forth training standards for mediators, and establishes other procedures.[46]

♦ An Indiana statute provides funding for community dispute resolution centers that handle both civil and criminal matters referred by the courts, as well as civil matters voluntarily submitted.[47] The centers are established under the power and authority of the chief justice of Indiana, whose office administers and supervises the overall program, selects centers, disburses funds, and adopts all necessary rules.[48]

Exercise

> Find out if your community has any ADR programs that are largely voluntary and funded through federal or state programs. If so, what types of disputes do they accept? How many per year? What are the fees involved? Do they offer ADR training?

Administrative Mediation

Most government services are delivered by administrative agencies at both the federal and state level, and like all organizations, they must not only make rules but also deal with complaints and disputes involving their clients, other agencies, and employees. In order to facilitate the fair and efficient handling of disputes and to ensure due process of law, more and more state government agencies are being required to employ mediation to hear complaints, enforce rules and resolve the conflict that will inevitably arise. Other factors that influence the increasing use of ADR among government agencies include:

a. The need to do more for less. Government agencies can no longer afford litigation, especially if it is unnecessary.

b. Public policy issues have become so complex that no one agency can unilaterally solve a problem; interagency solutions and collaborations are necessary.

c. The public is demanding input into issues that affect them.

d. Increasing diversity in the workforce requires the effective management of the differences that emerge.

Following are some examples of administrative laws and regulations that provide for mediation:

A. *Disputes Arising Between Agencies and Clients*

♦ The Texas Structural Pest Control Board gives pest control companies accused of violating applicable statutes and regulations the options of paying the penalty, attending a traditional hearing, or requesting a settlement conference.[49]

♦ In Ohio the state director of mental health oversees an agency that regulates all privately owned facilities and programs with whom the state contracts for mental health services. In that capacity, the director must approve all plans and contracts submitted by these private providers to the agency. If the director disapproves of a plan, and after the provider has had a chance to present its case, the director may refer the dispute to mediation, with the cost to be borne by the provider and the agency. In this case, the mediator has powers similar to an arbitrator in that he or she can make recommendations concerning how the dispute should be resolved.[50]

B.   *Disputes Among Agencies*

♦ The California Food and Agricultural Code provides that any dispute arising between the California State Fair and the local Agricultural District will be mediated and if no resolution is reached, the matter will be arbitrated by the Department of General Services.[51]

♦ Public utilities, including power, water, and sewage companies, are heavily regulated by government because their activities so profoundly and totally affect the health and safety of the public. For this reason, public utilities are often considered to be "quasi-public" agencies of government. Thus, if a dispute arises between two utilities, or a utility and a government board, regulations often require that such disputes be submitted to mediation in order to quickly resolve the matter for the benefit of the public.[52]

C.   *Disputes Between Agencies and Their Employees*

♦ Disputes between Nebraska state employees and the state over labor contracts must be submitted to continuing mediation at the request of either party if an early resolution is not achieved. A special master assigned to the case may evaluate the progress made and order additional mediation, if necessary.[53]

♦ The Texas Water Development Board, through its internal rules, has incorporated the use of mediation into the options available to employees as an alternative or prelude to internal grievance procedures.

Labor, Civil Rights, and Domestic Relations Mediation

By far the largest volume of state legislation prescribing the use of mediation outside the context of court-annexed ADR concerns three types of issues:

1. Labor and employment disputes involving both unionized and non-unionized labor;

2. Civil rights disputes involving discriminatory practices by individuals, companies and instruments of government; and

3. Domestic relations matters, especially those dealing with children.

A.   *Labor and Employment Mediation*

Almost every state has mediation statutes dealing with labor and employment. The purpose of labor mediation statutes is to provide a means of breaking an impasse that may occur in the process of collective bargaining between an employee organization or union, and an employer. In some states, these laws apply only to public employee groups such as police, firefighters, state hospital workers and so forth. In other states, labor mediation statutes deal with both public and private employee groups. These laws usually establish a labor relations board that intervenes when an impasse is reached. The board imposes a multi-step process to break the impasse and try to achieve settlement. Generally speaking, mediation is one of the first ADR methods attempted, and only if it is unsuccessful will arbitration or some other method involving third-party decision making be employed.[54]

B.   Civil Rights Mediation

Civil rights legislation that includes the use of mediation deals with disputes arising from discriminatory practices primarily in employment and housing, based on race, gender, disability and other protected classifications. The purpose of these statutes is not only to redress a grievance brought by an individual or group against an employer or landlord, but also to obtain the agreement of the employer or landlord to end the practice of discrimination altogether.

Most statutes establish a board or commission that receives and investigates complaints, and if discrimination is found, to eliminate it through the use of mediation between the charging party and the employer or landlord. The board or commission will also engage in dialogue with the party charged through the use of conference, conciliation, and other methods of persuasion. The result is a negotiated agreement with the employer or landlord to end the unlawful practice.[55]

C.   Domestic Relations Mediation

Mediation has long been used in the resolution of disputes involving child custody, visitation and support. Mediation is especially suited to resolving family conflict because it promotes joint decision making and helps preserve relationships between parents, all of which are in the best interest of the children involved. As the preamble to the Kansas domestic mediation statute declares, "The role of the mediator is to aid the parties in identifying the issues, reducing misunderstandings, clarifying priorities, exploring areas of compromise and finding points of agreement."[56]

Most domestic mediation statutes assume that a suit affecting the parent-child relationship is before the court. In some cases, the suit may be part of a divorce petition, while in others it is a stand-alone matter seeking to establish or modify a court order pertaining to custody, visitation, or support of a child. Generally, these statutes specify that before the court holds a full hearing and enters a final ruling, mediation may be ordered by the court on its own motion or on the motion of one of the parties to "enable the parties in a contested child custody, support or visitation proceedings to resolve disputes voluntarily."[57]

Nevertheless, the court has final authority on the matter and will review any agreement reached by the parties to determine if it is in the best interest of the child. If child abuse is suspected or alleged by either party, the court is generally forbidden from ordering mediation.

Some domestic mediation statutes, called "child dependency" or "parenting plan" statutes, seek to assist families to gain control over children who are before a court as truants, chronic runaways, or for other behavior indicating that they are uncontrollable by parents or guardians. Florida, for example, uses "diversion mediation" and other tactics to provide services to a family on a "continuum of increasing level of intensity and participation by the parents and child."[58] The purpose of these statutes is to forego judicial intervention until family mediation, counseling and other services have been exhausted. In this context, mediation plays a largely therapeutic role.

As compared with other mediation statutes, domestic statutes often specify the amount of training and other qualifications of family mediators. (See discussion of Mediator Qualifications and Training, below.) Many also expressly provide that the mediator is to reduce to writing any agreement reached by the parties and to present the agreement to the court after the parties have reviewed it with counsel and signed it. Some domestic statutes permit the court to fine parents who don't show up for mediation, and to impose sanctions if it determines that either parent did not make a good-faith effort to mediate. Possible sanctions include dismissing the action, rendering a default judgment, and assessing attorney fees and court costs.[59] Many states have enacted comprehensive domestic relations statutes, with which legal practitioners in family law should be thoroughly familiar.[60]

Mediation of Common Disputes

Another way that legislation has utilized ADR is to provide for mediation of common, and often minor disputes that often clog court dockets. These disputes tend to be both numerous and factually similar to one another. Therefore, the results reached by the courts or agencies involved are highly predictable, and the applicable law is well-known and well-established. By diverting these matters to mediation, legislators can lighten the load on the courts without denying justice to the parties or avoiding the court's obligation to rule on matters where the law needs to be clarified. Disputes covered by these statutes involve private parties who are in conflict with one another. If a court or government agency is involved, their role is to broker the dispute to ensure that the requirements of the law are met.

Examples of commonplace disputes covered by mediation legislation include:

A.　*Landlord-tenant disputes*

♦　A landlord and tenant may agree to mediation of disputes between them, and their written agreement shall be added to the rental agreement.[61]

♦　A county, city or town is authorized to establish a commission or agency that will mediate conflicts voluntarily submitted to it by landlords and tenants.[62]

B.　*Small claims*

♦　In Louisiana, a judge of small claims court may attempt to conciliate disputes and encourage fair settlements among the parties.[63]

♦　When a small claims action is commenced, the plaintiff shall be informed that the matter may be submitted to a magistrate for mediation and resolution at the request of either or both parties. Any agreement reached shall be entered as the judgment of the court.[64]

C.　*Automobile warranty claims*

♦　In North Dakota, a manufacturer has a duty to replace a defective passenger motor vehicle or refund the price. Nevertheless, this requirement does not apply if the purchaser has not first resorted to manufacturer-provided dispute resolution procedures.[65]

♦ Pennsylvania also requires that citizens exhaust manufacturer-provided dispute resolution procedures. However, these procedures are not binding on Pennsylvania purchasers, and in lieu of any settlement reached, a purchaser may pursue a remedy under state law, including additional [and presumably more neutral] mediation.[66]

D.   *Divorce*

♦ In Indiana any court with jurisdiction over domestic relations may establish a family relations division to offer counseling and conciliation to the parties.[67]

♦ New Hampshire provides that a court must suspend divorce proceedings while a couple voluntarily attempts to mediate an agreement. The parties have the responsibility to directly contract with a mediation provider of their own choosing.[68]

E.   *Workers' Compensation*

♦ The industrial commissioner in Iowa is required to adopt rules requiring that parties to an occupational injury dispute enter into mediation before being permitted to pursue a lawsuit. The rule further provides that the statute of limitations on the claim will be suspended for the duration of the mediation proceedings.

♦ In Maine, any workers' compensation controversy must be referred to a mediator who will be assigned to the case. Any agreement reached must be signed by the mediator and the parties. The mediator must file a written report to the appropriate board stating the legal issues involved in the dispute and, if no agreement is reached, the report must set forth the facts and legal issues. The parties are required to cooperate with the mediator and the mediator must report any failure to cooperate or to produce requested material. The board may sanction a noncooperating party by suspending the proceedings or assessing costs. An attorney who fails to cooperate may have his or her fees reduced. A party or party-representative who attends mediation but who does not have the authority to settle may be fined $100.[69]

F.   *Land use and other environmental concerns*

♦ Local environmental councils are required to make dispute resolution services available to resolve conflicts between units of government, developers, conservation and neighborhood interests arising under land use regulations.[70]

♦ When a municipality and the owner or operator of a regional low-level radioactive waste disposal facility are in conflict, they will be required to mediate their dispute, with a representative of the state's Office of Dispute Resolution serving as the mediator.[71]

G.   *Funeral and Cemetery Contracts*

◆ Florida cemeteries in excess of five acres must make every effort to resolve a consumer complaint. If the complaint is not resolved, the cemetery must advise the consumer of the right to seek investigation and mediation by the appropriate department of state government. That department will try first to resolve the matter by phone, and if unsuccessful, it will investigate and mediate the dispute.[72]

◆ The appropriate regulatory board of the state can dispose of minor consumer complaints against funeral homes by directly contacting the parties involved and mediating the dispute.[73]

Other examples of common, high-volume disputes that are covered by mediation statutes and regulations in most states include

◆ confiscation of property through eminent domain

◆ planning and zoning

◆ special education (disputes between parents and school boards)

◆ franchise agreements

◆ water rights

◆ new home construction

◆ mobile home parks

◆ home owner and condominium associations

◆ debtor/creditor

◆ doctor/patient.

Some disputes are peculiar to the state or region of the country. Thus, Midwestern states have many statutes dealing with the mediation of agricultural disputes, western states prescribe mediation for disputes involving water and timber rights, seaboard states have fishing-related statutes, while oil-producing states provide for mediation of disputes arising under oil and gas leases.

Legal advisors should be aware of the types of matters and disputes covered by state laws, and before recommending litigation, they should inform clients accordingly, including what the law requires in terms of compliance, and what resources may be provided to the parties in order to facilitate settlement. Often, the applicable statute provides the services of a mediator at little or no cost who is an official of some court or state agency. In other cases, the parties may select a mediator or mediation service of their own choosing. Community dispute resolution centers handle a great deal of "commonplace disputes." Because the legal issues involved in these disputes are often clear cut, paralegals and other nonattorney mediators can usually act as third-party neutrals without engaging in the unauthorized practice of law. (See Chapter Eight for a discussion of the unauthorized practice of law in mediation.)

Other Concerns Addressed by Mediation Law

The explosive growth in the use of mediation has raised questions on a variety of issues, which mediation legislation seeks to answer. Most of these questions involve issues of the fairness, quality, and accessibility of ADR. Through legislation, government seeks not only to endorse ADR but also to impose standards of practice that will insure participants as good a chance at justice as they would obtain through more traditional channels of the courts and administrative hearings. The concerns addressed by this legislation include

♦ whether mediation should be mandatory,

♦ the degree of confidentiality that should be afforded mediators and mediation proceedings,

♦ the enforceability of mediated agreements,

♦ the effect of mediation proceedings on the statute of limitations,

♦ the extent to which mediators should be liable for outcomes, and

♦ the extent to which mediators should be trained and certified.

Mandatory Participation in Mediation

Mediation, by its nature, is a voluntary endeavor. Therefore, to require people to participate in mediation appears contradictory. Furthermore, it would seem logical to assume that mediation will be an exercise in futility if one or both sides enters the process determined not to participate or to settle.[74] Studies have shown, however, that just getting the parties to talk to one another can be a catalyst to settlement.

For example, in 1991, the 101st District Court of Dallas County, Texas, surveyed several hundred cases it had referred to mediation. The survey found that a settlement rate of 80-85 percent occurred, regardless of whether both sides asked for mediation, only one side asked for mediation, or both sides objected to mediation. Thus, even though mediation requires a satisfactory level of participation by the parties in order to be successful,[75] wholehearted cooperation at the beginning of the process does not appear to be necessary to a favorable outcome.

Legislation dealing with mediation attempts to achieve meaningful participation in several ways.

♦ First, a court or other judicial or administrative body may be required to make mediation available to disputing parties.*

♦ Second, that court may or may not have discretion as to which cases to refer to mediation.** In some jurisdictions, courts are required to refer almost all cases to mediation.

♦ Third, if a court orders a case to mediation, the parties may or may not be required to participate. Many courts permit a party to oppose mediation provided the grounds for doing so are reasonable.*** In other courts, parties who do not show up for mediation can be sanctioned.▶

---

* Subject to the approval of the Chief Justice of the Supreme Court, the circuit court in a judicial district, ... may provide mediation . . . . for child custody and visitation disputes . . . . (Oregon Statutes § 107.755).

** After 30 days have passed following the appearance by all parties in any civil action, ... a judge of any district or circuit court may refer a civil dispute to mediation . . . . (Oregon Revised Statutes § 36.185).

◆ Fourth, parties engaged in mediation may or may not be required to participate "in good faith."▶

◆ Finally, there is the issue of whether participants can be required to reach an agreement through mediation. Some statutes require a mediator to make the settlement decision if the parties become deadlocked.[76]

Even when mediation is mandatory, the attitude of the attorneys and advocates toward mediation can enhance or undermine attempts to bring the parties together. Some advocates, especially if they are older litigators or older trial lawyers, still view the suggestion of mediation as an admission of weakness and may delay opening up settlement talks, hoping that the other side will go first.[77] As one writer put it, "real men don't mediate."[78]

Also, attorneys who earn most of their living through litigation are sometimes hostile toward ADR because it reduces billable hours, even though the economic impact on a lawyer's practice is not an appropriate basis for choosing any resolution strategy.* If an attorney feels that he or she cannot objectively employ ADR, especially where it is mandated, the attorney should resign from the case. Unfortunately, this is unlikely to happen.

Lack of support for mediation is most likely to be found in those jurisdictions that do not have court-annexed mediation. The presence of court-annexed ADR dramatically increases the use of mediation, improves the availability and competency level of local mediators, and can produce an increasing body of settlement successes that even the most jaundiced skeptic cannot overlook.

Paralegals may find themselves working in an environment where ADR is mandated in one way or another, but where their particular employer is skeptical about, and perhaps even hostile toward, any form of mandated negotiations. If the paralegal supports the use of ADR, his or her dilemma about responding to the employer and to the client will be compounded.

As mentioned above, ADR statutes often contain requirements that the parties and their advocates participate in mediation in good faith. Unfortunately, ADR statutes and codes of professional behavior offer little guidance regarding what constitutes adequate cooperation by the parties or their attorneys.

*** Any party may, within 10 days after receiving the notice [of referral to ADR], file a written objection to the referral. If the court finds that there is a reasonable basis for an objection filed . . . , the court may not refer the dispute [to ADR] (Texas Civil Practice and Remedies Code § 154.022(b)(c)).

▶ The court may impose an appropriate sanction upon a party's failure without good cause to appear for mediation after receiving notice of the scheduled time for mediation (Maine Revised Statutes Annotated § 581(4)).

▶ [It is the duty of the parties] to participate in good faith in the mediation, fact finding, arbitration and mediation-arbitration procedure required by this section (Maine Revised Statutes Annotated § 1285(1)(D)).

* On the other hand, seasoned litigators and trial lawyers may appreciate mediation more than those with less experience, simply because they understand the limits of legal remedies, which often do not provide clients with the benefits and relief to which they are entitled.

Furthermore, because the meaning of good faith is so nebulous, some commentators argue that it places undue pressure on the parties to settle, especially where the statute requires the mediator to report back to the court whether the parties participated in good faith.**

Attorneys/advocates can be sanctioned if they do not cooperate; therefore, it is usually in their professional and economic best interest to participate fully.*** However, if the parties themselves are uncooperative, this places considerable pressure on advocates to persuade them that mediation is worth the time and money.

In a 1994 Florida case, an insurance company failed to send a representative to mediation with the authority to settle the dispute. As a result, the trial court ordered the company's entire board of trustees to attend the next mediation session, and the appellate court upheld the decision.[79] As more and more courts annex mediation, they will be less likely to condone uncooperative behavior from parties or their advocates.

In the search for standards of "good faith" cooperation that are measurable and enforceable, one ADR professional has suggested three simple criteria:[80]

1. The parties or a party representative must attend the mediation.

2. The attending party must have authority to make settlement proposals and to settle the dispute.

3. Each party must submit a letter to the opponent and to the mediator prior to mediation outlining that party's position on each issue in the dispute.

The author argues that these criteria are objective and measurable, and a party who complies will be deemed to have cooperated in good faith. Furthermore, the criteria require enough involvement to give the process a chance, while providing room to retreat if the party or the advocate does not want to proceed any further. Finally, the exercise of preparing a position paper early in the dispute should prove helpful in negotiating a settlement, even if the parties do not go forward with mediation.

Confidentiality in Mediation

Confidentiality deals with the issue of what will be admissible as evidence in a proceeding before a court. Every jurisdiction has statutes dealing with admissibility. Some concern privileged communications arising out of certain types of relationships. For example, communications between a lawyer and client that the parties intend to be kept confidential may not be admitted into evidence for any purpose. The same is true for certain communications between a doctor and patient, and a husband and wife.

** "If the mediator and the parties [to a child neglect or dependency proceeding] agree that the parties are engaging in good faith mediation and inform the court thereof, the court may continue any pending hearing in the case to a date certain." (Colorado Revised Statutes § 19-3-310.5(6)(B)).

*** A federal court ordered the attorney and client to pay the other party's fees and costs for a hearing at which they failed to produce an insurance representative with authority to settle. [*Dvorak v. Shibata*, 123 FDR 608 (DC Neb.1988)].

Some statutes, however, override privilege, such as where suspicion or knowledge of child abuse is involved. As a general rule, offers to settle a claim are also not admissible. Therefore, if two parties negotiate in order to settle their dispute and the negotiations later break down, neither party can use the other party's offers as proof of liability or the amount of liability.

Generally, the confidentiality afforded settlement offers made during negotiations also applies to mediation. Some statutes, however, broaden the confidentiality of mediation to include anything else that occurs. These statutes seek to ensure that the mediator will be neutral, and also more effective, knowing that he or she cannot be forced to testify in court about what transpired. In Florida domestic relations mediations, for example, "Any information from the files, reports, case summaries, mediator's notes, or other communications or materials, oral or written, relating to a mediation proceeding.... and obtained by any person performing mediation duties" . . . . "is privileged and confidential . . . ."[81] This restriction can be waived, however, but only with the written consent of all parties to the proceeding.[82]

Confidentiality usually begins the moment a mediator or mediation service is contacted, regardless of whether the mediation is ultimately conducted or achieves settlement. For example, Kansas law provides that any matter disclosed in the process of setting up or conducting the mediation, conciliation, or arbitration of a civil dispute may not be disclosed by a mediator or that mediator's agents.[83]

Some statutes, however, apply certain limits on confidentiality. The duty to report child abuse, mentioned above, is one example. Threatened or actual violence during mediation is also not privileged.[84] Mediation in the context of labor disputes and criminal proceedings is also excepted in some states, in the interest of the public.[85] Courts have also refused to extend confidentiality to all that goes on in mediation. In *State v. Castellano*, a defendant accused of attempted murder who wanted to establish self-defense sought to subpoena a mediator who had heard the victim threaten the defendant during mediation of a prior dispute. The court allowed the subpoena on the grounds that the testimony that the defendant sought had nothing to do with offers to settle a claim, which is usually inadmissible evidence.[86]

Paralegals should be thoroughly familiar with how their state deals with confidentiality within the context of ADR proceedings. In reviewing a statute, ask yourself:

- ♦ What type of information does the statute cover?

- ♦ What are the limitations on the use of that information and are there any exceptions?

- ♦ What types of proceedings are included and how are they defined (e.g., mediation, conciliation, arbitration, etc.)?

- ♦ Who does the statute cover (e.g., just the mediator, anyone at the mediation, the mediator's agents)?

- ♦ Who may assert any privilege or protection afforded (e.g., generally the parties)?

Enforcement of Mediated Agreements

As a general rule, an agreement reached through mediation, written down and signed by the parties, is a contract and can be enforced in a court of law like any other contract. Nevertheless, the party seeking to enforce the agreement will need to file a lawsuit. In some cases, a court will enter a mediated agreement as the judgment of the court, in which case, the party attempting to enforce it will have a much wider range of enforcement actions available. Agreements reached in domestic relations matters such as divorce, child custody, visitation and support are almost always entered as the judgment of the court.

South Dakota has perhaps the most comprehensive policy concerning enforcement of mediated agreements. As a threshold matter, South Dakota law declares that "any person is subject to the jurisdiction of the courts of this state as to any cause of action arising from the doing personally, through any employee, through an agent or through a subsidiary, of any of the following acts: [including] commencing or participating in negotiations, mediation, arbitration or litigation involving subject matter located in whole or in part within the state."[87] In short, if you participate in mediation involving anything to do with South Dakota, reach agreement and later breach that agreement, you are subject to the jurisdiction of its courts.

Texas law is typical of the laws in most states. If the parties reach a settlement and execute a written agreement disposing of the dispute, the agreement is enforceable in the same manner as any other written contract. Texas courts have the discretion of incorporating the terms of the agreement in the court's final decree disposing of the case, thus giving the agreement the force of a court order.[88]

Conversely, in California, mediated business agreements are not enforceable in a court unless the agreement contains an express, written provision consented to by the parties that the agreement is enforceable by a court.[89] In Colorado, if the parties want their agreement to have the force of a court order, they must first submit it to the court.[90]

The remedies available to parties for breach of a mediated agreement depend upon the terms and nature of the agreement. Some mediated agreements contain liquidated damage clauses. If agreement is also a court order, the enforcing party can attach the property of the other party or seek specific performance. In the case of a mediated agreement regarding civil rights, the court can impose fines or other sanctions.

Under Tennessee law, violating the terms of a conciliation agreement made with the civil rights commission of the state is itself a discriminatory practice.[91]

A recent court decision in Texas dealt with the enforcement of settlement agreements reached in mediation. The case involved a written and signed settlement agreement where one of the parties changed her mind about the settlement before the court had entered a judgment that incorporated the agreement. When the other party asked the trial court to recognize the settlement agreement, it refused to do so. The appeals court upheld the trial court's decision. Furthermore, it found that the other party's remedy was through a breach of contract action.[92]

There is little support among legislators and courts for the enforcement of oral agreements made during mediation. Enforcement of an oral contract would require a court to hear testimony about what was said during mediation in order to determine when statements made ceased to be mere discussion and rose to the level of agreement. This would be not only an almost impossible task, hearing such testimony would breach the confidentiality of mediation that is protected by statute. Consequently, every state requires that mediated agreements be written down if they are to be enforceable in a court of law.

Effect of Mediation on the Statute of Limitations

The statute of limitations is the period of time between the event that gives rise to a claim (e.g., date of injury or discovery of the injury; date that a party breached a contract), and the date when a court or administrative agency can no longer hear the claim and provide a remedy. The policy behind statute of limitation laws is to promote timely resolution of disputes while evidence is still available, witnesses can still remember what took place, and so forth. The most common statute of limitations is two years, although some claims, such as fraud and breach of contract, have longer periods. Attorneys who fail to file their clients' suits within the applicable period are subject to claims of malpractice for which courts in the past have awarded multi-million-dollar verdicts. Attorneys may also be subject to sanction by their state, including suspension or revocation of their licenses to practice law.

Nearly two-thirds of the states have laws dealing with the effect of mediation on the statutes of limitations, at least for some claims. In the remaining states, and for all other claims, the law is silent. Obviously, a claimant would be unlikely to commence mediation to resolve a dispute if the statute was about to expire. Likewise, the other party would be inclined to withdraw from mediation if the statute expired in the interim, and the claimant could no longer resort to a court of law for a remedy.

In matters where suit has already been filed, the question arises whether instituting an ADR effort will postpone other deadlines such as discovery filings, pretrial hearings and so forth. Paralegals with responsibility for maintaining litigation schedules and meeting deadlines need to know the impact of ADR on these pretrial requirements. Local court rules in jurisdictions with court-annexed ADR usually cover these issues. In some cases, however, each judge may deal with these matters differently. Checking with the court coordinator should turn up the answer.

One of the issues concerning laws that permit an ADR proceeding to suspend a limitations period is determining when the proceeding begins and ends. Some laws are quite specific on the matter, while others are silent. For example, in California, conciliation of international disputes will extend all applicable limitation periods until the tenth day following the termination of the conciliation proceedings.[93]

Conciliation proceedings are deemed to have commenced as soon as one party requests conciliation and the other parties agree.[94] It is unclear, however, if the request and the agreement can be oral or if they must be in writing, and who has the authority to bind the parties. The same statute, however, provides four very explicit instructions on how the parties shall terminate the proceedings, including written declaration by the conciliator, written declaration by all of the parties, written declaration by one party, or by the parties signing a settlement agreement.[95]

Oklahoma law tolling the running of the statute of limitations during mediation has the opposite problem. It declares, that "[d]uring the period of [civil] mediation, any applicable statute of limitation shall be tolled as to the participants. Such tolling shall commence on the date the parties agree in writing to participate in mediation and shall end on the date mediation is officially terminated by the mediator."[96] The same statute provides that the parties must "enter into a written consent" to mediate, and that the consent must be in a form prescribed by the court.[97] At the other end of the process, however, no instructions are given as to what actions constitute "officially terminated by the mediator." Such questions are critical when only a few days remain in a waiting period during which a party can file suit, submit discovery or prepare for and attend a hearing. Once again, paralegals who are responsible for keeping litigation on track need to know the answers to these questions.

Mediator Liability

Generally speaking, a mediator is not subject to civil liability for acts or omissions in his or her role as a mediator. There are some exceptions, however, depending upon the state. Mediator liability is usually described in the language of intentional tort. Following are some examples of the range of protection from professional liability afforded to mediators by law:

♦ In California, there is no liability for any act or omission in the performance of the role of conciliator.[98]

♦ In Arizona, there is no liability except for acts or omissions that involve intentional misconduct or cause a substantial risk to the rights of others.[99]

♦ In Colorado, liability is limited to wanton or willful misconduct.[100]

♦ In Florida, mediators and arbitrators in suits affecting children will have judicial immunity in the same manner and to the same extent as a judge.[101]

♦ Officers, employees, and volunteers of Citizen Dispute Settlement Centers in Florida are liable only if the person acted in bad faith or with malicious purpose or in a manner exhibiting wanton and willful disregard of the rights, safety, or property of another.[102]

♦ In Hawaii, members of medical claim conciliation panels (who review and certify patient claims against doctors for malpractice) shall not be liable for libel, slander, or other defamation of character of any party to a medical claim action.[103]

Mediator Qualifications and Training

Mediator qualification and training is one of the most hotly debated issues in ADR today, and will likely continue to be debated well into the future. The issue is especially important to those who are concerned about people who turn to ADR because they cannot afford lawyers or a trip to the courthouse.[104] Often, it is only the mediator who can help parties protect their interests and preserve their rights. Yet, many mediators have no legal training at all. Others are concerned that no single set of standards or type of training could apply to all the possible situations in which mediation is used.[105]

What is needed and expected of a family mediator who often must broker an agreement in an atmosphere of high emotion is vastly different than what is required of a mediator of complex international business disputes or class action tort claims. Underlying these concerns about the quality of mediation is the fear that legislators and regulators, however well-intentioned, will impose rules that strip mediation of its flexibility, informality, and other advantages it now possesses.[106]

The most common approach to mediator qualifications is to prescribe entry-level requirements.[107] In Texas, for example, a mediator must have completed a minimum of 40 classroom hours of training in dispute resolution techniques from a source approved by the court appointing the mediator.[108] To qualify as a mediator in a dispute involving the parent-child relationship, the mediator must complete an additional 24 hours of training in the fields of family dynamics, child development, and family law.[109] By comparison, some states have no training requirements, while others ask for at least 60 hours. A few states try to solve the problem of training by requiring that mediators also be attorneys or that family mediators be professionals in the field of mental health.

Another approach to qualifications is to describe the qualities of a good mediator, which the appointing court can use to select those mediators to whom it refers cases. For example, Florida law provides that a family mediator "shall be a person with the appropriate attributes who can demonstrate sensitivity towards the parties involved and facilitate solutions to the problem, and may be a person trained or experienced in family counseling; or trained in conflict resolution for families."[110]

Paralegals who are interested in becoming mediators need to know the requirements of the programs where they hope to volunteer or market their services, and to obtain the necessary training. Similarly, all paralegals are encouraged to sign up for mediator training offered in their area, at least at the introductory level. By understanding local requirements, being able to recognize good mediation when they encounter it, and getting to know competent mediators in the area, a paralegal can better lend support to the attorneys and firms where they are employed.

Locating ADR Law

Paralegals should be thoroughly familiar with ADR law in the states where they work. In order to locate and understand local law, it is recommended that students consult *Mediation Law, Policy, Practice*, by Nancy H. Rogers and Craig A. McEwen, a two-volume set that contains topical appendices and reference tables listing laws and statutes dealing with mediation by state and federal jurisdiction. The set is updated annually.

Indices to state statutes should also lead the student to laws that govern the use of ADR under references such as "alternative dispute resolution," "arbitration," "mediation," "conciliation," and other similar terms. A word search in the appropriate library of LEXIS or Westlaw will locate ADR statutes, as well as court cases that have ruled on matters related to ADR. For copies of local rules, check with directors of any court-annexed ADR programs in your area.

Exercise   Using the indices to the statutes of your state, Westlaw, LEXIS, *Mediation Law, Policy, Practice*, by Nancy H. Rogers and Craig A. McEwen, or any other appropriate reference work, locate, review and summarize the law in your state dealing with each of the topics discussed above, including:

a.   community-based ADR programs

b.   examples of administrative mediation

c.   labor and employment mediation

d.   civil rights mediation

e.   domestic relations mediation

f.   examples of the use of mediation to resolve common disputes

g.   confidentiality in mediation

h.   enforcement of mediated agreements

i.   effect of mediation on the statute of limitation

j.   mediator qualifications and training

Sources

[1] See, *e.g.,* N.Y. Lab. Law § 141 (McKinney 1996).

[2] Railway Labor Act, 45 U.S.C.S. § 151 (Law Co-op 1992 & Supp. 1996).

[3] 29 U.S.C. § 6 (1994).

[4] N. Rogers and C. McEwen, *Mediation: Law, Policy, Practice*, 5-2 (1994).

[5] *Addresses on Conciliation*, ABA J 746-751 (1923).

[6] N. Rogers and C. McEwen, *supra*, at 5-2.

[7] J. Murray, A. Rau, and E. Sherman, *Processes of Dispute Resolution*, 273 (1989).

[8] 5 U.S.C.A. 571, notes (West 1996).

[9] 5 U.S.C. § 563 (1994).

[10] *Id.*

[11] *Id.*, at § 564.

[12] *Id.*, at § 566.

[13] *Id.*, at § 571(3).

[14] 5 U.S.C.A. 571, notes (West 1996).

[15] *Id.*, at § 2 (8).

[16] *Id.*, at § 3 (a).

[17] *Id.*, at § 3 (a)(2).

[18] 29 U.S.C. § 172 (1994).

[19] 29 U.S.C. § 172(a) (1994).

[20] *Id.*, at § 158(d).

[21] Labor Management Relations Act of 1947, 29 U.S.C. 7 (1994), as amended by the Administrative Dispute Resolution Act, 5 U.S.C. 571 (1994).

[22] 1 U.S.C. § 101.

[23] 42 U.S.C. § 2000g-1 (1994).

[24] *Id.*, at § 2000g-2(b).

[25] *Id.*, at § 3610.

[26] *Id.*, at § 2000e-5.

[27] *Id.*, at § 6103.

[28] *Id.*, at § 12212.

[29] 28 U.S.C. app. § 2(a)(1) (1994).

[30] *Id.*, at § 2(a)(3).

[31] *Id.*, at § 4(2).

[32] *Id.*, at § 4(3).

[33] *Id.*, at § 4(4).

[34] *Id.*, at § 4(7).

[35] 22 U.S.C. § 261 (1994).

[36] L. Singer, *Settling Disputes*, 165 (1994).

[37] Tex. Civ. Prac. & Rem. Code Ann. § 154.002 (West Supp. 1997).

[38] *Id.*, at § 154.003.

[39] *Id.*, at § 154.021.

[40] *Id.*, at §§ 154.023-154.027.

[41] *Id.*, at §§ 154.052-154.054.

[42] *Id.*, at §§ 154.071-154.073.

[43] Fla. Stat. Ann. ch. 44.201 (West 1988).

[44] Cal. Bus. & Prof. Code § 456-471.5 (West 1990).

[45] 805 Ill. Comp. Stat. 5/12.56 (1993).

[46] *Id.*, at 20.4-20.6.

[47] Ind. Code Ann. § 34-4 2.5-1 § 1 (West 1983 & Supp. 1996).

[48] *Id.*, at § 34-4-2.5-7.

[49] Tex. Civ. Stat. Ann. art. 135b-6 § 9A(a) (West Supp. 1996).

[50] Ohio Rev. Code Ann. § 5119.61 (Banks-Baldwin 1994).

[51] Cal. Food & Agric. Code Ann. § 4202 (West 1986).

[52] See, *e.g.,* Tenn. Code Ann. § 68-221-1011 (1991) (dealing with the disputes over the consolidation of waste water treatment facilities).

[53] Neb. Rev. Stat. § 81-1381-1382(e) (1994).

[54] See Ohio Rev. Code Ann. § 4117.01 (Banks-Baldwin 1994); N.Y. Lab. Law § 702 (McKinney 1986); and N.J. Rev. Stat. Ann. § 34:13A-4 (West 1994), for examples of typical labor mediation statutes.

[55] See Cal. Gov't Code § 12930 (West 1992); Colo. Rev. Stat. Ann. § 24-34-306 (West 1990); and Haw. Rev. Stat. § 368-3 (1994), for examples of civil rights statutes prescribing the use of mediation and other methods of ADR.

[56] Kan. Stat. Ann. § 23-601 (1995).

[57] N.D. Cent. Code § 14-09.1-01 (1991).

[58] Fla. Stat. Ann. ch. 39.42 (West 1988).

[59] Me. Rev. Stat. Ann. tit. 581(4) (West 1985 & Supp. 1996).

[60] See Wis. Stat. Ann. § 767.001 (West 1993); Minn. Stat. Ann. § 518.619 (West 1990); Cal. Fam. Code Ann. § 1815 (West 1994); and Ohio Rev. Code Ann. § 3105.091 (Banks-Baldwin 1994), for examples of typical domestic mediation statutes.

[61] Alaska Stat. § 34.03.345 (Michie 1995).

[62] Va. Code Ann. § 55-248.3 (Michie 1993).

[63] La. Rev. Stat. Ann. tit. 13 § 5208 (West 1991).

[64] Mass. Gen. Laws Ann. ch. 218 § 22 (West 1993).

[65] N.D. Cent. Code § 51-07-18 (1991).

[66] Pa. Stat. Ann. tit. 73 § 1959 (West 1993).

[67] Ind. Code §§ 3-1-11.5-19ff (1988).

[68] N.H. Rev. Stat. Ann. § 458:15-a (1992).

[69] Me. Rev. Stat. Ann. tit. 39-A § 313 (West 1985).

[70] N.Y. Envtl. Conserv. Law Ann. § 44-0107(17) (McKinney 1990).

[71] N.J. Rev. Stat. § 34 (1991).

[72] Fla. Stat. Ann. ch. 497.003. (West 1988).

[73] Mo. Rev. Stat. Ann. § 436.005 (West 1992).

[74] Winston, *Participation Standards in Mandatory Mediation Statutes, You Can Lead a Horse to Water....*, 11 Ohio St. J. Disp. Resol. 190 (1996).

[75] *Id.*, at 193.

[76] See, *e.g.*, Ky. Rev. Stat. Ann. § 353.5901 (Michie 1993).

[77] Winston, *supra*, at 192.

[78] Dauer, *Impediments in ADR*, 18 Colo. Law. § 39 (1989).

[79] *Physicians Protective Trust Fund v. Overman*, 636 So 2d 827, 829 (Fla App 1994).

[80] Winston, *supra*, at 201ff.

[81] Fla. Stat. Ann. § 61.183 (West 1988).

[82] *Id.*

[83] Kan. Stat. Ann. § 60-452a (1994)

[84] Ariz. Rev. Stat. Ann. § 12-2238D.

[85] For examples, see Mass. Gen. Laws Ann. ch. 233, § 23(C), ch. 150 § 10A(West 1993).

[86] *State v. Castellano*, 460 So.2d. 480 (Fla.Dist.Ct.App. 1984).

[87] S.D. Codified Laws § 15-7-2(11) (Michie 1984).

[88] Tex. Civ. Prac. & Rem. Code Ann. § 154.071(a)(b). (West Supp. 1997).

[89] Cal. Bus. & Prof. Code § 467.4.

[90] Colo. Rev. Stat. Ann. § 13-22-308 (West 1990).

[91] Tenn. Code Ann. § 4-21-301(5) (1991).

[92] *The Cadle Company v. Castle*, No. 05-94-00816-CV, (Tex. App.-Dallas, October 24, 1995).

[93] Cal. Civ. Proc. Code § 1297.382 (West 1997).

[94] *Id.*

[95] *Id.*, at §§ 1297.391, 392.

[96] Ok. Stat. Ann. tit. § 1806 (West 1993).

[97] *Id.*, at § 1894(A), (B).

[98] Cal. Civ. Proc. Code § 1297.432 (West 1993).

[99] Ariz. Rev. Stat. Ann. § 12-2238.

[100] Colo. Rev. Stat. Ann. § 13-33-305(6) (West 1990).

[101] Fla. Stat. Ann. ch. § 44.107 (West 1988).

[102] Fla. Stat. Ann. ch. § 44.201(6) (West 1988).

[103] Haw. Rev. Stat. § 671-17 (1994).

[104] N. Rogers and C. McEwen, *supra* note 4, at 11-1.

[105] *Id.*

[106] *Id.*

[107] *Id.*, at 11-4.

[108] Tex. Civ. Prac. & Rem. Code Ann. § 154.052(a) (West Supp. 1997).

[109] *Id.*, at § 154.052(b).

[110] Fla. Stat. Ann. ch. 39.428 (West 1988).

Chapter Five

Arbitration

Introduction

Arbitration is a method of dispute resolution where the parties refer the matter to an impartial third person (called an "arbitrator"), who renders a decision (called an "award"). The parties choose the arbitrator and agree in advance to abide by his or her award after a hearing at which both parties have had an opportunity to be heard.[1] Arbitration is informal and designed for quick, practical and economical settlements.[2] It is also private in most cases. The arbitrator's decision can be binding, or merely advisory, in which case it can be used to help the parties either negotiate a settlement, or proceed to trial.

Like mediation, arbitration can be completely voluntary or court-annexed. In addition, many federal and state laws provide for the use of arbitration and arbitration-like procedures for resolving disputes between government agencies and their employees, agencies and private citizens, and among agencies. (Chapter Four discusses in more detail the use of ADR, including arbitration, by agencies of the federal and state governments.)

Nevertheless, most arbitration occurs under the terms of private contracts that provide for the use of arbitration for any disputes arising between the parties as a result of their contractual relationship. For this reason, arbitration is the form of ADR used most often to resolve business disputes. For example:

1. Disputes between labor and management arising under collective bargaining agreements have long been submitted to arbitration.

2. Professional sports uses arbitration to decide salary issues and other terms of employment.

3. Construction contracts often contain arbitration clauses that govern the disposition of disputes between builders and customers.

4. The securities industry uses arbitration to resolve problems between brokers and their clients.

5. Contracts granting rights in patents, copyrights and trademarks almost always contain arbitration provisions.

6. Other examples include automobile warranties,[*] contracts between moving companies and their customers, and many types of sales agreements.

Arbitration clauses in business contracts serve the important function of a safety value, freeing the parties to conduct business in the knowledge that if a dispute does arise, they will be able to resolve it in an expeditious manner.[3]

---

[*] The American Arbitration Association serves as the administrative agency for arbitrations carried out under the lemon laws in Massachusetts, New York and Connecticut. Arbitrators are specially trained to handle lemon law cases and must render an award within two months after the case is first filed.

Arbitration is especially popular in the resolution of international commercial disputes,* in part because it bypasses the question of which country's laws will govern.

Beyond the commercial arena, arbitration provides a method for quickly and fairly settling conflict. The International Olympic Committee has instituted mandatory and binding arbitration beginning with the 1996 Olympics, to resolve disputes from drug testing to photo finishes. In order for athletes, coaches and officials to participate in the Olympic games, they must agree in writing to submit disputes to arbitration and be bound by the results.

Arbitration and Mediation Compared

Mediation and arbitration are often presented as comparable alternatives to dispute resolution. ADR agencies frequently offer both processes. Similarly, laws dealing with ADR often recommend both approaches. Some statutes even prescribe "mediation" and yet give the mediator the powers associated with arbitration. Despite the confusion, there are, nonetheless, vast differences between the two techniques.[4]

♦   To begin with, arbitration involves a decision made by a neutral third party who has the power to award a monetary amount that can include all forms of damages including attorneys' fees, interest, and in some states, punitive damages. In mediation, the decision is made by the parties and not the mediator, who has no power to award anything. Presumably, the settlement agreement forged by the parties will take into account those damages potentially available at trial, including attorneys' fees and so forth.

♦   Second, in order for arbitration to resolve a dispute, an arbitrator must hear evidence, proof, and arguments, and then employ logic, analysis and objective thinking to reach a decision. In contrast, a mediator is not concerned so much (or at all) about the merits of either side's case as about the parties' reaching reconciliation and agreement. In order to assist the parties in this quest, the mediator employs creative thinking, intuition, instinct, and other subjective factors, rather than relying purely on logic and objective standards.

♦   A third difference involves the focus of the proceedings. During arbitration, the focus is on the arbitrator, whom the parties try to convince of the merits of their respective cases. While the arbitrator may ask questions and seek out information, he or she is primarily a passive listener, albeit one with a great deal of power. In contrast, the focus of mediation is on the parties. Furthermore, the mediator is an active participant who devises tactics, often on the spot, to move the parties toward reconciliation.

---

*   A California statute prescribing arbitration of international commercial disputes defines an agreement as "commercial" if it is (a) a transaction for the supply or exchange of goods or services, (b) a distribution agreement, (c) a commercial representation or agency, (d) an exploitation agreement or concession, (e) a joint venture or other, related form of industrial or business cooperation, (f) the carriage of goods or passengers by air, sea, rail, or road, (g) construction, (h) insurance, (i) licensing, (j) factoring, (k) leasing, (l) consulting, (m) engineering, (n) finance, (o) banking, (p) the transfer of data or technology, (q) intellectual or industrial property, including trademarks, patents, copyrights, and software programs, and (r) professional services (California Code of Civil Procedure § 1297.16).

♦ Fourth, an arbitrator is usually knowledgeable about the subject matter of the dispute, and will use his or her specialized knowledge and experience to reach a decision. For example, environmental disputes will be arbitrated by an environmental engineer, medical malpractice complaints by a physician or hospital administrator, and international commercial disputes by an international business expert. Special expertise lends authority to an arbitrator and deters losing parties from seeking judicial review of the arbitrator's decision.

By contrast, a mediator is usually selected for his or her ability to communicate and to bring opposing parties together, rather than for specialized knowledge about the industry or other substantive aspects of the dispute. In fact, a mediator who is a specialist runs the risk of being expected to advise the parties on the best solution or even render a decision. Because the parties make the final decision in mediation, the mediator is not subject to judicial review.

♦ Fifth, the arbitrator is generally exempt from civil liability for failure to perform his or her duties with care or skill, or for making a bad decision.[5] An arbitrator functions in a quasi-judicial capacity and for this reason enjoys many of the same protections from liability that are afforded a judge. Nevertheless, an arbitrator can be sanctioned for failure to abide by the ethical norms that govern his or her behavior. (See below for a discussion of the ethics of arbitration.)

Mediators, on the other hand, can be held liable for negligence in their conduct as a mediator. However, courts are reluctant to find mediators negligent because the process leaves the settlement decision entirely up to the parties. Mediator behavior generally has to be found willful and wanton before a mediator will be found liable.

♦ Finally, arbitration and mediation are employed to resolve two different types of disputes. Arbitration is most appropriate where

- a misunderstanding has occurred in a contractual business transaction and the parties use arbitration to clarify the terms.

- in extreme situations, the parties are particularly difficult; negotiation has failed to produce settlement; and it is unlikely that further negotiations will be successful.

- the parties must answer to a diverse group whose interests are too divergent to be well-represented in traditional negotiation or mediation. Examples include labor unions, or the array of public and private parties involved in most environmental disputes. In these situations, a third-party decision may be the only workable alternative.

- one or both of the parties wants to decide the issue for all time and avoid having to relitigate or rearbitrate the dispute.

- in highly technical disputes, the parties can select an arbitrator with specialized knowledge.

Conversely, mediation is a better choice where

- there is a reasonable likelihood that the parties can negotiate a settlement, provided they have assistance from a neutral third party.

- the parties have mutual interests, and the range of settlement options from which they can choose is broad.

- the parties expect to have a continuing relationship after the current matter is settled.

- one or both of the parties wants the opportunity to relitigate or rearbitrate the matter if anyone fails to live up to the terms of the settlement agreement.

As compared with mediation, arbitration is almost never used to settle domestic relations disputes.

The Background of Arbitration

The story of arbitration is best understood against the backdrop of court adjudication. Early English law, on which United States law is based, did not favor arbitration.[6] The English courts were hostile toward arbitration because they viewed it as subversive to their authority and jurisdiction. They were unwilling to permit private parties to avoid the use of public courts through a contract to arbitrate.[7] Early arbitration laws limited its use to resolving disputes that had already occurred, but did not permit its use prospectively, that is, via an agreement to resolve future disputes that may arise between the parties to the agreement.[8]

Nevertheless, the popularity and use of arbitration grew, and by the 18th century it had gained a solid foothold in colonial America. During that era, many communities, including Boston, passed laws and resolutions promoting arbitration and discouraging litigation. George Washington is said to have added an arbitration clause to his will to resolve any disputes over how his estate should be distributed. By 1854, the United States Supreme Court had upheld the right of an arbitrator to issue binding judgments.[9] The Court declared that, "Arbitrators are judges chosen by the parties to decide the matters submitted to them, finally and without appeal. As a mode of settling disputes, it should receive every encouragement from courts of equity."[10]

Arbitration received a significant boost when violent labor disputes broke out in the late 19th century between workers on one side and industrial owners on the other. In response, Congress passed laws mandating the use of various arbitration-like techniques for resolving labor/management disputes. The government realized that the enormous power of labor unions and industry could be controlled only through self-government, which arbitration imposed. In 1926, the Railway Labor Act extended the use of arbitration to resolve labor disputes in the transportation industry. This Act was later amended to include airlines, which, like railroads, were considered critical to the national economy. Similarly, the War Labor Disputes Act of 1943 provided for the use of arbitration to settle disputes in industries involved in producing armaments and other material used in the national defense.

The return of millions of soldiers after World War II and the conversion to a peacetime economy led to passage in 1947 of the Taft-Hartley Labor-Management Relations Act, which created the National Labor Relations Board (NLRB). The job of the NLRB was to arbitrate allegations of unfair labor practices among unions and management.

Today, the vast majority of collective bargaining agreements between groups of employees and management require the use of arbitration to resolve disputes, including those arising between public employees and their governmental employers.

Modern Arbitration Law and Policy

Unlike mediation law, which focuses on establishing programs that promote and use mediation, modern arbitration law concerns itself primarily with legal issues, such as the enforceability of arbitration agreements. It also deals with the types of disputes that are suitable for arbitration, especially civil rights claims (e.g., laws prohibiting racial discrimination in employment).

One of the first federal laws dealing with arbitration of nonlabor matters was passed in 1925. Called the Federal Arbitration Act[11] (FAA), it made all arbitration clauses in contracts dealing with interstate commerce valid, irrevocable, and enforceable, except on grounds applicable to any other contract. In addition, it provided streamlined procedures for compelling arbitration where a party who has agreed to arbitrate fails to do so. Given the history of judicial resistance to arbitration, the FAA was designed to set the record straight on the issue of enforceability, at least as it pertained to contracts affecting commerce across state lines. The Supreme Court reinforced the FAA in 1984 when it held in *Southland Corp. v. Keating*,[12] that the FAA preempted contrary state law in contracts affecting interstate commerce. In 1995, the Supreme Court extended the reach of the FAA to contracts even remotely connected with interstate commerce. In an Alabama case involving a pest extermination company who did business in other states and who acquired its chemicals out-of-state, the Court struck down an Alabama law that made predispute arbitration agreements invalid and unenforceable.[13] By the mid-1990s nearly every state had adopted statutes similar to the FAA.

In 1955, the National Conference of Commissioners on Uniform State Laws drafted the Uniform Arbitration Act (UAA),* which sought to expand contractual validity to arbitration provisions in any contract. All 50 states now have statutes dealing with agreements to arbitrate and at least 35 have adopted the UAA.** The force of these statutes is to establish as a matter of law that any doubts concerning what issues may and may not be subject to arbitration should be resolved in favor of arbitration.

A considerable amount of federal legislation has also been enacted to promote the use of ADR techniques, including arbitration. These are the:

---

* The Uniform Arbitration Act is reprinted in Appendix 3.

** For a list of state arbitration laws, many of which are based on the UAA, see Appendix 4.

♦ Federal Mediation and Conciliation Service, which was created by Congress in 1947 and placed under the Department of Labor, and was designed to assist parties to resolve labor disputes. Over the years the Service has developed considerable skill, resources and successes with mediating and arbitrating difficult and complex matters. As a result, Congress has made the Service available to all federal agencies in the resolution of disputes.

♦ The Civil Justice Reform Act (CJRA), passed by Congress in 1990, requires every federal district court to devise a plan to curtail costs and shorten the time involved in most litigation. In response, every federal court provides for alternative dispute resolution, including arbitration. Similar legislation at the state level almost always includes arbitration in the mix of methods available.

♦ Administrative Dispute Resolution Act of 1990, requires each administrative agency of the federal government to adopt a policy that addresses the use of alternative means of dispute resolution and case management in connection with adjudication, rule making, enforcement actions, issuing and revoking licenses or permits, contract administration, and litigation. The goal of the Act is to promote faster, less expensive, and less contentious decisions, and lead to more creative, efficient, and sensible outcomes.

♦ Executive Order on Civil Justice Reform (1992), directs government litigators to make greater efforts to seek settlements prior to filing lawsuits against violators of federal laws and regulations. The Order encourages litigators to obtain ADR training and to use ADR techniques to obtain compliance and, thus, forego litigation. The agencies most affected include the Environmental Protection Agency, Federal Communication Commission, Internal Revenue Service, Interstate Commerce Commission, Department of Labor, Health and Human Services, Equal Employment Opportunity Commission and the Department of Justice.

A Typical Arbitration

The arbitration process consists of at least six stages, including:

♦ initiation

♦ selecting an arbitration sponsor

♦ prehearing meetings

♦ preparation

♦ hearing

♦ decision making and award

Initiation

Arbitration can be initiated in three ways:

♦ demanding arbitration under a previous agreement to arbitrate,

♦ agreeing to arbitrate at the time a dispute arises, or

♦ complying with court-ordered arbitration.

1. Demanding Arbitration

If the parties involved in a dispute have previously signed an agreement to arbitrate any disagreement between them, arbitration may be initiated by one of the parties unilaterally serving written notice upon the other that they want to use arbitration to resolve the current problem. The written notice is called a "demand." The demand will identify the contract containing the arbitration agreement being invoked by the complaining party. It will also contain a statement as to the nature of the dispute and the relief sought. If the agreement specifies that the arbitration is to be conducted according to the rules of the American Arbitration Association, or some other arbitration sponsor, the rules of that organization regarding initiation of arbitration will apply.

A typical arbitration clause in a contract would read as follows:

> Any controversy or claim arising out of or relating to this Agreement, the making or breach thereof, including any disputes, differences and/or controversies about which the parties may become deadlocked, shall be settled and finally determined by arbitration in [city, state] according to the then-existing, applicable Commercial Rules of the American Arbitration Association, and any judgment upon the award rendered by the arbitrators may be entered in any court having jurisdiction thereof.

A well-drafted clause will address how the arbitrator will be selected, the scope of discovery that will be allowed and other procedural rules to be followed, which state's laws will apply, and the type of remedies that the arbitrator can award. See Appendix 9 for other examples of contract clauses that provide for arbitration of disputes arising under a contract.

2. Agreeing to Arbitration

If no previous agreement has been reached between the parties to arbitrate, a written submission agreement can be entered into when a dispute arises. The "submission," by definition, must be agreed to by all of the parties. The submission will usually contain a statement about the matter in dispute, the amount of money involved (if applicable), and the remedy that the initiating party wants. It will also state the rules under which arbitration will be conducted, including whether arbitration is to be binding or nonbinding (merely advisory) and, if binding, whether the arbitrator's decision will be entered as the judgment of a court with jurisdiction over the matter.

The submission may also contain a statement of the rules of evidence to be followed in the arbitration hearing, what will happen at the hearing in terms of which side presents first, whether or not a court reporter will make a record of the proceedings, when the arbitrator will come to a decision and make the award, the extent to which the proceedings will be private and confidential, and who will pay the costs and fees associated with the arbitration. In other words, by choosing arbitration, the parties have the opportunity to fashion their own proceedings, and need not follow the formal rules of civil procedure that govern litigation and trial.

3. *Court Order to Arbitrate*

Just as a court can order the parties to a lawsuit to mediate their dispute, it can also order the parties into arbitration.* As with mediation, the parties may object to the order. Court-annexed arbitration is almost always nonbinding unless the parties agree to be bound by the arbitrator's decision, in which case the judge will generally enter the decision as the judgment of the court. If the parties choose not to abide by the arbitrator's decision and request a trial, court rules usually permit them to reopen arbitration at any point short of a decision by the court.

Courts will often establish a threshold for the referral of cases to arbitration. For example, the United States District Court for the Western District of Texas has mandatory referral to arbitration of cases that involve monetary claims of $150,000 or less, exclusive of interest, costs and attorneys' fees.[14] Certain types of cases are subject to discretionary referral by the court, while others require the consent of the parties.

Court-annexed arbitration rules usually contain provisions relating to selection and compensation of arbitrators. The court will almost always provide the parties with a list of approved arbitrators from which they may choose. Rules will also provide for procedural matters such as transcripts, submission of documents and other items into evidence, examination of witnesses, and so forth. Even though the parties in court-annexed arbitration generally do not have the freedom to establish the rules by which arbitration will be governed, court rules tend nevertheless to be much more informal and flexible than those required in civil litigation.

Furthermore, each court usually fashions its own rules, whereas the rules of civil procedure that control litigation and trial for each state, and the federal system, will apply to all of their courts. If the losing party in a court-annexed arbitration requests a trial after the arbitrator renders a nonbinding decision, the trial will be "de novo," meaning that the court will not rely on any record or transcript of the arbitration. Instead, the parties will be required to present their case in full to the court.

4. *Administrative Arbitration*

Arbitration and arbitration-like procedures are also used to resolve disputes arising between various parties and administrative agencies of government. For example, many states require arbitration to settle disputes between public employees, such as police and fire fighters, and the communities that employ them.[15] Some states, such as Arkansas, provide for the arbitration of disputes between private employers and their employees.[16] In Delaware, the Department of Agriculture will arbitrate disputes between agricultural producers and the companies that distribute their products.[17] See Chapter Four for a more complete discussion of the administrative uses of ADR.

---

* See, for example, California Business and Professional Code §§ 465 - 471.5; Connecticut General Statutes § 5, Public Act No. 93-108, 1993 Ct. ALS 108; 1993 Ct. P.A. 108; 1993 Ct. HB 6851.)

5. *Answering a Demand*

Depending upon the rules under which an arbitration is to be conducted, a party on whom a demand for arbitration has been made may or may not need to file an answer. This differs from litigation, where the defendant must always file a response to a plaintiff's complaint. If the defendant fails to do so, it is presumed that the defendant admits the plaintiff's claims, which entitles the plaintiff to a default judgment. Even if a party to arbitration is not required to file an answer, however, it may be in his or her best interest to do so. An answer sets forth any defenses that the nondemanding party has against the claims of the demanding party, as well as counter claims against the demanding party. By providing this information up front rather than revealing it for the first time at the hearing, both sides can be better prepared and the hearing won't have to be postponed while everyone scrambles to gather new evidence and formulate a response.

Selecting an Arbitration Sponsor

1. *Arbitration Sponsor*

Once a demand or submission has been prepared, or a court order to arbitrate has been received, the parties usually select an agency to sponsor the arbitration. As compared with mediation, third-party sponsorship of arbitration is critical. An arbitrator is forbidden by ethics and, in some cases, by law to confer alone with any of the parties or their representatives without the consent of the other parties. Thus, a neutral third party is needed to expedite arrangements for the arbitration. Also, because arbitration is a somewhat formal process that involves the gathering and exchange of evidence, and other procedural matters, the presence of a neutral agency to coordinate this process and to make sure that it proceeds amicably is very important.

Choices of agencies include national organizations such as the AAA, Judicial Arbitration & Mediation Services, Inc. (JAMS), Center for Public Resources (CPR), Endispute, or the National Association of Securities Dealers (NASD) (for securities disputes), to name a few. Additional agencies are available at the local level, both for-profit and not-for-profit, including agencies sponsored by local bar associations.

During preparation of a submission the parties will need to agree on which agency to use. If an arbitration clause in a contract is involved, the clause will usually specify an agency. In the case of court-ordered arbitration, the court may act as the sponsor and provide administrative services, or it may refer the parties to independent agencies available in the community.

2. *Rules*

Selection of an arbitration sponsor is often dependent upon the procedural rules that the organization can provide. Those rules deal with a wide variety of matters including how to

♦ initiate arbitration

♦ change or add a claim after filing

♦ select an arbitrator(s)

♦ request a prehearing conference

- fix the time and location of the hearing

- appoint an arbitrator

- challenge or waive a rule

- extend or postpone the hearing

- obtain a stenographic record of the hearing

- arrange for interpreters

- decide if witnesses will be required to swear an oath

- determine who shall attend the arbitration hearing

- communicate with the arbitrator

- reopen the hearing after it has been closed

- determine the time, form and scope of the award

- pay fees and determine what those fees will be, etc.

One of the advantages of arbitration over litigation is that it is more flexible with regard to the rules to be followed. The parties can decide to use the rules of the sponsoring agency, use the rules of another agency, or devise their own. In litigation, the parties must adhere to the formal rules of civil procedure for their particular jurisdiction. If the parties decide to devise some or all of the rules, they will generally insert them into the arbitration clause of their contract, or into the submission. In the case of court-annexed arbitration, the court will usually provide the rules under which arbitration will be conducted, as discussed above.

Arbitration sponsors often provide rules tailor-made to the dispute. For example, the AAA has rules for arbitrating disputes involving labor disagreements, construction contracts, securities agreements, textile and apparel industry matters, insurance claims, and international commercial transactions. Special rules are also available for agricultural, environment, and several other types of disputes.

3. *Arbitrator*

Selection of a sponsoring agency is based not only on the administrative services and rules it can provide, but also on the quality of arbitrators that it can make available. Agencies maintain lists and panels of qualified arbitrators from which parties can choose. Arbitration usually involves either a single arbitrator or a panel of three arbitrators whose selection is controlled completely, or to a large extent, by the parties. In this regard, arbitration differs significantly from litigation and trial, where the parties have little or no influence over which judge will hear their case.

In voluntary arbitration, arbitrators are most often selected from lists provided by the sponsoring agency or from one of many registries for qualified arbitrators. The federal government can provide lists of arbitrators through the Federal Mediation and Conciliation Service and the National Mediation Board. Privately, names and biographical information can be obtained from the *Directory of Arbitrators*, prepared by the Bureau of National Affairs, Inc., and from *Who's Who* (of arbitrators) published by Prentice-Hall, Inc. The American Arbitration Association (AAA) maintains a National Panel of Arbitrators containing more than 50,000 individuals throughout the United States and the rest of the world. Of course, the parties can also nominate an arbitrator on their own without the help of any agency or clearinghouse. In court-annexed arbitration the parties will select an arbitrator(s) from a list provided by the clerk.

4. AAA Rules for Selecting an Arbitrator

Parties who choose to abide by the rules of an independent ADR sponsor will usually select an arbitrator according to their rules from lists furnished by the organization. For example, the AAA, which is perhaps the most frequently subscribed ADR organization, provides that after a demand has been made by one of the parties, or a submission by both parties has been filed with the AAA, it will send to each party an identical list of five or more names of persons chosen by the AAA from its panel. The AAA will consider many factors in compiling the list, including whether the arbitrator is experienced in the subject matter of the dispute.

After receiving the list, the parties usually have ten days in which to strike any names, number the remaining names in order of preference, and return the list to the AAA. If one arbitrator is to be chosen, each party can strike three names without cause; and five names if a panel of arbitrators will be selected. If the list is not returned, the AAA will presume that all arbitrators are acceptable. The AAA will then invite an arbitrator to hear the dispute from the list of candidates acceptable to all of the parties. If none of the candidates are acceptable to both parties, the AAA will have the power to select an arbitrator(s) from names it has not submitted for pre-approval.[18] Once an arbitrator(s) is selected, he or she will work with the sponsor to set the time and place of the hearing. Arbitrators have more discretion in scheduling hearings than most trial judges, which is another strategic advantage of arbitration over litigation and trial.

Where a panel of arbitrators is used, AAA rules provide that each party's candidate will be invited, and the two arbitrators will select a third, "neutral" arbitrator who will participate in the final decision only if the other arbitrators cannot agree. As an alternative, the parties can ask the AAA to appoint a three-member panel from its approved list of arbitrators. Some commentators have noted that a panel approach is, in effect, a less efficient version of using a single arbitrator. It can also delay arbitration if a party instructs its chosen panel member to delay selecting a third, neutral member. However, under the AAA rules, the AAA can appoint a neutral arbitrator after a specified period of time.

5. Costs

Fees for arbitration are assessed by the sponsoring agency and are usually based on the amount in dispute. The sponsoring agency pays the arbitrator(s). The AAA, for example, charges the filing party a fee of $300 for a claim up to $25,000, while claims in excess of $5 million require a filing fee of $5,000. In addition, each day of arbitration carries a fee of $100 per party for a single arbitrator and $150 where an arbitration panel is used. A fee is also assessed for postponements.

Prehearing Meetings

Prehearing meetings consist of preliminary hearings and administrative conferences. Preliminary hearings are used to establish and clarify any substantive rules not already covered in the demand, submission or court order, or provided by the sponsoring agency. They are also used to determine the extent and schedule for the production of documents, the identification of any witnesses to be called, whether or not subpoenas will be required, and other substantive matters.

The preliminary hearing is attended by the arbitrator(s) and the parties or their representatives. As compared with pretrial hearings, however, discussion of the underlying merits of the various claims and defenses of the parties should be avoided at preliminary hearings. Instead, if a party has filed a motion attacking the validity of some claim, the arbitrator may ask for briefs to be submitted on the issue before the actual arbitration hearing. Ex parte conferences between the arbitrator and a party are strictly forbidden.

Administrative conferences are held by the sponsoring agency to expedite the arbitration process. They usually deal with such matters as time and location of the hearing, transmission of documents from one party to another and other procedural details. The arbitrator usually does not attend these meetings unless a substantive ruling is needed. Where the dispute is relatively straightforward, administrative conferences can be handled by phone. In large and more complex cases, several face-to-face conferences may be necessary.

Preparation

A case that is to be arbitrated must be thoroughly prepared. Arbitration is primarily a fact-finding process where each party presents his or her case to the arbitrator(s), who make(s) a decision based on the evidence presented. Preparing for arbitration is similar to preparing for a trial. Documents must be assembled, witnesses interviewed and depositions taken. The scope of allowable discovery will usually be determined by the arbitrator, by agreement of the parties, or both. Arbitrators generally have subpoena power and can order witnesses to appear and documents to be produced.

Unfortunately, an arbitrator has no inherent power to enforce orders and subpoenas. When a party does not comply, the other side must petition a court of law with jurisdiction via a motion for sanctions, motion for contempt, temporary restraining order, or other appropriate remedy. In this way, the civil courts are an invisible hand of control over the arbitration process.

Even though preparing for arbitration is similar to preparing for a trial, it differs in two important ways:

1. Arbitration does not rely on the precedents of past cases. Therefore, in researching the case, preparing evidence and formulating supporting arguments the attorney does not need to focus (or rely) on how the current case is similar to prior cases. Rather, the attorney will concentrate on assembling the best evidence so as to argue the case on its own merits.

2. Preparation for arbitration is usually not as extensive as preparation for trial, for several reasons:

   • First, the arbitrator is almost always experienced in the subject matter of the dispute; therefore, he or she does not need to be educated to the extent that a jury or a generalist judge must be educated.

   • Second, the arbitrator's decision is often based on issues of fairness or industry custom rather than legal precedence; therefore, it is unnecessary to prepare extensive legal arguments and assemble legal proof. For example, the issue of damages is primarily legal in nature, in that the law often dictates what type of damages are available in a case, and legal precedence establishes the range of recovery. The arbitrator, however, may choose to discount or disregard legal parameters in favor of standards more appropriate to the case at hand.

   • Third, the only items that are discoverable in arbitration are those that are absolutely necessary to the result. In litigation, however, it is customary to ask for a wide range of documents and take many depositions in the hope of turning up important evidence.

   • Fourth, because of the utility of arbitration, the parties are encouraged to stipulate as many facts as possible so that the hearing can center on facts and issues where an important difference of opinion exists between the parties.

The AAA makes the following suggestions concerning case preparation:[19]

♦ Assemble all documents and papers that you will need at the hearing. Always make photocopies for the arbitrator and the other party. . . . A checklist of documents and exhibits will be helpful toward your orderly presentation.

♦ If it will be necessary for the arbitrator to visit a building site or warehouse for on-the-spot investigation, make plans in advance.

♦ Interview all your witnesses. Make certain that each one understands the whole case and particularly the importance of his or her own testimony within it.

♦ Make a written summary of what each witness will prove.

♦ Study the case from the other side's point of view. Be prepared to answer the opposition's evidence.

Procedure for Oral Hearing In order to prepare for an arbitration hearing, several procedural decisions must be made. The following chart, adapted from one developed by the AAA, outlines six critical decisions based upon who gets to decide, who makes the arrangements, and who should be notified.

Decision	Who Decides	Who Arranges	Notice
Time	The arbitrator, at the convenience of the parties	The administrator of the agency (e.g., AAA) sponsoring the arbitration, after consulting with the parties and the arbitrator	At least ten days' notice before arbitration is given by the administrator, unless the parties agree otherwise
Representation	The individual party	The individual party	Three days' notice to other party, unless arbitration was initiated by counsel, in which case notice is deemed to have been given
Stenographic Record/ Interpreters	The requesting party	The requesting party	The requesting party notifies other party in advance of the hearing; may ask other side if it would share costs
Administrative Conference	Any party or the sponsoring agency	The administrator, after consulting with the parties, and the arbitrator if he or she needs to attend	The administrator notifies the parties, and the arbitrator if necessary, to confirm the date
Preliminary Hearing	Any party, the sponsoring agency or the arbitrator	The administrator, after consulting with the parties and the arbitrator	The administrator notifies the parties and the arbitrator to confirm the date
Who Attends Arbitration	Parties and their witnesses. Arbitrator decides if the interested persons may attend; may ask witnesses to leave during the testimony of others	Parties arrange for the attendance of their witnesses	Parties notify their own interested persons and witnesses
Affidavits and Documents	The arbitrator decides whether to receive such evidence when it is presented	Each party arranges to submit its own documents. If in the possession of other party, they may be requested directly	None is required
Subpoenas of Witnesses and Documents	The arbitrator issues subpoenas on showing of need by a party. In New York State, attorneys of record may also issue subpoenas.	The administrator obtains the signature of arbitrator on subpoena supplied by a party and returns subpoena to party for service	Subpoenas are served by parties directly on the witness or the custodian of documents
Inspection or Investigation	The arbitrator may decide on his or her own initiative or at the request of a party, if the arbitrator deems it necessary	The administrator	Parties are notified of time and place of inspection so that they can be present
Closing of Oral Hearings	Arbitrator closes hearing after both sides complete proofs and witnesses. If briefs, investigation or more data are required, hearings are kept open	Administrator arranges for receipt of post-hearing matters; makes record of closing of hearings on instructions from arbitrator	The administrator notifies parties of all official closing dates

Hearing An arbitration proceeding is an evidentiary-type hearing before an arbitrator. The parties have the option of waiving an oral hearing and having the matter decided on the basis of documentary evidence, but this is a rare exception. Unlike a trial, an arbitration hearing is not open to the public, but all people who have a direct interest in the case, in addition to the parties, can usually attend. A written record is not always made of the hearing, but if a party requires one, that party will have the responsibility to make arrangements for a stenographer to be present, and will bear the associated costs. Likewise, witnesses at an arbitration hearing usually do not take an oath unless required by law, the arbitrator, or on demand of one of the parties.

The location of the arbitration hearing will be agreed to by the parties and the arbitrator, and frequently will take place at the offices of the sponsor where there are facilities to conduct the hearing, segregate the witnesses, provide private working space for the parties and their representatives, and other such requirements. If a party fails to appear for an arbitration hearing, the arbitrator is usually authorized to proceed and will render an award based on the information that he or she has available about the absent party's case. There is generally no default judgment in arbitration for failure to appear.

1. Process

An arbitration hearing usually involves an opening statement by each of the parties to acquaint the arbitrator with the case and indicate what is to be proved. Who goes first is usually determined by the rules agreed to ahead of time. Those rules also determine whether evidence will be presented immediately after each statement or must wait until the other side has made their opening remarks. While each side may want to cross-examine the other side's witnesses, generally each party should try to establish its case by its own witnesses. Furthermore, no single party has the burden of proof at an arbitration hearing. Rather, each party must convince the arbitrator(s) of the correctness of his or her position. After presenting their evidence, the parties will make closing arguments and any rebuttal allowed by the rules and the arbitrator.

2. Evidence

Presentation of evidence is usually streamlined as compared with trial. First of all, documents will be treated as self-authenticating. This means that if a letter introduced into evidence is dated July 15, 1990, no testimony will be required to authenticate the letter or the date. Testimony will be introduced through the use of depositions and affidavits rather than in-person interviews. Likewise, testifying witnesses will be introduced via written biographical information rather than through a series of questions to establish identity and other similar background information.

Charts and graphs will be used to summarize voluminous data. Rather than extensive oral argument, the parties may be required to summarize their claims and defenses in the form of a written brief.

Even though presentation of evidence is streamlined, the arbitrator is free to hear any evidence that he or she deems necessary to understand the dispute and make a reasonable and informed decision. Thus, legal rules of evidence with regard to relevancy,* and hearsay** do not apply. Arbitration differs from litigation as well, in its emphasis on straightforward presentation of each party's case. Typical trial tactics including exaggeration, concealment of important facts, and the introduction of legal technicalities to delay the process or cover up weaknesses in one's case will not impress an arbitrator who is usually an expert in the subject matter of the dispute, and who has taken time out of a busy schedule to act as arbitrator.

3. *Timing*

The amount of time required by arbitration depends upon the time needed for each party to present his or her case. Of course, because presentations focus only on what is critical to the arbitrator's decision, arbitration hearings tend to take less time than trial proceedings. Furthermore, because arbitrators are usually paid only a nominal daily rate, everyone feels the pressure to proceed as efficiently as possible. Most hearing schedules are based on a five- or six-hour day, although some arbitrators prefer marathon sessions rather than returning the following day. If more than one day is needed, it is usually preferable to schedule additional sessions on consecutive days.

4. *Confidentiality*

Confidentiality of the proceedings and the arbitrator's final decision is determined in two ways:

♦ by agreement of the parties, the arbitrator, or both, and

♦ by the rules under which the arbitration is conducted.

American Arbitration Association rules guarantee complete privacy for both the proceedings and the award. Conversely, the rules of the National Association of Securities Dealers[20] and the New York Stock Exchange,[21] under which most securities disputes are arbitrated, provide for the disclosure of awards where the dispute involves a public customer (e.g., state school teacher's pension fund).

---

* According to the Federal Rules of Evidence, "relevant evidence" means evidence having any tendency to make the existence of any fact that is of consequence to the determination of the action more probable or less probable than it would be without the evidence (Rule 401). In other words, does the evidence tend to prove the matter sought to be proved? Evidence that is not relevant is not admissible (Rule 402). Furthermore, relevant evidence may be excluded if its probative value substantially outweighs the danger of unfair prejudice, confuses the issues, or misleads the jury, or if consideration would cause undue delay, waste time, or result in needless presentation of cumulative evidence (Rule 403).

** Hearsay is any statement made outside of the trial or hearing that is offered to prove whatever the statement claims (Federal Rules of Evidence Rule 801). For example, if a bystander goes home and tells his wife that the pedestrian was struck by a car exceeding the speed limit, his statement cannot be admitted into evidence to prove that the defendant was speeding. Subject to various exceptions, hearsay is not admissible (Rule 802).

Some rules will also permit agencies to provide parties who are looking for an arbitrator with a history of an arbitrator's awards, including the nature of the dispute and the parties involved. Because of the difference in treatment of confidentiality under various rules, parties are advised to consider what level of confidentiality they require before selecting the rules that will govern their arbitration.

Decision Making and Award

The arbitrator's decision is called an award and is usually issued no more than 30 days from the date of the hearing. If the matter is relatively simple, the award may be made at the close of the hearing. In cases where the matter is highly complex and the amount of evidence is voluminous, the arbitrator may take several weeks to render a decision. The purpose of the award is to fully and finally dispose of the case. Where a panel of arbitrators is involved, the decision is by a majority of the arbitrators or an average of all of the individual arbitrators' awards. If the arbitrators chosen by the parties are unable to reach a unanimous agreement, the neutral arbitrator will render a decision.

Where arbitration is voluntary, the arbitrator's decision will be based on standards selected by the parties. For example, the arbitration clause in a sales contract may state that an award should be based on standards of fairness, while a construction contract may require application of the customs of the trade. Court-annexed arbitration usually requires that decisions be made according to standards of fairness and applicable law.

The AAA Commercial Arbitration Rules provide that the arbitrator may grant any remedy or relief that he or she deems just and equitable and within the scope of the agreement of the parties. As compared with adjudication in a court of law, an arbitrator's award is also based on his or her experience and technical expertise, rather than solely on evidence presented by the parties. If the parties reach an agreement on their own during the course of arbitration, the arbitrator may set forth the terms of the settlement in what is called a "consent award."

Arbitration awards are always in writing, but they usually do not include a written opinion reviewing the arbitrator's rationale, unless the parties have requested one. Where the decision is binding, the law of arbitration provides only limited judicial review. As one writer put it, "[w]hen the arbitrators are properly selected, conduct an orderly hearing at which all parties have a fair chance to present their proofs and render an intelligible award within the scope of their authority, the courts will confirm and enforce the award."[22]

Nevertheless, because of the nature of arbitration proceedings, judicial review is never available on the basis of errors of law. Furthermore, judicial review is seldom if ever available on the basis of errors in admitting evidence, due in part to the lack of a stenographic record of the arbitration hearing.

In most cases, the arbitrator will render a final award and in so doing will relinquish control over the matter. However, in certain cases, the parties may agree to have the arbitrator retain jurisdiction over the case. For example, if the dispute involves the dissolution of a business partnership, the owners may want the arbitrator to retain control in the event that additional disagreements develop while the assets of the partnership are being sold off.

Damages Like a judge, an arbitrator can grant money damages. This includes punitive damages, unless the parties have expressly agreed otherwise, or state law governing the contract prohibits an arbitrator from awarding punitive damages. In 1995, however, the Supreme Court overruled New York common law that prevented an arbitral award of punitive damages in contracts affecting interstate commerce.[23] The New York law was based on the premise that only the state, through its courts, can punish. Given the Court's inclination to find that most contracts involve interstate commerce, it is unlikely that any state law prohibiting or limiting arbitral awards of punitive damages is unconstitutional.

In many cases, an arbitrator has much more flexibility in granting equitable relief as compared with a judge in a court of law. Equitable relief is another word for any remedy that is fair under the circumstances. An arbitrator can also grant specific performance, meaning that a party can be ordered to fulfill the obligations that he or she contracted to perform. Therefore, the range of relief available to an arbitrator is broader than what a law court can provide.

Appendix 8 contains a reprint of the AAA Commercial Arbitration Rules covering the topics discussed above, which students are encouraged to review.

Exercises

Review the mediation case study that begins on page 61 of Chapter Three, and answer the following questions:

1. Would arbitration have been an appropriate method to resolve this dispute? If not, why not? Is so, why?

2. If the contract involved had included an agreement to arbitrate, what should it have contained? Draft such an agreement.

3. As compared with mediation, how would arbitration have differed in terms of:
   a. qualifications and training of the third-party neutral?
   b. discovery?
   c. opening statements?

4. How would an arbitrator's decision in the matter likely have differed from the settlement reached by the parties in mediation?

The Role and Power of the Arbitrator

In the preceding description of a typical arbitration, we have seen that the arbitrator is a very powerful person. In fact, few judges have the power given to an arbitrator. For example:

1. An arbitrator has many of the same powers as a judge to fix the time and place of hearing, rule on evidence, issue subpoenas, direct the flow of information during the proceedings, and render a decision that is binding on the parties and fully enforceable. In most cases, however, an arbitrator's decision is unappealable, whereas any unfavorable decision by a judge can generally be appealed to a higher court.

2. An arbitrator can accept or decline to hear a dispute that has been submitted to his or her consideration for any reason or no reason at all. A judge, on the other hand, receives assignments randomly and can be excused only for cause, such as conflict of interest.

3. An arbitrator's power comes not from the state, but from the agreement of the parties to submit to the arbitrator's determination the outcome of their dispute. Thus, the arbitrator's only constituency is the parties, and he or she answers only to them. Judges, on the other hand, have direct responsibility to their jurisdiction, to the justice system, to the legal profession, to the public, and if elected, to their supporters.

4. The arbitrator's power is supported by law, which favors agreements among private parties to settle their disputes amicably and privately rather than resort to the courts.

5. The arbitrator's power is also supported by his or her expertise in the subject matter of the dispute. That expertise not only commands the respect and trust of the parties, it also enables the arbitrator to directly shape how a case is put together and presented. The power of a judge, on the other hand, to hear evidence and influence what goes on in the courtroom is restricted to the rules of procedure.

6. Finally, an arbitrator is not bound by legal precedent and can render an award that is tailored to the dispute. Conversely, a judge must always consider how similar cases have been decided in the past or face the prospect of having decisions overturned by a higher court.

Exercises

1. Arbitrators are often criticized for trying to give something to everybody in split-the-baby fashion. Assuming the accuracy of this observation, do you think arbitrators are merely being fickle? Or, are they trying to deal fairly with disputes that are usually not one-sided and where each party has some merit to its case? How do courts deal with two-sided disputes?

2. Are arbitrators beholden only to the parties that hire them, or are there other people and groups to which they are accountable?

3. If you were involved in a highly technical dispute and you could choose between a generalist judge whose decision was appealable and a specialist arbitrator whose decision would be final, which would you choose? Why?

4. If a school district is sued for discriminating against physically handicapped children, would you rather see the case decided by a judge or an arbitrator? Why?

The Role of the Attorney in Arbitration

Parties in arbitration are not always represented by an attorney or other advocate. If the dispute is simple, the evidence straightforward, and the parties subject to an arbitration clause in a contract, they may decide to contact the sponsor named in the contract and proceed to arbitration. Even parties who have no prior agreement to use ADR can ask a sponsoring agency to intervene. The agency will contact the other party to ascertain whether they are willing to arbitrate, explain the procedures involved, and then administer the case if the parties reach an agreement.[*]

---

[*] The American Arbitration Association will provide these services.

Parties involved in disputes with governmental regulatory agencies that use arbitration will attend on their own. Likewise, people with disputed claims against insurance carriers, car manufacturers and producers of similar consumer products who provide arbitrators to resolve customer claims, will often go to arbitration unaccompanied by counsel, especially if they can elect that the award be nonbinding. Therefore, if they do not get what they want from an arbitrator, they can always retain a lawyer and file a lawsuit.

Notwithstanding the above, most people who arbitrate their disputes are represented by counsel. Naturally, if the arbitration is ordered by the court pursuant to a lawsuit, an attorney is almost certainly involved. But even voluntary arbitration is likely to involve an attorney. First of all, the parties are apt to be business people who regularly use the services of an attorney. Furthermore, the dispute is likely to concern a commercial matter with a significant amount of money or property at stake. In many cases, the dispute will involve issues complex enough to require the services of a competent litigator to assemble and present evidence to an arbitrator who is also an expert.

The attorney plays a critical role in arbitration. Furthermore, many of the services that an attorney can provide a client are highly similar to those required by litigation. Nevertheless, there are differences, including the need to limit discovery to the essential information required, and to tailor the presentation, keeping in mind that the arbitrator is an expert in the subject matter. Following are some of the important tasks and roles played by an attorney.

1. Attorneys who draft contracts and other agreements should seriously consider including an ADR clause that requires the parties to submit disputes to mediation, arbitration, or a combination of the two, and recommend to their clients that such a clause be included in their contracts.

2. Attorneys should, upon being presented with a dispute, determine if the matter is subject to an agreement among the parties to resolve their differences through the use of arbitration. If so, the attorney should prepare and make a written demand based upon the rules and procedures contained in the agreement. If no such agreement has been made, the attorney should consider if arbitration would be appropriate under the circumstances and advise the client accordingly.

    Because a submission to arbitration requires the consent of all of the parties, the attorney for the complainant should contact the other parties, or their attorneys, to discuss the appropriateness of arbitration.

    If the parties decide not to submit the dispute to voluntary arbitration, the attorney will need to advise the client if court-ordered arbitration is a possibility and whether or not they should cooperate with or oppose such an order. If the matter concerns alleged regulatory violations, the attorney will need to determine if the government agency involved provides ADR as a means of resolving the matter before it resorts to more severe measures. If so, the attorney should contact the government agency regarding its arbitration procedures.

3. If the client is subject to a demand to arbitrate, the attorney can help the client resist the demand on legal grounds, such as the use of fraud by the other party to induce the client to sign the original contract, a claim that the client had no choice but to sign the agreement (e.g., "take-it-or-leave-it" contracts such as automobile sales agreements), the contract is unconscionable, and other similar defenses. The attorney also may need to prepare an answer to the demand, setting out defenses and any counterclaims.

4. If arbitration is desired or inevitable, the attorney can help the client select an arbitration sponsor based on the quality of its staff, the range of services it provides, the rules it uses, its operating practices and the characteristics of the arbitrators that it recommends. Once a sponsor is selected, the attorney will need to help the client choose an arbitrator by making inquiries and gathering information about the candidates.

5. The attorney will need to attend any preliminary hearings to deal with rules and discovery issues. The attorney is in the best position to determine what evidence is needed by the client, and also what evidence they may want to avoid relinquishing to the other side. Thus, the attorney will need to make persuasive arguments to the arbitrator regarding discovery orders. The attorney will also be responsible for preparing and transmitting discovery, conducting any depositions and evaluating documents and other items received from the other party.

6. The attorney will need to prepare for the arbitration hearing first by evaluating what will be needed to persuade the arbitrator of the merits of the client's case. The attorney will prepare exhibits, brief witnesses and draft the opening statement to persuasively inform the arbitrator of the critical issues at stake in the dispute, preview the evidence and explain why the arbitrator should see the problem from the client's perspective.

7. At the hearing, the attorney should counsel the client regarding any conflicts of interest revealed by the arbitrator and orchestrate any challenge to the arbitrator on that basis. Once the hearing begins, the attorney will bear the responsibility to present evidence, examine and cross examine witnesses and, in general, put on the client's case. The attorney will also prepare and make the closing statement, taking care to avoid overstatement or emotional arguments commonly seen at trial.

8. After the arbitrator makes an award, the attorney will counsel the client regarding whether to petition a court to enter the award as the judgment of the court. Entry of judgment will give the client a broader range of enforcement procedures in case the other party defaults.

9. Finally, the attorney will need to determine if the award can and should be appealed and, if so, to prepare such appeal.

The Role of the Paralegal in Arbitration

When providing support to an attorney whose clients are involved in arbitration, a paralegal will perform many of the same functions required to support litigation. This will include assisting in the preparation of demands and submissions, gathering and assembling documents and other discovery, coordinating transmission of documents to the other side, evaluating and summarizing documents and items received from the other party, preparing subpoenas, keeping track of schedules, preparing hearing exhibits, and other similar tasks.

Just as the paralegal should be thoroughly familiar with the rules of procedure that govern litigation and trial, he or she should also be familiar with the rules that will govern the arbitration. The paralegal will almost always attend administrative hearings on behalf of the client and counsel and will be responsible for coordinating administrative matters with the arbitration sponsor. Depending upon the level of involvement expected by the attorney, a paralegal may also assist in briefing witnesses and will attend the arbitration to provide continuing support to the process. Because an arbitration hearing is not a "legal" proceeding, in some cases, the paralegal may even assist in the presentation of the case.

In addition to supporting attorneys who represent parties involved in arbitration, paralegals have the opportunity to provide representation directly. As with mediation, there are very few obstacles preventing a nonattorney from representing a party at arbitration. The rules of several sponsoring agencies, including the AAA, provide for representation by "counsel or other authorized representative."[24] The Uniform Arbitration Act, on which many state arbitration laws are based, permits representation by counsel but does not forbid representation by a nonattorney.[25] Federal administrative agencies, as well as many at the state level, are required by law to develop rules and procedures permitting advocates who are not attorneys to represent clients in claims disputes and enforcement actions. Thus, paralegals are free to hold themselves out as advocates for parties involved in arbitration, subject, of course, to codes of ethics governing paralegal conduct, including those prohibiting the unauthorized practice of law.*

Finally, paralegals can serve as arbitrators, especially if they have expertise in the subject matter of the dispute. For example, a healthcare professional who is also trained as a paralegal could offer both medical and legal experience to disputants seeking an arbitrator for a medical malpractice claim.

The Ethics of Arbitration

The enormous growth in the use of arbitration to resolve a wider and wider variety of disputes raises serious concerns about standards of conduct for arbitrators. Because arbitration is largely a private enterprise, it is generally not accountable to any public system of justice. Yet, the public resorts more and more every day to arbitrators rather than the courts to determine its rights. This trend endows arbitrators with an ever increasing amount of responsibility to both the public, and the parties before them, to behave in a fair and ethical manner.

---

* See Chapter Eight for a discussion of the unauthorized practice of law.

Various codes of ethics and professional responsibility for arbitrators have been developed over the years. Labor arbitration is governed by the Code of Professional Responsibility for Arbitrators of Labor-Management Disputes. In 1977, the AAA and the American Bar Association (ABA) promulgated the Code of Ethics for Arbitrators in Commercial Disputes, to govern arbitrator conduct in situations where other codes do not apply. Because arbitrators serve in a quasi-judicial capacity, most arbitrator codes are modeled after codes of conduct for judges. Every jurisdiction has a judicial code, many of which are modeled, in turn, on the ABA Model Code of Judicial Conduct. Other sources of standards of conduct for arbitrators include laws that prescribe the use of arbitration by the courts or for specific types of disputes, which often contain provisions dealing with certain ethical issues such as confidentiality. Similarly, contract provisions calling for arbitration of disputes will also include ethical guidelines.

Following are listed the six canons of the AAA Code of Ethics for Arbitrators in Commercial Disputes, along with a summary of the several subpoints under each. The seventh canon concerns ethical considerations relating to arbitrators appointed by only one party. Appendix 12 contains a full reprint of the Code.

AAA Code of Ethics for Arbitrators in Commercial Disputes

CANON I. AN ARBITRATOR SHOULD UPHOLD THE INTEGRITY AND FAIRNESS OF THE ARBITRATION PROCESS.

Under Canon I, the arbitrator has a positive duty to recognize his or her solemn responsibility to society and the parties. That responsibility begins when an arbitration is solicited and continues after the arbitration is concluded. Although arbitrators can hold themselves out as arbitrators, they may not solicit appointments. Furthermore, they should accept appointment only if they are available. To avoid compromising an arbitration, an arbitrator should avoid any financial, business, professional, family or social relationships both during and for a reasonable time after the arbitration. An arbitrator should not be swayed by outside factors, should not exceed his or her authority, and should not permit delays and other abuses or disruption of the process.

CANON II. AN ARBITRATOR SHOULD DISCLOSE ANY INTEREST OR RELATIONSHIP LIKELY TO AFFECT IMPARTIALITY OR WHICH MIGHT CREATE AN APPEARANCE OF PARTIALITY OR BIAS.

Canon II is designed to get potential conflicts of interest on the table so that the parties can make a reasonable decision regarding whether or not to use the arbitrator selected or substitute another. Consequently, an arbitrator has a positive duty to disclose any financial, business, professional, family or social relationships that are likely to affect impartiality or which might reasonably create an appearance of partiality. Furthermore, the arbitrator must disclose conflicts when they become known, not just those that are apparent before the actual hearing. Nevertheless, once conflicts are disclosed, an arbitrator does not have to bow out as long as the parties agree and the arbitrator does not feel that he or she is compromised. This is a lower standard than the one applied to attorneys, who generally must withdraw regardless of whether or not they feel compromised. Furthermore, even when a client wants to retain an attorney regardless of any conflict, attorneys are still counseled to decline the representation.

CANON III.   AN ARBITRATOR, IN COMMUNICATING WITH THE PARTIES SHOULD AVOID IMPROPRIETY OR THE APPEARANCE OF IMPROPRIETY.

Canon III deals with the need to avoid communicating with one party without including all other parties in the communication. An arbitrator should avoid discussing the case without all parties being present. Likewise, letters and documents sent by the arbitrators to one party should be copied to all others, and communications received by the arbitrator from one party should also be copied to the others.

CANON IV.   AN ARBITRATOR SHOULD CONDUCT THE PROCEEDINGS FAIRLY AND DILIGENTLY.

Canon IV requires an arbitrator to be fair, evenhanded, diligent, prompt, patient and courteous. Parties should be treated equally with regard to notice, the right to be heard, and the right to counsel. Beyond mere procedural concerns, the arbitrator should determine if he or she has enough information to make a decision and if not, to delve more deeply into the case by asking questions, requesting documents and other measures. Canon IV also forbids an arbitrator from being privy to settlement negotiations that may commence between the parties.

CANON V.   AN ARBITRATOR SHOULD MAKE DECISIONS IN A JUST, INDEPENDENT AND DELIBERATE MANNER.

Under Canon V, an arbitrator is to decide only those issues submitted for determination. The decision should not be affected by any outside pressures, nor should it be delegated to anyone else. If the parties settle, the arbitrator may include the settlement award but is not required to do so.

CANON VI.   AN ARBITRATOR SHOULD BE FAITHFUL TO THE RELATIONSHIP OF TRUST AND CONFIDENTIALITY INHERENT IN THAT OFFICE.

Canon VI requires complete confidentiality of all matters relating to the arbitration. It also recognizes that the arbitrator is in a position of trust to the parties and should not use confidential information to gain any advantage for the arbitrator or anyone else. Canon VI also deals with the issue of fees, and counsels that fees should be determined and agreed to before the arbitrator accepts an appointment in order to avoid any coercion or other problem relating to payment.

CANON VII.   ETHICAL CONSIDERATIONS RELATING TO ARBITRATORS APPOINTED BY ONE PARTY.

Canon VII deals with the use of arbitration panels in which each party selects an arbitrator and they, in turn, select a (third) arbitrator. The canon recognizes that the members of a panel who are selected by a party are likely to be somewhat less neutral than the third arbitrator. Therefore, some ethical obligations do not apply to them. Specifically, they

♦   are permitted to be predisposed to the party that selected them, but they must act in good faith toward all of the parties.

♦ need not disclose conflicts in the same detail as required of neutral arbitrators, and they need not withdraw even if the party that did not select them requests it.

♦ may consult with the party that appointed them about the case, provided they inform the other party that such communications took place. Furthermore, they do not need to copy the other party on written communications sent or received.

Exercises

1. Compare the AAA Code of Ethics for Arbitrators in Commercial Disputes with the Code of Judicial Conduct for your state of residence. What similarities and differences do you find? What code imposes more stringent conflict-of-interest standards?

2. Review any laws in your state establishing court-annexed arbitration. What do these statutes say regarding the professional or ethical conduct of arbitrators? Review any state laws prescribing the use of arbitration to settle labor disputes. What standards are contained in these laws?

Conclusion

By and large, arbitration is the preferred method of resolving disputes that arise in commercial and industrial situations. In fact, it is safe to say that nearly every adult citizen who has ever contracted for services, opened a bank account, borrowed money, or obtained a credit card, has signed a contract that includes an agreement to arbitrate any disputes that may develop. Arbitration provides a businesslike way to evaluate the facts and interpret the terms of a contract. As compared with litigation, it is quick, economical, informal and private. It also preserves business relationships and can even improve how the parties do business in the future by clarifying the terms under which they cooperate. It can also motivate the parties to settle.

The American Arbitration Association reports that 30% of cases settle after the filing of a demand to arbitrate, due perhaps to the premise on which arbitration is based – that in any disagreement, both parties usually must bear a portion of the blame.

The next chapter will deal with various trial-like methods designed to promote settlement. It will also discuss how different ADR techniques have been combined to create new methods of resolving disputes.

Sources

[1] *Black's Law Dictionary* (6th ed. 1990).

[2] American Arbitration Association, A Guide to Arbitration for Business People, 3 (February 1993).

[3] A. Greenspan, *Handbook of Alternative Dispute Resolution*, 71 (1990).

[4] Arbitration vs. Mediation – Explaining the Differences, reprinted in A. *Alternatives to Litigation: Mediation, Arbitration, and the Art of Dispute Resolution*, at 104-106.

[5] *Id.*, at 110.

[6] B. Roth, R. Wulff, and C. Cooper, *The Alternative Dispute Resolution Practice Guide*, 2 (1993).

[7] *Id.*

[8] *Id.*

[9] *Burchell v. Marsh*, 58 U.S. (1 How.) 344 (1855).

[10] *Id.*, at 349.

[11] 9 USCA § 1 (West 1970).

[12] *Southland Corp. v. Keating*, 465 U.S. 1 (1984).

[13] *Allied-Bruce Terminix Co. v. Dobson*, 115 S. Ct 834 (1995).

[14] W.D. Tex. R. 300-9.

[15] See, *e.g.*, Colo. Rev. Stat. § 8-1-123 (West 1990).

[16] Ark. Code Ann. § 11-2-109 (Michie 1987).

[17] Del. Code Ann. tit. § 7701 (West Supp. 1993).

[18] American Arbitration Association, Commercial Arbitration Rules, Rule 13 (1996).

[19] American Arbitration Association, A Guide to Arbitration for Business People, 12 (1993).

[20] National Association of Securities Dealers, Compliance Manual: Rules of Fair Practice & Code Procedure 40(f) (July 1996).

[21] Dept. of Arbitration, N.Y.S.E. Arb. R. 127(f) (Sept. 1995).

[22] Points on a Continuum: Dispute Resolution Procedures and the Administrative Process, *reprinted in* A. Ordover, G. Flores, and A. Doneff, Alternatives to Litigation: Mediation, Arbitration, and the Art of Dispute Resolution, 123 (1993).

[23] *Mastrobuono v. Shearson Lehman Hutton, Inc.*, 115 S. Ct 1212 (1995).

[24] American Arbitration Association, Commercial Arbitration Rules, Rule 22 (1996).

[25] United States Arbitration Act, 9 U.S.C. § 6 (1994).

Chapter Six

Strategies for Settlement

Introduction

Although mediation and arbitration are the most frequently used forms of ADR that employ the assistance of neutral third parties, many other approaches have been developed that are tailor-made to particular disputes or disputants. Some of these are trial-like proceedings that result in a decision or opinion but are designed, nonetheless, to foster subsequent settlement talks between the parties. Like the ancient Anglo-Saxons who first went to court and then negotiated later in light of the outcome at law, many of the processes discussed below are designed to provide a dose of reality that prepares the parties to settle.

Because ADR is so flexible, many other approaches have been developed that combine the strengths of several methods. We have already seen how mediation is really a form of negotiation with assistance from a neutral third party. Likewise, arbitration borrows heavily from traditional litigation and trial techniques, but alters them in significant ways. Other variations of ADR combine mediation and arbitration to produce additional methods and hybrids. Several of these are also discussed below.

ADR advocates have devised a wide variety of programs to make ADR available to litigants and potential litigants at all levels of society. One of these – court-annexed ADR – has already been discussed at length in previous chapters. Others are discussed in the final section of this chapter.

Trial-Like ADR Methods

Of all of the methods for exploring settlement, minitrial is probably the most innovative and potentially useful method. While its application is limited, it provides a powerful tool for achieving mutually agreeable and lasting settlements in appropriate situations.

Minitrial

Minitrial, usually employed in large, complex cases, involves an exchange of information about the dispute conducted before a panel made up of senior executives of the disputing parties who then meet for settlement negotiations. The senior executives who comprise the panel are chosen because they have the authority to settle. Ideally, they will also have had little or no involvement in the dispute up to the point of minitrial. The information exchange occurs after a period of limited discovery and presents an abbreviated version of only the most important facts. If a lawsuit has been filed, there is generally a stay of those proceedings until the conclusion of the minitrial. Once the parties have agreed to employ minitrial, the period of time from their agreement to settlement might be as little as 90 days, although the length of the process will vary from case to case.

The first reported minitrial took place in the late 1970s concerning a patent infringement matter between two large public corporations, TRW and Telecredit. Telecredit had sued TRW for $6 million. Over the next three years the parties spent $500,000 on legal fees and other expenses and still were unable to resolve their differences. With trial seemingly inevitable, the lawyers for the parties invented the minitrial process in an attempt to avoid the courthouse. After a two-day minitrial the panel of executives from TRW and Telecredit negotiated a settlement in 30 minutes.

Since the TRW/Telecredit case, the minitrial has been used by other large corporations, government agencies and public institutions to resolve a wide variety of disputes. Nevertheless, the disputes most commonly submitted to minitrial have involved contract disagreements, patent infringement, and matters involving the federal government as a party. In the latter case, the government has routinely rejected binding arbitration as an appropriate forum for the resolution of disputes in which the government is involved. Minitrial offers the government an alternative to arbitration and litigation that is capable of dealing with complex technical disputes or multiparty matters that typify federal cases.

Minitrial contains elements of both conciliation and adjudication.[1] As compared with arbitration or trial, minitrial is a method of presenting a case for settlement by the parties rather than for a decision by a third party. Nevertheless, that presentation is usually adversarial in that each side presents only its strongest points and attempts to rebut the allegations of the other party. The panel members are then called upon to negotiate a settlement in light of the relative merits of each side's case.

The underlying goal of the minitrial presentations is to provide a basis on which the panel can assess the costs and risks of commencing or continuing litigation.[2] Because the panel is composed of senior executives who have not been involved in the litigation, they are better able to see the dispute in the context of broader company goals and interests. The panel of executives is usually moderated by an outside, neutral third party who presides over the case presentations and then meets with the executives to facilitate negotiation. In some cases, the neutral may be asked to present an opinion concerning the merits of each side's case or the terms of settlement proposed by the panel.

Uses for Minitrial
As with all types of ADR, minitrial is appropriate in some situations and not in others. Minitrial lends itself well to the following situations:

♦ Disputes where the parties, at least at the executive level, have the will to settle.[3]

♦ Disputes where the outstanding issues involve factual rather than purely legal questions or a mix of the two. Generally, if the dispute stems from different interpretations of the law, it can be disposed of more efficiently by filing a motion for summary judgment, which asks the court to rule on the nature of the law involved.[4]

♦ Disputes where the parties have had a long-term business relationship which they hope to continue.[5] Parties that know one another well have a stronger base on which to conduct negotiations. Furthermore, even though a minitrial is adversarial, its brevity and informality tend to mitigate the animosity that often develops during a trial.[6]

♦ Disputes where the cost of litigation and trial are likely to be very high.[7] This will generally mean cases where a large amount of money – usually exceeding $1 million – is at stake.

♦ Disputes that involve parties from more than one country. International parties are usually reluctant to try a case in another country's courts.[8]

♦ Disputes where the parties have differing estimations regarding the merits of their respective cases and would benefit from an adversarial presentation of the facts, which tends to expose the weaknesses of each party's position.[9]

♦ Disputes where senior decision makers with authority are available to settle a matter in the best interest of the organization.[10] Large corporations and institutions, both public and private, tend to fit this picture, simply because they are sizeable enough to insulate top executives from many of the day-to-day operations where disputes first arise. Consequently, these executives, though biased toward their own organizations, nevertheless can analyze the merits of the dispute much more dispassionately than the managers who have been embroiled in the matter. Due to their involvement, these lower-level managers will likely lack the perspective needed to see the path to settlement.[11]

♦ Disputes that would benefit from decision makers who are knowledgeable about the subject matter of the disagreement and about the customs of the industry also fit the minitrial scenario.[12] A panel made up of company executives clearly fits this profile. Disputes involving patents, high technology, construction contracts, and product liability are examples.[13]

Minitrial is likely to be unsuitable for cases that pit an individual against a large corporation or organization.[14] No matter how well represented, the individual's case is likely to be minimized by the brief presentation of the facts that characterize minitrials. Furthermore, if the matter involves personal injury, punitive damages are not available through a minitrial forum.[15] Finally, cases involving many parties are likely to be unsuitable for the use of minitrial due to the logistical problems of impaneling and carrying on negotiations involving executives from every organization represented.[16]

Initiating Minitrial

Like most forms of ADR, minitrial is usually voluntary. Any of the parties can propose minitrial at anytime during the life of a dispute. In more and more cases, however, the parties have agreed ahead of time to submit disputes arising under a contract or other transaction to minitrial, in which case, minitrial occurs early in the dispute and is initiated by notice of one party upon the other. Like most agreements to use ADR, minitrial agreements:

♦ establish the ground rules that will govern the process

♦ set out the need for discovery including any limits to be placed upon it

♦ establish a schedule for an exchange of documents

♦ provide for the format, site, and time for the proceeding

♦ provide for the selection of the neutral third party

♦ state the duties and responsibilities of the neutral third party

- set forth the conditions under which any party may terminate the proceeding or appeal the result

- provide for the confidentiality of the proceedings and the results, including the inadmissibility of any evidence in a subsequent trial and

- who will pay the costs and fees associated with the proceeding.

In addition, a minitrial agreement will specify who will serve on the panel from each disputing entity, by name, position or scope or responsibility. A minitrial agreement will also set forth a framework for the summary case presentations including whether live witnesses will be used and, if so, any limitations on cross-examination.

Agreements can be formal, or they may take the form of letters exchanged between the parties at the time that minitrial is proposed. In some cases, the neutral will propose the rules and, in others, the parties may agree to proceed under minitrial rules promulgated by one of several ADR organizations. For example, the American Arbitration Association (AAA) and Endispute (see Appendix 13 for additional information about these organizations) have both developed minitrial rules and procedures and will act as sponsor and facilitator for the proceedings in much the same way that they facilitate arbitration and mediation.

In addition to voluntary minitrials, some courts will order parties to engage in a minitrial before proceeding further with litigation. In these cases, the court may prescribe the rules and the format to be used. The advantage with rules being imposed from the outside is that the minitrial will not break down before it begins for lack of consensus about the process. Yet, studies have shown that parties are usually more satisfied with the outcome of a procedure in which they have significant control over the rules.[17]

Role of the Neutral Advisor

As discussed above, the panel of executives is usually moderated by a neutral third party. The neutral's knowledge and skills will depend upon the duties assigned to him or her by the parties' agreement.[18] For example, if the agreement requires the neutral to act as mediator during the panel negotiations, he or she should have extensive experience in mediating disputes involving complex matters. A requirement that the neutral render an opinion on the legal as well as factual merits of the case suggests that he or she should have legal training, or perhaps be a former judge. In some cases, the neutral may need to have extensive technical knowledge concerning the subject matter of the dispute, especially if he or she is expected to give an opinion on the most appropriate settlement option.

Executives on the Panel

A minitrial panel is usually composed of one executive from each party, as well as the neutral moderator. As discussed above, the executives assigned to serve on the negotiation panel should be senior-level managers with the authority to settle the case. Usually, this is not a problem with private organizations. However, if one of the parties is a governmental entity, such as a municipality, its representative on the panel may not be able to bind the municipality without the consent of an elected council. If the parties wish to employ a minitrial approach, their agreement will have to accommodate this contingency.

Because the executives will be negotiating with one another, it may be helpful if they have negotiation training. In lieu of this, the panel moderator can serve as mediator to facilitate the negotiation discussions. The panel members are usually permitted to invite other members of their management team to join them during negotiations. One or several sessions can be held until the parties reach agreement, or one or both break off discussions.

Preparing for Minitrial

A minitrial is an adversarial proceeding that requires thorough preparation. Because the parties are often large corporations, the attorney team is likely to include both inside and outside counsel to the companies. In many cases, a minitrial will be handled totally by the legal department of the corporation. In either situation, the active participation of inside counsel greatly improves access to information about the company and the ready availability of documentary evidence.

Discovery for a minitrial is abbreviated and limited to what is necessary for each party to put on its best case. The parties will confer and decide on a discovery schedule. If necessary, the neutral advisor will settle any disagreements that arise. All other discovery will be suspended until after the minitrial is concluded in the event that the parties do not settle. The attorneys will often prepare position papers and assemble critical documents that they will provide to the neutral advisor and which will usually be shared with the other side. They will also brief witnesses who are expected to testify and be cross-examined, and prepare any visual aids and other exhibits to enhance their presentations. Finally, the attorneys, the executive who will serve on the panel, and other key corporate decision makers will need to formulate settlement options.

Prior to the hearing, the executives on the panel will have access to position papers, to all discovery that has been exchanged, and to proprietary evidence gathered by their respective sides. Naturally, if any of this proprietary evidence is both damaging and also discoverable at a later date, it will certainly influence the bargaining position of the executive with knowledge of the evidence, and motivate him or her to settle rather than risk losing later at trial.

The Hearing

The hearing is typically called an "information exchange," which implies a cordial presentation of the facts of the case and the relevant evidence possessed by each side. Each party's counsel will present its best case in abbreviated form and the other party's counsel will be entitled to a rebuttal. The length and order of the presentations are usually determined by agreement. Witnesses, especially experts, are allowed. Slides, charts and other visual aids are typical. Each presentation usually proceeds uninterrupted. Executives on the panel are almost always permitted to ask questions of the other side, either during their rebuttal period, or throughout the hearing. The hearing concludes with closing arguments from each party's counsel. Minitrial proceedings are held in private and in most cases no stenographic record is made.

Settlement   Once a settlement is reached, the terms are set forth in a written agreement that is signed by the panel executives, preferably right after the conclusion of negotiations. As with all negotiated settlements, minitrial settlements, once signed, are legally binding and can be enforced in a court of law as any contract. If the parties have so stipulated, the terms of settlement will be kept confidential. Where one of the parties is a public entity, confidentiality is usually not possible and, therefore, is not so stipulated.

In the case of court-annexed minitrial, the agreement will usually be entered as the judgment of the court upon the request of the parties.

If negotiations fail, some minitrial agreements require a "cooling-off" period of several weeks before the parties can commence or continue litigation. The purpose is to give the executives an opportunity to think about the matter and initiate further negotiations before the cooling-off period expires. Expiration of the period does not preclude the parties from re-instituting negotiations at any point short of a court decision.

Sample Minitrial Schedule   The CPR Institute for Dispute Resolution (the "Institute"), a nonprofit organization of corporate counsel, lawyers, and law professors from leading companies, firms and law schools, has developed the following minitrial schedule, which is adapted and reprinted here with permission. The Institute also publishes its Model Minitrial Procedure, and Agreement to Initiate Minitrial Proceedings. See Appendix 13 for the address and telephone number of the Institute.

Sample Minitrial Schedule	
	Before the Information Exchange
Pre-Commencement	Parties' attorneys discuss possibility of minitrial and if agreed, select a Neutral Advisor [NA].
Commencement Date [CD]:	Parties sign initiating agreement.
CD + 10 Days:	Parties agree on Neutral Advisor [NA], if not named in the initiating agreement.
CD + 10 Days:	If litigation is pending, parties' attorneys move to stay proceedings.
CD + 15 Days:	Parties' attorneys agree on discovery plan including a 30-day discovery schedule.
CD + 20 Days:	Parties' attorneys send material on dispute to NA.
CD + 30 Days:	Parties' attorneys agree on place and date for minitrial.
CD + 30 Days:	Parties determine form of briefs and date for submission of briefs and exhibits.
CD + 45 Days:	Discovery is completed.
CD + 60 Days:	Parties exchange briefs and exhibits.
CD + 65 Days:	Parties give notice of advisors who will attend information exchange.
CD + 70 Days:	Information exchange begins.

Sample Minitrial Schedule		
At the Information Exchange		
CD + 70 Days:	9:00-12:00	Plaintiff's case-in-chief
	1:00-2:00	Defendant's rebuttal
	2:00-3:00	Open question and answer exchange
CD + 71 Days:	9:00-12:00	Defendant's case-in-chief
	1:00-2:00	Plaintiff's rebuttal
	2:00-3:00	Open question-and-answer exchange
Management Negotiations		
CD + 71 Days:	3:00-5:00	Negotiations
CD + 72-85 Days:	Negotiation period.	
CD + 85 Days:	Parties agree on settlement terms.	
CD + 90 Days:	A written settlement agreement is signed.	

Why Minitrial Over Arbitration or Mediation?

Minitrial offers large organizations several advantages over both arbitration and mediation.

♦ First of all, executives like to be in control rather than abdicate decision-making to third parties. Arbitration imposes a decision by an arbitrator, while mediation permits the neutral third party to exert significant influence over the final settlement. Minitrial, on the other hand, facilitates face-to-face negotiations between the principal parties, who are free to use the neutral advisor in any capacity they choose.

♦ Second, minitrial involves an objective, orderly, and businesslike presentation of a dispute that appeals to the nature of business executives. Arbitration is similar, but the emphasis is on persuading the arbitrator that your side should prevail rather than informing sound business decisions. A mediated settlement may also be unsatisfactory because the party representatives with authority to settle often do not have the information needed to make sound decisions, and the process does not allow for the presentation of all the required information. Mediation usually deemphasizes the legal and factual issues and seeks instead to explore more subjective issues such as motives and the underlying interests of the parties.

♦ Third, attorneys, including inside counsel to the parties, are comfortable with the presentation of the dispute in its legal context. Furthermore, the process casts the attorneys in roles familiar to them as trial advocates. Both arbitration and mediation often discount the rule of law in favor of other standards such as industry custom, fairness, and satisfaction. Furthermore, in mediation the lawyer's role is nonadversarial, which runs counter to a lawyer's training and experience.

Summary Jury Trial
Summary Jury Trial (SJT) is another trial-like method designed to foster settlement discussions between the parties. Unlike minitrial, which usually renders no third-party opinion, SJT provides disputants with an advisory verdict. Furthermore, the verdict is rendered by a "mock" jury, that is, nevertheless, drawn from the local jury pool. Consequently, the parties obtain a reasonable facsimile of the results that they will achieve at trial, which usually motivates the weaker side to proceed with settlement discussions.

Uses for SJT
SJT is a court-initiated process that is rooted in the Federal Rules of Civil Procedure (FRCP), which grants to each federal court the power to manage and control its docket.[19] The first reported use of SJT was in 1980 by the United States District Court for the Northern District of Ohio, which is credited with developing the process.[20] FRCP Rule 16(a) permits a court to hold pretrial conferences for the purpose, among others, of expediting the disposition of the action (Rule 16(a)(1)), and facilitating the settlement of the case (Rule 16(a)(5)). The Rule also permits participants to consider the use of extrajudicial procedures to resolve the dispute (Rule 16(c)(7)), and such other matters as may aid in the disposition of the action (Rule 16(c)(11)). The use of an advisory jury is specifically permitted in the Rules by motion of either the court or the parties (see FRCP Rule 39(c)).

SJT is useful where one or more of the parties has an unrealistic viewpoint about the merits of its case and will be influenced to settle only when the other side has presented their best evidence. In such cases, the attorneys are generally deadlocked and have exhausted traditional negotiations in their quest for settlement.

Judges, and parties, find SJT useful in those situations where there is disagreement or significant uncertainty about how a jury will respond to the evidence.[21] As Judge Lambros of the United States District Court for the Northern District of Ohio has commented, "The sole bar to settlement in many cases is the uncertainty of how a jury might perceive liability and damages."[22] This is especially true in cases where a jury must apply some standard of liability to a defendant's actions, such as the duty of "ordinary care" or the expectations of a "reasonable person."

Where punitive damages are sought in cases involving toxic waste, police brutality, employment discrimination, and other egregious activity, the plaintiff may be uncertain about how outraged a jury will be at the defendant's behavior. Judge Lambros points out that most parties assess their prospects at trial based on the outcome of supposedly similar cases handled by their attorneys.[23] Therefore, they are at the mercy of their counsel's experience, which may be insufficient or may not apply. SJT can be an effective way to overcome both uncertainty and inexperience.

SJT is especially helpful in large and complex cases, simply because it saves time and money. Like minitrial, SJT involves an abbreviated presentation of each party's best case. Thus, SJT can save the costs associated with a long drawn-out trial.

Unlike arbitration or minitrial, however, an SJT forum is composed of laypersons rather than experts. Therefore, enough evidence must be developed and presented to the jury so that it can render a reliable verdict. For this reason, some commentators believe that SJT is most effective only after the parties are substantially prepared for trial, including completing most discovery and finalizing all pending motions.[24] If this is the case, SJT may not be as efficient as other forms of ADR.

It goes without saying that SJT is inappropriate in cases where the parties have not demanded a jury trial. Likewise, SJT is inappropriate:

♦ where constitutional rights are involved that require formal court adjudication;

♦ where important precedent will be set;

♦ where a government agency or department is a party; and

♦ where the parties are too numerous or inaccessible to efficiently coordinate their participation.[25]

In addition, SJT is inappropriate in cases where witness credibility is the major concern, because most SJT proceedings expressly exclude testimony by live witnesses. However, the court can permit live testimony, which may be a prudent strategy if the primary issue of disagreement is how a jury will react to a critical witness.

Initiating SJT   As discussed above, SJT can be initiated by motion of either the court or the parties. Upon motion for an SJT, the court and counsel for the parties will determine if the process is appropriate to the case. If so, the judge will refer the matter to SJT by order of the court. The court order referring a case to SJT will often include a schedule for completing discovery and conducting the SJT, as well as procedural rules to be followed. Under the FRCP, and the rules of many of the states, a judge can order the parties to use SJT. However, it is questionable just how diligent the parties will be, given the intensity and amount of preparation required by an SJT proceeding. Throughout the federal district and circuit courts, there is disagreement regarding whether a court can actually require parties to use SJT over a party's objections.

Preparing for   Preparation for an SJT hearing is similar to preparing for trial. An SJT is an
SJT   abbreviated adversarial proceeding whose outcome affects the bargaining position of the parties.[26] Therefore, the attorneys will need to develop a persuasive presentation. Because no live witnesses are permitted, including the litigants, the presentation will need to include a review of the best evidence available that anticipates and rebuts what the other side will say.[27]

The parties will attend a pretrial hearing with the judge or magistrate assigned to the case and agree on a discovery schedule and other logistics for the SJT. Because no live witnesses are allowed, SJT discovery usually involves a few key depositions. As with minitrial, discovery is limited to only the most important documents, depositions and other evidence.

Depending upon the SJT rules of the jurisdiction, attorneys for the parties are usually required to prepare and submit trial briefs before the actual hearing covering the issues of law in the case. They also must prepare and submit jury instructions. In addition, they will need to develop exhibits, visuals and other material to aid their presentation. Finally, because SJT is primarily a settlement tool, the attorneys and their clients should clarify what the client hopes to obtain in the way of a settlement, and develop a realistic settlement range.

Choosing the Judge and Jury

The judge assigned to a case will often preside over the SJT, or will appoint a magistrate, a master, or other neutral third party to act in that capacity. The SJT is usually held in a courtroom to maintain the atmosphere of an actual trial. The parties will select a jury, generally made up of six members, from a panel of ten or more potential jurors. The panel will have been chosen from the court's regular jury pool. The court or counsel for the parties will question the ten potential jurors (called *voir dire*), and then the parties will each be allowed to eliminate two from the panel. The remaining six members of the panel will constitute the SJT jury. Due to the summary nature of the proceedings, *voir dire* is usually limited to 30 minutes.

The Hearing

During the hearing the attorneys will each be given approximately one hour, and longer if approved by the court, to present their case, along with a narrative overview of their proof and a summary of testimony that live witnesses are expected to give at trial. The allotted time includes rebuttal and closing arguments. Most SJTs last only four or five hours from opening to jury verdict.

The rules of evidence are somewhat relaxed during SJT. Likewise, formal objections to evidence are not encouraged. However, the judge will usually hear and consider objections if counsel deviates substantially from the rules of evidence.

Even though SJT uses a jury, the real purpose of the proceeding is to permit the parties to hear and compare their own case with that of their opponent's, and to observe the jury's reaction to the presentations. In this regard, SJT is similar in purpose to minitrial. Because SJT is designed to provide a dose of reality to the parties, most judges require that they attend the SJT. Furthermore, the parties in attendance must have authority to settle the case.

After each side presents its case, including rebuttal and closing argument, the jury is given an abbreviated charge and is sent off to deliberate. An SJT jury can return a consensus verdict or separate verdicts, depending upon the instructions of the court. In some cases, jurors may be asked to provide an opinion and/or rationale for their decision(s). Generally, no record is made of the SJT proceeding.

Settlement

Unlike minitrial, where negotiations take place immediately following presentation of the case, SJT usually does not provide for concurrent negotiations. However, because litigants are likely to be highly amenable to further negotiations immediately following the verdict, their attorneys may proceed to convene a negotiation session the same or following day.

In other cases, however, the attorneys together with the judge, may need additional time to evaluate the verdict. With a verdict in hand, a judge is in a position to press the attorneys to counsel settlement based on reality rather than on the attorneys' pretrial estimation of their chances.

In some situations, the parties will have stipulated that, if the jury reaches a unanimous verdict, it will be binding on the parties and entered as the judgment of the court. If this is the case, further negotiations will not be necessary, of course.

Advantages and Disadvantages of SJT

As compared with minitrial, SJT has had greater use and acceptance, largely because it has been embraced by the federal courts. Likewise, as an ADR technique, SJT has more widespread application than minitrial. Many state court systems include SJT as one of the ADR techniques to which judges may refer cases. Attorneys like SJT because it casts the dispute in its legal context, and calls upon them to play the familiar role of trial advocate.

Judges also like SJT because it provides a low, or no-risk method of realistically assessing a jury's reaction to a case without jeopardizing the right of the parties to a full-blown trial by jury. Furthermore, because SJT uses the same preparation required for trial, it does not add significantly to the cost of litigation. Finally, SJT provides the parties with the sense of having had their day in court and, therefore, they are more ready to proceed to serious negotiations.

One of the primary disadvantages of SJT concerns confidentiality. Like most other ADR proceedings, SJT sessions are not open to the public, and any settlement reached usually can be kept confidential. Jurors are cautioned not to discuss the case with anyone, and their names are sometimes kept secret. Nevertheless, courts generally cannot enforce juror confidentiality after an SJT is concluded, which means that the contents of the presentations, the verdict(s), and all jury deliberation are largely available. If the parties are unable to settle and proceed to trial, access to information from the SJT could jeopardize the ability of the parties to achieve a fair trial. This is especially critical in cases involving high-profile parties where media and public interest in the dispute is apt to be high.

In difficult cases where mediation has failed to achieve resolution and trial is contemplated, SJT can serve as an interim settlement method in order to avoid further litigation. For example, in 1996 a nonbinding summary jury trial helped settle a real estate case that had been pending for more than two years and had been to mediation five times. The parties were anticipating a two-week trial, when the judge ordered them to attempt settlement once more using SJT.

According to the account, neither the parties nor their lawyers believed that the effort would be productive.[28] The entire trial took less than five hours, not counting the time spent by the court selecting 12 jurors. Lawyers for each of the parties made 15-minute opening statements followed by presentation of the evidence, which took the plaintiff 45 minutes and the defendants about an hour. No witness took the stand, and the lawyers summarized their respective cases using enlarged key documents, deposition excerpts and a narrative description of pertinent facts. Each side was given 15 minutes of rebuttal and five minutes for closing arguments.

By 4 p.m. the case was in the hands of the jury, which took just 45 minutes to reach a verdict. The jury concluded that the sale of the property should proceed according to the contract involved. They also specified a price and recommended that each side should pay their own fees.

For the next hour, the lawyers were permitted to question the jurors who responded with a candid and often blunt assessment of the strengths and weaknesses of each side's case. After the jury was dismissed, the judge kept the parties in the courtroom and emphasized that if they did not settle, a traditional trial would commence in the morning. Not surprisingly, the two sides reached a settlement that night that was more or less consistent with the SJT verdict.

Legal Issues Concerning Summary Jury Trial

Because summary jury trials are often employed by both federal and state courts, questions often arise concerning the authority of a court to order an SJT, to compel the parties to attend and participate in SJT, and to keep the SJT proceedings and results confidential. Federal law empowers district courts to prescribe rules for the conduct of their business, and the Federal Rules of Civil Procedure permit district courts to make and amend local rules provided they are not inconsistent with other Federal Rules of Procedure. Federal Rule of Procedure 16 gives to trial courts the power to compel parties and their counsel to attend conferences designed to expedite the case and facilitate settlement, including using "special procedures" to assist in resolving the dispute. Many states have similar rules regarding the power and authority of their trial courts. The Alternative Dispute Resolution Act of 1998 now requires federal courts to establish ADR programs; however, it is unclear whether the requirements and restrictions of the Act include SJT.

Parties will sometimes object to court-ordered SJT on the grounds that it will force them to reveal confidential work product. As courts adopt more and more liberal discovery rules, however, this and similar arguments are losing their strength to persuade judges to bypass SJT for a full-blown trial. Other cases challenging the authority of the court to order SJT have been overturned on the grounds that SJT constitutes a form of settlement conference anticipated by Rule 16. Once SJT has been ordered, courts have also been given the power to compel attendance. For example, the Seventh Circuit Court of Appeals upheld a ruling ordering a New Jersey defendant to attend a SJT in Wisconsin, because any hardship to him was far outweighed by the burden on the court of an excessively long trial involving complex legal and factual issues.[29]

By law, trials are open to the public, which has raised questions about public access to summary jury trial proceedings and verdicts. The issue first arose in an Ohio federal district court case where the local media challenged the confidentiality of a court-ordered SJT. The Sixth Circuit rejected the challenge on the grounds that SJT was more akin to a settlement conference because it was nonbinding, and, therefore, the public had no right of access, even though the case involved public policy issues.[30] In 1996, the Sixth Circuit upheld its ruling in *Cincinnati Gas*, when it vacated an order to hold a SJT in public after the local media had once again challenged the confidentiality of the proceedings.[31] Agreements reached in SJT have been held confidential also on the grounds that confidentiality is necessary to maintain the utility of SJT as a settlement device.

Exercises

> 1. SJT is supposed to foster settlement by immersing parties in the trial experience. In what ways does SJT simulate a trial experience? In what ways does it appear to fall short of the real thing?
>
> 2. Typically, courts resort to SJT as a way to break a deadlock in negotiations. Is this the most efficient use of SJT, or should courts raise the possibility of SJT much earlier in the life of a lawsuit? What is the likely effect on the parties and their attorneys if they know from the start that an SJT is likely?
>
> 3. Why would a judge refer parties to SJT rather than mediation? In what ways, if at all, does the use of one preclude the other?
>
> 4. SJT and minitrial are often confused with each other. Discuss the similarities and differences between them.

Moderated Settlement Conference

Moderated Settlement Conference (MSC) is another trial-like process designed to encourage settlement. It appears to have been invented in Houston as part of the ongoing Texas experiment with ADR. Nevertheless, MSC is cropping up in other jurisdictions throughout the United States.

The uniqueness of MSC lies in the nature of the panel that hears the case presentations. While minitrial uses a panel composed of party executives, and SJT uses lay jurors, MSC employs the services of three experienced attorneys who evaluate the legal merits of the case. The strength of MSC is that it assists the parties to define the central issues of a lawsuit, and to provide them with a professional evaluation of the strengths and weaknesses of their case.

Uses of MSC

Like SJT, MSC has a wide application. MSC has been used successfully in domestic relations matters, personal injury cases, consumer litigation, commercial disputes, and anytime a neutral opinion regarding the application of the law to the facts of a case would be beneficial.[32] Furthermore, MSC can be used to evaluate the entire case or a portion of it, such as comparative negligence, the amount of damages, the merits of a counterclaim or cross-claim, and so forth. By deciding or eliminating ancillary matters, subsequent negotiations or trial can focus on the most critical issues.

MSC can even be used prior to filing suit or to determine whether or not to appeal an adverse verdict. Furthermore, the success of MSC does not require that the parties be interested in settling. Even a battle-thirsty litigant can see value in obtaining a professional evaluation of his or her case, only to be swayed toward settling when the evaluation reveals problems.

In short, MSC is appropriate whenever a neutral, lawyerly evaluation of the merits of a case would be helpful.[33] As with other ADR methods, MSC is inappropriate where the need to establish legal precedent through a court-rendered decision is paramount.

Initiating MSC

Prior to filing suit, either party can contact the other to discuss the possibility of using MSC as a method of exchanging information about the case and for exploring early settlement possibilities. If a lawsuit has been filed, a moderated settlement conference can be initiated by motion of either of the parties, or on motion of the court. A party can oppose the use of MSC, generally by filing a written objection with the court within some specified period of time. Sometimes a party will be amenable to ADR but will object to the form of ADR that has been proposed. It is up to the parties and the court to determine which method of ADR is most appropriate in each case.

After it has been determined to proceed with MSC, the judge or court coordinator will set a date, time, and place for the conference. Sometimes an MSC will take place in a local courtroom to lend an air of authenticity to the proceedings. Nevertheless, like most ADR proceedings, an MSC will be held in private and the results will be kept confidential. The judge assigned to the case will learn about the results of the case only from the next step taken by the parties; a motion to dismiss, to nonsuit, to enter the settlement as the judgment of the court, or a request to reinstate the case on the trial docket.

Appointing the Panel

An MSC panel is made up of three attorneys, at least two of whom are experienced in the law of the case before them. Thus, a personal injury case will be heard by attorneys with practice experience in personal injury, while a contract case will be presented to a panel with business litigation experience. The litigants will be given a list of potential panel members, called "moderators," from which they will strike the names of those they do not want to use.

Reasons for striking a name include conflict of interest or some appearance of bias. Once the parties have indicated their preferences, the court will select the panel. One member will usually be appointed administrator to oversee the details of arranging for the conference. Moderators generally serve on a volunteer basis, although most ADR statutes permit the court to require compensation if appropriate.

Preparing for the Conference

An MSC is an adversarial proceeding in which each side presents its best case in abbreviated form. In this regard, MSC is identical to minitrial and SJT. The attorneys and their clients should begin by thoroughly reviewing their case, including the facts, legal issues, and remedies sought. The attorneys will then prepare a summary case memorandum for the moderator panel covering any stipulated facts, issues and facts that are in dispute, legal theories relied on and the status of settlement discussions. Often, the memorandum will be prepared jointly. If not, each side should prepare a memorandum and share it with the other party as well as the moderators.

The summary case memorandum is generally the only party-provided material that the moderators will see before the conference. If the case is particularly complex, the moderators may request copies of depositions and other documents and also review pertinent statutes and case law on their own.

In addition to preparing the case memorandum, attorneys for the litigants will need to prepare exhibits, visuals, and other aids to their presentation. The only live witnesses allowed at an MSC are the litigants who, if they are expected to testify, should also be prepared. Finally, the attorneys and their clients should clarify what the client hopes to obtain in the way of a settlement and develop a realistic settlement range.

The Conference As compared with minitrial and SJT, a moderated settlement conference is an even more abbreviated presentation of the facts and arguments of each side's case. An MSC begins with a brief opening statement by one of the panel members. Attorneys for plaintiff then have up to 30 minutes to present their case, followed by defendant's presentation of equal length. After the panel has questioned both sides, the plaintiff and defendant each have five minutes to sum up. Panel deliberations generally take another 30 minutes, followed by presentation of their opinion(s). Unless the case is particularly complex, most MSCs last no more than four hours.

During the question-and-answer period, the panel is free to ask questions of the attorneys and their clients. Because MSC is designed to foster settlement, it is imperative that the parties attend and have the authority to settle the case. The panel will evaluate whatever the parties have asked them for, from level of liability to amount of damages. If one side is considering appeal, the panel will deliver an opinion on the probability of the appeals court sustaining the lower court's decision.

Settlement Armed with the panel's opinion about the merits of the case, the parties enter the settlement phase. If they reach agreement, the accord will be written down and executed. As with most settlement agreements, the parties can decide whether to simply dismiss the case or ask the court to enter an agreed judgment. If the panel's opinion is unanimous, the parties can agree ahead of time to accept it and settle the case accordingly.

Even if the parties do not settle, an MSC can help to narrow the issues at trial, which saves time and money on additional discovery. An MSC can also result in more facts being stipulated, thus eliminating the need to prove them up. Furthermore, little if any of the preparation for MSC is wasted when the case later goes to trial. MSC is an excellent approach for the new litigator because it enables them to obtain an evaluation of the case from experienced attorneys.

Private Judging Private judging is included in this text because it is, in one sense, an alternative method of dispute resolution. Nevertheless, it is like traditional litigation and trial in that it results in a judge-rendered decision that is binding on the parties. Furthermore, it does not, like the other ADR methods and hybrids considered in this chapter, directly and intentionally promote settlement. In fact, private judging may tend to dilute many of the pressures to settle that come with the costs and delays associated with public justice.

Private judging involves the use of an attorney, former judge, or a nonattorney expert paid by the parties to perform an adjudicative role as temporary judge or referee.[34] Private judging assumes that a lawsuit has been filed. However, the parties have determined that the public court system cannot deal optimally with the dispute.[35] Therefore, on motion of the parties, a private judge stipulated in the motion is appointed by the court to hear the case.

Private judging is provided for by statute in approximately one-half of the states. Some of the earliest statutes go back to the 19th century in New York (1848) and California (1872). Statutes vary from jurisdiction to jurisdiction in terms of the qualifications required of the judges, the matters that can be referred to private judges, whether or not a jury trial is available, and whether or not a private judge can award attorneys' fees.

Private judging is not to be confused with an appointment by the court of a referee or master to either handle pretrial matters, or actually hear the case and propose a possible outcome to the judge. In these situations, the referee or master is chosen by the court and serves at its behest. Furthermore, the decisions of referees and masters are purely advisory and usually must be ratified by the judge. In private judging, on the other hand, the judge is chosen by the parties and is accountable to them. In addition, the decision of the private judge is final and cannot be overruled by the public trial court that appointed the private jurist. As with any other decision at the trial court level, a private trial verdict can be challenged only on appeal to the next highest court.

Uses of Private Judging

Private judging has been used in a wide variety of cases from highly complex commercial disputes to family and domestic matters. However, it is better suited to some matters than to others.

♦ First, private judging may be the answer in cases where a quick decision is needed. An example would be a dispute involving distribution rights of a recently released video that will have to be withheld from the market until a decision is reached, resulting in lost profits for everyone involved. Conversely, a domestic relations case where there is a risk that one of the parents may flee with a child is probably not a good choice for private judging, simply because you want the full weight of the court behind you.

♦ Second, private judging lends itself to cases that are highly technical or complex, because the parties can select a judge who has expertise in judging similar matters and who will make the case a top priority.

♦ Private judging is a good choice where the parties want a court-rendered judgment but also want the trial to be closed to the press and the public. For example, where the defendant's reputation may be damaged by evidence to be presented at trial, private judging offers privacy and confidentiality. Critics of private judging point out, however, that cases involving matters of public policy, such as environmental violations, should be aired openly and the violators should not be given the protection afforded by private judging.

♦ Finally, privately judged trials are a good choice in matters involving many parties and witnesses where the logistics and costs of assembling them for trial are more reasonable when the parties control the schedule.

Initiating a Private Judge Trial

In most jurisdictions, a motion for a private judge must be agreed to by all of the parties. If a party desires to use a private judge, their attorney should contact counsel for the other side and discuss the possibility, along with suggested candidates. Once they have reached agreement and recruited a private judge, a motion to the court requesting a referral should be prepared.

A motion for a private judge generally must contain a waiver of a right to a trial by jury. It must also state the issues that the parties want the private judge to consider, the proposed time and place of trial, and the name of the proposed judge. The court will consider the motion, taking into account the nature of the dispute, its complexity, the number of parties involved, whether enough discovery has been made to permit an accurate evaluation of the case, the extent of past negotiations, and the status of the case on the trial court docket.[36] A judge who concurs with the motion will enter a referral order.

Selecting the Judge   Often the parties will know of a judge they want to use. If not, organizations such as the American Arbitration Association, Endispute, and the Center for Public Resources maintain lists and resumes of private judges available in most major urban jurisdictions in the United States. Once the parties agree on a candidate, they should contact the judge jointly, or request that the listing agency coordinate the request.

The qualifications of a private judge may be prescribed by statute. For example, in Texas a private judge must be a former or retired district court judge who has sat for a minimum of four years as a district or appeals court jurist, has not left the judgeship under questionable circumstances, has substantial experience in an area of specialty, and has complied with a continuing legal education requirement.[37]

The litigants pay the private judge an hourly rate. Therefore, the fees charged by a judge may be another factor to consider in selecting a private jurist. In the public courts the services of judges are paid by taxpayers.

The Trial   Trials conducted by a private judge may take place in a courtroom or at the offices of the judge. The rules of civil procedure and evidence for the jurisdiction will apply, and a court reporter will be present to create a record of the event. Nevertheless, some of the formality associated with a public trial including the dress code are usually relaxed. For example, it is unlikely that the judge will wear a robe. The judge generally has all of the powers of a public court judge conducting a bench trial, except perhaps the power to find someone in contempt of court. As indicated above, the judge's verdict is binding on the parties and enforceable as any other judgment.

Advantages of Private Judging   There are many advantages to using a private judge.

♦ First, litigants choose who hears their case rather than taking their chances with the process of randomly assigning cases employed by most public court systems. The skill and reputation of a judge is a critical factor in the outcome of any case.

♦ Second, litigants are also likely to be more satisfied or accepting of a private judge's verdict, simply because they have selected the decision maker. Greater satisfaction means less money spent on costly appeals or on enforcement actions.

♦ Third, private judges are usually experienced in hearing the types of disputes they adjudicate. Thus, the parties do not have to bear the expense of educating a generalist judge or jury. Furthermore, the judge is likely to be more interested in the matter and, therefore, more likely to render a well thought-out decision.

♦ Fourth, because the litigants have a high degree of control over when the trial takes place, the expense associated with assembling witnesses to accommodate the schedule of the court is minimized. Also, litigants spend less money on legal fees paid to attorneys who must keep refreshing their memory of the matter while awaiting trial one, two or three years away.

♦ Fifth, the parties have the benefit of presenting all pretrial motions and discovery matters to the same judge who will preside at the trial. This achieves more consistency of results and serves to educate the judge about the case. In a traditional trial, several different masters and referees may hear motions, rather than the judge who will preside over the trial.

♦ Finally, private judge trials are usually confidential, at least until a judgment is rendered. For parties who want a full blown trial but also desire privacy, private judging may be the best choice.

Disadvantages of Private Judging

Despite the advantages of private judging, there are several disadvantages that litigants should consider before choosing this approach:

♦ First, one of the key disadvantages of private judging is the unavailability in most jurisdictions of a private jury trial. Thus, a privately judged trial is always a bench trial. In matters where litigants feel they will achieve more from a jury, especially in the way of damages, they will simply have to forego the other advantages of private judging and wait their turn in public court.

♦ Another disadvantage is the possibility of selecting a judge who will not perform as expected. Sometimes a private jurist will prove to be more deferential to one side than the other, especially if he or she has received business in the past from one of the attorneys involved. In other situations, the judge may prolong the trial in order to earn a larger fee, or simply take an inordinate amount of time to issue a decision. A mandamus action is generally not available to redress these problems, and they may not be apparent in the record in case a party desires to appeal an adverse verdict.

Comparison of Private Judging to Arbitration

Private judging has often been compared to binding arbitration. In both, the parties seek a binding decision by a selected third party. The private judge, like the arbitrator, is apt to be an expert in the subject matter of the dispute. Also, both private judging and arbitration provide flexibility in scheduling so as to accommodate the parties.

There are differences, however:

♦ First, a trial presided over by a private judge is identical to a traditional trial in length, formality, rules of procedure, and rules of evidence. By comparison, the arbitration hearing is often informal and run according to rules selected or developed by the parties. Furthermore, arbitration usually takes less time than trial because the parties present only their best evidence. Also, live witness testimony is limited in arbitration.

♦ Second, the private judge must apply substantive law, while an arbitrator can disregard legal precedence and craft a decision based on alternative standards.

♦ Third, the decision of a private judge can be appealed to a higher court, while an arbitrator's award can be challenged only in limited situations.

♦ Fourth, the private court decision is enforceable as any other judgment, whereas an arbitrator's decision must be enforced in a special proceeding for that purpose.

♦ Fifth, private judging has broad application, including matters where the stakes are high. By comparison, because the decision of the arbitrator is largely unappealable, arbitration is seldom used in "bet-the-farm" situations.

Early Neutral Evaluation

Courts have long been aware that parties involved in a dispute, as well as their attorneys, usually have a one-sided view of the conflict that prevents them from pursuing settlement early in the life of a lawsuit. Furthermore, the parties are often unrealistic about the strengths and weakness of their case. Consequently, they will not be open to strategies that encourage settlement, such as negotiation, mediation, or any of the techniques discussed in this chapter unless an experienced, neutral fact finder evaluates the case and offers an opinion about its merits. In order to aid in the process, courts have developed a variety of techniques to provide evaluation services to disputants.

Early neutral evaluation (ENE) is one of the best known methods. ENE refers to a variety of programs used in various federal and state courts since the early 1980s that are designed to encourage the parties to a lawsuit to resolve their differences as early as possible. The authority to institute these programs is derived from the inherent power of a court to control its docket. In federal court such power comes from:

♦ Federal Rules of Civil Procedure Rule 16(a)(5) (FRCP) to "facilitate the settlement of the case;"

♦ FRCP Rule 16(c)(7) to take appropriate action with respect to "the identification of witnesses and documents, the need and schedule for filing and exchanging pretrial briefs, and the date or dates for further conferences . . .;" and

♦ FRCP Rule (16)(c)(9) to take appropriate action with respect to settlement and the use of special procedures to assist in resolving the dispute when authorized by statute or local rule."

The authority in state courts to institute ENE programs is derived from rules that are similar to the federal rules.

The first ENE program was developed in 1982 in the United States District Court for the Northern District of California. A committee organized by the court evaluated litigation and identified several factors that make it difficult for attorneys and their clients to resolve their disputes early rather than later, after considerable monetary and psychological expense. Specifically, the committee determined that:

♦ Pleadings, made up of the complaint, the answer and any counterclaims and cross claims, typically do not provide any significant detail to explain what the parties' positions are and what they are relying on to support those positions. Even federal pleadings, which generally must be more specific than state court pleadings, still don't communicate needed information. Consequently, the parties must launch an expensive process of gathering information simply to understand their opponent's point of view.[38]

♦   The psychological barriers that exist between the parties as a result of their dispute, as well as the lack of time that most disputants have to focus on resolving their problems, make it difficult for the parties and their attorneys to discuss the dispute with the other party. To the disputants who are often angry and in pursuit of justice, it is easier to pay an attorney to launch a formal discovery process than to confront their opponent.[39]

ENE involves a confidential case evaluation conference ordered by the court. In most ENE programs, the parties are required to attend along with their attorneys. In other programs, the parties are permitted to send representatives with the authority to make decisions about issues to pursue, discovery, and settlement.

The ENE conference is presided over by an "evaluator" who is an attorney or former judge chosen and appointed by the court. Ideally, the evaluator has had extensive experience in litigating, trying, or hearing civil disputes of similar size and scope as the present case. In some courts, the ENE conference occurs after suit has been filed but prior to any scheduling conference before the judge. In others, the ENE is held after limited discovery, while in some courts, ENE does not occur until discovery is complete. In the latter case, the benefits of ENE to save on discovery costs are largely unrealized and make sense only in those matters where there is a high probability of disposing of some or all of the lawsuit via a motion to dismiss or motion for summary judgment. Such situations are rare, however.

Frequently, the parties are required to submit a brief paper to the neutral evaluator prior to the ENE conference outlining their position(s) and the legal theories and evidence to support those positions. At the conference, each party is usually given up to 30 minutes to present its positions, at which point the neutral evaluator:

♦   helps the parties to identify the most important legal theories that support the client's position;

♦   assists the parties to clarify the facts;

♦   evaluates the strengths and weaknesses of the arguments and evidence;

♦   estimates the likelihood of liability and range of possible damages; and

♦   proposes a discovery plan aimed at gathering the information needed to settle the matter.

One of the important goals of the evaluator is to whittle the case down to manageable size. Thus, the evaluator will encourage the parties to stipulate to those facts on which they agree. He or she will also encourage the parties to compromise and settle ancillary issues where they are already close to agreement. Cases that are reduced to their essentials will reduce the time and expense associated with discovery, pretrial hearings and trial itself. They are also easier to settle because the parties can focus on what is most important.

As with any strategy that gets the parties together and talking to one another, ENE provides many benefits. In addition to those discussed above, ENE:

♦   Motivates the attorneys to investigate the case early on rather than fire off admissions, interrogatories, and requests for production of documents in knee-jerk fashion;

- ◆ Provides the parties with the opportunity to share information with one another rather than play "hide the ball";

- ◆ Gets the clients involved in the process as strategists and decision makers;

- ◆ Simulates for clients the experience of "having their day in court"; and

- ◆ Gives each side a better understanding of their opponent's position, as well as a neutral evaluation of the strengths and weaknesses of each side's case.

Typically, a neutral evaluator remains available to the parties throughout the course of a lawsuit if the parties and the court agrees. For example, after more discovery has been taken, the parties may want the evaluator to estimate liability and damages again.

Although a neutral evaluator has no power to issue binding orders of any kind, he or she can play a key role in shaping the course of the lawsuit by streamlining discovery and influencing how the parties view their positions relative to one another. Furthermore, by coaxing the parties to stipulate facts, eliminate ancillary issues and agree on joint discovery, the evaluator can change the goal of the parties to one of settlement rather than trial.

Exercises

> 1. How is ENE similar to mediation in its aims? How is it different? Compare and contrast the role and power of the ENE evaluator to that of a mediator.
>
> 2. In what way is ENE similar to Moderated Settlement Conference? Is it a substitute for MSE or does ENE serve other purposes? Compare and contrast the role and power of the ENE evaluator to that of the MSE panel.
>
> 3. What are the advantages of ENE over pre-trial management conferences before the judge? Does ENE serve other purposes?
>
> 4. Does the federal district court in your area provide for ENE? If so, obtain a copy of its general rule and orders for ENE. Find out if any of the state district courts in your area use ENE or similar early disposition strategies aimed at clarifying issues and outlining future discovery.

ADR Hybrids

As we have seen throughout this text, ADR exists because of the need and desire to promote the amicable settlement of disputes. Sometimes, however, no one method of ADR can completely satisfy the special circumstances of a particular set of parties. Consequently, new methods are devised to meet these needs. The techniques discussed in this chapter combine elements of trial with elements of ADR in order to promote agreement. Likewise, additional methods of ADR have been created that borrow elements from various types of ADR. These hybrid methods usually try to combine the strengths of each traditional ADR method from which they borrow.

Med-Arb

Med-Arb, which dates back at least to 1972, is an approach to dispute resolution that combines mediation with binding arbitration. Not surprisingly, it was first proposed in the context of labor disputes where arbitration has long been the acceptable method of resolving disagreements.

In Med-Arb, the mediator serves as arbitrator if mediation breaks down and becomes deadlocked on any or all of the issues. The authority of the mediator to both mediate and, if necessary, to also make a final binding decision, is granted by the parties in the Med-Arb agreement, and encompasses only those issues contained in the agreement.

Thus, a settlement reached through Med-Arb can combine consensus reached through mediation on some of the issues, and one or more decisions by the mediator/arbitrator on other issues where the parties were unable to agree. The mediator/arbitrator is the only one with the power to declare a deadlock with regard to an issue, thereby reserving its resolution for the arbitration phase. Generally, all aspects of the settlement, whether reached through mediation or arbitration, are enforceable as an ordinary arbitration award.

Med-Arb has several advantages over just mediation or just arbitration. These include:

♦ Greater flexibility in designing the process, because the parties can borrow from both mediation and arbitration.

♦ Assurance that the effort will not be wasted, because a binding decision will result, one way or another.

♦ More incentive to be both thorough and honest with the mediator, knowing that if agreement is not reached, the same person will be making the final decision.

♦ More incentive to settle during mediation, knowing that if agreement is not reached, someone else will make the decision for you.

♦ If arbitration is required, the elimination of most, if not all of the hearing phase, because the mediator/arbitrator has already heard the parties' stories and evaluated the evidence.

♦ As stated above, a decision that will have the force of an arbitration award, as compared with a mediated agreement which is enforceable merely as a contract.

Consideration of Med-Arb occurs in several ways. In some situations, the parties will want Med-Arb from the very beginning, while in others, the parties will agree first to mediate, or to arbitrate and then realize that their dispute may not be adequately served by just one method. For example, they may have chosen arbitration because they desire a final and binding decision made by an expert. However, they realize that some of the issues involved are amenable to negotiation provided a neutral party aids their discussions. Conversely, the parties may have selected mediation and then become concerned that trial may still be necessary if they cannot agree.

One of the criticisms of Med-Arb is that the parties will have revealed their true positions to the mediator/arbitrator during mediation, thus compromising his or her neutrality if later called upon to make a final and binding decision. Some argue, however, that knowledge of the parties' bottom lines will likely help the arbitrator to make a decision that is more satisfying to everyone. By knowing each party's settlement range, the arbitrator is more likely to avoid a decision that tries to give a little something to everybody but satisfies no one.

Another criticism of Med-Arb is that a mediator typically does not study the law applicable to the dispute, nor makes judgments about the quality of the evidence presented. Consequently, he or she is likely to make a bad decision if called upon to render an award as an arbitrator.

Med-Then-Arb   Med-Then-Arb is a process that is similar to Med-Arb, except that it uses a different third-party to arbitrate any issues that have not been resolved through mediation. Med-Then-Arb was developed out of concern for the lack of neutrality that a mediator/arbitrator will have as a result of learning each party's confidential positions during private caucuses. It is also a response to the dearth of neutral third parties who are qualified as both mediators and arbitrators.

The primary criticism of Med-Then-Arb is the high cost in both time and money of having to educate the arbitrator about the dispute. One way to avoid these drawbacks is to appoint both an arbitrator and mediator who serve together during the mediation. The arbitrator, however, does not participate in any private caucuses and is not informed of what transpires in them. If the parties are unable to reach agreement during mediation, the arbitrator takes over and decides any unresolved issues. This approach has been called Co-Med-Arb.

Arb-Med   Arb-Med reverses the process of Med-Arb and begins with traditional arbitration first. Before issuing a final decision, the arbitrator/mediator attempts to mediate the dispute, or at least those issues where a negotiated agreement appears possible.

Arb-Med has many drawbacks. First, it is more expensive than Med-Arb because it requires formal presentation of each party's case and evidence. Second, the parties are less likely to be flexible about their position and settlement ranges after formally presenting their case at an arbitration hearing. Third, the parties are highly likely to treat the mediation phase as a time to influence the arbitrator/mediator's decision rather than to mediate in good faith.

One way to avoid these drawbacks is to appoint a "shadow mediator" who will sit in on an arbitration proceeding. If an issue arises that appears to be more amenable to mediation or, if one of the parties desires to mediate a particular issue, the shadow mediator will take over and attempt to resolve the matter before the arbitration continues. As with Med-Then-Arb, this method is expensive because it requires paying two neutral third parties.

Concilio-Arbitration   Concilio-Arbitration is a method that involves mediation, after which the mediator issues a draft award on any matters left unresolved. The award can be accepted by all of the parties or rejected by all of the parties. However, if one party rejects the award, arbitration or litigation will ensue. Unless the rejecting party is able to significantly improve his or her results (usually by one-third) as compared with the award, the rejecting party will be responsible for all costs associated with the arbitration or litigation.

"Baseball Arbitration"   Baseball arbitration refers to a variation on standard arbitration where the arbitrator receives an offer submitted by each of the parties after presentation of each party's case, and decides on which offer should constitute the award. This approach assumes that none of the parties will submit too outlandish a bid for fear of having it rejected by the arbitrator. It also eliminates "split-the-difference" decisions by an arbitrator who wants to try and satisfy everyone.

There are several variations on baseball arbitration, including "last offer" arbitration where the arbitrator selects as the award the last offer presented by one of the parties. If preceded by mediation, this approach is called "medaloa" (*med*iation *a*nd *l*ast *o*ffer *a*rbitration).

Another variation is "high-low" arbitration where the parties agree ahead of time on what the award will be if the defendant is found liable or not liable. If the arbitrator determines that the defendant is liable, the award is the higher amount; if not liable, the award is the lower amount. The plaintiff gets something and the defendant is protected from unlimited liability.

ADR Programs

Proponents of ADR who believe that it offers many people the best hope they have of resolving their disputes amicably have long sought to make ADR available to citizens involved in all types of conflict and at all levels of society. Court-annexed ADR, which is increasing in the United States, represents one of the most aggressive attempts by the judicial and legal establishment to espouse ADR and to provide encouragement for its use. Some courts have gone farther, however. The following discussion describes two additional approaches used by various court systems to promote the use of ADR.

Multi-Door Courthouse

Multi-door courthouse is the name given to a concept proposed by Harvard law professor Frank E. A. Sanders in 1976 at the first Pound Conference, which was convened by the American Bar Association to discuss ADR. Professor Sanders envisioned a dispute resolution system that encompassed a variety of processes and that would utilize the method most appropriate to each dispute.

Professor Sanders' proposal led to the development in 1982 of three "test markets" under the sponsorship of the American Bar Association for the multi-door courthouse concept. Sites selected included Houston, Texas; Tulsa, Oklahoma; and Washington D.C. Although each location developed a unique approach, all three involved the successful coordination of a variety of dispute resolution services and processes.[40] Since then, other programs styled on one or more of these early models have been developed in several jurisdictions throughout the United States.

Most multi-door courthouse programs involve a central intake office or department, usually administered by the federal, county or city court(s), which interviews citizens who have complaints and then recommends one or more methods for resolving the dispute. In many situations, recommendations are likely to include a referral to a legal or community resource, such as a justice of the peace, small claims court, legal aid service, lawyer referral program, district attorney, community dispute resolution center, family counseling service, battered women's shelter, and others.

In some multi-door courthouse programs, intake specialists are trained to conciliate disputes on the spot or over the telephone. More complex disputes, or matters where suit has already been filed are evaluated by the intake specialists for referral to an appropriate ADR process, often by order of the court. In some cases, the parties may be counseled to forego ADR and proceed to trial, especially if the dispute involves differing interpretations of the applicable law, which only a judge can decide.

In order to recommend the best approach for resolving a dispute, intake personnel will seek to understand the history of the conflicts including how long the problem has existed, who is involved, how serious the problem is, and what efforts have been made so far to resolve the matter.[41]

Other factors considered include the financial strength of the parties, their willingness to participate in resolving the dispute, whether physical threats or property damage has occurred or may occur in the future, and how much evidence must be assembled to support either party's side of the argument.[42]

The Multi-Door Division of the Superior Court of the District of Columbia has developed a system for matching lawsuits with the most appropriate ADR method. The system takes into account ten "objective" factors and nine "subjective" factors. Based on the court's experience with ADR over many years, the system weighs each factor as to whether it suggests the use of mediation, arbitration or some form of neutral case evaluation (NCE). The following table, which is based on the Washington D.C. court's model, matches each factor to the preferred ADR method. (The number of asterisks indicates the level of preference.)

OBJECTIVE FACTORS	MED	ARB	NCE
Dispute involves multiple plaintiffs or defendants	*		
One or more party is pro se	*		
Case involves more than monetary issues	**		
Relationship between the parties will continue	***		
Dispute involves highly technical/scientific questions		*	*
More than one issue is involved	*		
Insurance company is partially or totally liable		*	*
Case involves a contract dispute	*		
Case involves tort where liability is in question		*	*
Case involves tort where liability is not in question		**	*
SUBJECTIVE FACTORS	MED	ARB	NCE
Parties desire a quick resolution		*	
Party(s) want to keep the outcome private	*		*
Parties desire the nonbinding opinion of an expert			**
Parties desire to minimize pretrial discovery		*	
Parties want to have a say in the outcome of the case	*		
Parties desire to preserve their relationship	*		
Parties desire a binding opinion by neutral third party		**	
Party wants to avoid negotiating with other side		*	*
Parties want someone to decide "right or wrong"		*	*

Settlement Week   Settlement week, like multi-door courthouse programs, is another court-created initiative designed to foster the resolution of disputes through the use of ADR. During a typical settlement week, the civil courts in a jurisdiction will suspend their normal dockets and make the courthouse building and personnel available to litigants who desire to have their cases considered by a neutral third party. Volunteer mediators and other neutrals will provide their services free of charge to litigants who sign up to participate. Once a party has elected to participate, cooperation and participation by the other party may or may not be required, depending upon the jurisdiction. ADR techniques employed during settlement week can include most of the recognized methods; however, mediation is the most frequently requested and utilized form. Most court systems that sponsor settlement week will hold at least two per year.

In some jurisdictions, settlement week is created by statute,[43] while in others it is initiated by the courts as part of their inherent power to control their dockets. Frequently, the local bar association is a co-sponsor of settlement week and provides training for mediators, and certain administrative services. Although most civil cases are regarded as amenable to settlement week mechanisms, some jurisdictions use settlement week to clear older cases from their dockets that otherwise are likely candidates for dismissal for want of prosecution. Rates of settlement during settlement week vary widely from jurisdiction to jurisdiction, and often depend upon whether the local courts already refer the majority of civil cases to ADR. In addition to completely settling cases, settlement week can also help to narrow the issues of pending lawsuits.

Settlement week offers legal professionals the opportunity to be trained in mediation, usually at little or no cost, as well as to practice their mediation skills several times in one week with a variety of different matters. Because many of the other functions related to planning and executing a settlement week are performed by volunteers, these events provide an excellent way to meet and interact with other persons in the jurisdiction who are influential in ADR. These include attorneys, mediators, arbitrators, judges, court coordinators, and local bar association officials who provide ADR leadership. Volunteers also get to observe firsthand the response of litigants to ADR, so as to be better able to tailor ADR to their own clients and practice.

This chapter has discussed variations on ADR designed to fit the needs of particular disputes and parties. The next chapter will explore the use of various ADR techniques within the context of particular industries and types of disputes.

Sources

[1] B. Roth, R. Wulff, C. Cooper, *The Alternative Dispute Resolution Practice Guide*, § 38:1-2 (1993).

[2] *Id.*, at § 38:6-9.

[3] *Id.*, at § 38:5-6.

[4] *Id.*, at § 38-5-7.

[5] *Alternative Dispute Resolution Techniques*, §3,020 (W. Hancock ed. 1996).

[6] *Id.*

[7] *Id.*, at 3.020-3.021.

[8] *Id.*, at 3.021.

[9] B. Roth, R. Wulff, C. Cooper, *supra*, at §38:5-7.

[10] *Id.*, at § 35:5-6.

[11] *Id.*, at § 38:5-7.

[12] *Id.*

[13] W. Hancock, *supra*, at 3.021-3.022.

[14] *Id.*, at 3.022.

[15] *Id.*

[16] *Id.*, at 3.023.

[17] *Id.*, at 3.009.

[18] B. Roth, R. Wulff, C. Cooper, *supra*, at §38:7-10-11.

[19] T. Lambros, The Summary Jury Trial and Other Alternative Methods of Dispute Resolution, A Report to the Judicial Conference of the United States Committee on the Operation of the Jury System (1984), *reprinted in* Alternative Dispute Resolution Techniques, §7.011 (W. Hancock ed. 1996).

[20] A. Greenspan, *Handbook of Alternative Dispute Resolution*, 75 (1990).

[21] T. Lambros, *supra*, at 7.010.

[22] T. Lambros, as reprinted in W. Hancock, at 7.010.

[23] *Id.*

[24] Note, *Constitutional Law/Alternative Dispute Resolution – Summary Jury Trials: Should the Public Have Access?*, Fla. St. U. LL. Rev. 1069, 1072 (1989).

[25] A. Greenspan, *supra*, at 77.

[26] Branton, St. Mary's Alternative Dispute Resolution Institute, Alternative Dispute Resolution and the Attorney, at I-9 (1988).

[27] A. Greenspan, *supra*, at 79.

[28] Bill Rhea and Talmage Boston, *The Dallas Morning News*, December 29, 1996

[29] *G. Heileman Brewing v. Joseph Oat Corp.* 871 F.2d 648 (7th Cir. 1989) *(en banc)*.

[30] *Cincinnati Gas & Electric Co. v. General Electric Co.,* 854 F.2d 900 (6th Cir. 1989).

[31] *In re Cincinnati Enquirer,* 94 F.3d 198 (6th Cir. 1996).

[32] *See generally* A. Greenspan, *supra*. (The discussion regarding Model Settlement Conference is generally derived from Chapter 7.)

[33] *Id.*, at 104.

[34] B. Roth,, R. Wulff, C. Cooper, *The Alternative Dispute Resolution Practice Guide*, § 40:1(1993).

[35] *Id.*

[36] *Downey v. Gregory*, 757 S.W.2d 524, 525 (Tex. App.–Houston [1st Dist.] 1988, no writ).

[37] Tex. Civ. Prac. & Rem. Code Ann. § 151.003 (West Supp. 1997).

[38] *ADR and the Courts: A Manual for Judges and Lawyers* 166 (E. Fine ed. 1987).

[39] *Id.*

[40] A. Greenspan, *supra*, at 295.

[41] *Id.*, at 296.

[42] *Id.*

[43] See, *e.g.*, Tex. Civ. Prac. & Rem. Code § 155.001 (West Supp. 1997).

Chapter Seven

Application of ADR to Specific Disputes

Introduction

So far, we have discussed the various methods of ADR generally, with only minimal reference to the needs of particular types of disputes. Yet, one of the advantages of ADR is its flexibility to adapt and change to the needs of the issues and the parties. Not only does ADR encompass a wide variety of techniques from which disputants can choose, but each technique can be tailored to the particular controversy.

For the purposes of selecting the most appropriate ADR technique and adapting that technique to the matter, disputes can be categorized in many ways as to:

♦ *complexity* (e.g., contract dispute over the paving of a parking lot versus the building of a high-rise office building);

♦ *industry* (e.g., construction, securities, apparel industry, farming);

♦ *legal category* (e.g., contract, medical malpractice, criminal, family law);

♦ *domain* (e.g., public versus private; local versus interstate; national versus international); and

♦ *topic* (e.g., domestic, employment, commercial).

It is beyond the scope of this text to cover the use of ADR in all of the major industries and areas of law to which it is applied. Nevertheless, the following discussion is designed to give the student a better understanding of how ADR is adapted to specific types of disputes by focusing on the use of ADR in seven distinct contexts, including:

1. Construction industry disputes

2. Labor and employment disputes

3. Family law/domestic disputes

4. Criminal matters

5. Securities disputes

6. Environmental disputes

7. Community conflicts

Construction industry disputes, and labor and employment matters will be discussed in considerable detail to show how ADR is specifically adapted to fit the conflict. Family law and criminal matters will be covered less thoroughly, but with enough detail to help the reader understand how ADR can be tailored to the dispute. The discussion concerning securities and environmental disputes will raise the issues that ADR must address if it is to be successful in these arenas. Finally, the material on community conflicts will introduce the reader to the growing use of ADR in preventing and resolving grass roots problems through the use of voluntary and not-for-profit dispute resolution services.

Construction Industry Disputes

Construction disputes are an example of categorizing a matter by industry. They are also likely to be highly complex. Depending upon the project, construction disputes may have public as well as private dimensions. Examples of construction disputes with a public dimension include the construction of a bridge, a water treatment plant, or an airport. Finally, a construction dispute exemplifies the use of ADR in the realm of commerce.

The Origin of Construction Disputes

A construction project is considered by many a dispute waiting to happen. There are several reasons that this is the case.[1]

1. First of all, many owners and developers are inexperienced in handling construction projects. Consequently, they plan poorly and fail to build in quality controls along the way.

2. Second, owners and developers often accept bids based on the lowest price rather than on the completeness of the bid, or the quality and expertise of the contractor/bidder.

3. Third, most owners and project sponsors have no prior relationship with their various contractors and suppliers, and will have none in the future. Consequently, they have no past dealings to help guide them through the current impasse, and no strong incentive to seek to ensure an amicable relationship beyond the current project.

4. Fourth, problems that arise often have many causes that are difficult and costly to trace and that engender a "pass-the-buck" mentality. ("It's the plumber's fault, not mine.")

5. Fifth, construction plans and specifications generally cannot anticipate all of the changes in circumstances that necessitate many modifications during the life of a project, and disputes inevitably arise over the nature, scope, and responsibility for those modifications.

6. Finally, construction projects are usually undergirded by a host of sureties/insurance companies who are loath to pay out on claims arising from delays, extra work, and plan changes unless those claims are well-proven and unambiguous.

The construction industry has developed a process of altering building plans called "change-orders," whereby contractors and owners attempt to informally negotiate needed modifications as a project progresses. However, when negotiations break down, the parties often turn to litigation. Construction disputes, like most commercial disputes, almost always involve breach of contract or similar allegations, although tort claims involving injuries to workers are also common.

Characteristics of Construction Disputes

Construction disputes share many of the same characteristics as other types of commercial disputes; however, they have certain peculiar characteristics that tend to increase the cost of litigation:

a. First of all, construction disputes usually concern many events, transactions, and episodes that span an extended period of time. Consequently, the task of telling the story to a jury will also take a considerable amount of time and expense.

b. Construction disputes involve many different people, all of whom are potential witnesses. Litigation will, therefore, involve dozens of depositions, and many days in the courtroom examining and cross-examining witnesses.

c. Construction projects generate masses of paperwork, from the original requests for proposals and contractors' bids to blueprints and other drawings, specifications, cost estimates, schedules, purchase orders, inspection reports, correspondence, and much more. Much of this paperwork is subject to discovery when a dispute erupts into litigation.

d. Construction projects always involve countless oral exchanges between the parties that materially affect the project. Unfortunately, these exchanges often have not been reduced to written memoranda. Consequently, difficult factual issues will likely arise due to conflicting accounts of what was said. Likewise, legal issues concerning contract terms, parol evidence, reliance on oral statements, and so forth must also be briefed, heard and decided.

e. Many of the issues involved in a construction dispute are highly technical in nature in that they concern engineering principles that are not easily apprehended by an untrained layperson. Other issues involve complex and time-honored industry practices that must be explained to a judge and jury before they can understand what has occurred and make intelligent decisions. This complexity not only increases the potential for appealable error; it also increases the need for expert witnesses to explain and authenticate these practices.

f. Finally, although construction is highly time-sensitive, not even the most efficient court docket can accommodate the need of the parties for a quick resolution. In addition, the complexity of construction disputes usually increases the incidence of evidentiary hearings and other pretrial proceedings, as compared with other types of disputes. Consequently, it is not unusual for trial to be postponed for 24 months or longer. In the meantime, the project stagnates, in turn giving rise to additional disputes. For example, lessees of space will breach their leases in the new but uncompleted building because they must rent somewhere else, and suppliers of materials will refuse to deliver materials at the contract price because their costs have increased in the interim.

Arbitration of Construction Disputes

Because resolving construction disputes through litigation is so inefficient, the construction industry has used other forms of settling disputes for a long time. Binding arbitration is one form of ADR that has been used for many decades to resolve construction disputes. Several ADR agencies publish arbitration rules and procedures for construction disputes, most notably the American Arbitration Association (AAA), which also publishes *The Guide for Construction Industry Arbitrators*. Construction industry arbitration falls under the category of "commercial arbitration," and in this regard is highly similar to the arbitration of other types of complex business disputes. Nevertheless, construction arbitration presents some special issues.

Enforceability of Arbitration Clauses

Most construction contracts include arbitration clauses whereby the parties agree ahead of time to use binding arbitration to resolve any disputes arising under the contract. These clauses are likely to be universally enforceable under the Federal Arbitration Act, because most projects involve materials and even labor that has crossed state lines. In some cases, the parties are from different states.[2] Because the courts favor arbitration, any provision for its application will usually be interpreted broadly.[3] Furthermore, even if a party opposing arbitration claims the contract is illegal or was obtained by fraud, many courts will sever the arbitration clause from the broader contract and enforce it.[4]

Parties to Construction Arbitration

Construction disputes involve not only the parties to the contract that has been breached, but also related parties, as well. These may include subcontractors who supposedly did shoddy work, architects who drew blueprints with alleged errors, or suppliers who provided materials that the contractor claims were faulty. Unfortunately, each of these parties may be operating under separate contracts that may not include arbitration clauses or, if they do, the clauses may have provisions that are contradictory to the arbitration provisions involved in the principal suit.

When situations such as these arise, and the various parties cannot agree on which arbitration rules to apply, it is usually left to a court to decide before arbitration can proceed. At issue is whether parties can be bound by decisions reached in an arbitration that proceeded under rules that they did not agree to.[5] One solution is for the general contractor to require that all contracts involved in a single project contain the same arbitration provisions.

Also of concern is whether parties who are subject to different arbitration provisions can be compelled to participate in a consolidated arbitration. Unfortunately, courts are also divided on this issue.[6] Failure to consolidate can strip arbitration of its advantages and make litigation and trial the more efficient method of resolving construction disputes, simply because a judge has the power to combine actions and claims arising from the same events.

Location and Timing

Just as parties disagree about the rules for arbitration, they sometimes disagree about where the sessions are to take place. If the parties cannot agree on a location, they may abdicate the decision to the sponsoring agency (e.g., AAA) or to the general contractor, provided the location chosen is not so inconvenient to one of the parties as to cause some unacceptable disadvantage. Likewise, timing can also raise issues of fairness, especially for subcontractors who have a small stake in the matter but who may be compelled to attend the entire proceedings.[7] In response to this problem, construction arbitrators will often conduct special proceedings to hear small stakeholders.[8] Arbitrators will also devise expedited hearings to quickly resolve disputes that arise mid-project and that threaten to shut the project down. For example, the AAA Construction Industry Arbitration Rules, Rule 53, provides for notice of arbitration by telephone rather than in writing.

Mediation of Construction Disputes

Although arbitration is the traditional form of ADR used in the construction industry, mediation is gaining in popularity. Because mediation is nonbinding, some parties will attempt mediation first and resort to arbitration or some other form of ADR only if mediation fails to achieve a satisfactory resolution. Several ADR agencies, including the AAA, publish mediation rules for the construction industry.

There are several reasons that mediation works in the construction industry.

1. People in the construction industry expect conflicts to arise and are skilled at negotiating their differences and solving problems together. Consequently, they approach mediation with a better attitude and more confidence than the average litigant.

2. The parties involved in construction disputes are likely to have joint interests far beyond the minimum requirements of the law that can be exploited in mediation. At the very least, they want to finish the project so that the sponsor can get the benefit of project being built, and the contractor can get paid.

3. In a project lasting many months and even years, the parties have a strong need to maintain a good working relationship, which mediation can repair and preserve.

4. Mediation can better serve small stakeholders who can participate with less preparation and expense, and who can withdraw if they feel pressured to accept an unfair settlement.

5. Mediation accommodates the need to reach a resolution quickly so that construction can continue. As compared with litigation and even arbitration, mediation can be organized quickly and requires much less discovery and preparation. If it doesn't work, little time and effort have been lost, and the parties can proceed to arbitration, minitrial, moderated settlement conference or to court.

Mediation of construction disputes highly resembles mediation as described in Chapter Three. However, there are some critical differences.

1. First, the mediator is likely to have substantial experience in the construction industry. Given the complexity of construction disputes, such experience will usually save a substantial amount of time and expense for the parties.

2. Second, because construction disputes are document-intensive, the mediator will most likely be called on to facilitate the amicable exchange of discovery.

3. Third, presentations in joint sessions are likely to last several hours due to the complexity of the issues. Furthermore, where multiple parties are involved in the suit, there may be more than just two presentations.

4. Fourth, private caucuses are apt to involve shuttling between several different parties rather than merely two. Likewise, any agreement reached will involve multiple interests.

5. Finally, the mediator is likely to be called on to render an advisory opinion on the matter.

Labor and Employment Disputes

The use of ADR to resolve disputes between organized labor and management has a long tradition extending back into the nineteenth century. More recently, ADR has gained prominence as an effective way to resolve disputes between employees and employers outside of the organized labor context.

Organized Labor Disputes

Organized labor disputes involve the rights of workers to organize, and to bargain as a group with their employers over the terms of employment. The negotiation process that results in a written agreement between employers and labor is called "collective bargaining." Collective bargaining agreements usually cover a period of years, and deal with such matters as wage rates, benefits, vacation policy, seniority and a host of other matters. The rights of employees to organize and to engage in collective bargaining are guaranteed by a host of well-known legislation including the Norris-LaGuardia Act of 1932 (29 U.S.C. §§ 101-115), the National Labor Relations Act of 1935 (28 U.S.C. §§ 151-169), the Labor Management Relations Act of 1947 (29 U.S.C. §§ 141-97), and other laws. Groups of employees that organize for the purpose of bargaining with their employers are not required to form a "union," although many do. Unions serve a variety of purposes, including to aid the employees in organizing and calling a strike if the employer fails to bargain in good faith or to live up to a collective bargaining agreement.

Organized labor disputes almost always concern major segments of the economy such as auto manufacturing, steel production, or transportation. They also may involve large numbers of workers associated by a common employer, by skill such as bricklayer or plumber, or by industry such as autoworkers. The plaintiffs in labor disputes are usually groups rather than individuals, while defendants are often major employers (e.g., an urban school board, a large corporation). Because of the significance of these entities to the national economy, labor disputes have a strong public dimension. Some readers may recall the air traffic controllers' strike of the early 1980s that affected every major airport in the country and thousands of noncontroller employees as well as millions of passengers. Nevertheless, labor disputes are not necessarily complex matters, in that they often involve only a limited number of parties (e.g,. the union and a company), and the issues are clearly defined (e.g., hourly wage increase).

The Resolution of Organized Labor Disputes

The resolution of labor disputes is usually governed by the terms of collective-bargaining agreements between the employee group and their employer(s), which almost always contain ADR provisions. Disputes occur usually because the employer allegedly has failed to live up to the terms of a collective bargaining agreement. It is beyond the scope of this book to address the subject of collective bargaining, which is a fully developed area of law and practice usually referred to as "labor law." Labor law attorneys are often highly skilled and experienced negotiators who forge agreements between labor and management, and who represent one or the other during arbitration when disputes arise under an agreement.

The Origin of Employment Disputes

In contrast to labor matters, employment disputes usually involve one, or a small group of aggrieved employees and one employer. Employee claims arise under a host of federal statutes including the:

◆ Equal Pay Act of 1963[9]

◆ Title VII of the Civil Rights Act of 1964[10]

◆ Age Discrimination in Employment Act (ADEA)[11]

◆ Older Workers Benefit Protection Act[12]

◆ Americans With Disabilities Act (ADA)[13]

◆ Family and Medical Leave Act of 1993 (FMLA),[14] and the

◆ Employee Retirement Income Security Act of 1974 as amended (ERISA).[15]

Employee claims also arise under state laws that govern the hiring, firing, treatment, and safety of employees. In addition, employees may have common-law contract claims related to hiring, fair treatment and firing, as well as common-law tort claims for on-the-job injuries and other torts attributable to the employer.

The high incidence of employment-related claims is a function of the increasing number of rights given to employees by legislation, such as that listed above. The incidence of claims is also a function of an uncertain economy. Where jobs are hard to find, employees are more likely to fight for the right to obtain and keep their jobs, as well as to be treated fairly. Conversely, when jobs are plentiful, employees are more likely to move on to another employer and leave the dispute with their former employer behind.

Characteristics of Employment Disputes

Employment disputes have several characteristics that must be taken into account when assessing the merits of ADR over litigation.

1. First of all, although employment disputes often concern private matters, if an employee's civil rights have been violated, such as job discrimination based on ethnicity or handicap, a dispute may contain elements of concern to the public. Employers generally will have a high interest in keeping such matters confidential, while aggrieved employees will welcome public exposure of the defendant employer.

2. Second, even though the incidence of employment disputes is high, the incidence of resolution is low. Only a tiny fraction of employment disputes is considered litigable by plaintiff's attorneys who handle employment litigation. Consequently, most grievances go unresolved. This tends to undermine employee morale and productivity, which has, in turn, fueled the development of internal, employer-sponsored grievance mechanisms.

3. Employment claims are costly to litigate. They often involve allegations that can only be proven by circumstantial evidence, which can be expensive to assemble. For example, to prove that a minority employee has been discriminated against in promotions and salary, that employee may be required to commission a statistical survey of employee files to prove a pattern of similar discrimination by the employer against other minority employees. For employers, the loss of executive time adds significantly to their costs of litigation.

4. Employment related lawsuits often involve large jury verdicts. Most jurors tend to identify with employee/plaintiffs rather than employers, and will award significant damages, especially in wrongful discharge and sexual harassment cases. Because of this, employers tend to prefer ADR over trial.

5. As compared with organized labor disputes, employment disputes frequently do not involve any written agreement between the employer and employee to arbitrate or mediate conflicts that arise between them. This is especially true if the employer is a small, private company. As a result, the only way for an employee to obtain a hearing may be to file a lawsuit.

6. Depending upon the employer involved, more and more employment disputes are being resolved internally. In response to the frequency and cost of employment litigation, many companies are developing internal grievance procedures. Some company procedures permit employees to be assisted in bringing their grievance by outside parties such as attorneys, paralegals, representatives of civil rights groups and others. Where workplace procedures exist, the courts will generally require an employee to exhaust these internal mechanisms before filing suit. Additionally, where a lawsuit has been filed, voluntary agreements between the parties to resolve the matter through ADR is also increasing, due to the need to preserve goodwill in the workplace.

Specific Types of Employment Disputes

Employment disputes can involve a host of claims, each with their own special characteristics and problems that must be taken into account when choosing the most appropriate forum for resolution.[16]

1. Sexual Harassment Claims

As the number of women in the work place has increased, sexual harassment has also grown. This is especially true in work settings typically composed exclusively of men, such as construction, docks and loading platforms, firefighting, and so forth. Bringing a sexual harassment claim is risky because the claimant knows that other employees will likely rally around the accused and isolate the claimant. In most cases, the accused is often superior in rank to the accuser, which exacerbates the claimant's feelings of fear and isolation.

Furthermore, company management is likely to side with the accused, who will almost always deny the allegations. Thus, the claimant risks the loss of a job or some other sanction, even if the claims are later determined to be justified. Likewise, the employer risks paying huge damages due to the sympathy of juries and the often sensational and egregious facts surrounding an employee's claims of sexual harassment.

Because of these fears, ADR is often the best way to resolve sexual harassment matters. Depending upon the method chosen, the aggrieved employee can raise all of these concerns and negotiate an outcome that not only provides monetary compensation for any injuries suffered, but also protects his or her job and future career options. In addition, the employee may be able to insist on measures to be taken by the employer to reduce the incidence of sexual harassment in the future. Sometimes, what an employee really wants is for the accused to understand and admit the behavior, apologize, and promise not to do it again, a remedy that is likely to be available only through ADR.

2. Discrimination Claims

Employment discrimination claims usually involve allegations of failure to hire or promote based on race, gender, or age, as well as national origin and religion. Passage of the Americans With Disabilities Act (ADA) has significantly increased the number of claims based on handicap. As the American work force becomes more and more diverse, it is highly likely that legislators at both the federal and state levels will extend protection to other groups as well. As compared with employer prohibitions against sexual harassment, prohibitions against discrimination are often in writing and can be found on employment applications and on signs throughout the workplace declaring the company an "equal opportunity employer." Consequently, discrimination will usually be attributed to the employer and can't be blamed on some chauvinist employee who didn't know any better.

Furthermore, public disapproval of discrimination is strong and, if proven, damages are likely to be high. For these reasons, the employee will often view his or her grievance in terms of the larger cause, while the employer will try to keep the dispute narrowly focused on the employee's claim. Also, the employee will welcome public attention, while the employer will desire confidentiality. In short, the employee is apt to want to go to court, while the employer will prefer an alternative. In these types of cases, a neutral third party called in to resolve the matter often must become an advocate for the process and convince the employee that ADR can produce a satisfactory conclusion. Nevertheless, if ADR is binding, there is a high likelihood that a dissatisfied employee will appeal the award, thereby attracting the public exposure the employer wanted to avoid.

3. *Wrongful Discharge Claims*

Claims based on wrongful firing account for a significant portion of employment disputes. Unlike statutory sexual harassment and discrimination claims, however, they are usually based on state common law principles. The common law of most jurisdictions still favors the notion that employment is "at-will," meaning that an employer can terminate an employee at any time for any reason or no reason at all. Even though there has been significant erosion of this doctrine in recent years, the claimant often has the difficult task of first proving that he or she can be fired only for just cause. In addition, because the claimant is now a "former employee," internal grievance procedures may no longer be available. Likewise, neither party has the pressure of an ongoing relationship to protect. Because of these factors, many wrongful discharge claims are never brought.

For those wrongful discharge claims that are filed as a lawsuit, however, the primary interest of the claimant is likely to be monetary, in that he or she seeks to be compensated for wages lost as a result of the wrongful termination. If ADR is employed, the focus will be on whether the employee was fired justly or unjustly, and on the relative value of the claims being made. At best, the issue of whether the employment was at-will or not will have been resolved via a motion for summary judgment made by the employer. If not, ADR is likely to be unsuccessful simply because it is not designed to resolve matters of law.

Predispute Agreements to Informally Resolve Employment Disputes

With an American work force well in excess of 100 million, disputes between employers and employees are commonplace. For many employers, preventing and defending lawsuits brought by employees constitute most of the time and money they spend on litigation and related matters. For this reason, more and more companies require employees to sign agreements to forego their legal claims in a judicial court and instead to submit employment disputes to some binding form of ADR, usually arbitration.

As compared with predispute agreements between other types of parties, agreements in the context of employment are somewhat suspect. This is due in part, to the perceived disparity of power between employers on the one hand and employees on the other. A job applicant with a family to feed and bills to pay is in a difficult position to refuse to sign a predispute arbitration agreement as a condition of employment. Because of the disparity in bargaining power between employers and employees, courts have traditionally been reluctant to enforce predispute agreements to use binding ADR in this context. Nevertheless, an employee seeking to avoid binding ADR pursuant to a predispute agreement generally must prove that he or she signed the agreement under coercion, or that the agreement is unduly oppressive or unconscionable.[17] For example, if the agreement requires that an employee submit his or her dispute to an arbitrator hired by the employer, a pre-dispute ADR agreement will likely not be enforceable if it appears that the arbitrator is so closely controlled by the employer as to raise the issue of bias.[18]

The Use of Binding ADR in Resolving Statutory Claims

Courts have been especially reluctant in the past to enforce predispute ADR agreements between employers and employers over claims arising under statute. There are two primary reasons for this reluctance.

1. First, statutes dealing with employment, such as the Age Discrimination in Employment Act (ADEA), provide employees with legal rights, and with causes of action in a court of law if those rights are violated. Substituting binding ADR has been viewed as a way for employers to circumvent the scrutiny of the courts in such matters.

2. Second, the Federal Arbitration Act (FAA), which provides for the enforcement of pre-dispute arbitration agreements in matters involving interstate commerce, specifically excludes contracts of employment.[19]

In a landmark decision in 1991, the United States Supreme Court opened a wide door to the enforceability of predispute agreements concerning statutory employee rights. In the case of *Gilmer v. Interstate/Johnson Lane Corp.*,[20] the Court ruled that arbitration was a valid forum for the resolution of a discrimination claim brought under the ADEA. The Court stated that:

> "[B]y agreeing to arbitrate a statutory claim, a party does not forgo the substantive rights afforded by the statute; it only submits to their resolution in an arbitral, rather than a judicial forum."[21]

Because federal policy favors ADR generally, and arbitration in particular, the Court also found that arbitration of a statutory claim is appropriate "unless Congress itself has evinced an intention to preclude a waiver of judicial remedies of the statutory rights at issue."[22] In other words, unless the text of the statute, its purpose, or its legislative history provide otherwise, arbitration is an acceptable substitute forum for hearing statutory employment claims.[23] Recent legislation dealing with employment, such as the Civil Rights Act of 1991[24] and the ADA,[25] have specifically included provisions encouraging the use of ADR to resolve disputes that may arise under its terms.

The *Gilmer* decision did not specifically deal with the issue of whether predispute agreements made between an employer and employee constitute "contracts of employment" under the FAA. In fact, the jurists in the majority avoided the question by finding that the agreement involved was not a contract of employment. However, the minority in *Gilmer* dissented on the grounds that any agreement to arbitrate between an employer and employee is indeed a contract of employment and therefore, is outside the scope of the FAA.[26] In other words, the jurists in the minority felt that the FAA precludes enforcement. Since *Gilmer*, federal appeals courts have split on the issue, and the matter remains open. One way for employers to avoid the problem of unenforceability is to separate the agreement to use ADR for employment related disputes from agreements regarding other terms of employment.[27]

Arbitration of Employment Disputes

Most predispute agreements between employers and employees specify the use of binding arbitration rather than some other form of ADR. Several organizations publish rules and procedures for arbitrating employment related disputes, including the Center for Public Resources, Inc. (business and corporate employers), the New York Stock Exchange (securities industry employers) and the AAA (all employers). In 1999, the American Arbitration Association published its *National Rules for the Resolution of Employment Disputes* (Including Arbitration and Mediation Rules).

Additional Issues Concerning the Arbitration of Employment Disputes

In addition to the issue of enforceability of predispute agreements, discussed above, there are other concerns related to the arbitration of employment disputes.[28]

1. Where the parties have agreed, predispute, to arbitrate, they must determine the scope of their agreement. This includes the parties to be bound, the causes of action covered, and any provisions for counterclaims. Ideally, an agreement should cover the officers, directors, employees and agents of the employer, as well as any third parties involved who agree to be bound by the arbitrator's decision. It should also bind a former employer, where the employee has quit or been terminated.[29] Causes of action should cover statutory and common law claims, and legitimate employer counterclaims against the employee should be permitted. For example, the employer may seek to recover company funds or property in the control of the employee.

2. The method of choosing the arbitrator must be as neutral as possible. As discussed above, the assumed disparity of bargaining power between the employer and employee can cause an arbitration award to be set aside if a court finds that the employer has unduly influenced the selection of the arbitrator(s).

3. In disputes involving alleged wrongful termination, the parties often must first determine whether termination is at the will of the employer or whether just cause for termination must be proved. Traditionally, employment has been considered "at-will." Where employment termination is for just cause only, the employer generally has the burden of proving that the decision to terminate was justified, even though it is the employer that has been sued.

4. Given the uncertainty over the arbitrability of statutory claims, the parties will want to consider the possibility of asking a court to give significant weight to any arbitration award if the matter is later litigated.

5. Confidentiality is especially important in the arbitration of employment disputes, and in fact is one of the primary reasons why employers prefer to arbitrate. The fear is that if news of the claim or the award becomes common knowledge, other employees will be encouraged to bring similar claims. Therefore, the parties should agree on whether the results will be kept confidential.

6. Discovery is generally limited in employment arbitration, and the arbitrator is often given broad powers to control it. This works to the advantage of all the parties, but especially employees who often cannot afford the associated costs. Nevertheless, discovery should not be so limited as to hamstring employees who do not have the same access to pertinent records as the employer.

7. Arbitrators in the employment setting are often given the power to entertain motions for summary judgment where issues of law rather than fact may resolve all or part of the matter. For example, in a wrongful termination dispute where a former employee asserts that he or she can be fired only for just cause and the employer asserts the opposite, a motion for summary judgment could resolve the entire case. Arbitrators are also frequently given the power to issue injunctive relief, for example, to enjoin a claimant-employee from revealing trade secrets or in other ways to damage the employer during the pendency of the dispute.

8. Finally, the remedies available to an arbitrator in the employment context must not be too limited so as to render any award nonbinding or unenforceable. Furthermore, given the possibility of receiving substantial punitive damages from a jury, employees may be reluctant to fully participate in arbitration unless the stakes are high enough. The risk in any case is that regardless of the arbitrator's award, an employee will overestimate the value and strength of his or her claim and appeal the arbitrator's award in the hopes of receiving more from a jury.

Mediation of Labor and Employment Disputes

Mediation of labor and employment disputes can occur at several levels and serve several purposes.

Labor Mediation

In the context of collective bargaining agreements, a provision to mediate first is often inserted into the agreement. This provision permits the use of mediation to resolve the entire dispute before resorting to arbitration, which is usually more time-consuming and expensive. It will also permit the use of mediation to resolve peripheral issues so that arbitration can focus on the most important matters. Reaching agreement through mediation on at least some of the issues can help to avert a strike.

In 1947 Congress created the Federal Mediation and Conciliation Service (FMCS) under the Department of Labor. The purpose of the FMCS was to "assist parties to labor disputes in industries affecting commerce to settle such disputes through conciliation and mediation."[30] It was seen as an enhancement to the obligation of labor and management to bargain collectively over issues of unfair labor practices.[31] The FMCS has developed considerable skill over the years at mediating labor disputes and can provide parties with mediation procedures and rules, as well as the names of qualified mediators.

Many states have developed comprehensive statutory schemes to encourage and even require mediation of disputes involving public employees. Some of these groups are unionized, such as teachers, sanitation workers, state government employees, and so forth, while other are not. In either case, however, mediation can usually be initiated at the request of either party. The purpose of these statutes is to provide a means of breaking an impasse that may occur in the process of collective bargaining between an employee organization or union, and an employer.

Predispute Agreements to Mediate

Just as collective bargaining agreements will contain mediation provisions, agreements between individual employees and employers will also contain similar provisions to mediate first before proceeding to arbitration. These clauses serve the same purpose as they do in the context of union and organized labor agreements.

Post-Dispute Mediation

Mediation can also occur after a dispute has arisen but before a lawsuit has been filed. This is especially true in disputes involving employees who are still on the job and who desire to continue working for the employer. Because these disputes often involve sensitive issues such as sexual harassment, mediation provides many advantages, including confidentiality, which is usually important to all of the parties. It also provides an opportunity to inform and even rehabilitate the employee(s) whose offending actions have given rise to the dispute, provided he or she participates in the mediation session. It can even be used to encourage the offending party to apologize. Finally, mediation can help the parties identify joint interests and develop creative solutions so that the problem does not occur again.

Post-Lawsuit Mediation

Once a lawsuit has been filed, mediation can take place in an attempt to resolve the matter prior to trial. This is most likely to occur in jurisdictions where the courts have the power to refer parties to mediation. Nevertheless, more and more litigants are voluntarily using mediation because of the advantages it provides.

Special Issues in Mediating Employment Claims

Employment mediation highly resembles mediation as described in Chapter Three. Nevertheless, there are some special issues and concerns that arise in the employment context.

1. Employment mediation frequently involves the use of private caucuses due to the disparity of bargaining power between the employer and the employee. The employer usually has more money and is likely to be better represented that the employee-plaintiff. Furthermore, the employee may be less well-educated, and in other respects feel intimidated by the employer.

2. The opening session in employment mediation is likely to be acrimonious, with both sides seeking to paint the other in the worst possible light. For example, the employer may try to prove that the employee is a deadbeat, or that the employee solicited the sexual attention now complained of. The mediator will need to work hard to focus the parties on the issues and to stress that mediation does not involve proving one's case.

3. As discussed above, confidentiality concerning both the mediation session(s) and the results is especially crucial in the employment context in order to avoid ruining anyone's reputation or to encourage other employees to bring similar claims. The mediator or the parties' attorneys should caution the clients that breach of confidentiality could lead to additional claims by one against the other for defamation, slander or breach of the agreement.

4. In employment mediation, the plaintiff will likely want to preserve the goodwill of the employer, if for no other reason than to obtain a letter of recommendation or to clean up the employee's personnel file. Thus, the plaintiff may be timid or less than candid. The mediator will need to draw out the plaintiff and to stress that only by being open and candid will the mediation succeed, to everyone's benefit.

Future of ADR in Employment Setting

The use of ADR in the employment setting is one of the fastest growing "sub-industries" within the ADR movement, and offers many exciting, challenging, and highly remunerative career opportunities. There are several reasons for the increasing use of ADR to solve employer/employee disputes. The robust economy of the 1990s caused thousands of companies to grow beyond their ability to effectively manage the workplace environment, and many new companies came on line with only minimal policies and procedures in place regarding conduct at work and the handling of grievances. At the same time, worker expectations grew and with it the potential for problems and complaints. In addition, the increasing diversity in the workforce, including the influx of foreign workers has raised a whole new set of employment issues and challenges that companies must address.

On the legal front, the types of actions for which employers can be held accountable continue to increase, and jury awards for alleged employer misbehavior often reach seven figures. At the same time, trial courts, especially at the federal level, are deciding more and more cases at the summary judgment stage, while appeals courts are routinely reducing and even reversing large jury award. In short, risks abound for both plaintiffs and defendants determined to pursue litigation and trial rather than settle their grievances.

ADR consultants can offer critical help to companies and institutions in tailoring ombuds programs designed to investigate complaints, and in structuring grievance procedures to address problems before they explode into costly litigation. ADR neutrals can also offer their services as mediators, arbitrators, and advisors for actual problems and complaints when they arise.

Family Disputes

Family-related disputes, including divorce and child custody, account for a significant number of all civil disputes filed in state courts each year. In fact, the number is so great and the issues so specialized that most urban jurisdictions have courts devoted to purely family law matters. These courts, in turn, spawn various services aimed at assisting families in crisis. Likewise, attorneys who practice in the area of family law often devote themselves completely to domestic relations matters.

Characteristics of Family Disputes

Family law matters involve a variety of special needs and circumstances. Unfortunately, the traditional court system is ill-equipped, despite its specialization, to determine what is in the best interest of a child, or how the parties should fairly divide the assets and liabilities of a lifetime of living together.

1. First of all, family disputes are likely to be highly emotional and acrimonious. The parties are often not speaking to one another and they do not trust each other in any respect. Nevertheless, they are compelled to make critical decisions about their own futures and the future of their children.

2. There is likely to be an imbalance of power between the parties, characterized most often by a dominant husband who holds the purse strings and most of the economic power, and a wife who is facing the prospect of a significantly lower standard of living for herself and her children. In some states, such as Texas, her prospect for a settlement amounts to one-half of all marital property, which may amount to little or nothing, and alimony only by proving that she is almost completely unemployable.

3. Marriage is largely a private matter, and spouses tend to keep their marital problems private. However, when divorce enters the picture, spouses often want a public airing of their stories of misunderstanding, mistreatment, and abuse. Therefore, many relish the opportunity to "tell it to the judge." For some, the process of divorce will be incomplete and inconclusive until they have had their day in court, or some reasonable substitute thereof.

4. Many individuals involved in divorce and child custody disputes are not represented by counsel, often because they cannot afford it. This places additional pressure on the courts and others involved to make sure that people are informed of their rights and do not acquiesce to undue pressure from their spouse or other parties adverse to their interests.

Mediating Family Law Disputes

ADR in the context of family disputes almost always means mediation. Mediation is highly suited to resolving family conflict because it promotes joint decision making and helps preserve relationships between the parties. This is especially important when children are involved. The role of the mediator is to aid the parties in identifying the issues, reducing misunderstandings, clarifying priorities, exploring areas of compromise and finding points of agreement. In this regard, the mediator often plays a therapeutic role, which accounts for why family law mediators are, by and large, mental health care professionals rather than lawyers.[*]

Family law mediation is mostly voluntary, and in fact, represents one of the earliest uses of mediation. Today, the overwhelming majority of marital disputes are resolved through mediation.[32] Family mediation has, in fact, spawned an entire industry aimed at providing conciliation and related services to families in crisis.

---

[*] As early as 1983, a survey reported at 21 Conciliation Courts Rev, No. 1, at 1, that 78% of private divorce mediators and 90% of public-sector divorce mediators were health care professionals, while only 15% and 1%, respectively, were lawyers. Even though the number of lawyers conducting divorce mediation has likely increased since then, persons with mental health backgrounds still account for the majority of such mediators, largely because state statutes often require professional mental health certification.

On the national level, several organizations support family ADR, including the Academy of Family Mediators and the Association of Family and Conciliation Courts.

Locally, many community-based mediation services as well as private practices offer information, assist with the gathering and developing financial information and budgets, draft settlement agreements, assist with preparing legal paperwork for filing, and provide mediators and mediation facilities.

Over time, courts have coopted mediation because of its successful track record at producing fair agreements between warring spouses in less time than traditional litigation and trial. Of the state courts throughout the United Stated devoted exclusively to family law matters, about one in ten had a mediation program by the mid-1990s.[33] Although courts can refer divorcing parties to mediation, divorce mediation remains largely voluntary. However, some family courts can compel mediation of divorce, dissolution, or annulment actions,[34] and most have the power to compel participation by people involved in child custody and visitation disputes.[35]

Many states have statutes regulating the use of mediation in family disputes. These statutes usually cover not only who is required to participate, but also the enforceability of any agreement reached, the liability of the mediator, and the qualifications of the mediator. See Chapter Three for a discussion of qualification standards for mediators, including those involved in family law matters. Also see Chapter Four for additional information regarding domestic relations mediation statutes.

Special Issues in Mediating Family Disputes

Family law mediation differs from mediation of other types of disputes in several ways.

1. Mediation in the context of family disputes has therapeutic dimensions in that it often must help the parties deal with their emotions and move through them in order to reach agreement. The mediator is also likely to coach the participants in how to communicate with one another, especially if issues concerning their children are involved. Also, family mediation is likely to require multiple sessions, due to the emotions involved and the number of distinct issues that must be addressed (3-5 sessions is common). Nevertheless, mediation is not therapy, and the mediator should never lose sight of the legal issues involved, including the need for fairness as defined not only by the parties, but by the law.

2. Many family dispute mediations are not attended by counsel for the parties, which raises issues of fairness. Attorneys are often not present for two reasons. First, some state statutes mandating mediation in the context of custody and visitation matters prohibit the attendance of counsel. Second, as indicated above, more and more parties cannot afford counsel and must negotiate the process on their own. The absence of counsel can exacerbate any imbalance of power between the spouses, which the mediator must be sensitive to and strive to equalize.

3. In cases where attorneys are not available at the mediation session, the mediator must decide if the parties are informed sufficiently of their legal rights to proceed or whether the mediation session should be postponed while competent legal advice can be obtained. In some cases, the mediator may resort to providing legal advice and in so doing runs the risk of the unauthorized practice of law. A mediator can avoid this problem by providing printed material prepared by an attorney or bar association, for example, that summarizes the applicable law.

4. Where property settlements and child support matters are mediated along with issues of custody and visitation, a mediator needs to be sensitive to the possibility of the parties trading economic concessions for custody and visitation privileges. Judges are likely to disallow settlements that suggest one party has bought access to the children.

5. The parties involved in family dispute mediation are likely to feel a high degree of pressure to settle, especially if the well being of children is involved and/or one or both of the parties cannot afford a trial. Trial usually means additional delays and costs, therefore, mediation may be the only way to settle a dispute early and with a minimum of expense.

6. As compared with other types of mediation, the parties in a family dispute are apt to view the opposing counsel or representative with hostility and as aiding and abetting an unfair result. Consequently, party representatives should be low key during joint sessions and appear as neutral as possible.

7. Because of the high degree of unexpressed and unresolved hostility usually involved in divorce, the parties should be given the opportunity throughout to vent their feelings. In this regard, telling the mediator often serves as a substitute for telling the judge. Nevertheless, the mediator will need to control the process so that matters do not get out of hand and sabotage the process.

8. Divorcing parties are likely to be sensitive to the gender of the mediator because they assume that a male will side with the husband while a woman will side with the wife. For this reason, comediation of family disputes is common, with a team made up of both a male and female mediator.

ADR and Criminal Justice

ADR is generally associated with civil law disputes. But with increasing frequency ADR is finding its way into the criminal justice system, providing alternative processes at each step, from early intervention and prevention through pretrial hearings to sentencing and even afterwards during incarceration. The purpose that ADR serves within the criminal justice system is to achieve more accountability among offenders and increase satisfaction of victims by involving them directly in the criminal justice process.[36]

The commission of a crime causes enormous conflict among the parties involved. With a criminal matter, those parties include the accused on the one side and the state in the person the prosecutor on the other, as well as the victim and the broader community. The criminal wants to be treated fairly and to minimize the consequences of his or her actions. He or she may even desire the forgiveness of the victim or the victim's family or the restoration of a previous relationship with the parties. On the other side of the dispute, the state wants to do justice and punish criminal activity. The victim seeks restitution, healing, and sometimes revenge. The community seeks protection and ultimately the assurance that the criminal's future behavior will be lawful. Unfortunately, the criminal justice system is ill equipped to negotiate the conflicting expectations of the parties. Often, the biggest loser is the victim who gets shut out of the process at every juncture. The system is compelled to deal with criminal behavior that has already occurred, and is not prepared to hold the criminal accountable to the victim or to consider how to alter the criminal's future behavior.

ADR in the Criminal Justice System

The use of ADR in the criminal justice system, generally in the form of mediation, can occur at four points in the process.

Preventing Crime

First, mediation is used in community-related programs to prevent criminal activity and to insure that conflicts between neighbors do not escalate into violence. Community dispute resolution centers offer assistance to families, local businesses, consumers, and others. Gang intervention programs use mediation to negotiate the resolution of conflict between and within groups. Mediation skills are also taught in the schools to children and teens to help them resolve their disputes peacefully and also how to intervene in and mediate the disputes of their peers.

Pretrial Mediation

Once a crime has occurred, mediation is also used at the pretrial phase in a variety of ways. So far, most pretrial mediation occurs in the context of offenses involving property crimes and simple assault where the offender is a minor and the victim(s) is an adult. Nevertheless, some jurisdictions are applying the technique to more serious crimes, as well.

1. At the preliminary hearing, mediation can replace the traditional plea bargain between the prosecutor and counsel for the offender. A neutral mediator will meet with the attorneys and the offender to negotiate the plea, punishment and restitution. As with civil mediators, the criminal justice mediator will gather information about the case and the offender that will help the parties impose a proper sanction without unnecessarily inflicting or diminishing the charge. Most important, because the offender participates, it is hoped that he or she will be less likely to view the sanction as imposed wholly from the outside, and will therefore, be more likely to comply with the plea bargain and restitution agreement.

2. Pretrial mediation is also used to orchestrate confrontations between offenders and their victims. The purpose is for each to see the other as individuals in order to negotiate restitution and promote compliance with any agreement reached. Used in this manner, mediation gives the victim an active and positive role in the process of justice. Depending upon the jurisdiction, victim-offender agreements may be binding upon all the parties, or they may be merely advisory. In the case of first-time young offenders, if the victim is satisfied that the young person understands the gravity of his or her actions and agrees to repay the victim in some appropriate manner, the victim will often drop the charges. Thus, mediation can be a complete substitute for the court process.

3. Mediation is also used to renegotiate probation and restitution in cases where the offender has not fully complied with the agreement, or conversely, where his or her behavior has been especially meritorious. The parties will include not only the offender, counsel, and the victim, but also the probation or community corrections officer.

Sentencing

A third point where mediation is applied is at sentencing, and can be applied to any crime. Because victims often feel revictimized by inappropriate sentences, mediation is used to mitigate this outcome. The process is designed to provide a forum for the judge to meet face-to-face with victims to hear their concerns. As a result, victims are more likely to feel that justice has been done. If the victim and offender have negotiated at least some of the components of the sentence among themselves, to the extent that their agreement is advisory only, the judge may impose a less severe sentence in terms of length and conditions of incarceration.

Post-Sentencing

Finally, mediation is used in prison to facilitate meetings between violent offenders and their victims. These mediations are almost always at the request of the victim. Furthermore, they do not change the status of the criminal or in any way reduce the sentence imposed. The purpose of these prison mediations is to help heal the emotional wounds of the victim and to provide the opportunity to the criminal to apologize and make peace with the victim and the victim's family.

Most ADR programs involving criminal offenses are sponsored by private organizations such as local dispute resolution centers and victim-offenders groups. However, more and more courts and probation programs are embracing ADR techniques, and this trend is expected to continue.[37]

The use of ADR in the context of criminal offenses is highly controversial and will likely remain so for a long time to come. Opponents consider the use of ADR as another way to coddle criminals and expand their rights. Proponents, on the other hand, stress the power of ADR to achieve accountability on the part of offenders, and especially to include victims in the justice process in a way that not only promotes their healing but also forces the system to impose sentences that realistically "fit the crime." Thus, they claim that ADR is actually harder on criminals than traditional approaches and results in tougher sentences. Furthermore, ADR provides another alternative to "cookie cutter" justice that treats every offender the same regardless of age, gender, background, crime, or prior record.

Victim-Offender Mediation

Both pretrial and post-trial encounters between offenders and their victims account for a substantial amount of mediations in the criminal context. Although mediation involving many different types of offenders and crimes has been successful, most involve younger offenders with few prior convictions, and no major mental health or substance abuse problems.[38] As indicated above, sometimes these encounters are initiated by the victims or their families in an attempt to come to terms with the crime. However, many are initiated by community, police, or court program personnel who offer services to crime victims including mediation with the offender. Consequently, one of the most important steps in achieving success in these mediations is to explain the process, including the benefits and the risks to both victims and offenders, and to gain their support and trust in the process. Of paramount importance in victim-offender mediation is that the victim not be again victimized by the experience. Consequently, it is critical that none of the parties be coerced into participating.[39]

Securities Disputes

Like the construction industry, the securities industry[40] makes extensive use of ADR, especially arbitration and mediation, to solve customer disputes, disputes with employees, and conflict among member firms. In 1817, the New York Stock Exchange (NYSE) provided in its constitution that inter-dealer disputes concerning the purchase of stock would be resolved by a majority of the NYSE Board. This procedure was extended in 1872 to nonmembers of the NYSE who could initiate arbitration with members concerning disputes between them. In 1968, the National Association of Securities Dealers (NASD) began to use arbitration extensively to resolve problems between members and their customers. In 1977, the Securities Industry Conference on Arbitration (SICA) was formed by the NASD and other industry groups to handle both customer and intra-industry matters. SICA developed a Uniform Code of Arbitration and a manual for arbitrators. By the mid-1990s, thousands of disputes were being heard under these rules in sessions sponsored by the NASD. In addition, the American Arbitration Association hears several hundred securities-related disputes under its Securities Arbitration Rules. Most securities disputes take an average of from seven to nine months to reach the arbitration hearing, depending upon complexity, and two days' worth of sessions to reach a resolution.[41]

Predispute Agreements   Many securities arbitrations arise due to predispute arbitration agreements incorporated into sales or margin agreements between customers and a brokerage firm. Dealers who do business with one another also sign agreements that frequently contain arbitration provisions. Likewise, employees of securities firms sign agreements to arbitrate employment disputes with their employers. Consequently, when a dispute arises in any of these arenas, the parties are contractually bound to submit the matter to binding arbitration.

When no predispute arbitration agreement exists, an aggrieved customer or dealer may choose to file a lawsuit. Alternatively, he or she may decide to voluntarily use SICA, AAA or some other industry procedures for arbitration of the matter. In more and more situations, however, parties are using mediation. One of the primary attractions of this method over arbitration is the cost savings associated with discovery and preparation for an arbitration hearing. Mediation is especially useful in resolving disputes between a customer and a broker over such matters as an investment recommended by the broker that went sour, extensive trading activity designed to generate commissions, failing to tell a customer important facts about an investment, and other similar matters involving breach of fiduciary duty or professional negligence.[42]

Securities Arbitration   The mediation of securities disputes proceed much like any other commercial or business mediation. In contrast, securities arbitration has some special aspects that parties need to consider.

1. First of all, the rules for arbitration of securities disputes vary on several key points, depending upon which organization promulgated them. Therefore, parties and their counsels should be aware of the rules that apply. If the rules can be selected by the parties, they also must decide on which set of rules is most favorable to the parties involved.

2. Second, securities arbitration often requires that the aggrieved party file a claim setting forth the facts of the dispute in detail, supporting documentation and a calculation of damages. The respondent must file an answer in twenty days. Both the claim and the answer can later be amended. Thus, the commencement of securities arbitration highly resembles the filing of a lawsuit.

3. Third, the arbitrators involved are frequently not associated with the securities industry. Furthermore, in matters where the amount in controversy is greater than $25,000, the NASD Code requires the use of a panel of three arbitrators.

4. Fourth, the award may or may not be confidential, depending upon the rules being used. The AAA rules keep all awards private, the NASD rules reveal awards in matters involving public customers (e.g., state employee's pension fund), while NYSE rules reveal the awards made to both public and private customers.

5. Finally, the failure of an industry member to satisfy an award can lead to the suspension or revocation of its license to do business. Thus, securities arbitration has a built in enforcement mechanism that is not available in many other industries.

Environmental Disputes

Environmental disputes usually involve clean-up of accidents or pollution, location of hazardous waste sites, enforcement or promulgation of regulations, preservation of resources and wilderness areas and other similar matters. Environmental disputes are unique from most other types of disputes in that they involve a large and divergent number of individuals and groups, many of whom are not directly involved in negotiating an outcome to a dispute. Furthermore, they raise questions concerning critical public policy issues. Finally, environmental conflict often concerns highly complex matters that require specialized knowledge to understand. For these and other reasons, environmental disputes are difficult to resolve in any forum, including a court of law. But they offer some special challenges when considering the use of ADR as an appropriate dispute resolution mechanism.

Parties to the Conflict

Environmental conflict usually pits an alleged polluter or exploiter against not one, but many people and interest groups. For example, a chemical spill near a residential neighborhood will implicate the residents, insurance carriers, local government, state and national regulatory agencies, emergency response groups, health care providers, citizen organizations, elected officials at various levels, employees and stockholders of the polluter, and many more. In addition, the media will likely be present trying to report on the matter and make sense of the various interests. Unfortunately, only a few of the parties affected will actually sit down at the bargaining table. Nevertheless, those who are absent and unrepresented will often be able to delay resolution of the case. Involving as many people as possible in solving the problems that an environmental event creates is the challenge facing those who attempt to craft an effective approach to resolving the dispute.

Public Policy Issues

An environmental issue or event raises many questions that any resolution process must deal with if valid solutions are to be identified and implemented. An act of pollution, for example, will always cause property damage and may also injure or kill citizens. This will result in claims usually in the form of lawsuits filed by individuals, property owners, insurance providers, governmental groups, and anyone else who believes they have been immediately harmed. In the case of air pollution or down stream water pollution, claimants may live hundreds of miles away and across state lines. Thus, claims may arise in many jurisdictions, both state and federal. Those claiming that the event will have long term negative effects may also file on behalf of themselves or as representatives of the community or some other constituency. Regulators will also bring actions against the polluter that may include administrative, civil and criminal proceedings. In short, one event can give rise to dozens of divergent actions in many different forums. The most effective technique(s) for resolving these claims will likely be the one that consolidates as many actions and issues as possible into one joint endeavor. Furthermore, the best technique(s) will deal with both present and future implications, public and private concerns, local and outlying effects, and other seemingly contradictory interests.

Beyond the damages issues, environmental emergencies and problems almost always bring into question the effectiveness of laws and regulation dealing with the environment and how well they are being enforced. Business interests and those allied with them economically and politically will often use the opportunity to press for relaxation of standards on the grounds that industry, if left to its own devises, can better regulate itself. Those on the other side will call for more stringent standards and penalties, and blame regulators for failing to enforce existing law so as to prevent emergencies in the first place. Dispute resolution of the immediate claims will take place in this broader arena of public policy concerns and will both influence and be influenced by them.

Complexity   The discussion above demonstrates the complexity of environmental disputes in terms of the large number of people involved and the divergent interests, both public and private, that are at issue. In addition, these disputes often involve complex scientific and engineering matters that only highly trained people can fully understand. Resolving environmental matters effectively requires the use of techniques that can accommodate complex testimony.

Unlike other areas of conflict, environmental disputes do not lend themselves to a particular ADR procedure or set of rules as with construction, securities, labor, employment and other dispute categories. Given the vast number of interests involved in any environmental event, ADR can be used to dispose of collateral issues and parties. Mediation techniques are especially promising in the environmental arena in that they are designed to identify joint interests among highly different parties and concerns. Arbitration is also promising through the use of arbitrators with specialized knowledge but also with some of the powers of a civil judge to require parties to appear and participate in the resolution of the matter. ADR has proved so effective in resolving these complex disputes that many states have enacted statutes to encourage the use of ADR in the context of environmental conflicts.[43]

Community-Based Dispute Resolution   The use of alternative dispute resolution, both formal and informal, to both prevent and also to settle disputes among individual citizens before they escalate into violence or lawsuits is as old as human existence. In both Chapters One and Three, we reviewed some of that history. In Chapter Four we discussed how government has encouraged the use of community-based dispute resolution to solve problems between neighbors, merchants and their customers, classmates, and within families, by passing laws establishing community relations programs and centers, including:

◆   Federal law created the Community Relations Service to provide assistance to communities and persons therein in resolving disputes, disagreements, or difficulties relating to discriminatory practices in housing,[44] in federally assisted programs due to age,[45] in employment,[46] due to disability,[47] and in other ways.[48]

♦ The Dispute Resolution Act provides assistance to the various states to establish community-based dispute resolution mechanisms that will promote the expeditious settlement of minor disputes by offering low threat, flexible forums for their settlement. The Act specifically provides that times and locations of community-based services are to be convenient,[49] that provision should be made for people with language barriers and disabilities,[50] that the procedures be readily understandable,[51] and that the availability of community-based ADR be well publicized.[52] These programs often provide the training ground for new mediators.

♦ Various state programs establish new community-based mediation programs aimed at promoting peace and preserving community values. In fact, nearly every state has passed some sort of legislation aimed at promoting the use of ADR at the community level, often by providing funding to private, non-profit dispute resolution centers.[53] Although these centers handle a certain number of disputes from "walk-in" clients, most of their activity comes from law enforcement agencies, the courts, the state attorney, legal aid, tenant associations, consumer hotlines, and other agencies. In some jurisdictions, community dispute resolution centers participate actively in multi-door courthouse programs, discussed in Chapter Six, and may even act as the clearinghouse for new disputes and litigation.

One of the first community-based programs of the modern era was developed in 1970 in Columbus, Ohio, by the law professors of the Capital University School of Law. Law students were trained to mediate disputes among citizens who often went to the local prosecutor's office looking for assistance. The program flourished and by 1989 was handling nearly 60,000 cases annually. Today, hundreds of similar programs exist in all large U.S. cities and many other places as well. Some deal primarily with neighbor and family disputes, while others offer an array of resolution techniques, usually at low cost, to all sorts of parties and disputes. The American Bar Association maintains a list of these programs in its *Dispute Resolution Program Directory*.

Types of Disputes Disputes that are especially amenable to resolution by a community dispute resolution program include disputes between:

♦ Neighbors over boundary lines, noise, etc.

♦ Family members, especially couples, and also parents and their teenage children

♦ Parents of minor children over court-ordered visitation issues or child support

♦ Customer complaints about shoddy products, failure to perform services, credit terms, and so forth

♦ Landlord/tenant matters including eviction, failure to maintain premises, etc.

♦ Property owners and trespassers

♦ Victims of assault and their assailants

♦ Employers and employees, involving wrongful discharge, accusations of theft and other wrongdoing, etc.

♦ Teachers and students, over discipline problems and expulsion of the student from school

♦ Schools and parents, over failure to provide essential services to students with special needs, inappropriate disciplinary measures, etc.

♦ An injured party and the tortfeasor, especially where the tortfeasor is uninsured (e.g., uninsured driver who damages another person's car and/or causes physical injury)

♦ Insurance carriers and policyholders, over payment of small claims.

Conciliation and mediation tend to be the primary forms of ADR that community dispute resolution programs provide. However, more and more are also providing both binding and nonbinding arbitration, as well as moderated settlement conferences. Some centers offer specialized services, such as property division counseling for divorcing couples, victim/offender encounters, and management of restitution agreements.

Advantages of Community Dispute Resolution

One of the advantages that community programs provide is speedy resolution of problems. Sometimes, a staff member or volunteer mediator will telephone the other party during the initial intake interview with a new client and seek to resolve the matter over the phone. For cases where a formal mediation or arbitration session is required, the session will often be scheduled within ten days of intake.

Community centers provide ancillary services as well, including by helping the parties draft a memorandum of their agreement,* and by referring parties to other providers including family services, credit counselors, mental health professional, law enforcement mechanisms, and attorney referral services. In some situations, a center will act as the trustee for money that one party owes to another.

Dispute resolution centers almost always sponsor mediator training for their volunteer mediators. In addition, some provide such training to others in the community who are close to conflict, including teachers, students, ministers, gang members, police and so forth. Community dispute resolution centers often provide would-be professional mediators with their initial training and opportunity to practice their skills.

The final chapter will deal with the important issue of the unauthorized practice of law among practitioners of alternative dispute resolution. It will also discuss some of the career opportunities available to nonlawyers in the ADR industry. The chapter will conclude with some observations by the authors of this book concerning the future of alternative dispute resolution in the United States and its role in our system of justice.

Sources

1 *Alternative Dispute Resolution Techniques*, 51.041 (W. Hancock ed. 1989).
2 See *e.g.*, *Blanks v. Midstate Constructors, Inc.*, 610 S.W. 2d 220 (Tex. Civ. App. 1980).
3 W. Hancock, *supra*, at 51.029.

---

* See Chapter Eight for a discussion of the unauthorized practice of law in the context of drafting settlement agreements.

[4] *Alternative Dispute Resolution Techniques*, at 51.025 (W. Hancock ed. 1996). See, *e.g.*, *Weinrott v. Carp*, 298 N.E.2d 42 (N.Y. 1973).

[5] See *e.g*, *J&S Constr. Co. v. Travelers Indem. Co.*, 520 F.2d 809 (9th Cir. 1975) (a contractor's surety was required to pay due to the contractor's breach, even though the surety did not participate in the arbitration). Other courts have reached opposite results, see *Transamerica Ins. Co. v. Yonkers Contracting Co.* 267 N.Y.S.2d 669 (Sup. Ct. 1966).

[6] *Compare Grover-Diamond Associates v. American Arbitration Assn.*, 211 N.W.2d 787 (Minn. 1973) (consolidation ordered where there were common questions involved, and the various arbitration agreements did not prohibit consolidation); *Stop & Shop Cos. v. Gilbance Bldg. Co.*, 304 N.E.2d 429 (Mass. 1973) (consolidation denied in absence of agreement among the parties to consolidate).

[7] B. Roth, R. Wulff, C. Cooper, *The Alternative Dispute Resolution Practice Guide*, § 16:13 (1993).

[8] *Id.*

[9] 29 U.S.C. § 206(d)(1994).

[10] 42 U.S.C. § 2000e (1994).

[11] 29 U.S.C. § 621 (1994).

[12] 29 U.S.C. § 623 (1994).

[13] 42 U.S.C. § 12101(1994).

[14] 29 U.S.C. § 2601 (1994).

[15] 88 U.S.S. at Large 829.

[16] See E. Galton, *Mediation, A Texas Practice Guide*, at § 18.4 (1993), for a more complete discussion of employment disputes.

[17] *See, e.g., Graham v. Scissor-Tail, Inc.*, 623 P.2d 165 (Cal 1981)(in bank).

[18] *Id.*, at 180.

[19] 9 U.S.C. § 1 (1994).

[20] *Gilmer v. Interstate/Johnson Lane Corp.*, 111 S.Ct 1647 (1991),114 L. Ed. 2d 26 (1991).

[21] *Id.*, at 1652, quoting *Mitsubishi Motors Corp. v. Soler Chrysler-Plymouth, Inc.*,469 U.S. 916 (1985), concerning the arbitration of a claim arising under the Sherman Act.

[22] *Id.*

[23] *Id.*

[24] 42 U.S.C. § 1981a (1994).

[25] 42 U.S.C. § 12212 (1994).

[26] *Gilmer v. Interstate/Johnson Lane Corp.*,111 S.Ct. 1647 (1991). 114 L. Ed. 2d 26 (1991).

[27] B. Roth, R. Wulff, and C. Cooper, *The Alternative Dispute Resolution Practice Guide*, § 17.10 (1993).

[28] *Id.*, at § 17.12 - 17.33.

[29] *Id.*

[30] 29 U.S.C. § 172(a)(1994).

[31] *Id.*, at § 158(d).

[32] B. Roth, R. Wulff, and C. Cooper, The Alternative Dispute Resolution Practice Guide, § 31.2 (1993).

[33] Pearson, Family Mediation, *in* National Symposium on Court-Connected Dispute Resolution Research, A Report on Current Research Findings – Implications for Courts and Future Research Needs, 51 (Keilitz ed 1994).

[34] See *e.g.*, Me. Rev. Stat. Ann. tit. 19 § 636, 665 (1985 and Supp. 1996): Alaska Stat. § 25.24.060 (1994).

[35] *Id.*

[36] See *e.g.*, Kan. Stat. Ann. § 23-603 (1995), Cal. Civ. Code Ann. § 4351.5(3) (West 1983); *compare* N.D. Cent. Code § 14-09, 1-5 (1991) and Alaska Stat. § 25.24.060(c) (1994) (preventing a mediator from excluding attorneys from the mediation session).

[37] Gibson, *Fighting Crime with ADR*, 12 Tex. Trial Law. 45 (May 20, 1986).

[38] A. Greenspan, *Handbook of Alternative Dispute Resolution*, at § 17.3.(1990).

[39] *Id.*, at § 17.5.

[40] Securities matters include the purchase and sale of stock, bonds, U.S. government paper (e.g., treasury bills), commercial paper, shares of limited partnerships, etc.

[41] ADR Guide, § 21.2.

[42] B. Roth, R. Wulff, and C. Cooper, *supra* note 32, at § 21.2.

[43] *Id.*, at § 35.2

[44] See *e.g.*, Va. Code Ann. § 10.1-1434 (Michie 1993); Ohio Rev. Code Ann. §.1521.03 (Banks-Baldwin 1994).

[45] 28 U.S.C. § 3610(1994).

[46] *Id.*, at § 2000e-5.

[47] *Id.*, at § 12212.

[48] 42 U.S.C. § 2000g-1.

[49] 42 U.S.C. §2000g-1 (1994).

[50] *Id.*, at § 4(3).

[51] *Id.*, at § 4(4).

[52] *Id.*, at § 4(7).

[53] See N. Rogers and C. McEwen, *Mediation Law, Policy & Practice,* Appendix B (2[d]. ed. 1994), for a listing of state community ADR statutes.

Chapter Eight

The Role of the Paralegal in ADR

Introduction

ADR is a complex topic, and like any new and promising system or body of knowledge, it is changing and growing daily. One result of the enormous growth in ADR is its emergence as both an institution and an industry. ADR is an institution in that it encompasses rules, regulations, and professional organizations and practitioners. Furthermore, it enjoys official recognition by other major institutions such as labor unions, large corporations and, of course, the courts. ADR is also an industry in that it has spawned hundreds of for-profit and not-for-profit businesses, employs thousands of people in many different positions and roles, sponsors large numbers of training seminars, and in other ways generates revenue. This concluding chapter will summarize the role of the paralegal in ADR, explore the issue of ethics, including the unauthorized practice of law, and conclude with a look at one ADR system in action and how well it has lived up to the promise of ADR.

The Role of the Paralegal in ADR

Throughout this text, we have discussed the role of the paralegal in ADR. Our focus has been primarily on paralegals as support staff to attorneys who use ADR to help clients resolve disputes. We have also talked about paralegals who support attorneys and others who are professional mediators, arbitrators or private judges. And to some extent, we have discussed the paralegal as client advocate. More and more paralegals accompany clients to administrative hearings, ADR proceedings, and other nonjudicial forums that permit the use of nonattorney advocates. For example, most federal government agencies who provide services directly to citizens must permit parties to be represented by people other than attorneys. Consequently, in certain situations paralegals may serve as advocates in ADR proceedings before government agencies. Finally, we have looked at ways in which paralegals can serve as mediators and arbitrators, most often in the context of community dispute resolution.

Supporting Litigation

By far the biggest role that paralegals play in ADR is in their support of litigators whose cases involve the use of ADR at some stage in the process. In most situations, trial is not a foregone conclusion and, therefore, litigation and ADR run on parallel tracks as the case proceeds. At any point in the process, the parties may be preparing for trial, preparing for mediation, and negotiating a possible resolution of the matter, all at the same time. Therefore, it is critical for paralegals to perform their duties in such a way that does not weaken or sabotage any of the resolution strategies available. For example, in dealing with the other side, an effective paralegal will avoid disclosing important information about the client and the case while at the same time signaling a willingness to hear and consider what the other side wants.

In the context of litigation, paralegals frequently have ongoing contact with clients, as well as with the support staff from the other side. Thus, they can provide valuable assistance to attorneys in gathering both objective and subjective information about the case, and in providing feedback about the client's needs and desires. This information can be important to the attorney in determining the most appropriate strategy for resolving the case. The paralegal can also gather information about similar cases, likely jury awards, and the needs and desires of the other side, all of which is critical in assessing what outcome the opponent will consider acceptable.

In the context of formal negotiation and mediation, attorneys will sometimes employ the use of settlement brochures, which outline the strengths of the client's case and set forth a realistic and supportable rationale for what the client wants. Settlement brochures are often prepared by paralegals who are relied upon by busy attorneys to distill complex information and package the client's case in a creative and persuasive manner. In so doing, a paralegal can influence how a case is presented, and thus play an important role in how it is ultimately resolved. Similarly, paralegals assist attorneys in preparing position papers that mediators often request from the parties prior to mediation. In so doing, they can influence the course and outcome of mediation.

Typically it is paralegals who help arrange for mediation, arbitration, and other ADR processes. They need to know the rules under which sessions will be conducted. Effective paralegals will insist that all rules be scrupulously followed. They should also learn as much as possible about the logistics of each session, especially when it is up to the ADR neutral and/or the other party to make most of the arrangements. Adequate location, facilities, food and beverages, and other similar concerns are critical to providing an environment conducive to settlement.

Paralegals often participate in negotiations, mediations, and other ADR proceedings in order to assist where needed and to provide another set of eyes and ears. Consequently, it is important for them to understand the ADR technique being employed in each case in order to lend effective support to the client and the process. Training in negotiation and mediation is important in helping paralegals develop listening and observation skills necessary to effectively participate in these processes.

Exercise

Appendix 13 contains a list of competencies of a civil litigation paralegal. Review the list and identify which activities support ADR. How? Of those activities that support ADR, discuss how the paralegal can perform each one in such a way that supports both the adversarial nature of litigation and the cooperative nature of ADR.

Ethical Responsibilities of Paralegals in ADR

Paralegals who are employed by attorneys have a broader range of rules and ethical guidelines to follow than their employers. First and foremost, paralegals are governed by the same rules of conduct and professional responsibility that apply to attorneys who employ them. These include the rules of professional conduct and codes of professionalism promulgated in each state, generally by the group or organization that has jurisdiction over such matters. Typically, this is the state bar association, or an agency of state government. In many states, those rules are based on models developed by the American Bar Association.

Under these rules and codes, attorneys and their staff are admonished to represent clients zealously, be honest and trustworthy, avoid conflicts of interest, and maintain the client's confidentiality. In addition, attorneys are required to supervise the work of their support staff in such a way as to ensure that applicable rules and codes are not violated.[1]

In addition to the rules that govern the behavior of attorneys, paralegals are also guided by rules developed by paralegal organizations. The National Association of Legal Assistants, Inc. (NALA) has promulgated *Model Standards and Guidelines for Utilization of Legal Assistants* and a *Code of Ethics and Professional Responsibility*. The National Federation of Paralegal Associations (NFPA) has developed its *Model Code of Ethics and Professional Responsibility*.

NALA's *Model Standards* are aimed at attorneys and legal departments of companies or agencies who employ paralegals. Thus, they emphasize the limits of what a paralegal may do in that context. For example, a paralegal may not establish an attorney-client relationship, give legal opinions or advice, set legal fees, represent a client before a court, or in other ways practice law. In addition, clients are to be informed of the paralegal's position and role as a nonattorney member of the team. When performing work that an attorney could do, the paralegal is to be supervised by an attorney. Finally, the *Model Standards* impose on legal employers the responsibility of continuing education for the paralegal in substantive matters. NALA's *Code of Ethics and Responsibility* contains similar provisions, but it applies directly to the paralegal rather than the employer. NFPA's *Model Code* covers the same topics as NALA's *Code*, but adds considerably more detail.

All of these standards and codes contain provisions directly applicable to paralegals involved in one way or another in ADR. Several provisions concern the unauthorized practice of law, which is discussed below. Following are provisions of NFPA's *Model Code of Ethics and Professional Responsibility* that are applicable to the conduct of paralegals involved in ADR.

CANON 1.   A paralegal shall achieve and maintain a high level of competency.

> EC-1.1 A paralegal shall achieve competency through education, training, and work experience.
> EC-1.2 A paralegal shall participate in continuing education to keep informed of current legal, technical, and general developments.

CANON 2.   A paralegal shall maintain a high level of personal and professional integrity.

> EC-2.1 A paralegal shall not engage in any *ex parte* communications involving the courts or any other adjudicatory body in an attempt to exert undue influence or to obtain advantage for the benefit of only one party.

CANON 4.   **A paralegal shall serve the public interest by contributing to the delivery of quality legal services and the improvement of the legal system.**

EC-4.1 A paralegal shall be sensitive to the needs of the public and shall promote the development and implementation of programs that address those needs.

EC-4.2 A paralegal shall support *bona fide* efforts to meet the need for legal services by those unable to pay reasonable and customary fees; for example, participation in *pro bono* projects and volunteer work.

EC-4.3 A paralegal shall support efforts to improve the system and shall assist in making changes.

CANON 5.   **A paralegal shall preserve all confidential information provided by the client or acquired from other sources before, during, or after the course of the professional relationship.**

CANON 7.   **A paralegal shall not engage in the unauthorized practice of law.**

CANON 8.   **A paralegal shall avoid conflicts of interest and shall disclose any possible conflict to the employer or client, as well as to the prospective employers of clients.**

Exercises

Below are several situations to which the Canons, above, may apply. For each situation, identify the applicable Canon. How does it apply to the situation? How should a paralegal respond?

Situation 1:   A paralegal is hired by a law firm to support several business litigators. The local jurisdiction has an aggressive program of court-annexed ADR, and most law suits are referred to mediation. Unfortunately, the paralegal has no training or experience in ADR.

Situation 2:   A paralegal telephones the clerk of court in order to learn if and when the judge intends to assign a mediator to a particular case. During the conversation, the paralegal mentions the names of two mediators with whom that paralegal's law firm has achieved good results for their clients.

Situation 3:   A paralegal is employed by a law firm that consistently resists efforts to engage in any form of ADR, and when compelled to do so, is uncooperative nearly to the point of bad faith.

Situation 4:   A paralegal moves to a jurisdiction that has several community dispute resolution centers badly in need of volunteer mediators.

Situation 5:   A paralegal who works for a law firm with several litigation cases that have bogged down for various reasons learns that the local courts intend to hold a settlement week.

> Situation 6:   While making arrangements for a mediation session with the secretary of an attorney for the other side in a lawsuit, a paralegal mentions that his firm's client has complained about all the legal fees and is hopeful that the case can be settled during mediation.
>
> Situation 7:   A paralegal learns that her law firm has just taken on the defense of an insurance carrier in a personal injury case. The case involves a plaintiff who was recently a party in a consumer dispute that the paralegal mediated as a volunteer at a local community dispute resolution center.

Emerging Opportunities in ADR

Today, more and more positions involving ADR responsibilities are being created in both the public and private sector. Paralegals who are trained in both the law and in ADR are especially qualified to fill many of these positions, for two reasons. First, employers such as law firms, corporate legal departments, and government agencies are directly involved with prosecuting disputes that have been defined in legal terms and, therefore, they need and value staff who are trained to think "legally." Second, even when a position involves primarily disputes that appear to be "extralegal," (e.g., disputes between neighbors, parents and children, gangs), the resolution of these disputes must take into account the respective legal rights of the parties.

Examples of positions for ADR specialists include the following:

♦ Court systems that make active use of ADR employ coordinators to develop standards for and pools of competent mediators, conduct mediator orientation and training programs, conduct settlement weeks and, overall, to ensure that each individual court within the system is assigning cases to mediation and in other ways is making effective use of ADR.

♦ Community dispute resolution agencies, discussed in Chapter VII, hire ADR specialists to plan, develop and administer the agency, raise funds, train staff, develop business for the agency by communicating its presence and availability to constituents, and to serve as mediators and arbitrators.

♦ Large corporations who have internal legal departments often employ ADR coordinators who ensure that ADR is used effectively in litigation matters in which the corporation is a party, who train inside lawyers and other staff in ADR, and who work with human resources to develop internal grievance programs and procedures and to resolve employee disputes using ADR techniques.

♦ Law firms often engage ADR specialists to assist litigators and trial lawyers in their use of and participation in ADR, to evaluate individual cases and to identify if and how ADR can be used to move a matter toward resolution, to orient and train staff in ADR, and even to develop an ADR practice within the firm.

♦ Government agencies that provide services directly to citizens (e.g., Social Security Administration) frequently employ individuals in a wide variety of roles to administer ADR programs, train staff, and conduct arbitration and mediation sessions with agency constituents.

♦ Police departments employ ADR specialists to develop and administer programs designed to diffuse tension within a community and in so doing to prevent crime. These specialists work actively with established community agencies such as community centers, local churches and schools, women's and children's centers, gang intervention programs, and others.

♦ School systems have created positions for specialists who are qualified to promote peace and improve discipline in schools where conflict among students, disputes between students and teachers, gang violence, property damage, truancy and other critical problems are present or threatened.

♦ Hospitals and health care systems employ mediators to help resolve disputes with patients before they escalate into benefits and malpractice claims.

Exercise

> Make a survey of the opportunities for employment in the ADR field in your area. Contact each of the following institutions or organizations to learn about their use of ADR professionals, whether as employees, consultants or third-party neutrals.
> a.   the civil courts
> b.   community dispute resolution agencies
> c.   major corporations
> d.   law firms
> e.   local offices of government agencies
> f.   police department
> g.   local school districts
> h.   local hospitals and health care systems
> i.   labor unions

The Unauthorized Practice of Law

Generally, ADR is independent of the courts and does not constitute the practice of law. Consequently, serving in the role of a neutral third party in an ADR proceeding is usually not considered the practice of law. In addition, most ADR proceedings result in settlements that are not reviewed by a court. This is true even when the proceeding has been ordered by the court.* If a lawsuit has been filed, the complaining parties will usually move to dismiss the suit once settlement has been reached, thus terminating the court's jurisdiction over the matter.

Despite ADR's theoretical independence from the law, it usually occurs in the context of a real or threatened lawsuit. Most disputes have legal underpinnings, whether or not the parties are aware of the legal rights and defenses that they possess. If the parties are represented by counsel, they will likely have been apprised of the applicable law. In this situation, an ADR neutral may still get involved in helping the attorneys to draft a settlement agreement.

If only one party is represented, however, the unrepresented party is apt to be less knowledgeable about his or her rights and defenses, and may look to the ADR neutral to provide that information and to help draft a final settlement agreement. Also, the neutral may be tempted to actually provide legal advice to any party who appears to be operating at a significant disadvantage due to lack of counsel.

---

* Most settlements reached in family law cases (e.g., divorce, child visitation and support, etc.) are reviewed by a court and entered as the court's judgment in the case. Consequently, they are enforceable by contempt if either party violates the agreement.

Where both parties are *pro se*, the ADR neutral is apt to be the only person involved who is aware of the legal issues and who possesses the skills to achieve a clear settlement and draft a cogent agreement that will be legally enforceable.

Unfortunately, when an ADR neutral offers legal information, gives legal advice, or contributes to the drafting of a settlement agreement, he or she may be engaging in the unauthorized practice of law, depending upon the jurisdiction. Even when the neutral is licensed to practice law, the fact that he or she is engaging in activity that even appears to favor one party over the other may compromise a neutral position. In an attempt to "level the playing field," the neutral may inadvertently champion the cause of one of the parties and give them the advantage.

Some jurisdictions prohibit any advising or drafting by an ADR neutral, while most offer little or no guidance. Often the only rules available are codes of professional responsibility that prohibit lawyers from representing parties that have conflicting interests, unless the parties are informed of the conflict and agree to the representation ahead of time.[*] These rules anticipate a situation where two parties hire one attorney, as is often the case, for example, with business partners who desire to exercise a buy-sell agreement, or a divorcing couple who seek an amicable divorce. A lawyer in this position must maintain neutrality while assessing each party's understanding of his or her rights. If either of the parties does not understand their rights and obligations, the attorney has to decide whether, or how to provided the needed information or advice so that negotiations can proceed fairly.

An ADR neutral is sometimes placed in a similar situation when either of the parties lacks a sufficient understanding of his or her rights and obligations to make good settlement decisions. While the ADR neutral does not owe either party a duty of loyalty, as is the case with counsel hired by a party, the neutral is still required to be honest and to provide an adequate level of service.[2]

One approach is to permit the ADR neutral to provide legal information but not to give legal advice. For example, the neutral may explain the provisions of the applicable statute to a divorcing couple concerning what property is considered to be "marital property." But the neutral may not advise either party about how the law applies to their particular situation.[3] Also, the neutral can assist in drafting an agreement, but he or she should advise the parties not to sign it until each has consulted with an attorney.[4]

A review of state laws and bar association rules concerning what an ADR neutral may and may not do in terms of providing legal information, and in drafting agreements reveals that there is much confusion and ambiguity on the topic and consequently very little agreement, both within and among groups. Furthermore, the landscape is constantly changing as each group and jurisdiction gains more experience and insight, amending the rules accordingly.

---

[*] See, for example, the Model Rules of the American Bar Association, which permit "intermediation" by a lawyer between parties with conflicting interests only when informed consent has been obtained and when there is "little risk of material prejudice to the interests of any of the clients if the contemplated resolution is unsuccessful." ABA Model Rules of Professional Conduct, Rule 2.2(a)(3) (1983).

Exercises

1. Imagine a mediation between a business owner and a customer who claims to have been defrauded by the business owner.

   a. What if both parties are represented by counsel but the business owner's attorney is very competent while the customer's attorney is inexperienced in consumer law? What challenges does the mediator face? How should the mediator respond?

   b. What if the business owner is represented by counsel but the customer is acting on her own behalf? Assume further that the customer is unaware of consumer legislation that would make it quite easy to prove that her claims are justified. How should the mediator respond? What potential liability does the mediator face if she informs the customer of her rights under the law? If she fails to inform the customer? What liability if the mediator stops the mediation?

2. Research the laws and rules in your state or jurisdiction concerning the unauthorized practice of law that apply to ADR neutrals and proceedings. To whom do they apply? Do they clarify or confuse the situation? Who enforces them? Has there been any attempt to enforce them and, if so, what was the outcome? How would you draft the rules?

When a neutral is not licensed to practice law, any offering of legal information, advice or other services is especially suspect. According to Canon 6 of NALA's *Code of Ethics and Professional Responsibility*, "A legal assistant shall not engage in the unauthorized practice of law and shall assist in preventing the unauthorized practice of law." Likewise, the *Model Code of Ethics and Professional Responsibility* promulgated by NFPA, Canon 7, states, "A paralegal shall not engage in the unauthorized practice of law," and further, "A paralegal shall comply with the applicable legal authority governing the unauthorized practice of law" (Canon 7, EC-7.1).

The issue of the unauthorized practice of law by nonlawyers is not new. Accountants who advise clients on tax law matters and real estate agents who review documents, draft amendments to standard contracts, and advise on matters concerning property law have often been accused of practicing law without a license. Likewise, financial and insurance consultants who advise clients on estate planning matters have faced similar accusations.

Today, most state legislatures and courts distinguish between situations involving purely transactional matters (buying property, filing tax returns, purchasing insurance) from matters involving litigation. With the former, they are typically more lenient because transaction professionals serve the good of consumers who prefer to deal with only one person in order to buy a house or an insurance policy, or have their tax returns prepared.

Courts also look at whether the consumer has been charged for the legal advice given. If not, they are more likely to permit the sharing of legal information and advice in these situations.

In the context of ADR, courts generally have permitted nonlawyer neutrals to assist in the preparation of settlement agreements but have been less lenient with regard to the provision of legal advice during the proceeding. They argue that nonlawyers are unlikely to understand all of the legal issues involved in a dispute or whether a question involves simple or complex answers. In contrast, ADR neutrals are appropriate participants in the task of drafting settlement agreements. Because they have been an integral part of the settlement process, they are apt to have a clear understanding of what the parties want and also what they want to avoid. Nevertheless, a nonlawyer neutral should always advise the parties to have any agreement reviewed by an attorney before signing it.

Raising concerns about the unauthorized practice of law in the context of ADR has been a defense against ADR by attorneys and other members of the legal establishment who feel that ADR will take away business. This is especially true in those jurisdictions where ADR is not well established. Nevertheless, as the discussion above demonstrates, the issue is real and deserves careful consideration and analysis.

Exercises

1. Do you agree that parties to a dispute need information about the law in order to assess the fairness of any settlement offers made by the other side? Why or why not? In what ways does the nature of the dispute make knowledge of one's legal rights more or less important? For example, compare a dispute between a mechanic and a car owner over allegedly unnecessary repairs to a dispute between divorcing parents over the custody and visitation of their children.

2. Discuss how a mediator can make sure the parties are adequately informed about the law involved in their dispute in each of the following situations:
   - ✓ The mediator doesn't know the law involved.
   - ✓ The mediator knows the law but is prohibited by state law or professional rules of conduct from giving legal advice.
   - ✓ One of the parties is represented by counsel and the other is not.

3. In situations where parties are not represented by counsel, mediators are often permitted to distribute brochures that discuss the applicable law. How adequate would this approach be to informing people of their legal rights in a dispute between a mechanic and a car owner over allegedly unnecessary repairs? In a dispute between divorcing parents over the custody and visitation of their children?

The Promise and Reality of ADR

The modern ADR movement began with great promises. Some of those promises have been fulfilled, some have been forgotten or amended, and some await fulfillment. What is apparent is that the effectiveness of ADR, and its ability to live up to its potential depend to a great extent upon the ADR resources available to disputants. This, in turn, is dependent upon how well-developed the ADR system is in any given locale.

Where ADR has been legitimized by legislation and fully annexed by the courts, it is likely to be a full-blown industry comprising a wide variety of agencies, experts, training, and other mechanisms. It will also provide a ready supply of individual mediators, arbitrators and other neutrals competing for ADR business. Issues such as the unauthorized practice of law, the appropriateness of ADR to solve different types of disputes, or whether ADR is siphoning off litigation business will likely have been resolved.

Conversely, in areas of the country where the local courts have not fully embraced ADR, where few agencies provide ADR services, or where very few experienced practitioners offer their help as neutral third parties, ADR will be an insignificant and often distrusted part of the local justice system. This is especially true in towns and rural districts that may be too small to support the infrastructure necessary to enable ADR to be a viable alternative to traditional litigation. Nevertheless, many urban areas around the United States have yet to fully embrace ADR and, in those places, it remains only a future promise.

Paralegals working on cases where ADR is anticipated and who practice in jurisdictions where ADR is a well-developed industry will find a ready supply of expertise, assistance, and training. However, paralegals in less well-developed districts may find even the most basic services lacking. For example, it may be difficult to find a competent mediator, or proper facilities for conducting a mediation. The attorneys as well as the clients may need extensive orientation in how the particular ADR process involved will work and what results to expect. Likewise, the attorneys may participate without having properly prepared a presentation of their clients' cases. In areas where ADR is not well-supported, moderated settlement conference, summary jury trial, and other trial-like processes are likely to be beyond the sophistication of local practitioners. By taking a course or reading this book, a paralegal may know more about ADR already than many attorneys and judges in those jurisdictions across the country where ADR is seldom used. Consequently, paralegals who practice in these jurisdictions have much to offer in support of ADR, but also face a more difficult task than their counterparts in places where ADR is a full partner in the system of justice.

Case Study of an ADR System in the Making

Throughout this book, many references have been made to ADR as it is practiced in Dallas County, Texas, where the authors of this text practice law. Based on the authors' personal knowledge and research, the development of ADR in Dallas County is in many ways typical of its development in other urban areas in the United States. Following is a discussion between the authors about the Dallas ADR scene and its development over the past decade. The reader is encouraged to compare the similarities and differences between what has occurred in Dallas, Texas, and the particular jurisdiction where he or she works.

The Early Years

Susan: Grant, you've been an integral part of the local ADR scene for over ten years here in Dallas. What's going on here and what do you see happening in the future?

Grant: As you know, the Texas legislature created court-annexed ADR in 1987. In response, local courts around the state drafted rules and procedures concerning how they would implement the new laws. The Dallas civil courts, for the most part, decided to actively refer as many cases as possible to mediation. Perhaps this was so because ADR wasn't particularly new to Dallas. For many years prior to 1987, we had Dispute Mediation Services of Dallas County, a public agency that dealt primarily with what I call the "barking dog," neighbor-type cases. They also handled a lot of small consumer complaints. Also, the American Arbitration Association had always been active in Dallas, although their focus was primarily on arbitration, with mediation sort of an afterthought back in the 1980s. Concurrently, the U.S. Arbitration and Mediation Service dealt primarily with major insurance carriers. They mediated a fair number of insurance cases, both prelawsuit and post-filing.

Starting in 1988, the Dallas Bar Association business law section, in conjunction with the Dallas Trial Lawyers Association, cosponsored the first settlement week in Dallas County. As the vice-chair that year of settlement week, I was responsible for preparing and conducting the first training for mediators. The courts arbitrarily selected about 30 or 40 cases per court, for a total of about 600 or 700 cases, and referred them all to mediation. The mediations were conducted by *pro bono* attorneys during settlement week. We ended up that year with about a 55% to 65% settlement rate. In 1989, settlement week resulted in over 800 cases being mediated, of which approximately 60% settled. By 1992, as I recall, settlement week went by the boards, primarily because cases were being referred to mediation in other ways. As a program to dispose of 400 or 500 cases at a time, it no longer exists. However, it taught us about the power of ADR to settle cases and made believers out of many judges and lawyers.

Susan: You said that settlement week was replaced by other means of referring cases to ADR. Could you explain what you mean?

Grant: After the first settlement week in 1988, more formal efforts were begun by the Dallas Bar Association to establish an organized training program for lawyers so that they could be appointed mediators by the court on a compensated basis. Starting in 1989, several civil judges began to deliberately refer cases to mediation. Currently, three of our thirteen district court judges pretty much refer almost all of their cases to mediation. Most of the rest refer cases on a more selective basis. And a few courts basically let the lawyers direct how they want to do it. That translates into over 10,000 cases annually being referred to mediation by Dallas judges.

The ADR System Today

Susan: Would you characterize the ADR system here in Dallas as mature, as compared to other locations you are aware of?

Grant: Well, the ADR system in Dallas County certainly is a mature system, but that doesn't mean it is necessarily a perfect system, or that we don't have a long way to go. What it means is that we've grown beyond the initial enthusiasm we had in 1988. We don't have the same missionary zeal we did back then in terms of lofty principles about peacemaking and cost-effective civil justice and things of this nature. There was a vision at that time of substantial reductions in the numbers of cases, not necessarily because of diversion of existing cases, but more in terms of diversion of disputes to mediation prior to their becoming lawsuits. For the most part, preventing lawsuits through ADR hasn't happened.

Susan: Earlier you said that all of the district court judges in Dallas County refer cases to mediation, at least to some extent. Yet, I've noticed that it's difficult to enforce a mediation order if one of the parties doesn't want to cooperate. In your opinion, are Dallas County judges losing interest or faith in ADR? What's the problem?

Grant: When judges in Dallas County sign orders to refer cases to mediation, most of them defer to the parties and their counsel to schedule the session, show up, and participate meaningfully. Today, judges tend to see their referral of cases as administrative rather than adjudicative. It's usually the job of the court coordinator to make sure that orders are issued and signed and that mediators are assigned to pending cases. The judges view the matter as off the court's plate until they get a letter saying the case either did or did not settle.

In 1988 through 1991 or so, many lawyers resisted mediation because it was new; therefore, judges became very actively involved in making sure their mediation orders were enforced and followed. When it became apparent that the ADR system was here to stay, attorneys stopped resisting, and judges turned their attention to other litigation abuses.

Many attorneys in Dallas County believe in the ADR system, and they give it a chance. In this sense, the system works. Others, however, treat mediation like a mandatory but unnecessary stage in the litigation process. Consequently, they tend to ride roughshod over the mediator, who is just trying to follow the court's directive. The mediator is perceived as lacking the authority of the court, despite the judge's order. I don't think that attitude is necessarily malicious. It's just a fact that when litigation counsel is busy, they deal with the squeakiest wheel first. Federal judges get top priority and somewhere down the list, below the county court clerk, is the mediator. A mediator can waste a lot of time trying to get a session scheduled and, in this regard, becomes an unpaid member of the court administrative team for the ADR process. And if the parties don't show up, the mediator may not get paid.

Enforcement of Mediation Orders

Susan: Do you think we're going to see more attempts to enforce mediation orders in Dallas County?

Grant: I see more efforts to avoid mediation than I do to enforce it. As far as meaningful participation in mediation – the obligation to negotiate in good faith – that was pretty much gutted by some recent court decisions. Basically, the court can order you to show up, but it can't force you to cooperate. I don't think we're going to see parties sanctioned for bad faith participation in mediation, unless it involves something serious like serving process at the mediation or physically assaulting someone. You don't see very many motions to compel mediation but you certainly see some to avoid it, either because one of the parties wants to postpone mediation or they don't like the mediator appointed. Where we are seeing motions to compel ADR is in the enforcement of mediation and arbitration clauses in contracts. So far, the courts are looking favorably on such clauses and tend to enforce them.

Availability of Qualified Mediators

Susan: Because of court-annexed mediation, there seem to be many people putting themselves out there as mediators. How would you characterize the local supply of qualified mediators?

Grant: Back in the late 1980s and early 1990s, there was a land-rush mentality about mediation. Everybody thought they could jump into it and make a full-time living, which didn't prove to be the case. Today, there are probably about eight or ten mediators in Dallas who truly can say they earn a very substantial income doing it full time. There's a middle group who earn a fair amount, and then there's everybody else who gets two or three cases per month.

I have to admit I didn't envision the huge supply of mediators. At the same time, I hoped there would have been more demand for the services of mediators. The demand for mediation peaked early and appears to have remained the same since then. It's essentially a function of the number of cases filed in local courts. What this means is that cases are spread out over a broad range of mediators, some of whom have questionable qualifications and little or no real experience. As a result, we're seeing a certain amount of dissatisfaction among parties and attorneys, and more complaints. So, the overall quality as a whole is probably going down on mediation. I'd estimate that today, we have about 50 or 60 mediators in town who are very competent and qualified.

Susan: Some of the critics of ADR claim that it wouldn't be needed if attorneys were better trained at negotiating, and that mediation in particular is justified only when lawyers don't know how to settle cases on their own. In their view, mediation is a public service to help lawyers who don't know how to negotiate. Do you agree with that assessment?

Grant: I find that a good deal of the time I spend in mediation is adjusting and correcting the destructive negotiating style of lawyers and their counsel. So, to that extent, a mediator serves a good purpose. Put in a more positive tone, mediation is appropriate when heretofore unassisted efforts to negotiate a settlement by the parties and their attorneys have proved unproductive. Nevertheless, negotiations fail for a lot of reasons, not just because the attorneys involved don't know what they're doing. Furthermore, negotiating isn't easy, and I think that expecting all attorneys to be good at it is unrealistic. Also, mediation can sometimes achieve results that traditional negotiating cannot.

Presuit   **Susan:**   It surprises me that at the same time that the Texas legislature
Mediation   was creating court-annexed ADR, the vision in the law community here was more in terms of reducing court case loads by preventing disputes from becoming lawsuits.

Grant: The two ideas went hand in hand. The initial concept was to deal first with what was in the courthouse and then, ultimately, through education, to create the awareness among clients and lawyers that the courthouse was the last place they'd want to be and that they'd be better off mediating or arbitrating disputes rather then suing. At first, this appeared to be happening. Maybe every tenth or twelfth mediation case would involve a prelawsuit dispute.

In the last couple of years, however, I've seen very few of those come in and, when they do, they tend to be as a result of presuit mediation clauses that parties have put into their contracts. So, in that sense, the early education is paying off. The other area that is producing presuit mediation and arbitration is in real estate. It's become standard practice in the real estate industry here in Dallas to use mediation addenda in contracts. That's one area I know where there has been good implementation of presuit mediation clauses.

Susan: Realistically though, isn't it true that when a conflict gets serious enough for a client to call an attorney, it's too late to consider presuit mediation?

Grant: There's a saying that "hiring a lawyer means never having to say you're sorry." What that means is that once you've decided to seek counsel over a dispute, generally most of the goodwill probably is gone, there's a lot of anxiety, and maybe just downright contempt for the other side. So the last thing you want to hear about is getting together to kiss and make up and go on down the road. Instead, you're ready to legally draw and quarter the other side.

Here's where an attorney should play the role of quasi-mediator with his or her own client, allow the client to vent, get if off their chest, and then through a structured interview, talk about the practical aspects of what the dispute is, the damages involved, the costs associated with filing suit, and the alternatives, whether it be negotiation, mediation, or arbitration. I think a lawyer owes a duty to clients to walk them through the alternatives. Just as a surgeon has a duty to discuss the risks involved with surgery and the alternatives, I think a lawyer owes the same kind of duty to clients.

Susan: Okay, so attorneys owe a duty to their clients to inform them of alternatives to litigation, but you're saying that it's not happening very often. Why not? Is it lack of education of our attorneys; is it economics; what's the problem?

Grant: Probably all of the above. I think it's a lack of continuing education among counsel. They assume that because they've had five or six cases referred to mediation, they are all experts on mediation. The last thing lawyers want to do these days is to go to an ADR seminar. As a result, a lot of lawyers are not continuing to educate themselves on this issue, or the legalities of the process. They are relying on what they may have learned in some of the training back in 1988 or 1990. Consequently, they are unaware of the improvements in ADR techniques, and of the developing law of ADR.

Second, the glut of attorneys combined with the fact that fewer matters are being referred out by the larger firms means that everybody is looking at the bottom line. Litigation pays the bills, and whether or not it's conscious or unconscious, attorneys may be acceding to clients' desires to sue rather than consider alternatives.

Susan: Are there other reasons why you think that so few disputes are referred to mediation before they turn into lawsuits?

Grant: Another important reason is that the gatekeepers, meaning attorneys, have lost some of their enthusiasm for the process. Consequently, they don't suggest to their clients that they should consider mediation. I know in my own practice, every contract I draft has a mediation and arbitration clause in it unless I am directed to take it out by my client and/or by the other party. Even so, it never ceases to amaze and surprise me when one or both of the parties to a contract rejects the ADR clause out of hand, even though keeping it in is seldom thought of as a deal-killer. Typically, the parties are more interested in the current economic consequences of the contract than they are in the long term. They either can't imagine themselves getting into a dispute, or they think they'll get better results at the courthouse.

I blame this attitude on a lack of education and consciousness raising among both the general populace and the business community. If people were more aware of the tangible benefits of ADR, I think they would be requesting their lawyers to consider it more. Or when their lawyers suggest it, they would be less likely to reject it out of hand as they are doing at this time.

Settlement Strategy

Susan: If most ADR is going to occur after suit has been filed, when should it occur in the life of a lawsuit?

Grant: I've always said that settlement is a state of mind and that each side must equally want to consider it and be in a position to settle. That may be on the first day suit is filed. It may not be until the appellate process. Generally speaking, most people do not want to consider settlement without some appreciation of the facts of the case, which are gathered through discovery. It's somewhat difficult for a lawyer to assist clients in valuing their case based on a lot of unknowns. I think the client would rightfully wonder whether he or she was getting good advice if the attorney encouraged them to accept an offer before the facts had been properly developed.

On the other hand, I've said many times that if you give me a lawsuit long enough, I can lose it for anybody. In other words, if you keep digging into the facts, eventually you'll discover a lot of bad facts that aren't good for your client's case. If you had settled six months ago, those bad facts would not have come out. So there's no one right time or good time; it's a judgment call, and the decision to settle has to be made by the client and by the lawyer.

Typically, though, most lawsuits settle where basic fact discovery has been completed, expert discovery has been completed, and if there's a dispositive motion to be heard, such as a motion for summary judgment, it's been heard. The only thing left to be done, other than preparing for trial, is taking the depositions of ancillary or collateral witnesses. I think that's probably the most logical place to mediate a case that's already in court.

Susan: Given the fact that typically 90% of all civil cases settle before trial, do you think that cases settle sooner with mediation?

Grant: Cases certainly settle quicker with mediation because of what I describe as the compression of the space and time continuum. Traditional negotiation means that the parties must make offers and counteroffers by letter, phone or fax over the course of several days or weeks. Mediation, on the other hand, compresses the space to the distance across a table, and the time to a few seconds or minutes. When everybody involved has nothing else to do but concentrate on the case, with no phones ringing or other distractions, that dynamic alone will assist a case in settling more quickly.

Yes, I think that mediation allows a case to be settled sooner and, for that reason alone, it is worthwhile, because it saves time and money and permits clients to get on with doing what they do best rather than trying lawsuits.

Susan: You are currently the chair of the Dallas Bar Association ADR section. In your administration, what do you want to accomplish?

Grant: Basically, I think the overall theme and focus is going to be "mediation revisited." Like the PBS series, "Brideshead Revisited," where the main character returned to the Brideshead estate in England to relive better times before World War II, I want to go back and revisit the beginning of ADR in Dallas County. What were we originally trying to accomplish? Have we done that, or have we diverted from it, and why?

One area where I know we have missed the boat is in educating the public about ADR. I think there has been an immense amount of education of lawyers but I don't have a sense that the public has really been brought into the process. What I'd like to do is take ADR to the people – come up with a way to distribute the message to the public. Whether it's a speakers bureau, appearances on TV or radio, or advertising, I want to develop a better public awareness. I'd also like to work actively with some of the groups who are working on lawsuit reform, with the idea that probably the best way to reform lawsuits is to mediate them instead.

Mediating Complex Disputes

Susan: The use of mediation to resolve complex cases is usually viewed as an indication that the system, or at least the skills of a mediator, have matured. You mediate a lot of complex cases. How do you feel about the use of mediation to solve complex disputes?

Grant: When you talk about a complex mediation, it generally means a case that involves complex issues of fact and law, complex parties or both. Parties are complex in number, in temperament, or both. So probably the most complex case is one involving complex facts and law, and multiple parties all of whom hate each other. That's the best mediation to have, because it means that the parties are looking to the mediator to come up with some way out of the quagmire. What separates the mediation masters from the journeymen out there is the ability to go beyond the two person, slip-and-fall or breach of contract case, deal with multiple parties and multiple legal issues and not be befuddled by it – to be able to help the participants to find a common thread among all these diverse interests that will enable them to resolve their differences.

Qualities of a Good Mediator

Susan: You said earlier that you think there are maybe 50 or 60 "master mediators" in Dallas County. Is there anything that these people have in common other than just numbers of mediations under their belt?

| **Grant:** | They have lots of training, have conducted lots of mediations, and they are all bright, articulate people. I've always said that mediators *are*, they are not made. All the training in the world will not make a manipulative person into a good mediator. |

I look for some core qualifications or characteristics, which I've summed up as my "PFC" principle. "P" means that a mediator is a pleasantly persistent individual. That means that they do what it takes to get the job done, but they do it without offending people.

The "F" means that a mediator is a flexible individual. They have the ability to respond to changes, they're not frustrated by the lack of continuity, or the lack of stability. In fact, they feed on and revel in situations that are uncertain.

Lastly, the "C" means a good mediator is by nature a consensus seeker. In other words, the mediator has the ability to look at the swamp out there and can pull out of it some earth and some sunshine and, in effect, make a universe in which the parties can coexist.

If people have those qualities to start with, with some training and experience, they can make good mediators. But if they don't have those core qualities, it doesn't matter how much training and experience they have.

How Paralegals Support ADR

Susan: This book will be used primarily by students who are training to become paralegals. How does a paralegal support ADR and what training is needed to help that paralegal do a better job?

Grant: Well, in general, I think a paralegal supports ADR in the same manner he or she supports litigation, which is to perform the tasks requested by the litigation counsel. In addition, the paralegal can contribute to settlement through the preparation of the settlement brochure or mediation presentation. This requires the assembly and arrangement of various exhibits, the creation of graphics, overheads, visual aids, and so forth to use during the mediation. If you've got dozens of depositions, someone's got to go through them and pull out the pearls of fact that bear heavily on the settlement value of the case. In this regard, I see paralegals having a continuing responsibility to be aware that even though they must be ready to engage in a two-week trial of a case, at the same time they need to be ready to condense everything down to a half-hour presentation for mediation. I'd like to see more education of paralegals, and attorneys for that matter, in distinguishing between facts that prove the case and those that give clues to what a party really wants to have happen. They also need training in how to present a case for settlement.

In addition to these skills and duties, sometimes legal issues come up during settlement that the paralegal is called on to flesh out, and otherwise be another hand for the litigator while he or she is busy in the ADR session. This might involve calling up a witness or an expert, or getting some clarification on an issue, or getting additional documents or evidence. These are the kinds of tasks that a paralegal is trained to do, and that can be critical to the success of any ADR session.

Unauthorized Practice of Law

Susan: One more question. Do you have any concerns for the future about the unauthorized practice of law by nonattorney-mediators?

Grant: Probably not in any area except maybe in family law. There are some mediators out there who will assist parties in resolving their cases who are not lawyers and the parties don't have lawyers with them. In general, I don't have a real problem with that. ADR is a customer-complaint-driven system. In other words, I assume that if someone perceives they've been taken advantage of by a mediator who is not a lawyer, they will complain and that's how the issue gets raised. I think if it were a problem we'd know about it.

Regarding my concern about family law, there are a lot of psychologists and social workers out there who mediate divorce cases. I think the ones who do it correctly either direct their clients to the law library or bookstore to get their own legal information and forms and/or admonish them to hire an attorney. I have heard of situations where the psychologist or social worker would actually assist in drafting agreed *pro se* pleadings and, if so, I think that's probably crossing the line. But again, if it was a real problem, I think someone from the family law section of the Dallas Bar Association who has more of a vested interest would bring the problem to the forefront and, to my knowledge, this is not happening.

Exercises

1. What not-for-profit ADR agencies such as the American Arbitration Association have offices in your area and how long have they been operating?

2. Approximately what percentage of civil cases filed each year in the state civil courts in your area employ some form of ADR prior to trial? What forms of ADR are most popular? What results?

3. Do the civil courts in your area conduct settlement weeks? If so, describe how and when they are conducted. What results?

4. Approximately how many trained ADR neutrals market their services in your area? What training is available? What training is required and by whom?

5. Do the civil court judges in your area refer cases to ADR? If so, describe the administrative process involved, including how cases are selected for ADR, what ADR method is mandated, who actually selects the ADR neutral, how the parties and the ADR neutral are informed of the referral, how much time the parties are given to conclude an ADR proceeding, and what reporting must be done to the court regarding the outcome. If possible, obtain copies of any sample paperwork involved.

6. What sort of educational material is disseminated in your area informing the public of the availability of ADR to resolve disputes? Obtain copies if possible.

7. Talk to one or more attorneys or judges in your area about the attitude in the local legal community about ADR. What do they like about ADR? What are their criticisms? What is their prognosis regarding the future of ADR in your locale?

Sources

[1] Model Rules of Professional Conduct, Rule 5.3 (1983)
[2] N. Rogers and C. McEwen, *Mediation: Law, Policy & Practice*, §10:02 (1994).
[3] See, for example, the ABA Standards of Practice for Lawyer-Mediators in Family Disputes, Standard IVC.
[4] *Id.* at VI.

List of Appendices

Dispute Resolution Act

DISPUTE RESOLUTION ACT
United States Code
Title 28 Appendix
[Selected Portions]

§ 1 Short title

This Act may be cited as the "Dispute Resolution Act."

§ 2 Congressional findings and declaration of purpose

    (a)   The Congress Finds and declares that –

        (1)   for the majority of Americans, mechanisms for the resolution of minor disputes are largely unavailable, inaccessible, ineffective, expensive, or unfair;

        (2)   the inadequacies of dispute resolution mechanisms in the United States have resulted in dissatisfaction and many types of inadequately resolved grievances and disputes;

        (3)   each individual dispute, such as that between neighbors, a consumer and seller, and a landlord and tenant, for which adequate resolution mechanisms do not exist may be of relatively small social or economic magnitude, but taken collectively such disputes are of enormous social and economic consequence;

        (4)   there is a lack of necessary resources or expertise in many areas of the Nation to develop new or improved consumer dispute resolution mechanisms, neighborhood dispute resolution mechanisms, and other necessary dispute resolution mechanisms;

        (5)   the inadequacy of dispute resolution mechanisms throughout the United States is contrary to the general welfare of the people;

        (6)   neighborhood, local, or community based dispute resolution mechanisms can provide and promote expeditious, inexpensive, equitable, and voluntary resolution of disputes, as well as serve as models for other dispute resolution mechanisms; and

        (7)   the utilization of neighborhood, local, or community resources, including volunteers (and particularly senior citizens) and available building space such as space in public facilities, can provide for accessible, cost-effective resolution of minor disputes.

    (b)   It is the purpose of this Act to assist the States and other interested parties in providing to all persons convenient access to dispute resolution mechanisms which are effective, fair, inexpensive, and expeditious.

§ 4 Criteria for dispute resolution mechanisms

Any grant recipient which desires to use any financial assistance received under this Act in connection with establishing or maintaining a dispute resolution mechanism shall provide satisfactory assurances to the Attorney General that the dispute resolution mechanism will provide for –

        (1)   assistance to persons using the dispute resolution mechanism;

(2)   the resolution of disputes at times and locations which are convenient to persons the dispute resolution mechanism is intended to serve;

(3)   adequate arrangements for participation by persons who are limited by language barriers or other disabilities;

(4)   reasonable, fair, and readily understandable forms, rules, and procedures, which shall include, where appropriate, those which would –

> (A)   ensure that all parties to a dispute are directly involved in the resolution of the dispute, and that the resolution is adequately implemented;
>
> (B)   promote, where feasible, the voluntary resolution of disputes, including the resolution of disputes by the parties before resorting to the dispute resolution mechanism established by the grant recipient;
>
> (C)   promote the resolution of disputes by persons not ordinarily involved in the judicial system;
>
> (D)   provide an easy way for any person to determine the proper name in which, and the proper procedure by which, any person may be made a party to a dispute resolution proceeding;
>
> (E)   permit the use of dispute resolution mechanisms by the business community if state law permits; and
>
> (F)   ensure reasonable privacy protection for individuals involved in the dispute resolution process;

(5)   the dissemination of information relating to the availability, location, and use of other redress mechanisms in the event that dispute resolution efforts fail or the dispute involved does not come within the jurisdiction of the dispute resolution mechanism;

(6)   consultation and cooperation with the community and with governmental agencies; and

(7)   the establishment of programs or procedures for effectively, economically, and appropriately communicating to disputants the availability and location of the dispute resolution mechanism.

Administrative Dispute Resolution Act

ADMINISTRATIVE DISPUTE RESOLUTION ACT
United States Code
Public Law No. 101-552
[Selected Portions]

Sec. 1 Short Title

This Act may be cited as the "Administrative Dispute Resolution Act."

Sec. 2 Findings.

The Congress finds that –
    (1)   administrative procedure, as embodied in chapter 5 of title 5, United States Code, and other statutes, is intended to offer a prompt, expert, and inexpensive means of resolving disputes as an alternative to litigation in the Federal courts;
    (2)   administrative proceedings have become increasingly formal, costly, and lengthy resulting in unnecessary expenditures of time and in a decreased likelihood of achieving consensual resolution of disputes;
    (3)   alternative means of dispute resolution have been used in the private sector for many years and, in appropriate circumstances, have yielded decisions that are faster, less expensive, and less contentious;
    (4)   such alternative means can lead to more creative, efficient, and sensible outcomes;
    (5)   such alternative means may be used advantageously in a wide variety of administrative programs;
    (6)   explicit authorization of the use of well-tested dispute resolution techniques will eliminate ambiguity of agency authority under existing law;
    (7)   Federal agencies may not only receive the benefit of techniques that were developed in the private sector, but may also take the lead in the further development and refinement of such techniques; and
    (8)   the availability of a wide range of dispute resolution procedures, and an increased understanding of the most effective use of such procedures, will enhance the operation of the Government and better serve the public.

Sec. 3 Promotion of alternative means of dispute resolution.

    (a)   Promulgation of agency policy. Each agency shall adopt a policy that addresses the use of alternative means of dispute resolution and case management. In developing such a policy, each agency shall –
    (1)   consult with the Administrative Conference of the United States and the Federal Mediation and Conciliation Service; and
    (2)   examine alternative means of resolving disputes in connection with –
        (A)   formal and informal adjudications;
        (B)   rulemakings;
        (C)   enforcement actions;

(D)   issuing and revoking licenses or permits;
(E)   contract administration;
(F)   litigation brought by or against the agency; and
(G)   other agency actions

(b)   Dispute resolution specialists. The head of each agency shall designate a senior official to be the dispute resolution specialist of the agency. Such official shall be responsible for the implementation of –

(1)   the provisions of this Act and the amendments made by this Act; and
(2)   the agency policy developed under subsection (a).

(c)   Training. Each agency shall provide for training on a regular basis for the dispute resolution specialist of the agency and other employees involved in implementing the policy of the agency developed under subsection (a). Such training should encompass the theory and practice of negotiation, mediation, arbitration, or related techniques. The dispute resolution specialist shall periodically recommend to the agency head agency employees who would benefit from similar training.

(d)   Procedures for grants and contracts.

(1)   Each agency shall review each of its standard agreements for contracts, grants, and other assistance and shall determine whether to amend any such standard agreements authorize and encourage the use of alternative means of dispute resolution.

(2)   (A)   Within 1 year after the date of the enactment of this Act, the Federal Acquisition Regulation shall be amended, as necessary, to carry out this Act and the amendments made by this Act.

(B)   For purposes of this section, the term "Federal Acquisition Regulation" means the single system of Government-wide procurement regulation referred to in section 6(a) of the Office of Federal Procurement Policy Act (41 USC § 405(a)).

Sec. 4 Administrative procedures.

(a)   Administrative hearings. Section 556(c) of title 5, United States Code, is amended –

(1)   in paragraph (6) by inserting before the semicolon at the end thereof the following: "or by the use of alternative means of dispute resolution as provided in subchapter IV of this chapter; and

(2)   by redesignating paragraphs (7) through (9) as paragraphs (9) though (11), respectively, and inserting after paragraph (6) the following new paragraphs:

(7)   inform the parties as to the availability of one or more alternative means of dispute resolution, and encourage use of such methods;

(8)   require the attendance at any conference held pursuant to paragraph (6) of at least one representative of each party who has authority to negotiate concerning resolution of issues in controversy."

(b)   Alternative means of dispute resolution. Chapter 5 of title 5, United States Code, is amended by adding at the end the following new subchapter:

SUBCHAPTER IV – ALTERNATIVE MEANS OF DISPUTE RESOLUTION IN THE ADMINISTRATIVE PROCESS

...

Sec. 7 Federal mediation and conciliation service.

Section 203 of the Labor Management Relations Act, 1947 (29 USC § 173) is amended by adding at the end the following new subsection:

...

(f)   The Service may make its services available to Federal agencies to aid in the resolution of disputes under the provisions of subchapter IV of chapter 5 of title 5, United States Code. Functions performed by the Service may include assisting parties to disputes related to administrative programs, training persons in skills and procedures employed in alternative means of dispute resolution, and furnishing officers and employees of the Service to act as neutrals. Only officers and employees who are qualified in accordance with section 573 of title 5, United States Code, may be assigned to act as neutrals. The Service Shall consult with the Administrative Conference of the and other agencies in maintaining rosters of neutrals and arbitrators, and to adopt such procedures and rules as are necessary to carry out the services authorized in this subsection.

Sec. 8 Government tort and other claims.

(a)   Federal tort claims, Section 2672 of title 28, United States Code, is amended by adding at the end of the first paragraph the following: "Notwithstanding the proviso contained in the preceding sentence, any award, compromise, or settlement may be effected without the prior written approval of the Attorney General or his or her designee, to the extent that the Attorney General delegates to the head of the agency the authority to make such award, compromise, or settlement. Such delegations may not exceed the authority delegated by the Attorney General to the attorneys to settle claims for money damages against the United States. Each Federal agency may use arbitration, or other alternative means of dispute resolution under the provisions of subchapter IV of chapter 5 of title 5, to settle any tort claim against the united States, to the extent of the agency's authority to award, compromise, or settle such claim without the prior written promise, or settle such claim without the prior written approval of the Attorney General or his or her designee.

(b)   Claims of the government. Section 3711(a)(2) of title 31, United States Code, is amended by striking out "$20,000 (excluding interest)" and inserting in lieu thereof "100,000 (excluding interest) or such higher amount as the Attorney General may from time to time prescribe."

Sec. 9 Use of nonattorneys.

(a)   Representation of parties. Each agency, in developing a policy on the use of alternative means of dispute resolution under this Act, shall develop a policy with regard to the representation by persons other than attorneys of parties in alternative dispute resolution proceedings and shall identify any of its administrative programs with numerous claims or disputes before the agency and determine –
(1)   the extent to which individuals are represented or assisted by attorneys or by persons who are not attorneys; and
(2)   whether the subject areas of the applicable proceedings or the procedures are so complex or specialized that only attorneys may adequately provide such representation or assistance.

(b)   Representation and assistance by nonattorneys. A person who is not an attorney may provide representation or assistance to any individual in a claim or dispute with an agency, if—

(1)   such claim or dispute concerns an administrative program identified under subsection (a);

(2)   such agency determines that the proceeding or procedure does not necessitate representation or assistance by an attorney under subsection (a)(2); and

(3)   such person meets any requirement of the agency to provide representation or assistance in such a claim or dispute.

(c)   Disqualification of representation or assistance. Any agency that adopts regulations under subchapter IV of chapter 5 of title 5, United States Code, to permit representation or assistance by persons who are not attorneys shall review the rules of practice before such agency to—

(1)   ensure that any rules pertaining to disqualification of attorneys from practicing before the agency shall also apply, as appropriate, to other persons who provide representation or assistance; and

(2)   establish effective agency procedures for enforcing such rules of practice and for receiving complaints from affected persons.

Sec. 10 Definitions.

As used in this Act, the terms "agency," "administrative program," and "alternative means of dispute resolution" have the meanings given such terms in section 581 of title 5, United States Code, as added by section 4(b) of this Act.

Sec. 11 Sunset provision.

The authority of agencies to use dispute resolution proceedings under this Act and the amendments made by this Act shall terminate on October 1, 1995, except that such authority shall continue in effect with respect to then pending proceedings which, in the judgment of the agencies that are parties to the dispute resolution proceedings, require such continuation, until such proceedings terminate.

Uniform Arbitration Act

UNIFORM ARBITRATION ACT

§ 1. Validity of Arbitration Agreement

A written agreement to submit any existing controversy to arbitration or a provision in a written contract to submit to arbitration any controversy thereafter arising between parties is valid, enforceable and irrevocable, save upon such grounds as exist at law or in equity for the revocation of any contract. This act also applies to arbitration agreements between employers and employees or between their respective representatives (unless otherwise provided in the agreement).

§ 2. Proceedings to Compel or Stay Arbitration

(a)   On application of a party showing an agreement described in Section 1, and the opposing party's refusal to arbitrate, the Court shall order the parties to proceed with arbitration, but if the opposing party denies the existence of the agreement to arbitrate, the Court shall proceed summarily to the determination of the issue so raised and shall order arbitration if found for the moving party, otherwise, the application shall be denied.

(b)   On application, the court may stay an arbitration proceeding commenced or threatened on a showing that there is no agreement to arbitrate. Such an issue, when in substantial and bona fide dispute, shall be forthwith and summarily tried and the stay ordered if found for the moving party. If found for the opposing party, the court shall order the parties to proceed to arbitration.

(c)   If an issue referable to arbitration under the alleged agreement is involved in an action or proceeding pending in a court having jurisdiction to hear applications under subdivision (a) of this Section, the application shall be made therein. Otherwise and subject to Section 18, the application may be made in any court of competent jurisdiction.

(d)   Any action or proceeding involving an issue subject to arbitration shall be stayed if an order for arbitration of an application therefor has been made under this section or, if the issue is severable, the stay may be with respect thereto only. When the application is made in such action or proceeding, the order for arbitration shall include such stay.

(e)   An order for arbitration shall not be refused on the ground that the claim in issue lacks merit or bona fides or because any fault or grounds for the claim sought to be arbitrated have not been shown.

§ 3. Appointment of Arbitrators by Court

If the arbitration agreement provides a method of appointment of arbitrators, this method shall be followed. In the absence thereof, or if the agreed method fails or for any reason cannot be followed, or when an arbitrator appointed fails or is unable to act and his successor has not been duly appointed, the court on application of a party shall appoint one or more arbitrators. An arbitrator so appointed has all the powers of one specifically named in the agreement.

§ 4. Majority Action by Arbitrators

The powers of the arbitrators may be exercised by a majority unless otherwise provided by the agreement or by this act.

§ 5. Hearing

Unless otherwise provided by the agreement:

(a)   The arbitrators shall appoint a time and place for the hearing and cause notification to the parties to be served personally or by registered mail not less than five days before the hearing. Appearance at the hearing waives such notice. The arbitrators on request of a party and for good cause, or upon their own motion may postpone the hearing to a time not later than the date fixed by the agreement for making the award unless the parties consent to a later date. The arbitrators may hear and determine the controversy upon the evidence produced notwithstanding the failure of a party duly notified to appear. The court on application may direct the arbitrators to proceed promptly with the hearing and determination of the controversy.

(b)   The parties are entitled to be heard, to present evidence material to the controversy and to cross-examine witnesses appearing at the hearing.

(c)   The hearing shall be conducted by all the arbitrators but a majority may determine any question and render a final award. If, during the course of the hearing, an arbitrator for any reason ceases to act, the remaining arbitrator or arbitrators appointed to act as neutrals may continue with the hearing and determination of the controversy.

§ 6. Representation by Attorney

A party has the right to be represented by an attorney at any proceeding or hearing under this act. A waiver thereof prior to the proceeding or hearing is ineffective.

§ 7. Witnesses, Subpoenas, Depositions

(a)   The arbitrators may issue (cause to be issued) subpoenas for the attendance of witnesses and for the production of books, records, documents and other evidence, and shall have the power to administer oaths. Subpoenas so issued shall be served, and upon application to the Court by a party or the arbitrators, enforced, in the manner provided by law for the service and enforcement of subpoenas in a civil action.

(b)   On application of a party and for use as evidence, the arbitrators may permit a deposition to be taken, in the manner and upon the terms designated by the arbitrators, of a witness who cannot be subpoenaed or is unable to attend the hearing.

(c)   All provisions of law compelling a person under subpoena to testify are applicable.

(d)   Fees for attendance as a witness shall be the same as for a witness in the.....Court.

§ 8. Award

(a)   The award shall be in writing and signed by the arbitrators joining in the award. The arbitrator shall deliver a copy to each party personally or by registered mail, or as provided in the agreement.

(b)   An award shall be made within the time fixed therefor by the agreement or, if not so fixed, within such time as the court orders on application of a party. The parties may extend the time in writing either before or after the expiration thereof. A party waives the objection that an award was not made within the time required unless he notifies the arbitrators of his objection prior to the delivery of the award to him.

§ 9. Change of Award by Arbitrators

On application of a party or, if an application to the court is pending under Sections 11, 12 or 13, on submission to the arbitrators by the court under such conditions as the court may order, the arbitrators may modify or correct the award upon the grounds stated in paragraphs (1) and (3) of subdivision (a) of Section 13, or for the purpose of clarifying the award. The application shall be made within twenty days after delivery of the award to the applicant. Written notice thereof shall be given forthwith to the opposing party, stating he must serve his objections thereto, if any, within ten days from the notice. The award so modified or corrected is subject to the provisions of Sections 11, 12 and 13.

§ 10. Fees and Expenses of Arbitration

Unless otherwise provided in the agreement to arbitrate, the arbitrators' expenses and fees, together with other expenses, not including counsel fees, incurred in the conduct of arbitration, shall be paid as provided in the award.

§ 11. Confirmation of an Award

Upon application of a party, the Court shall confirm an award, unless within the time limits hereinafter imposed grounds are urged for vacating or modifying or correcting the award, in which case the court shall proceed as provided in Sections 12 and 13.

§ 12. Vacating an Award

(a)   Upon application of a party, the court shall vacate an award where:

  (1)   The award was procured by corruption, fraud or other undue means;
  (2)   There was evident partiality by an arbitrator appointed as a neutral or corruption in any of the arbitrators or misconduct prejudicing the rights of any party;
  (3)   The arbitrators exceeded their powers;
  (4)   The arbitrators refused to postpone the hearing upon sufficient cause being shown thereof or refused to hear evidence material to the controversy or otherwise so conducted the hearing, contrary to the provisions of Section 5, as to prejudice substantially the rights of a party; or
  (5)   There was no arbitration agreement and the issue was not adversely determined in proceedings under Section 2 and the party did not participate in the arbitration hearing without raising the objection;

but the fact that the relief was such that it could not or would not be granted by a court of law or equity is not ground for vacating or refusing to confirm the award.

(b)   An application under this Section shall be made within ninety days after delivery of a copy of the award to the applicant, except that, if predicated upon corruption, fraud or other undue means, it shall be made within ninety days after such grounds are known or should have been known.

(c)   In vacating the award on grounds other than stated in clause (5) of Subsection (a) the court may order a rehearing before new arbitrators chosen as provided in the agreement, or in the absence thereof, by the court in accordance with Section 3, or if the award is vacated on grounds set forth in clauses (3) and (4) of Subsection (a) the court may order a rehearing before the arbitrators who made the award or their successors appointed in accordance with Section 3. The time within which the agreement requires the award to be made is applicable to the rehearing and commences from the date of the order.

(d)   If the application to vacate is denied and no motion to modify or correct the award is pending, the court shall confirm the award. As amended Aug. 1956.

§ 13. Modification or Correction of Award

(a)   Upon application made within ninety days after delivery of a copy of the award to the applicant, the court shall modify or correct the award where:

> (1)   There was an evident miscalculation of figures or an evident mistake in the description of any person, thing or property referred to in the award;
> (2)   The arbitrators have awarded upon a matter not submitted to them and the award may be corrected without affecting the merits of the decision upon the issues submitted; or
> (3)   The award is imperfect in a matter of form, not affecting the merits of the controversy.

(b)   If the application is granted, the court shall modify and correct the award so as to effect its intent and shall confirm the award as so modified and corrected. Otherwise, the court shall confirm the award as made.

(c)   An application to modify or correct an award may be joined in the alternative with an application to vacate the award.

§ 14. Judgment or Decree on Award

Upon the granting of an order confirming, modifying or correcting an award, judgment or decree shall be entered in conformity therewith and be enforced as any other judgment or decree. Costs of the application and of the proceedings subsequent thereto, and disbursements may be awarded by the court.

§ 15. Judgment Roll, Docketing

(a)   On entry of judgment or decree, the clerk shall prepare the judgment roll consisting, to the extent filed, of the following:

> (1)   The agreement and each written extension of the time within which to make the award;
> (2)   The award;
> (3)   A copy of the order confirming, modifying or correcting the award; and

(4)   A copy of the judgment or decree.

(b)   The judgment or decree may be docketed as if rendered in an action.

§ 16. Applications to Court

Except as otherwise provided, an application to the court under this act shall be by motion and shall be heard in the manner and upon the notice provided by law or rule of court for the making and hearing of motions. Unless the parties have agreed otherwise, notice of an initial application for an order shall be served in the manner provided by law for the service of a summons in an action.

§ 17. Court, Jurisdiction

The term "court" means any court of competent jurisdiction of this State. The making of an agreement described in Section 1 providing for arbitration in this State confers jurisdiction on the court to enforce the agreement under this Act and to enter judgment on an award thereunder.

§ 18. Venue

An initial application shall be made to the court of the [county] in which the agreement provides the arbitration hearing shall be held or, if the hearing has been held, in the county in which it was held. Otherwise the application shall be made in the [county] where the adverse party resides or has a place of business or, if he has no residence or place of business in this State, to the court of any [county]. All subsequent application shall be made to the court hearing the initial application unless the court otherwise directs.

§ 19. Appeals

(a)   An appeal may be taken from:

    (1)   An order denying an application to compel arbitration made under Section 2;
    (2)   An order granting an application to stay arbitration made under Section 2(b);
    (3)   An order confirming or denying confirmation of an award;
    (4)   An order modifying or correcting an award;
    (5)   An order vacating an award without directing a rehearing; or
    (6)   A judgment or decree entered pursuant to the provisions of this act.

(b)   The appeal shall be taken in the manner and to the same extent as from orders or judgments in a civil action.

§ 20. Act Not Retroactive

This act applies only to agreements made subsequent to the taking effect of this act.

§ 21. Uniformity of Interpretation

This act shall be so construed as to effectuate its general purpose to make uniform the law of those states which enact it.

§ 22. Constitutionality

In any provision of this act or the application thereof to any person or circumstance is held invalid, the invalidity shall not affect other provisions or applications of the act which can be given effect without the invalid provision or application, and to this end the provisions of this act are severable.

§ 23. Short Title

This act may be cited as the Uniform Arbitration Act.

§ 24. Repeal

All acts or parts of acts which are inconsistent with the provisions of this act are hereby repealed.

§ 25. Time of Taking Effect

This act shall take effect.....

State Arbitration Statutes

Ala. Code tit. 7, ch 19, §§6-6-1 *et seq.* (1977 & Supp. 1993).

Alaska Stat. § 09.43.010 (1962 & Supp. 1992).

Ariz. Rev. Stat. Ann. §§ 12-1501 *et seq.* (West 1982 & Supp. 1993).

Ark. Stat. Ann. §§ 16-108-201 *et seq.* (1987 & Supp. 1992).

Cal. Civ. Proc. Code §§ 1280 *et seq.* (Deering 1981 & Supp. 1993).

Colo. Rev. Stat. §§ 13-22-201 *et seq.* (West 1989 & Supp. 1993).

Conn. Gen. Stat. §§ 52-408 *et seq.* (West 1991 & Supp. 1992).

Del. Code Ann. tit. 10, §§ 5701 *et seq.* (1975 & Supp. 1992).

D.C. Code tit. 16 §§ 16-4301 *et seq.* (Michie 1981 & Supp. 1992).

Fla. Stat. §§ 682.01 *et seq.* (West 1992).

Ga. Code Ann. §§ 9-9-1 *et seq.* (Construction disputes only)(1982 & Supp. 1992).

Haw. Rev. Stat. §§ 658-1 *et seq.* (Michie 1988 & Supp. 1992).

Idaho Code §§ 7-901 *et seq.* (Michie 1948 & Supp. 1992).

Ill. Rev. Stat. ch. 710, ILCS § 5 *et seq.* (West 1992).

Ind. Code Ann. §§ 34-4-1-1 *et seq.* (West 1983 & Supp. 1993).

Iowa Code §§ 679A.1 *et seq.* (West 1987 & Supp. 1992).

Kan. Stat. Ann. §§ 5-401 *et seq.* (1990).

Ky. Rev. Stat. Ann. §§ 417.045 *et seq.* (Michie 1971 & Supp. 1992).

La. Rev. Stat. Ann. §§ 9:4201 *et seq.* (West 1992).

Me. Rev. Stat. Ann. tit. 14, §§ 5927 *et seq.* (West 1980 & Supp. 1993).

Md. Cts. & Jud. Proc. Code Ann. §§ 3-201 *et seq.* (Michie 1992).

Mass. Gen. Laws Ann. ch. 251, §§ 1 *et seq.* (West 1988 & Supp. 1992).

Mich. Comp. Laws §§ 600.5001 *et seq.* (West 1992).

Minn. Stat. Ann. §§ 572.08 *et seq.* (West 1993).

Miss. Code Ann. §§ 11-15-101 *et seq.* (Construction disputes only)(1991).

Mo. Ann. Stat. §§ 435.350 *et seq.* (West 1992).

Mont. Code Ann. §§ 27-5-111 *et seq.* (1978 & Supp. 1991).

Neb. Rev. Stat. §§ 25-2601 *et seq.* (1954 & Supp. 1992).

Nev. Rev. Stat. §§ 38.015 *et seq.* (Michie 1986 & Supp. 1991).

N.C. Gen. Stat. §§ 1-567.1 *et seq.* (Michie 1944 & Supp. 1992).

N.D. Cent. Code tit. 32, chs. 32-29 §§ 32-29.2-01 *et seq.* (Michie 1987 & Supp. 1992).

N.H. Rev. Stat. Ann. §§ 542:1 *et seq.* (Equity 1991).

N.J. Stat. Ann. §§ 2A:24-1 *et seq.* (West 1992).

N.M. Stat. Ann. §§ 44-7-1 *et seq.* (1978 & Supp. 1992).

N.Y. Civ. Prac. L.& R. §§ 7501 *et seq.* (McKinney 1980 & Supp. 1993).

Ohio Rev. Code Ann. §§ 2711.01 *et seq.* (Anderson 1912 & Sup. 1992).

Okla. Stat. Ann. tit. 15, §§ 801 *et seq.* (West 1993).

Or. Rev. Stat. §§ 36.300 *et seq.* (1991).

Pa. Con. Stat. Ann. tit. 42, ch. 73, §§ 7301 *et seq.* (West 1982 & Supp. 1992).

R.I. Gen. Laws §§ 10-3-1 *et seq.* (Michie 1957 & Supp. 1992).

S.C. Code §§ 15-48-10 *et seq.* (1991).

S.D. Codified Laws Ann. §§ 21-25A-1 *et seq.* (1968 & Supp. 1992).

Tenn. Code Ann. §§ 29-5-301 *et seq.* (1955 & Supp. 1992).

Tex. Rev. Civ. Stat. Ann. tit. 10, Art. 224 *et seq.* (Vernon 1973 & Supp. 1992).

Utah Code Ann. §§ 78-31a-1 *et seq.* (Michie 1986 & Supp. 1992).

Vt. Stat. Ann. tit. 12, §§ 5651 *et seq.* (1991).

Va. Code Ann. §§ 8.01-581.01 *et seq.* (Michie 1992).

Wash. Rev. Code Ann. §§ 7.04.010 *et seq.* (West 1992).

W. Va. Code of 1966, ch. 55, §§ 55-10-1 to 55-10-8 (Michie 1966 & Supp. 1992).

Wis. Stat. Ann. §§ 788.01 *et seq.* (West 1992).

Wyo. Stat. §§ 1-36-101 *et seq.* (1977 & Supp. 1992).

See also P.R. Laws. Ann. tit. 32, §§ 3201 *et seq.* (1991).

Reprinted from *Alternative Dispute Resolution Practice Guide*, by Lawyers Cooperative

Sample Mediation Order

PLAINTIFF	)	BASIC JUDICIAL DISTRICT COURT
	)	
V.	)	
	)	
DEFENDANT	)	_____ COUNTY, _____

MEDIATION ORDER

This case is appropriate for mediation pursuant to Section 154.001 et seq. of the Texas Civil Practice and Remedies Code. [Name and Phone Number of Mediator] is appointed Mediator in the above case and all counsel are directed to contact mediator to arrange the logistics of mediation within 7 days from the date of this Order. Any objection to this Order must be filed and served upon all parties and the mediator, and a hearing must be requested within 10 days from the date of this Order; an objection that is neither timely filed nor ruled upon before the scheduled mediation may be waived.

Mediation is a mandatory but nonbinding settlement conference, conducted with the assistance of the mediator. Mediation is private, confidential and privileged from process and discovery. After mediation, the court will be advised by the mediator, parties and counsel, only that the case did or did not settle. The mediator shall not be a witness nor may the mediator's records be subpoenaed of used as evidence. No subpoenas, citations, writs or other process shall be served at or near the location of any mediation session, upon any person entering, leaving or attending any mediation session.

The mediator will negotiate a reasonable fee with the parties which shall be divided and borne equally by the parties unless agreed otherwise, paid by the parties directly to the mediator, and taxed as costs. If the parties do not agree upon the fee requested by the mediator, the court will set a reasonable fee, which shall be taxed as costs. Each party and their counsel will be bound by the rules for mediation printed on the reverse hereof, and shall complete the information forms as are furnished by the mediator.

Named parties shall be present during the entire mediation process and each corporate party must be represented by an executive officer with authority to negotiate a settlement. Counsel, the parties and the mediator shall agree upon a mediation date within 20 days from the date of this order. If no date can be agreed upon within the 20 day period, the mediator shall select a date for the mediation and all parties shall appear as directed by the mediator.

The date scheduled by the mediator is incorporated in this Order as the date upon which the mediation shall occur. In any event, the mediation shall be conducted no later than [DATE] .

Failure or refusal to attend the mediation as scheduled may result in the imposition of sanctions, as permitted by law, which may include dismissal or default judgment. Failure to mediate will not be considered cause for continuance of the trial date. Referral to mediation is neither a substitute for nor a cause for delay of trial, and the case will be tried if not settled.

A report regarding the outcome of the mediation session is to be mailed by the mediator to the court, with a copy to the ADR Coordinator, immediately after the mediation session.

Signed this ____ day of _____, 20___

_____
JUDGE PRESIDING

cc: Counsel of Record
    Mediator

Mediation Order form used by the Civil District Courts of Dallas County, Texas.

Premediation Submissions Checklist

I. Brief Statement of Issues and Positions

A. Include a factual summary.

B. If the sequence of events is essential (almost always in medical negligence cases), include a chronology of events. Even if the case does not resolve, such chronology will be helpful at trial.

C. What are the legal issues in dispute?

D. What is your position on such legal issues?

E. What are the factual issues in dispute?

F. What is your position on these factual issues?

II. Copies of Current, Live Pleadings

A. Include only the most recent amended affirmative and defensive pleadings.

B. Include, subject to confidentiality, pleadings that may be filed if the matter is not resolved; i.e., a motion for summary judgment.

C. If a motion for summary judgment, a brief in support of such motion, and/or an opposing motion and brief are on file, include such pleadings in this section.

III. Pertinent Appellate Decisions

A. Those decisions most supportive of your position.

B. Those decisions that oppose your position, to whatever degree.

C. In cases in which a legal point has not been finally resolved or there are conflicting opinions, include the following:

    1. Helpful law review articles.

    2. Recent seminar articles.

    3. Opinions from other jurisdictions.

IV. Critical Documentary Evidence (this will vary from case to case)

A. The contract or correspondence that creates an agreement.

B. Medical bills (essential in a personal injury (PI) mediation).

C. Physicians' reports or medical records (PI).

D. Reports regarding future medical expenses and treatment (PI).

E. Lost wage statements (PI).

F. Reports on future lost earnings and possible employment opportunities or lack thereof (PI).

G. A life expectancy table (PI).

H. Reports from treating psychiatrists, psychologists, counselors, etc.

I. Economist reports.

J. Excerpts from critical expert/witness reports or depositions.

K. A chronology.

L. Critical photographs.

M. Any models, charts, diagrams, etc.

N. "Day in the life" videos.

O. Curriculum vitae for important experts.

P. Invoices that support alleged damages.

Reprinted from *Mediation: A Texas Practice Guide* by Eric Galton © 1993 by American Lawyer Media LP, 1-800-456-5484 ext. 157.

Q. Time sheets, report summaries, and the like that support attorney's fees.

R. Excerpts from responses to interrogatories, requests for production, or requests for admissions.

V. Negotiation History

A. Outline the series of demands and offers.

B. Indicate clearly which party made the last bid.

C. Include any history of any informal negotiations that have not resulted in a specific proposal.

D. Include your best educated guess as to what the other side might be willing to pay or take and why you think so.

VI. Objective Strength/Weakness Analysis

A. From a *factual* perspective, outline your strengths and weaknesses. For example, do your witnesses make good credible presentations? Or do your witnesses testify poorly? Are they then subject to rigorous cross-examination? Do you have a strong expert? What about the other side's witnesses?

B. From a legal perspective, what are your strengths *and* weaknesses? What potential legal problems do you have; i.e., limitations, causation, immunity, etc?

C. Does the venue play any part in your assessment of strengths and weaknesses? Are juries liberal? Conservative? What is the orientation of the judge?

D. How quickly will your case come to trial?

E. Is an appeal possible, likely, or certain?

F. Has the other side committed a procedural blunder?

G. Insurance coverage problems.

VII. Subjective Factors

A. Do the parties dislike each other intensely? Why?

B. Did the parties, prior to dispute, enjoy a positive relationship? Why and on what basis?

C. Have any of the parties developed a personality problem with any of the counsel? Why?

D. Is there a personality problem between counsel? Why?

E. What is the negotiating style of your client? The other side?

F. What are your client's non-monetary interests and needs?

G. What are the sensitive, sore spot issues? Why?

H. Does your client have unrealistic expectations? The other side? Why?

I. Are there political, personal, or emotional issues fueling this dispute?

J. Why do you think settlement at mediation is in your client's interests? The other side's interests?

AAA Commercial Mediation Rules

AMERICAN ARBITRATION ASSOCIATION
COMMERCIAL MEDIATION RULES
Amended and in Effect January 1, 1992

1. Agreement of Parties

Whenever, by stipulation or in their contract, the parties have provided for mediation or conciliation of existing or future disputes under the auspices of the American Arbitration Association (AAA) or under these rules, they shall be deemed to have made these rules, as amended and in effect as of the date of the submission of the dispute, a part of their agreement.

2. Initiation of Mediation

Any party or parties to a dispute may initiate mediation by filing with the AAA a submission to mediation or written request for mediation pursuant to these rules, together with the appropriate administrative fee contained in the Fee Schedule. Where there is no submission to mediation or contract providing for mediation, a party may request the AAA to invite another party to join in a submission to mediation. Upon receipt of such a request, the AAA will contact the other parties involved in the dispute and attempt to obtain a submission to mediation.

3. Request for Mediation

A request for mediation shall contain a brief statement of the nature of the dispute and the names, addresses, and telephone numbers of all parties to the dispute and those who will represent them, if any, in the mediation. The initiating party shall simultaneously file two copies of the request with the AAA and one copy with every other party to the dispute.

4. Appointment of Mediator

Upon receipt of a request for mediation, the AAA will appoint a qualified mediator to serve. Normally, a single mediator will be appointed unless the parties agree otherwise or the AAA determines otherwise. If the agreement of the parties names a mediator or specifies a method of appointing a mediator, that designation or method shall be followed.

5. Qualifications of Mediator

No person shall serve as a mediator in any dispute in which that person has any financial or personal interest in the result of the mediation, except by the written consent of all parties. Prior to accepting an appointment, the prospective mediator shall disclose any circumstances likely to create a presumption of bias or prevent a prompt meeting with the parties. Upon receipt of such information, the AAA shall either replace the mediator or immediately communicate the information to the parties for their comments. In the event that the parties disagree as to whether the mediator shall serve, the AAA will appoint another mediator. The AAA is authorized to appoint another mediator if the appointed mediator is unable to serve promptly.

6. Vacancies

If any mediator shall become unwilling or unable to serve, the AAA will appoint another mediator, unless the parties agree otherwise.

7.   Representation

Any party may be represented by persons of the party's choice. The names and addresses of such persons shall be communicated in writing to all parties and to the AAA.

8.   Date, Time, and Place of Mediation

The mediator shall fix the date and the time of each mediation session. The mediation shall be held at the appropriate regional office of the AAA, or at any other convenient location agreeable to the mediator and the parties, as the mediator shall determine.

9.   Identification of Matters in Dispute

At least ten days prior to the first scheduled mediation session, each party shall provide the mediator with a brief memorandum setting forth its position with regard to the issues that need to be resolved. At the discretion of the mediator, such memoranda may be mutually exchanged by the parties.

At the first session, the parties will be expected to produce all information reasonably required for the mediator to understand the issues presented.

The mediator may require any party to supplement such information.

10.   Authority of Mediator

The mediator does not have the authority to impose a settlement on the parties but will attempt to help them reach a satisfactory resolution of their dispute. The mediator is authorized to conduct joint and separate meetings with the parties and to make oral and written recommendations for settlement. Whenever necessary, the mediator may also obtain expert advice concerning technical aspects of the dispute, provided that the parties agree and assume the expenses of obtaining such advice. Arrangements for obtaining such advice shall be made by the mediator or the parties, as the mediator shall determine.

The mediator is authorized to end the mediation whenever, in the judgment of the mediator, further efforts at mediation would not contribute to a resolution of the dispute between the parties.

11.   Privacy

Mediation sessions are private. The parties and their representatives may attend mediation sessions. Other persons may attend only with the permission of the parties and with the consent of the mediator.

12.   Confidentiality

Confidential information disclosed to a mediator by the parties or by witnesses in the course of the mediation shall not be divulged by the mediator. All records, reports, or other documents received by a mediator while serving in that capacity shall be confidential. The mediator shall not be compelled to divulge such records or to testify in regard to the mediation in any adversary proceeding or judicial forum.

The parties shall maintain the confidentiality of the mediation and shall not rely on, or introduce as evidence in any arbitral, judicial, or other proceeding:

      (a) views expressed or suggestions made by another party with respect to a possible settlement of the dispute;

      (b) admissions made by another party in the course of the mediation proceedings;

      (c) proposals made or views expressed by the mediator; or

      (d) the fact that another party had or had not indicated willingness to accept a proposal for settlement made by the mediator.

13.   No Stenographic Record

There shall be no stenographic record of the mediation process.

14.   Termination of Mediation

The mediation shall be terminated:

(a) by the execution of a settlement agreement by the parties;

(b) by a written declaration of the mediator to the effect that further efforts at mediation are no longer worthwhile; or

(c) by written declaration of a party or parties to the effect that the mediation proceedings are terminated.

15.   Exclusion of Liability

Neither the AAA nor any mediator is a necessary party in judicial proceedings relating to the mediation.

Neither the AAA nor any mediator shall be liable to any party for any act or omission in connection with any mediation conducted under these rules.

16.   Interpretation and Application of Rules

The mediator shall interpret and apply these rules insofar as they relate to the mediator's duties and responsibilities. All other rules shall be interpreted and applied by the AAA.

17.   Expenses

The expenses of witnesses for either side shall be paid by the party producing such witnesses. All other expenses of the mediation, including required traveling and other expenses of the mediator and representatives of the AAA, and the expenses of any witness and the cost of any proofs or expert advice produced at the direct request of the mediator, shall be borne equally by the parties unless they agree otherwise.

Reprinted with permission from *Commercial Mediation Rules*, January 1, 1993, American Arbitration Association.

AAA Commercial Arbitration Rules

American Arbitration Association's Commercial Arbitration Rules
as Amended and Effective on July 1, 1996

1. **Agreement of Parties**
    The parties shall be deemed to have made these rules a part of their arbitration agreement whenever they have provided for arbitration by the American Arbitration Association (hereinafter AAA) or under its Commercial Arbitration Rules. These rules and any amendment of them shall apply in the form obtained at the time the demand for arbitration or submission agreement is received by the AAA. The parties, by written agreement, may vary the procedures set forth in these rules.

2. **Name of Tribunal**
    Any tribunal constituted by the parties for the settlement of their dispute under these rules shall be called the Commercial Arbitration Tribunal.

3. **Administrator and Delegation of Duties**
    When parties agree to arbitrate under these rules, or when they provide for arbitration by the AAA and an arbitration is initiated under these rules, they thereby authorize the AAA to administer the arbitration. The authority and duties of the AAA are prescribed in the agreement of the parties and in these rules, and may be carried out through such of the AAA's representatives as it may direct.

4. **National Panel of Arbitrators**
    The AAA shall establish and maintain a National Panel of Commercial Arbitrators and shall appoint arbitrators as provided in these rules.

5. **Regional Offices**
    The AAA may, in its discretion, assign the administration of an arbitration to any of its regional offices.

6. **Initiation under an Arbitration Provision in a Contract**
    Arbitration under an arbitration provision in a contract shall be initiated in the following manner:
    a. the initiating party (hereinafter claimant) shall, within the time period, if any, specified in the contract(s), give written notice to the other party (hereinafter respondent) of its intention to arbitrate (demand), which notice shall contain a statement setting forth the nature of the dispute, the amount involved, if any, the remedy sought, and the hearing locale requested, and
    b. shall file at any regional office of the AAA three copies of the notice and three copies of the arbitration provisions of the contract, together with the appropriate filing fee as provided in the schedule on page 27.

    The AAA shall give notice of such filing to the respondent or respondents. A respondent may file an answering statement in duplicate with the AAA within ten days after notice from the AAA, in which event the respondent shall at the same time send a copy of the answering statement to the claimant. If a counterclaim is asserted, it shall contain a statement setting forth the nature of the counterclaim, the amount involved, if any, and the remedy sought. If a counterclaim is made, the appropriate fee provided in the schedule on page 27 shall be forwarded to the AAA with the answering statement. If no answering statement is filed within the stated time, it will be treated as a denial of the claim. Failure to file an answering statement shall not operate to delay the arbitration.

Reprinted from *Commercial Arbitration Rules*, July 1, 1996, American Arbitration Association.

7. **Initiation under a Submission**

Parties to any existing dispute may commence an arbitration under these rules by filing at any regional office of the AAA three copies of a written submission to arbitrate under these rules, signed by the parties. It shall contain a statement of the matter in dispute, the amount involved, if any, the remedy sought, and the hearing locale requested, together with the appropriate filing fee as provided with the schedule on page 27.

8. **Changes of Claim**

After filing of a claim, if either party desires to make any new or different claim or counterclaim, it shall be made in writing and filed with the AAA, and a copy shall be mailed to the other party, who shall have a period of ten days from the date of such mailing within which to file an answer with the AAA. After the arbitrator is appointed, however, no new or different claim may be submitted except with the arbitrator's consent.

9. **Applicable Procedures**

Unless the AAA in its discretion determines otherwise, the Expedited Procedures shall be applied in any case where no disclosed claim or counterclaim exceeds $50,000, exclusive of interest and arbitration costs. Parties may also agree to use the Expedited Procedures in cases involving claims in excess of $50,000. The Expedited Procedures shall be applied as described in Sections 53 through 57 of these rules, in addition to any other portion of these rules that is not in conflict with the Expedited Procedures. All other cases shall be administered in accordance with Sections 1 through 52 of these rules.

10. **Administrative Conference, Preliminary Hearing, and Mediation Conference**

At the request of any party or at the discretion of the AAA, an administrative conference with the AAA and the parties and/or their representatives will be scheduled in appropriate cases to expedite the arbitration proceedings. There is no administrative fee for this service.

In large or complex cases, at the request of any party or at the discretion of the arbitrator or the AAA, a preliminary hearing with the parties and/or their representatives and the arbitrator may be scheduled by the arbitrator to specify the issues to be resolved, to stipulate to uncontested facts, and to consider any other matters that will expedite the arbitration proceedings. Consistent with the expedited nature of arbitration, the arbitrator may, at the preliminary hearing establish (i) the extent of and schedule for the production of relevant documents and other information, (ii) the identification of any witnesses to be called, and (iii) a schedule for further hearings to resolve the dispute. There is no administrative fee for the first preliminary hearing.

With the consent of the parties, the AAA at any stage of the proceedings may arrange a mediation conference under the Commercial Mediation Rules, in order to facilitate settlement. The mediator shall not be an arbitrator appointed to the case. Where the parties to a pending arbitration agree to mediate under the AAA's rules, no additional administrative fee is required to initiate mediation.

11. **Fixing of Locale**

The parties may mutually agree on the locale where the arbitration is to be held. If any party requests that the hearing be held in a specific locale and the other party files no objection thereto within ten days after notice of the request has been sent to it by the AAA, the locale shall be the one requested. If a party objects to the locale requested by the party, the AAA shall have the power to determine the locale and its decision shall be final and binding.

12. **Qualifications of an Arbitrator**

Any neutral arbitrator appointed pursuant to Section 13, 14, 15, or 54, or selected by mutual choice of the parties or their appointees, shall be subject to disqualification for the reasons specified in Section 19. If the parties specifically so agree in writing, the arbitrator shall not be subject to disqualification for those reasons.

Unless the parties agree otherwise, an arbitrator selected unilaterally by one party is a party-appointed arbitrator and is not subject to disqualification pursuant to Section 19.

The term "arbitrator" in these rules refers to the arbitration panel, whether composed of one or more arbitrators and whether the arbitrators are neutral or party appointed.

13. **Appointment from Panel**

If the parties have not appointed an arbitrator and have not provided any other method of appointment, the arbitrator shall be appointed in the following manner: immediately after the filing of the demand or submission, the AAA shall send simultaneously to each party to the dispute an identical list of names of persons chosen from the panel.

Each party to the dispute shall have ten days from the transmittal date in which to strike names objected to, number the remaining names in order of preference, and return the list to the AAA. In a single-arbitrator case, each party may strike three names on a peremptory basis. In a multiarbitrator case, each party may strike five names on a preemptor basis. If a party does not return the list within the time specified, all persons named therein shall be deemed acceptable. From among the persons who have been approved on both lists, and in accordance with the designated order of mutual preference, the AAA shall invite the acceptance of an arbitrator to serve. If the parties fail to agree on any of the persons named, or if acceptable arbitrators are unable to act, or if for any other reason the appointment cannot be made from the submitted lists, the AAA shall have the power to make the appointment from among other members of the panel without the submission of additional lists.

14. **Direct Appointment by a Party**

If the agreement of the parties names an arbitrator or specifies a method of appointing an arbitrator, that designation or method shall be followed. The notice of appointment, with the name and address of the arbitrator, shall be filed with the AAA by the appointing party. Upon the request of any appointing party, the AAA shall submit a list of members of the panel from which the party may, if it so desires, make the appointment.

If the agreement specifies a period of time within which an arbitrator shall be appointed and any party fails to make the appointment within that period, the AAA shall make the appointment.

If no period of time is specified in the agreement, the AAA shall notify the party to make the appointment. If within ten days thereafter an arbitrator has not been appointed by a party, the AAA shall make the appointment.

15. **Appointment of Neutral Arbitrator by Party-Appointed Arbitrators or Parties**

If the parties have selected party-appointed arbitrators, or if such arbitrators have been appointed as provided in Section 14, and the parties have authorized them to appoint a neutral arbitrator within a specified time and no appointment is made within that time or any agreed extension, the AAA may appoint a neutral arbitrator, who shall act as chairperson.

If no period of time is specified for appointment of the neutral arbitrator and the party-appointed arbitrators or the parties do not make the appointment within ten days from the date of the appointment of the last party-appointed arbitrator, the AAA may appoint the neutral arbitrator, who shall act as chairperson.

If the parties have agreed that their party-appointed arbitrators shall appoint the neutral arbitrator from the panel, the AAA shall furnish to the party-appointed arbitrators, in the manner provided in Section 13, a list selected from the panel, and the appointment of the neutral arbitrator shall be made as provided in that section.

16. **Nationality of Arbitrator in International Arbitration**

Where the parties are nationals or residents of different countries, any neutral arbitrator shall, upon the request of either party, be appointed from among the nationals of a country other than that of any of the parties. The request must be made prior to the time set for the appointment of the arbitrator as agreed by the parties or set by these rules.

17.   **Number of Arbitrators**

If the arbitration agreement does not specify the number of arbitrators, the dispute shall be heard and determined by one arbitrator, unless the AAA, in its discretion, directs that a greater number of arbitrators be appointed.

18.   **Notice to Arbitrator of Appointment**

Notice of the appointment of the neutral arbitrator, whether appointed mutually by the parties or by the AAA, shall be sent to the arbitrator by the AAA, together with a copy of these rules, and the signed acceptance of the arbitrator shall be filed with the AAA prior to the opening of the first hearing.

19.   **Disclosure and Challenge Procedure**

Any person appointed as neutral arbitrator shall disclose to the AAA any circumstance likely to affect impartiality, including any bias or any financial or personal interest in the result of the arbitration or any past or present relationship with the parties or their representatives. Upon receipt of such information from the arbitrator or another source, the AAA shall communicate the information to the parties and, if it deems it appropriate to do so, to the arbitrator and others. Upon objection of a party to the continued service of a neutral arbitrator, the AAA shall determine whether the arbitrator should be disqualified and shall inform the parties of its decision, which shall be conclusive.

20.   **Vacancies**

If for any reason an arbitrator is unable to perform the duties of the office, the AAA may, on proof satisfactory to it, declare the office vacant. Vacancies shall be filled in accordance with the applicable provisions of these rules.

In the event of a vacancy in a panel of neutral arbitrators after the hearings have commenced, the remaining arbitrator or arbitrators may continue with the hearing and determination of the controversy, unless the parties agree otherwise.

21.   **Date, Time, and Place of Hearing**

The arbitrator shall set the date, time, and place for each hearing. The AAA shall send a notice of hearing to the parties at least ten days in advance of the hearing date, unless otherwise agreed by the parties.

22.   **Representation**

Any party may be represented by counsel or other authorized representative. A party intending to be so represented shall notify the other party and the AAA of the name and address of the representative at least three days prior to the date set for the hearing at which that person is first to appear. When such a representative initiates an arbitration or responds for a party, notice is deemed to have been given.

23.   **Stenographic Record**

Any party desiring a stenographic record shall make arrangements directly with a stenographer and shall notify the other parties of these arrangements in advance of the hearing. The requesting party or parties shall pay the cost of the record. If the transcript is agreed by the parties to be, or determined by the arbitrator to be, the official record of the proceeding, it must be made available to the arbitrator and to the other parties for inspection, at a date, time, and place determined by the arbitrator.

24.   **Interpreters**

Any party wishing an interpreter shall make all arrangements directly with the interpreter and shall assume the costs of the service.

25.   **Attendance at Hearings**

The arbitrator shall maintain the privacy of the hearings unless the law provides to the contrary. Any person having a direct interest in the arbitration is entitled to attend hearings. The arbitrator shall otherwise have the power to require the exclusion of any witness, other than a party or other essential person, during the testimony of any other witness. It shall be discretionary with the arbitrator to be determine the propriety of the attendance of any other person.

26. **Postponements**
    The arbitrator for good cause shown may postpone any hearing upon request of a party or upon the arbitrator's own initiative, and shall also grant such postponement when all the parties agree.

27. **Oaths**
    Before proceeding with the first hearing, each arbitrator may take an oath of office and, if required by law, shall do so. The arbitrator may require witnesses to testify under oath administered by any duly qualified person and, if it is required by law or requested by any party, shall do so.

28. **Majority Decision**
    All decisions of the arbitrators must be by a majority. The award must also be made by a majority unless the concurrence of all is expressly required by the arbitration agreement or by law.

29. **Order of Proceedings and Communication with Arbitrator**
    A hearing shall be opened by the filing of the oath of the arbitrator, where required; by the recording of the date, time, and place of the hearing, and the presence of the arbitrator, the parties, and their representatives, if any; and by the receipt by the arbitrator of the statement of the claim and the answering statement, if any.

    The arbitrator may, at the beginning of the hearing, ask for statements clarifying the issues involved. In some cases, part or all of the above will have been accomplished at the preliminary hearing conducted by the arbitrator pursuant to Section 10.

    The complaining party shall then present evidence to support its claim. The defending party shall then present evidence supporting its defense. Witnesses for each party shall submit to questions or other examination. The arbitrator has the discretion to vary this procedure but shall afford a full and equal opportunity to all parties for the presentation of any material and relevant evidence.

    Exhibits, when offered by either party, may be received in evidence by the arbitrator.

    The names and addresses of all witnesses and a description of the exhibits in the order received shall be made a part of the record.

    There shall be no direct communication between the parties and a neutral arbitrator other than at oral hearing, unless the parties and the arbitrator agree otherwise. Any other oral or written communication from the parties to the neutral arbitrator shall be directed to the AAA for transmittal to the arbitrator.

30. **Arbitration in the Absence of a Party or Representative**
    Unless the law provides to the contrary, the arbitration may proceed in the absence of any party or representative who, after due notice, fails to be present or fails to obtain a postponement. An award shall not be made solely on the default of a party The arbitrator shall require the party who is present to submit such evidence as the arbitrator may require for the making of an award.

31. **Evidence**
    The parties may offer such evidence as is relevant and material to the dispute and shall produce such evidence as the arbitrator may deem necessary to an understanding and determination of the dispute. An arbitrator or other person authorized by law to subpoena witnesses or documents may do so upon the request of any party or independently.

    The arbitrator shall be the judge of the relevance and materiality of the evidence offered, and conformity to legal rules of evidence shall not be necessary. All evidence shall be taken in the presence of all of the arbitrators and all of the parties, except where any of the parties is absent in default or has waived the right to be present.

32. **Evidence by Affidavit and Posthearing Filing of Documents or Other Evidence**
    The arbitrator may receive and consider the evidence of witnesses by affidavit, but shall give it only such weight as the arbitrator deems it entitled to after consideration of any objection made to its admission.

If the parties agree or the arbitrator directs that documents or other evidence be submitted to the arbitrator after the hearing, the documents or other evidence shall be filed with the AAA for transmission to the arbitrator. All parties shall be afforded an opportunity to examine such documents or other evidence.

33.   Inspection or Investigation

An arbitrator finding it necessary to make an inspection or investigation in connection with the arbitration shall direct the AAA to so advise the parties. The arbitrator shall set the date and time and the AAA shall notify the parties. Any party who so desires may be present at such an inspection or investigation. The arbitrator shall make a verbal or written report to the parties and afford them an opportunity to comment.

34.   Interim Measures

The arbitrator may issue such orders for interim relief as may be deemed necessary to safeguard the property that is the subject matter of the arbitration, without prejudice to the rights of the parties or to the final determination of the dispute.

35.   Closing of Hearing

The arbitrator shall specifically inquire of all parties whether they have any further proofs to offer or witnesses to be heard. Upon receiving negative replies or if satisfied that the record is complete, the arbitrator shall declare the hearing closed.

If briefs are to be filed, the hearing shall be declared closed as of the final date set by the arbitrator for the receipt of briefs. If documents are to be filed as provided in Section 32 and the date set for their receipt is later than that set for the receipt of briefs, the later date shall be the date of closing the hearing. The time limit within which the arbitrator is required to make the award shall commence to run, in the absence of other agreements by the parties, upon the closing of the hearing.

36.   Reopening of Hearing

The hearing may be reopened on the arbitrator's initiative, or upon application of a party, at any time before the award is made. If reopening the hearing would prevent the making of the award within the specific time agreed on by the parties in the contract(s) out of which the controversy has arisen, the matter may not be reopened unless the parties agree on an extension of time. When no specific date is fixed in the contract, the arbitrator may reopen the hearing and shall have thirty days from the closing of the reopened hearing within which to make an award.

37.   Waiver of Oral Hearing

The parties may provide, by written agreement, for the waiver of oral hearings in any case. If the parties are unable to agree as to the procedure, the AAA shall specify a fair and equitable procedure.

38.   Waiver of Rules

Any party who proceeds with the arbitration after knowledge that any provision or requirement of these rules has not been complied with and who fails to state an objection in writing shall be deemed to have waived the right to object.

39.   Extensions of Time

The parties may modify any period of time by mutual agreement. The AAA or the arbitrator may for good cause extend any period of time established by these rules, except the time for making the award. The AAA shall notify the parties of any extension.

40.   Serving of Notice

Each party shall be deemed to have consented that any papers, notices, or process necessary or proper for the initiation or continuation of an arbitration under these rules; for any court action in connection therewith; or for the entry of judgment on any award made under these rules may be served on a party by mail addressed to the party or its representative at the last known address or by personal service, in or outside the state where the arbitration is to be held, provided that reasonable opportunity to be heard with regard thereto has been granted to the party.

The AAA and the parties may also use facsimile transmission, telex, telegram, or other written forms of electronic communication to give the notices required by the rules.

41. **Time of Award**
The award shall be made promptly by the arbitrator and, unless otherwise agreed by the parties or specified by law, no later than thirty days from the date of closing the hearing, or, if oral hearings have been waived, from the date of the AAA's transmittal of the final statements and proofs to the arbitrator.

42. **Form of Award**
The award shall be in writing and shall be signed by a majority of the arbitrators. It shall be executed in the manner required by law.

43. **Scope of Award**
The arbitrator may grant any remedy or relief that the arbitrator deems just and equitable and within the scope of the agreement of the parties, including, but not limited to, specific performance of a contract. The arbitrator shall, in the award, assess arbitration fees, expenses, and compensation as provided in Sections 48, 49, and 50 in favor of any party and, in the event that any administrative fees or expenses are due the AAA, in favor of the AAA.

44. **Award upon Settlement**
If the parties settle their dispute during the course of the arbitration, the arbitrator may set forth the terms of the agreed settlement in an award. Such an award is referred to as a consent award.

45. **Delivery of Award to Parties**
Parties shall accept as legal delivery of the award the placing of the award or a true copy thereof in the mail addressed to a party or its representative at the last known address, personal service of the award, or the filing of the award in any other manner that is permitted by law.

46. **Release of Documents for Judicial Proceedings**
The AAA shall, upon the written request of a party, furnish to the party, at its expense, certified copies of any papers in the AAA's possession that may be required in judicial proceedings relating to the arbitration.

47. **Applications to Court and Exclusion of Liability**
   a.   No judicial proceeding by a party relating to the subject matter of the arbitration shall be deemed a waiver of the party's right to arbitrate.
   b.   Neither the AAA nor any arbitrator in a proceeding under these rules is a necessary party in judicial proceedings relating to the arbitration.
   c.   Parties to these rules shall be deemed to have consented that judgment upon the arbitration award may be entered in any federal or state court having jurisdiction thereof.
   d.   Neither the AAA nor any arbitrator shall be liable to any party for any act or omission in connection with any arbitration conducted under these rules.

48. **Administrative Fees**
As a not-for-profit organization, the AAA shall prescribe filing and other administrative fees and service charges to compensate it for the cost of providing administrative services. The fees in effect when the fee or charge is incurred shall be applicable.

The filing fee shall be advanced by the initiating party or parties, subject to final apportionment by the arbitrator in the award.

The AAA may, in the event of extreme hardship on the part of any party, defer or reduce the administrative fees.

49. **Expenses**
The expenses of witnesses for either side shall be paid by the party producing such witnesses. All other expenses of the arbitration, including required travel and other expenses of the arbitrator, AAA

representatives, and any witness and the cost of any proof produced at the direct request of the arbitrator, shall be borne equally by the parties, unless they agree otherwise or unless the arbitrator in the award assesses such expenses or any part thereof against any specified party or parties.

50. **Neutral Arbitrator's Compensation**
Unless the parties agree otherwise, members of the National Panel of Commercial Arbitrators appointed as neutrals on cases administered under the Expedited Procedures with claims not exceeding $10,000, will customarily serve without compensation for the first day of service. Thereafter, arbitrators shall receive compensation as set forth herein.

Arbitrators shall charge a rate consistent with the arbitrator's stated rate of compensation, beginning with the first day of hearing in all cases with claims exceeding $10,000.

If there is disagreement concerning the terms of compensation, an appropriate rate shall be established with the arbitrator by the Association and confirm to the parties.

Any arrangement for the compensation of a neutral arbitrator shall be made through the AAA and not directly between the parties and the arbitrator.

51. **Deposits**
The AAA may require the parties to deposit in advance of any hearings such sums of money as it deems necessary to cover the expense of the arbitration, including the arbitrator's fee, if any, and shall render an accounting to the parties and return any unexpended balance at the conclusion of the case.

52. **Interpretation and Application of Rules**
The arbitrator shall interpret and apply these rules insofar as they relate to the arbitrator's powers and duties. When there is more than one arbitrator and a difference arises among them concerning the meaning or application of these rules, it shall be decided by a majority vote. If that is not possible, either an arbitrator or a party may refer the question to the AAA for final decision. All other rules shall be interpreted and applied by the AAA.

Expedited Procedures

53. **Notice by Telephone**
The parties shall accept all notices from the AAA by telephone. Such notices by the AAA shall subsequently be confirmed in writing to the parties. Should there be a failure to confirm in writing any notice hereunder, the proceeding shall nonetheless be valid if notice has, in fact, been given by telephone.

54. **Appointment and Qualifications Arbitrator**
   a.   Where no disclosed claim or counterclaim exceeds $50,000, exclusive of interest and arbitration costs, the AAA shall appoint a single arbitrator, from the National Panel of Commercial Arbitrators, without submission of lists of proposed arbitrators.
   b.   Where all parties request that a list of proposed arbitrators be sent, the AAA upon payment of the service charge as provided in the Administrative Fees shall submit simultaneously to each party an identical list of five proposed arbitrators, drawn from the National Panel of Commercial Arbitrators, from which one arbitrator shall be appointed. Each party may strike two names from the list on a peremptory basis. The list is returnable to the AAA within seven days from the date of the AAA's mailing to the parties.

   If for any reason the appointment of an arbitrator cannot be made from the list, the AAA may make the appointment from among other members of the panel without the submission of additional lists.

   c.   The parties will be given notice by telephone by the AAA of the appointment of the arbitrator, who shall be subject to disqualification for the reasons specified in Section 19. The parties shall notify the AAA, by telephone, within seven days of any objection to the arbitrator appointed.

Any objection by a party to the arbitrator shall be confirmed in writing to the AAA with a copy to the other party or parties.

55. **Date, Time, and Place of Hearing**
The arbitrator shall set the date, time, and place of the hearing. The AAA will notify the parties by telephone, at least seven days in advance of the hearing date. A formal notice of hearing will also be sent by the AAA to the parties.

56. **The Hearing**
Generally, the hearing shall be completed within one day, unless the dispute is resolved by submission of documents under Section 37. The arbitrator, for good cause shown, may schedule an additional hearing to be held within seven days.

57. **Time of Award**
Unless otherwise agreed by the parties, the award shall be rendered not later than fourteen days from the date of the closing of the hearing.

ADMINISTRATIVE FEES

The administrative fees of the AAA are based on the amount of the claim or counterclaim. Arbitrator compensation is not included in this schedule. Unless the parties agree otherwise, arbitrator compensation and administrative fees are subject to allocation by the arbitrator in the award.

Filing Fees
A nonrefundable filing fee is payable in full by a filing party when a claim, counterclaim or additional claim is filed, as provided below.

Amount of Claim	Filing Fee
Up to $10,000	$500
Above $10.000 to $50,000	$750
Above $50,000 to $100,000	$1,250
Above $100,000 to $250,000	$2,000
Above $250,000 to $500,000	$3,500
Above $500,000 to $1,000,000	$5,000
Above $1,000,000 to $5,000,000	$7,000

When no amount can be stated at the time of filing, the minimum fee is $2,000, subject to increase when the claim or counterclaim is disclosed.

When a claim or counterclaim is not for a monetary amount, an appropriate filing fee will be determined by the AAA.

The minimum filing fee for any case having three or more arbitrators is $2,000.

The administrative fee for claims in excess of $5,000,000 will be negotiated.

Expedited Procedures, outlined in sections 53-57 of the rules, are applied in any case where no disclosed claim or counterclaim exceeds $50,000, exclusive of interest and arbitration cost. Under those procedures, arbitrators are directly appointed by the AAA. Where the parties request a list of proposed arbitrators under those procedures, a service charge of $150 will be payable by each party. There is no hearing fee for the initial hearing in cases in which no party's claim exceeds $10,000, administered under the Expedited Procedures.

Hearing Fees
For each day of hearing held before a single arbitrator, an administrative fee of $150 is payable by each party. For each day of hearing held before a multiarbitrator panel, an administrative fee of $250 is payable by each party. There is no AAA hearing fee for the initial Procedural Hearing.

Postponement/Cancellation Fees
A fee of $150 is payable by a party causing a postponement of any hearing scheduled before a single arbitrator. A fee of $250 is payable by a party causing a postponement of any hearing scheduled before a multiarbitrator panel.

Suspension for Nonpayment
If arbitrator compensation of administrative charges have not been paid in full, the administrator may so inform the parties in order that one of them may advance the required payment. If such payments are not made, the tribunal may order the suspension or termination of the proceedings. If no arbitrator has yet been appointed, the administrator may suspend the proceedings.

Sample ADR Contractual Clauses

Sample Presuit Arbitration Agreement
Standard Contract

Any controversy or claim arising out of or relating to this Agreement, the making or breach thereof, shall be settled and finally determined by arbitration in (city, state), according to the then-existing, applicable (sponsor rules), and any judgment upon the award rendered by the arbitrators may be entered in any court having jurisdiction thereof.

Sample Presuit Arbitration Agreement
Purchase Agreement

NOTICE: BY SIGNING IN THE SPACE BELOW YOU ARE AGREEING TO HAVE ANY DISPUTE ARISING OUT OF THIS PURCHASE AGEEMENT DECIDED BY NEUTRAL ARBITRATION AND YOU ARE GIVING UP THE RIGHTS YOU MIGHT POSSESS TO HAVE THE DISPUTE LITIGATED IN A COURT OR JURY TRIAL. BY INITIALING IN THE SPACE BELOW YOU ARE GIVING UP YOUR JUDICIAL RIGHTS TO DISCOVERY AND APPEAL, UNLESS THOSE RIGHTS ARE SPECIFICALLY INCLUDED IN THE RULES UNDER WHICH THE DISPUTE IS ARBITRATED. IF YOU REFUSE TO SUBMIT TO ARBITRATION AFTER AGREEING TO THIS PROVISION, YOU MAY BE COMPELLED TO ARBITRATE BY AUTHORITY OF A COURT OF LAW. YOUR AGREEMENT TO THIS ARBITRATION PROVISION IS VOLUNTARY. YOU HAVE READ AND UNDERSTAND THE FOREGOING AND AGREE TO SUBMIT DISPUTES ARISING OUT OF THIS PURCHASE AGREEMENT TO NEUTRAL ARBITRATION.

Sample Presuit Mediation Agreement
Standard Contract

If a dispute arises out of or relates to this contract, or the breach thereof, and if said dispute cannot be settled through negotiation, the parties agree first to try in good faith to settle the dispute by mediation under the (rules) before resorting to arbitration, litigation or some other dispute resolution procedure.

Sample Presuit Negotiation Agreement
Executive Agreement

The parties shall attempt in good faith to resolve any dispute arising out of or relating to this agreement promptly by negotiation between executives of the companies who are parties to this agreement. If the matter has not been resolved within 60 days of a parties request for negotiation, any party to the controversy can initiate mediation or arbitration as provided herein.

Ethical Standards of Professional Responsibility

ETHICAL STANDARDS OF PROFESSIONAL RESPONSIBILITY
Society of Professionals in Dispute Resolution
Adopted June 1986

General Responsibilities

Neutrals have a duty to the parties, to the profession, and to themselves. They should be honest and unbiased, act in good faith, be diligent, and not seek to advance their own interests at the expense of their parties.

Neutrals must act fairly in dealing with the parties, have no personal interest in the terms of the settlement, show no bias toward individuals and institutions involved in the dispute, be reasonably available as requested by the parties, and be certain that the parties are informed of the process in which they are involved.

Responsibilities to the Parties

1.   **Impartiality**. The neutral must maintain impartiality toward all parties. Impartiality means freedom from favoritism or bias either by word or by action and a commitment to serve all parties as opposed to a single party.

2.   **Informed Consent**. The neutral has an obligation to assure that all parties understand the nature of the process, the procedures, the particular role of the neutral, and the parties' relationship to the neutral.

3.   **Confidentiality**. Maintaining confidentiality is critical to the dispute resolution process. Confidentiality encourages candor, a full exploration of the issues, and a neutral's acceptability. There may be some types of cases, however, in which confidentiality is not protected. In such cases, the neutral must advise the parties, when appropriate in the dispute resolution process, that the confidentiality of the proceedings cannot necessarily be maintained. Except in such instances, the neutral must resist all attempts to cause him or her to reveal any information outside the process. A commitment by the neutral to hold information in confidence within the process also must be honored.

4.   **Conflict of Interest.** The neutral must refrain from entering or continuing in any dispute if he or she believes or perceives that participation as a neutral would be a clear conflict of interest and any circumstances that may reasonably raise a question as to the neutral's impartiality. The duty to disclose is a continuing obligation throughout the process.

5.   **Promptness.** The neutral shall exert every reasonable effort to expedite the process.

6.   **The Settlement and Its Consequences.** The dispute resolution process belongs to the parties. The neutral has no vested interest in the terms of a settlement, but must be satisfied that agreements in which he or she has participated will not impugn the integrity of the process. The neutral has a responsibility to see that the parties consider the terms of a settlement. If the neutral is concerned about the possible consequences of a proposed agreement, and the needs of the parties dictate, the neutral must inform the parties of that concern.

Reprinted from *Ethical Standards of Professional Responsibility,* 1986. Society of Professionals in Dispute Resolution

In adhering to this standard, the neutral may find it advisable to educate the parties, to refer one or more parties for specialized advice, or to withdraw from the case. In no case, however, shall the neutral violate Section 3, Confidentiality, of these standards.

Unrepresented Interests

The neutral must consider circumstances where interests are not represented in the process. The neutral has an obligation, where in his or her judgment the needs of parties dictate, to assure that such interests have been considered by the principal parties.

Use of Multiple Procedures

The use of more than one dispute resolution procedure by the same neutral involves additional responsibilities. Where the use of more than one procedure is initially contemplated, the neutral must take care at the outset to advise the parties of the nature of the procedures and the consequences of revealing information during any one procedure which the neutral may later use for decision making or may share with another decision maker. Where the use of more than one procedure is contemplated after the initiation of the dispute resolution process, the neutral must explain the consequences and afford the parties an opportunity to select another neutral for the subsequent procedures. It is also incumbent upon the neutral to advise the parties of the transition from one dispute resolution to another.

Background and Qualifications

A neutral should accept responsibility only in cases where the neutral has sufficient knowledge regarding the appropriate process and subject matter to be effective. A neutral has a responsibility to maintain and improve his or her professional skills.

Disclosure of Fees

It is the duty of the neutral to explain to the parties at the outset of the process the bases of compensation, fees and charges, if any.

Support of the Profession

The experienced neutral should participate in the development of new practitioners in the field and engage in efforts to educate the public about the value and use of neutral dispute resolution procedures. The neutral should provide *pro bono* services, where appropriate.

Responsibilities of Neutrals Working on the Same Case

In the event that more than one neutral is involved in the resolution of a dispute, each has an obligation to inform the others regarding his or her entry in the case, Neutrals working with the same parties should maintain an open and professional relationship with each other

Advertising and Solicitation

A neutral must be aware that some forms of advertisement and solicitations are inappropriate and in some conflict resolution disciplines, such as labor arbitration, are impermissible. All advertising must honestly represent the services to be rendered. No claims of specific results or promises which imply favor of one side or another for the purpose of obtaining business should be made. No commissions, rebates, or other similar forms of remuneration should be given or received by a neutral for the referral of clients.

Model Standards of Conduct for Mediators

I.   Self-Determination: A Mediator Shall Recognize that Mediation is Based on the Principle of Self-Determination by the Parties.

Self-determination is the fundamental principle of mediation. It requires that the mediation process rely upon the ability of the parties to reach a voluntary, uncoerced agreement. Any party may withdraw from mediation at any time.

COMMENTS:

- ◆ The mediator may provide information about the process, raise issues, and help parties explore options. The primary role of the mediator is to facilitate a voluntary resolution of a dispute. Parties shall be given the opportunity to consider all proposed options.
- ◆ A mediator cannot personally ensure that each party has made a fully informed choice to reach a particular agreement, but it is a good practice for the mediator to make the parties aware of the importance of consulting other professionals, where appropriate, to help them make informed decisions.

II.   Impartiality: A Mediator shall Conduct the Mediation in an Impartial Manner.

The concept of mediator impartiality is central to the mediation process. A mediator shall mediate only those matters in which she or he can remain impartial and evenhanded. If at any time the mediator is unable to conduct the process in an impartial manner, the mediator is obligated to withdraw.

COMMENTS:

- ◆ A mediator shall avoid conduct that gives the appearance of partiality toward one of the parties. The quality of the mediation process is enhanced when the parties have confidence in the impartiality of the mediator.
- ◆ When mediators are appointed by a court or institution, the appointing agency shall make reasonable efforts to ensure that mediators serve impartially.
- ◆ A mediator should guard against partiality or prejudice based on the parties' personal characteristics, background or performance at the mediation.

III.   Conflicts of Interest: A mediator Shall Disclose all Actual and Potential Conflicts of Interest Reasonably Known to the Mediator. After Disclosure, the Mediator Shall Decline to Mediate unless all Parties choose to Retain the Mediator. The Need to Protect Against Conflicts of Interest also Governs Conduct that Occurs During and After the Mediation.

A conflict of interest is a dealing or relationship that might create an impression of possible bias. The basic approach to questions of conflict of interest is consistent with the concept of self-determination. The mediator has a responsibility to disclose all actual and potential conflicts that are reasonably known to the mediator and could reasonably be seen as raising a question about impartiality. If all parties agree to mediate after being informed of conflicts, the mediator may proceed with the mediation. If, however, the conflict of interest casts serious doubt on the integrity of the process, the mediator shall decline to proceed.

Reprinted from *Model Standards of Conduct for Mediation,* 1995, American Arbitration Association, American Bar Association, Society of Professionals in Dispute Resolution.

A mediator must avoid the appearance of conflict of interest both during and after the mediation. Without the consent of all parties, a mediator shall not subsequently establish a professional relationship with one of the parties in a related matter, or in an unrelated matter under circumstances which would raise legitimate questions about the integrity of the mediation process.

COMMENTS:

- A mediator shall avoid conflicts of interest in recommending the services of other professionals. A mediator may make reference to professional referral services or associations which maintain rosters of qualified professionals.
- Potential conflicts of interest may arise between administrators of mediation programs and mediators and there may be strong pressures on the mediator to settle a particular case or cases. The mediator's commitment must be to the parties and the process. Pressure from outside of the mediation process should never influence the mediator to coerce parties to settle.

IV. Competence: A Mediator Shall Mediate Only When the Mediator Has the Necessary Qualifications to Satisfy the Reasonable Expectations of the Parties.

Any person may be selected as a mediator, provided that the parties are satisfied with the mediator's qualifications. Training and experience in mediation, however, are often necessary for effective mediation. A person who offers herself or himself as available to serve as a mediator gives parties and the public the expectation that she or he has the competency to mediate effectively. In court-connected or other forms of mandated mediation, it is essential that mediators assigned to the parties have the requisite training and experience.

COMMENTS:

- Mediators should have information available for the parties regarding their relevant training, education and experience.
- The requirements for appearing on a list of mediators must be made public and available to interested persons.
- When mediators are appointed by a court or institution, the appointing agency shall make reasonable efforts to ensure that each mediator is qualified for the particular mediation.

V. Confidentiality: A Mediator Shall Maintain the Reasonable Expectations of the Parties with Regard to Confidentiality.

The reasonable expectations of the parties with regard to confidentiality shall be met by the mediator. The parties' expectations of confidentiality depend on the circumstances of the mediation and any agreements they may make. The mediator shall not disclose any matter that a party expects to be confidential unless given permission by all parties or unless required by law or other public policy.

COMMENTS:

- The parties may make their own rules with respect to confidentiality, or the accepted practice of an individual mediator or institution may dictate a particular set of expectations. Since the parties' expectations regarding confidentiality are important, the mediator should discuss these expectations with the parties.
- If the mediator holds private sessions with a party, the nature of these sessions with regard to confidentiality should be discussed prior to undertaking such sessions.
- In order to protect the integrity of the mediation, a mediator should avoid communicating information about how the parties acted in the mediation process, the merits of the case, or settlement offers. The mediator may report, if required, whether parties appeared at a scheduled mediation.
- Where the parties have agreed that all or a portion of the information disclosed during a mediation is confidential, the parties' agreement should be respected by the mediator.

♦ Confidentiality should not be construed to limit or prohibit the effective monitoring, research, or evaluation of mediation programs by responsible persons. Under appropriate circumstances, researchers may be permitted to obtain access to statistical data and, with the permission of the parties, to individual case files, observations of live mediations, and interviews with participants.

VI.   Quality of the Process: A Mediator Shall Conduct the Mediation Fairly, Diligently, and in a Manner Consistent with the Principle of Self-Determination by the Parties.

A mediator shall work to ensure a quality process and to encourage mutual respect among the parties. A quality process requires a commitment by the mediator to diligence and procedural fairness. There should be adequate opportunity for each party in the mediation to participate in the discussions. The parties decide when and under what conditions they will reach an agreement or terminate a mediation.

♦ A mediator may agree to mediate only when he or she is prepared to commit the attention essential to an effective mediation.
♦ Mediators should only accept cases when they can satisfy the reasonable expectations of the parties concerning the timing of the process. A mediator should not allow a mediation to be unduly delayed by the parties or their representatives.
♦ The primary purpose of a mediator is to facilitate the parties' voluntary agreement. This role differs substantially from other professional-client relationships. Mixing the role of a mediator and the role of a professional advising a client is problematic, and mediators must strive to distinguish between the roles. A mediator should, therefore, refrain from providing professional advice. Where appropriate, a mediator should recommend that parties seek outside professional advice, or consider resolving their dispute through arbitration, counseling, neutral evaluation, or other processes. A mediator who undertakes, at the request of the parties, an additional dispute resolution role in the same matter assumes increased responsibilities and obligations that may be governed by the standards of other professions.
♦ A mediator shall withdraw from a mediation when incapable of serving or when unable to remain impartial.
♦ A mediator shall withdraw from a mediation or postpone a session if the mediation is being used to further illegal conduct, or if a party is unable to participate due to drug, alcohol or other physical or mental incapacity.
♦ Mediators should not permit their behavior in the mediation process to be guided by a desire for a high settlement rate.

VII.   Advertising and Solicitation: A Mediator Shall Be Truthful in Advertising and Solicitation for Mediation.

Advertising or any other communication with the public concerning services offered or regarding the education, training, and expertise of the mediator shall be truthful. Mediators shall refrain from promises and guarantees of results.

COMMENTS:

♦ It is imperative that communication with the public educate and instill confidence in the process.
♦ In an advertisement or other communication to the public, a mediator may make reference to meeting state, national, or private organization qualifications only if the entity referred to has a procedure for qualifying mediators and the mediator has been duly granted the requisite status.

VIII.   Fees: A Mediator Shall Fully Disclose and Explain the Basis of Compensation, Fees, and Charges to the Parties.

The parties should be provided sufficient information about fees at the outset of a mediation to determine if they wish to retain the services of a mediator. If a mediator charges fees, the fees shall be reasonable, considering, among other things, the mediation service, the type and complexity of the matter, the expertise of the mediator, the time required, and the rates customary in the community. The better practice in reaching an understanding about fees is to set down the arrangements in a written agreement.

COMMENTS:

♦ A mediator who withdraws from a mediation should return any unearned fee to the parties.

♦ A mediator should not enter into a fee agreement which is contingent upon the result of the mediation or amount of the settlement.

♦ A mediator should not accept a fee for referral of a matter to another mediator or to any other person.

IX.   Obligations to the Mediation Process: Mediators Have a Duty to Improve the Practice of Mediation.

COMMENT:

♦ Mediators are regarded as knowledgeable in the process of mediation. They have an obligation to use their knowledge to help educate the public about mediation; to make mediation accessible to those who would like to use it; to correct abuses; and to improve their professional skills and abilities.

Code of Ethics for Arbitrators in Commercial Disputes

THE CODE OF ETHICS FOR ARBITRATORS IN COMMERCIAL DISPUTES
American Arbitration Association

CANON I

AN ARBITRATOR SHOULD UPHOLD THE INTEGRITY AND FAIRNESS OF THE ARBITRATION PROCESS.

A.   Fair and just processes for resolving disputes are indispensable in our society. Commercial arbitration is an important method for deciding many types of disputes. In order for commercial arbitration to be effective, there must be broad public confidence in the integrity and fairness of the process. Therefore, an arbitrator has a responsibility not only to the parties but also to the process of arbitration itself, and must observe high standards of conduct so that the integrity and fairness of the process will be preserved. Accordingly, an arbitrator should recognize a responsibility to the public, to the parties whose rights will be decided, and to all other participants in the proceeding. The provisions of this code should be construed and applied to further these objectives.

B.   It is inconsistent with the integrity of the arbitration process for persons to solicit appointment for themselves. However, a person may indicate a general willingness to serve as an arbitrator.

C.   Persons should accept appointment as arbitrators only if they believe that they can be available to conduct the arbitration promptly.

D.   After accepting appointment and while serving as an arbitrator, a person should avoid entering into any financial, business, professional, family or social relationship, or acquiring any financial or personal interest, which is likely to affect impartiality or which might reasonably create the appearance of partiality or bias. For a reasonable period of time after the decision of a case, persons who have served as arbitrators should avoid entering into any such relationship, or acquiring any such interest, in circumstances which might reasonably create the appearance that they had been influenced in the arbitration by the anticipation or expectation of the relationship or interest.

E.   Arbitrators should conduct themselves in a way that is fair to all parties and should not be swayed by outside pressure, by public clamor, by fear of criticism or by self-interest.

F.   When an arbitrator's authority is derived from an agreement of the parties, the arbitrator should neither exceed that authority nor do less than is required to exercise that authority completely. Where the agreement of the parties sets forth procedures to be followed in conducting the arbitration or refers to rules to be followed, it is the obligation of the arbitrator to comply with such procedures or rules.

Reprinted from *The Code of Ethics for Arbitrators in Commercial Disputes,* March 1996, American Arbitration Association.

G.   An arbitrator should make all reasonable efforts to prevent delaying tactics, harassment of parties or other participants, or other abuse or disruption of the arbitration process.

H.   The ethical obligations of a arbitrator begin upon acceptance of the appointment and continue throughout all stages of the proceeding. In addition, wherever specifically set forth in this code, certain ethical obligations begin as soon as a person is requested to serve as an arbitrator and certain ethical obligations continue even after the decision in the case has been given to the parties.

CANON II

AN ARBITRATOR SHOULD DISCLOSE ANY INTEREST OR RELATIONSHIP LIKELY TO AFFECT IMPARTIALITY OR WHICH MIGHT CREATE AN APPEARANCE OF PARTIALITY OR BIAS.

Introductory Note

This code reflects the prevailing principle that arbitrators should disclose the existence of interests or relationships that are likely to affect their impartiality or that might reasonably create an appearance that they are biased against one party or favorable to another. These provisions of the code are intended to be applied realistically so that the burden of detailed disclosure does not become so great that it is impractical for persons in the business world to be arbitrators, thereby depriving parties of the services of those who might be best informed and qualified to decide particular types of case.[1]

This code does not limit the freedom of parties to agree on whomever they choose as an arbitrator. When parties, with knowledge of a person's interests and relationships, nevertheless desire that individual to serve as an arbitrator, that person may properly serve.

Disclosure

A.   Persons who are requested to serve as arbitrators should, before accepting, disclose

(1)   any direct or indirect financial or personal interest in the outcome of the arbitration;

(2)   any existing or past financial, business, professional, family or social relationships which are likely to affect impartiality or which might reasonably create an appearance of partiality or bias. Persons requested to serve as arbitrators should disclose any such relationships which they personally have with any party or its lawyer, or with any individual whom they have been told will be a witness. They should also disclose any such relationships involving members of their families or their current employers, partners or business associates.

---

[1] In applying the provisions of this code relating to disclosure, it might be helpful to recall the words of the concurring opinion, in a case decided by the U.S. Supreme Court, that arbitrators "should err on the side of disclosure" because "it is better that the relationship be disclosed at the outset when the parties are free to reject the arbitrator or accept him with knowledge of the relationship." At the same time, it must be recognized that "an arbitrator's business relationships may be diverse indeed, involving more or less remote commercial connections with great numbers of people." Accordingly, an arbitrator "cannot be expected to provide the parties with his complete and unexpurgated business biography," nor is an arbitrator called on to disclose interests or relationships that are merely "trivial" (a concurring opinion in *Commonwealth Coatings Corp. v. Continental Casualty Co.*, 393 U.S. 145, 151-152, 1968).

B.   Persons who are requested to accept appointment as arbitrators should make a reasonable effort to inform themselves of any interests or relationships described in the preceding paragraph A.

C.   The obligation to disclose interests or relationships described in the preceding paragraph A is a continuing duty which requires a person who accepts appointment as an arbitrator to disclose, at any stage of the arbitration, any such interests or relationships which may arise, or which are recalled or discovered.

D.   Disclosure should be made to all parties unless other procedures for disclosure are provided in the rules or practices of an institution which is administering the arbitration. Where more than one arbitrator has been appointed, each should inform the others of the interests and relationships which have been disclosed.

E.   In the event that an arbitrator is requested by all parties to withdraw, the arbitrator should do so. In the event that an arbitrator is requested to withdraw by less than all of the parties because of alleged partiality or bias, the arbitrator should withdraw unless either of the following circumstances exists.

(1)   If an agreement of the parties, or arbitration rules agreed to by the parties, establishes procedures for determining challenges to arbitrators, then those procedures should be followed; or,

(2)   if the arbitrator, after carefully considering the matter, determines that the reason for the challenge is not substantial, and that he or she can nevertheless act and decide the case impartially and fairly, and that withdrawal would cause unfair delay or expense to another party or would be contrary to the ends of justice.

CANON III

AN ARBITRATOR IN COMMUNICATING WITH THE PARTIES SHOULD AVOID IMPROPRIETY OR THE APPEARANCE OF IMPROPRIETY.

A.   If an agreement of the parties or applicable arbitration rules referred to in that agreement, establishes the manner or content of communications between the arbitrator and the parties, the arbitrator should follow those procedures notwithstanding any contrary provision of the following paragraphs B and C.

B.   Unless otherwise provided in applicable arbitration rules or in an agreement of the parties, arbitrators should not discuss a case with any party in the absence of each other party, except in any of the following circumstances.

(1)   Discussions may be had with a party concerning such matters as setting the time and place of hearings or making other arrangements for the conduct of the proceedings. However, the arbitrator should promptly inform each other party of the discussion and should not make any final determination concerning the matter discussed before giving each absent party an opportunity to express its views.

(2)   If a party fails to be present at a hearing after having been given due notice, the arbitrator may discuss the case with any party who is present.

(3)   If all parties request or consent to it, such discussion may take place.

C.   Unless otherwise provided in applicable arbitration rules or in an agreement of the parties, whenever an arbitrator communicates in writing with one party, the arbitrator should at the same time send a copy of the communication to each other party. Whenever the arbitrator receives any written communication concerning the case from one party which has not already been sent to each other party, the arbitrator should do so.

CANON IV

AN ARBITRATOR SHOULD CONDUCT THE PROCEEDINGS FAIRLY AND DILIGENTLY.

A.   An arbitrator should conduct the proceedings in an evenhanded manner and treat all parties with equality and fairness at all stages of the proceedings.

B.   An arbitrator should perform duties diligently and conclude the case as promptly as the circumstances reasonably permit.

C.   An arbitrator should be patient and courteous to the parties, to their lawyers and to the witnesses and should encourage similar conduct by all participants in the proceedings.

D.   Unless otherwise agreed by the parties or provided in arbitration rules agreed to by the parties, an arbitrator should accord to all parties the right to appear in person and to be heard after due notice of the time and place of hearing.

E.   An arbitrator should not deny any party the opportunity to be represented by counsel.

F.   If a party fails to appear after due notice, an arbitrator should proceed with the arbitration when authorized to do so by the agreement of the parties, the rules agreed to by the parties or by law. However, an arbitrator should do so only after receiving assurance that notice has been given to the absent party.

G.   When an arbitrator determines that more information than has been presented by the parties is required to decide the case, it is not improper for the arbitrator to ask questions, call witnesses, and request documents or other evidence.

H.   It is not improper for an arbitrator to suggest to the parties that they discuss the possibility of settlement of the case. However, an arbitrator should not be present or otherwise participate in the settlement discussions unless requested to do so by all parties. An arbitrator should not exert pressure on any party to settle.

I.   Nothing in this code is intended to prevent a person from acting as a mediator or conciliator of a dispute in which he or she has been appointed as arbitrator, if requested to do so by all parties or where authorized or required to do so by applicable laws or rules.

J.   When there is more than one arbitrator, the arbitrators should afford each other the full opportunity to participate in all aspects of the proceedings.

CANON V

AN ARBITRATOR SHOULD MAKE DECISIONS IN A JUST, INDEPENDENT AND DELIBERATE MANNER.

A.   An arbitrator should, after careful deliberation, decide all issues submitted for determination. An arbitrator should decide no other issues.

B.   An arbitrator should decide all matters justly, exercising independent judgment, and should not permit outside pressure to affect the decision.

C.   An arbitrator should not delegate the duty to decide to any other person.

D.   In the event that all parties agree upon a settlement of issues in dispute and request an arbitrator to embody that agreement in an award, an arbitrator may do so, but is not required to do so unless satisfied with the propriety of the terms of settlement. Whenever an arbitrator embodies a settlement by the parties in an award, the arbitrator should state in the award that it is based on an agreement of the parties.

CANON VI

AN ARBITRATOR SHOULD BE FAITHFUL TO THE RELATIONSHIP OF TRUST AND CONFIDENTIALITY INHERENT IN THAT OFFICE.

A.   An arbitrator is in a relationship of trust to the parties and should not, at any time, use confidential information acquired during the arbitration proceeding to gain personal advantage or advantage for others, or to affect adversely the interests of another.

B.   Unless otherwise agreed by the parties, or required by applicable rules or law, an arbitrator should keep confidential all matters relating to the arbitration proceedings and decision.

C.   It is not proper at any time for an arbitrator to inform anyone of the decision in advance of the time it is given to all parties. In a case in which there is more than one arbitrator, it is not proper at any time for an arbitrator to inform anyone concerning the deliberations of the arbitrators. After an arbitration award has been made, it is not proper for an arbitrator to assist in postarbitral proceedings, except as is required by law.

D.   In many types of arbitration it is customary practice for the arbitrators to serve without pay. However, in some types of cases it is customary for arbitrators to receive compensation for their services and reimbursement for their expenses. In cases in which any such payments are to be made, all persons who are requested to serve, or who are serving as arbitrators, should be governed by the same high standards of integrity and fairness as apply to their other activities in the case. Accordingly, such persons should scrupulously avoid bargaining with parties over the amount of payments or engaging in any communications concerning payments which would create an appearance of coercion or other impropriety. In the absence of governing provisions in the agreement of the parties or in rules agreed to by the parties or in applicable law, certain practices, relating to payments are generally recognized as being preferable in order to preserve the integrity and fairness of the arbitration process. These practices include the following.

(1)   It is preferable that before the arbitrator finally accepts appointment the basis of payment be established and that all parties be informed thereof in writing.

(2)   In cases conducted under the rules or administration of an institution that is available to assist in making arrangements for payments, the payments should be arranged by the institution to avoid the necessity for communication by the arbitrators directly with the parties concerning the subject.

(3)   In cases where no institution is available to assist in making arrangement for payments, it is preferable that any discussion with arbitrators concerning payments should take place in the presence of all parties.

CANON VII

ETHICAL CONSIDERATION RELATING TO ARBITRATORS APPOINTED BY ONE PARTY

Introductory Note

In some types of arbitration in which there are three arbitrators, it is customary for each party, acting alone, to appoint one arbitrator. The third arbitrator is then appointed by agreement either of the parties or of the two arbitrators, or, failing such agreement, by an independent institution or individual. In some of these types of arbitration, all three arbitrators are customarily considered to be neutral and are expected to observe the same standards of ethical conduct. However, there are also many types off tripartite arbitration in which it has been the practice that the two arbitrators appointed by the parties are not considered to be neutral and are expected to observe many—but not all—of the same ethical standards as the neutral third arbitrator. For purposes of this code, an arbitrator appointed by one party who is not expected to observe all of the same standards as the third arbitrator is called a "nonneutral arbitrator." This Canon VII describes the ethical obligations that nonneutral party-appointed arbitrators should observe and those that are not applicable to them.

In all arbitrations in which there are two or more party-appointed arbitrators, it is important for everyone concerned to know from the start whether the two party-appointed arbitrators are to be neutrals or nonneutrals. In such arbitrations, the two party-appointed arbitrators should be considered nonneutrals unless both parties inform the arbitrators that all three arbitrators are to be neutral or unless the contract, the applicable arbitration rules, or any governing law requires that all three arbitrators be neutral.

It should be noted that, in cases conducted outside the United States, the applicable law might require that all arbitrators be neutral. Accordingly, in such cases, the governing law should be considered before applying any of the following provisions relating to nonneutral party-appointed arbitrators.

A.   *Obligations under Canon I*

Nonneutral party-appointed arbitrators should observe all of the obligations of Canon I to uphold the integrity and fairness of the arbitration process, subject to the following provisions.

(1)   Nonneutral arbitrators may be predisposed toward the party who appointed them but in all other respects are obligated to act in good faith and with integrity and fairness. For example, nonneutral arbitrators should not engage in delaying tactics or harassment of any party or witness and should not knowingly make untrue or misleading statements to the other arbitrators.

(2)   The provisions of Canon I.D. relating to relationships and interests are not applicable to nonneutral arbitrators.

B.   *Obligations under Canon II*

Nonneutral party-appointed arbitrators should disclose to all parties, and to the other arbitrators, all interests and relationships which Canon II requires be disclosed. Disclosure as required by Canon I is for the benefit not only of the party who appointed the nonneutral arbitrator, but also for the benefit of the other parties and arbitrators so that they may know of any bias which may exist or appear to exist. However, this obligation is subject to the following provisions.

(1)   Disclosure by nonneutral arbitrators should be sufficient to describe the general nature and scope of any interest or relationship, but need not include as detailed information as is expected from persons appointed as neutral arbitrators.

(2)   Nonneutral arbitrators are not obliged to withdraw if requested to do so by the party who did not appoint them, notwithstanding the provisions of Canon II.E.

C.   *Obligations under Canon III*

Nonneutral party-appointed arbitrators should observe all of the obligations of Canon III concerning communications with parties, subject only to the following provisions.

(1)   In an arbitration in which the two party-appointed arbitrators are expected to appoint the third arbitrator, nonneutral arbitrators may consult with the party who appointed them concerning the acceptability of persons under consideration for appointment as the third arbitrator.

(2)   Nonneutral arbitrators may communicate with the party who appointed them concerning any other aspect of the case, provided they first inform the other arbitrators and the parties that they intend to do so. If such communication occurred prior to the time the person was appointed as arbitrator, or prior to the first hearing or other meeting to the parties with the arbitrators, the nonneutral arbitrator should, at the first hearing or meeting, disclose the fact that such communication has taken place, In complying with the provisions of this paragraph, it is sufficient that there be disclosure of the fact that such communication has occurred without disclosing the content of the communication. It is also sufficient to disclose at any time the intention to follow the procedure of having such communication in the future and there is no requirement thereafter that there be disclosure before each separate occasion on which such a communication occurs.

(3)   When nonneutral arbitrators communicate in writing with the party who appointed them concerning any matter as to which communication is permitted under this code, they are not required to send copies of any such written communication to any other party or arbitrator.

D.   *Obligations under Canon IV*

Nonneutral party-appointed arbitrators should observe all of the obligations of Cannon IV to conduct the proceedings fairly and diligently.

E.   *Obligations under Canon V*

Nonneutral party-appointed arbitrators should observe all of the obligations of Canon V concerning making decisions, subject only to the following provision.

(1)   Nonneutral arbitrators are permitted to be predisposed toward deciding in favor of the party who appointed them.

F.   *Obligations under Canon VI*

Nonneutral party-appointed arbitrators should observe all of the obligations of Canon VI to be faithful to the relationship of trust inherent in the office of arbitrator, subject only to the following provision.

(1)   Nonneutral arbitrators are not subject to the provisions of Canon VI.D with respect to any payments by the party who appointed them.

ADR Organizations

The following list contains the names, addresses and telephone numbers of the major ADR organizations in the United States. Because ADR is a fast growing industry, new organizations and centers are forming all of the time. Readers are encouraged to check with their local and state bar associations, and law schools for the names of organizations in their area devoted to ADR. Also, the world wide web contains the home pages of many ADR organizations, which can be identified and accessed by searching on common ADR terms (e.g., mediation, arbitration, ADR, dispute resolution) through your favorite internet browser.

American Arbitration Association (AAA)
140 West 51st Street
New York, NY 10020-1203
Telephone: (212) 484-4000
Fax: (212) 307-4387
http://www.adr.org/
(provides a panel of neutrals, plus rules, procedures, facilities, administrative services, research, publications and training. Check your phone book for the local AAA office)

American Bar Association
Section of Dispute Resolution
740 Fifteenth Street, N.W.
Washington, D.C. 20005-1009
Telephone: (202) 662-1681
Fax: (202) 662-1032
E-mail: dispute@attmail.com
http://www.abanet.org/dispute/home.html
(provides rules, procedures, research, and education)

Society of Professionals in Dispute Resolution (SPIDR)
815 Fifteenth Street, N.W., Suite 530
Washington, D.C. 20005
Telephone: (202) 783-7277
Fax: (202) 783-7281
http://www.spidr.org
(provides a roster of trained neutrals, plus ADR rules, procedures, research, publications and education)

CPR Institute for Dispute Resolution
366 Madison Avenue
New York, NY 19917
Telephone: (212) 949-6490
Fax: (212) 949-8859
E-mail: info@cpradr.org
http://www.cpadr.org
(coalition of general counsel for major corporations, law firm partners and legal scholars; provides a roster of neutrals, plus research, education, and publications)

Federal Mediation and Conciliation Service
2100 K Street, NW
Washington, DC 20427
http://www.fmcs.gov
(provides arbitration panels to hear disputes, plus training and communications programs in collective
bargaining, as well as funding to establish or expand labor-management committees)

JAMS/Endispute, Inc.
Telephone: (800) 352-5267
http://www.jams-endispute.com
(provides a roster of professional ADR neutrals, plus administrative services to facilitate the use of ADR.
Check your phone book for the local JAMS/Endispute office)

National Institute for Dispute Resolution (NIDR)
1726 M Street, NW, Suite 500
Washington, DC 20036
Telephone: (202) 466-4764
Fax: (202) 466-4769
E-mail: nidr@igc.apc.org
http:www.nidr.org
(provides consultation, education, training, and publications aimed at youth conflict resolution,
improving justice in American courts, and other public issues related to dispute resolution)

Other ADR Web Sites

http://adir.com
http://www.americord.com
http://www.mediate.org
http://www.cdsusa.org
http://www.cfrd.com
http://www.Colorado.edu/conflict
http://www.conflict-resolution.net
http://hg.org/adr
http://www.lanl.gov/ombuds
http://www.mediate.com
http://www.naarb.org
http://stfombuds.berkeley.edu
http://www.technologymediation.com
http://www.usam.com
http://www.wipo.org

Competencies of a Civil Litigation Paralegal

- Arrange for an outside investigator

- Handle computerized research for source materials

- Conduct factual research

- Conduct an initial client interview

- Draft demand letters

- Photograph accident scenes, evidence, and/or the parties

- Locate, interview, and obtain statements of witnesses

- Trace documents and physical evidence

- Search records from private and public sources.

- Draft documents including complaints, answers, interrogatories, requests for production of documents, affidavits, motions for extension of time, trial briefs, *voir dire* questions, jury instructions, etc.

- Review client files, gather and organize factual data

- Prepare and serve *subpoenas* and *subpoena duces tecum*

- Index/abstract documents

- Review documents for responsiveness to production requests

- Prepare statistical and economic information

- Review and summarize medical and other records

- Index and summarize depositions and deposition exhibits

- Keep current with procedures and local, state, and federal courts

- Organize witness files

- Arrange for publication of legal notices

- Maintain court calendar (docket) on tickler system

- Arrange for extensions of time by telephone, letter, or motion

- Meet with a client to prepare answers to interrogatories and obtain a client's documents to be produced: medical records, wage and wage loss information, tax statements, photographs, bills or expenses that were incurred because of the lawsuit, etc.

- Attend and organize document productions

- Attend on-site and expert inspections

- Prepare, organize, and supervise document control systems

Reprinted from *Paralegal Internship Manual* by Charles P. Nemeth, 1996, Dallas, Pearson Publications Company.

♦ Create database and procedures for computerized systems

♦ Input information into database

♦ Research facts for depositions

♦ Draft outline and questions for depositions

♦ Prepare witnesses for deposition

♦ Schedule, attend, and take notes at depositions

♦ Organize exhibits and request copies of a transcript

♦ Follow up after a deposition for additional information

♦ Segregate and record documents not to be produced and privileged materials, for attorney's review

♦ Locate expert witnesses; interview and prepare reports

♦ Prepare statistical/factual memoranda

♦ Prepare status reports on a case to be submitted to the client

♦ Compile product history; obtain information about similar products, market surveys, and industrial statistics in product liability cases

♦ Draft legal memoranda or briefs

♦ Perform legal research, cite check, and Shepardize

♦ Review and analyze a case continually for further discovery

♦ Prepare and exchange names of witnesses and exhibit lists

♦ Prepare trial notebooks and witness files

♦ Prepare graphs, charts, etc.

♦ Arrange for a court reporter and computerized transcript

♦ Prepare, mark, and index exhibits

♦ Prepare outlines of anticipated testimony

♦ Meet with witnesses, help in preparation of witnesses and client testimony, and coordinate attendance at the trial.

♦ Help in analysis of video and audio evidence at the trial

♦ Draft pretrial statements, settlement calculations (including comparative analysis of potential settlement terms) and a settlement conference memo

♦ Obtain the jury list and do biographical research on each juror

♦ Draft a bill of costs

♦ Draft settlement documents, including releases, dismissals, and satisfaction

♦ Maintain a list of exhibits offered, admitted, or objected to

♦ Prepare digests, abstracts, indices and/or summaries of transcripts

♦ Attend trial: take notes of testimony, and reaction of jurors, witnesses, and counsel; organize exhibits, documents, coordination of witnesses and experts

♦ Help in jury selection: prepare *voir dire* questions, observe jurors' reactions and responses, and review and analyze jurors' questionnaires

- Prepare draft of document list and testimony used to impeach opposition witnesses

- Help in preparing witnesses

- Gather documents and pertinent information with which to familiarize the witness with the issues and facts of the case.

- Draft notice of appeal

- Order hearing transcript; prepare recap or outline of transcripts

- Set up timetable for filings

- Help in preparation of record on appeal

Index

B

D